The Women of Suye Mura

The Women

Robert J. Smith &

# of Suye Mura

Ella Lury Wiswell

The University of Chicago Press

Chicago and London

HQ
1765
.S93
S63
1982

Robert J. Smith, Goldwin Smith Professor of
Anthropology and former chairman of the
department at Cornell University, is the author
of *Ancestor Worship in Contemporary Japan* and
Kurusu: The Price of Progress in a Japanese Village.
Ella Lury Wiswell is emerita professor of
European Languages at the University of
Hawaii. Her most recent publication is a
translation of V. M. Golvonin's *Around the World
on the Kamchatka 1817–1819*.

The University of Chicago Press, Chicago 60637
The University of Chicago Press, Ltd., London
©1982 by The University of Chicago
All rights reserved. Published 1982
Printed in the United States of America

89 88 87 86 85 84 83 82   5 4 3 2 1

Publication of *The Women of Suye Mura* was aided by a
grant from the Goldwin Smith Professorship and by the
Hull Memorial Publication Fund of Cornell University.
This assistance is gratefully acknowledged.

Some passages from Ella Wiswell's journal quoted in this
volume first appeared in Robert J. Smith, "Japanese
Village Women: Suye-mura 1935–1936," *Journal of Japanese
Studies* 7, no. 2 (1981).

Library of Congress Cataloging in Publication Data

Smith, Robert John, 1927–
  The women of Suye Mura.

  Bibliography: p.
  Includes index.
    1. Women—Japan—Sue-mura (Kumamoto-ken, Japan)—
Social conditions. 2. Sue-mura (Kumamoto-ken, Japan)
—Social conditions. I. Wiswell, Ella Lury. II. Title.
HQ1765.S93S63   305.4'2'09522   82-2708
ISBN 0-226-76344-7   AACR2
ISBN 0-226-76345-7 (pbk.)

Contents

In memory of John and Clare Embree, who also knew

Suye Mura

Preface

This book is based on field research conducted forty-five years ago by Ella Lury Wiswell. Were that circumstance in itself not sufficiently unusual to require some explanation, the complicated train of events that has led to this publication is well worth recounting.

In the fall of 1935, John and Ella Embree arrived in Japan with their infant daughter, Clare, to undertake a study of an agricultural community, the first project of its kind in that country. After completing several preliminary surveys of likely districts, they settled on the village of Suye, a collection of agricultural and commercial hamlets in Kumamoto Prefecture on the southernmost island of Kyushu. The Embrees found a house and lived in the community for a year. During their stay they collected between them more than two thousand pages of typescript notes, took quantities of photographs, and assembled a variety of documents and miscellaneous material. It is a unique resource, for there is no other corpus of data, secured by direct observation, on the day-to-day behavior of Japanese villagers before the Pacific War. Furthermore, it should not go unremarked that to this day the study of Suye is the only one ever carried out by a married couple of any nationality during a year's residence in a Japanese rural community.

They left Japan in the winter of 1936, and three years later John Embree's book on the village began its career as a durable classic.[1] Although a few additional publications appeared,[2] his turn to Southeast Asian in-

1. John F. Embree, *Suye Mura: A Japanese Village* (Chicago: University of Chicago Press, 1939).

2. a. "Some Social Functions of Religion in Rural Japan," *American Journal of Sociology* 47, no. 2 (September 1941): 184–89.

   b. *Japanese Peasant Songs*. (Philadelphia: Memoirs of the American Folklore Society, no. 38, 1944).

   c. "Sanitation and Health in a Japanese Village," *Journal of the Washington Academy of Sciences* 34, no. 4 (April 1944): 97–108.

terests shortly before he joined the faculty of Yale University, and his tragic death in 1950 at the age of forty-two, in an accident that also took the life of their only child, made the book the sole major publication on Suye.

There the matter rested until 1965, when I first met my coauthor when she was on a visit to Ithaca, New York. In the course of our conversation, she said that she had in her possession all of her late husband's field notes as well as her own, and that she had been hoping to find someone who might be interested in making use of them. The arrangements were soon made to have them shipped to my office. There were, as she had said, two sets of notes, approximately half of them her own, both in the form of daily journals. A cursory reading of them soon brought the entirely unanticipated realization that while hers had been drawn on in the preparation of *Suye Mura*, the bulk of the material they contained lay outside the scope of the book.

The two journals differ quite strikingly. Embree's is clearly the product of a field project undertaken in the heyday of Robert Redfield's and A. R. Radcliffe-Brown's influence in the Department of Anthropology at the University of Chicago. Accordingly, it focuses on community structure, ritual and economic relations, and community-level analysis generally. Ella Wiswell's is more personal, and less concerned with structure and organization than with the business of everyday life. But it is not in these respects that the greatest contrast lies. John Embree spoke no Japanese, and his journal reveals the problems that arise from the use of an interpreter and necessarily heavy reliance on the observation of behavior. Ella Wiswell, on the other hand, had come to Japan from Russia at the age of ten, and was able to conduct all of her interviews and conversations in Japanese. What she wrote down has pungency, is often poignant, and always conveys a sense of immediacy.

In the years that followed our first meeting, a combination of circumstances prevented us from turning to the Suye data, but in the fall and winter of 1978 we were able to begin work in Honolulu, where I was visiting and Wiswell now lives. This book is, then, the result of an unusual kind of collaboration between two people of very different backgrounds and training, brought together by the sheerest of coincidences. Wiswell knew the Suye of forty-five years ago very well indeed, and has been there twice since the end of World War II. I know it only through her eyes and the record she set down, and through the writings of John Embree and others who subsequently conducted research in the community.[3]

---

d. "Japanese Administration at the Local Level," *Applied Anthropology* 3, no. 4 (September 1944): 11–18.

3. a. Arthur F. Raper et al., *The Japanese Village in Transition* (Tokyo: General Headquarters, Supreme Commander for the Allied Powers, Natural Resources Section, Report Number 136, 1950).

b. Roger I. Yoshino, *Selected Social Changes in a Japanese Village* (unpublished Ph.D. dissertation, University of Southern California, 1955).

This book can be read in several ways. It is above all an excursion back in time, to a version of Japanese society that will seem very remote to those who know only contemporary Japan. It is also an account of an extraordinary anthropological field study by a young foreign couple, conducted at a time in Japan's history when that society's view of outsiders was very different from what it has since become. And it is about women, seen through the eyes of a woman at a time when there was not the slightest thought of the appropriateness of advocacy in the discipline, and no "anthropology of women." The collection of the data was dictated by the character of anthropology and its definitions of the problems and tasks facing it as they were guiding and shaping research almost two generations ago. It is inevitable, therefore, that these field materials should be silent on many issues of concern to contemporary anthropology. These shortcomings are more than compensated for, we believe, by the character of the materials we do have.

We are indebted to an anonymous reader for pointing out that most of the voluminous anthropological literature on women—and Japan is no exception—deals with their *structural* position vis-à-vis men. It focuses on their access to resources, the degree of their autonomy and power in the domestic and public domains, their participation in the labor market, and so on. We rarely get accounts of how women feel about things—their likes and dislikes or their hopes and fears. John Embree's monograph on Suye is an excellent structural analysis; Wiswell's journal complements it perfectly.

This same reader also observes that the journal is unique because the Embrees were the only foreign anthropologists to work in prewar Japan. More important, it will remain so because there no longer exist any communities in Japan where the same kind of intimacy can be established between researcher and residents. As I discovered when I returned to a farming village in 1975,[4] most able-bodied men and women have become commuters who leave the place all day to work outside, leaving the houses and streets virtually empty. They are thus much less involved in their neighbors' affairs, have much less information on what is going on in the village, and so cannot provide the variety of views and gossip concerning

---

c. Roger I. Yoshino, "A Re-study of Suye Mura: An Investigation of Social Change," *Research Studies, State College of Washington* 24, no. 2 (1956): 182.

d. Ushijima Morimitsu, *Suye Mura in Transition* (unpublished M.A. dissertation, Atlanta University, 1958).

e. Ushijima Morimitsu, *Henbō suru Suye mura (Suye Mura in Transition: A Fundamental Study of Socio-cultural Change)* (Kyoto: Minerva shobō, 1971). In Japanese, with a twenty-eight page summary by the author and a foreword by Ella Lury Wiswell, both in English.

Smith (1981) has presented a preliminary version of a fraction of the materials in an earlier publication.

4. See Smith (1978, 114–30) for the manifold ways in which regular nonfarm employment has altered the character of interaction among the residents of a small agricultural hamlet on the island of Shikoku in western Japan.

a given event, person, or situation that they once could. People who live in contemporary Japanese villages are just not that close any more. They are very busy and are much involved in their workplace and relations with fellow employees far from the community where they live. Furthermore, it is doubtful that women today would talk as freely to anyone as the women of Suye did to the Embrees. The richness of the journal derives in no small part from being based on day-to-day close observation and conversations with a great many people, rather than on the kind of more or less formal interviewing that characterizes much of the postwar anthropological research on Japan.

In a few places, I have introduced passages from John Embree's journal to supplement or confirm a point under discussion. Virtually all of the quotations in the following pages, however, are edited excerpts from Ella Wiswell's journal. Chronology has been abandoned in favor of topical treatment, it should be noted, and it has been my task to convert the journal into field notes from which this text has been constructed. Because the form of presentation is somewhat unusual, let me give a brief account of it. The passages in double quotation marks are taken directly from the journals, edited to reduce redundancy and to clarify where necessary. Materials between single quotation marks within these passages are quotations from conversations and comments made by the villagers. Parenthetical passages are in the original. Bracketed ones are mine, as is the balance of the text. Thus:

> That was precisely what had happened. "Of the Maehara change of wives the women thought favorably. This one is said to be a good worker and not 'an *okusan* type' [by implication a lady] like the one who has left. She gave a *kao mishiri* [a 'face-showing' party given by one who moves into a new community] when she arrived. 'At Maehara's,' they laughed, 'they have to throw such a party because the wives change so often.' (I learned later that his real wife—the first one—is not officially registered as such.)"

There remains one issue to be disposed of before we proceed. As the reader will soon see, much of the book touches on the intimate aspects of life in Suye. Our decision to alter names of people (since they are pseudonyms we have omitted the usual diacritical marks) and, further, to conceal identities by switching occupations of individuals and transposing their hamlets of residence does not entirely absolve us of the charge that we have revealed too much. We have discussed the problem at great length, and concluded that there are compelling reasons for bringing the material to light. These are taken up in some detail in the introduction. As for the raw field data, the entire collection is to be placed in the Cornell University Archives under seal until, as the saying goes, all the principals are dead.

Acknowledgments

This book quite literally would never have been written had it not been for the unfailing hospitality and sense of the fitness of things that led Lauriston and Ruth Sharp to invite us to their home, where we first met. Many people have offered assistance of various kinds during the preparation of the manuscript. Yoshida Teigo, J. Victor Koschmann, Sherman G. Cochran, and Richard J. Smethurst helped us identify some dialect words, place names, and other references. Above all, however, we must acknowledge the comments and criticisms made by L. Keith Brown, Kazuko Smith, and Margery Wolf, who contributed much patient advice on ways to improve our original unwieldy manuscript. They have not always prevailed, but our debt to them is great.

Introduction

The foreigner's stereotypical view of the Japanese woman is easily drawn. Compliant, long-suffering, nurturant, and charming in her childlike way, she is thought to conform to the Confucian injunction to obey her father in her youth, her husband in her adulthood, and, at the end of her life, her grown son. Child-centered and restricted in her interests and actions to the domestic realm, she routinely appears in fiction as victim, pawn, and tragic heroine. Madame Butterfly, Madame Chrysanthemum, and the impossible Mariko of *Shōgun* have all contributed to the popular perception of the Japanese woman. It is surely noteworthy that there are no comparable fictional figures of Japanese men in the literature of the Western world.

Scholars of Japan have more accurately shown us the complexities of the position of women in that society, but they are for the most part men and women—Japanese and foreign alike—from urban backgrounds. Much of what they tell us is based on conjecture as to what rural women must have been like, for they lack direct acquaintance with them and are innocent even of vicarious experience of their lives.

There is, of course, a special danger for the foreigner who attempts to deal with the issue, for inevitably we bring to the task of analyzing the position of women in Japanese society our understanding of women's position in our own. For a vivid illustration of the powerful biasing effect of our expectations, consider the remarkable result of a translation exercise given recently to a small class of male and female American students of the Japanese language. They were asked to translate the following sentence: *Beddo mo daidokoro no dōgu mo tsuite inai apāto o kanai ga sōdan sezu ni karite shimai mashita.* Some rendered it as follows: "Without consulting my wife, I rented an apartment that had neither bed nor kitchen appliances." Others had it: "Without consulting his wife, he rented an apartment that had neither bed nor kitchen appliances." While both are wrong, the sentence is absolutely unambiguous. It says: "Without consulting me, my wife rented an apartment that had neither bed nor kitchen appliances." It clearly had never occurred to these American students that a wife in any country might be empowered to do any such thing, and their bias overrode their otherwise firm control of the Japanese language.

Which is only to make the point that we must take great care to guard against the most common error made in analyses of sex roles in other societies. Domains of responsibility are differently allocated, and authority is often exercised in contexts where our perceptions do not lead us to expect to find it. Certainly no one who knows Japanese white-collar urban families would be in the least likely to make the mistake in translation just given, for they will be well aware that in Japan major decisions connected with the domestic unit are commonly taken by the wife rather than by the husband, whose authority and concerns lie elsewhere.

Because Japanese society has been so strikingly transformed in the period since the Meiji Restoration in 1868, many observers have been concerned to analyze the changes that have occurred in the position of women in it. One dominant theme of this literature relates to the implications for women's roles of the development of capitalism in Japan. Another is the degree to which the government deliberately legislated women into a subordinate position. It is, for example, widely asserted that from the beginning of the Meiji period, the authorities assiduously and successfully promoted the ideals of the old warrior class as the model for the society at large. The Civil Code of 1898 is said to exemplify this tendency particularly, imposing on all classes the household and family system of the samurai class, and the educational system is said to have been designed to reenforce the notion of women as filial daughters, obedient wives, and compliant mothers. It is further argued that among the old commoner classes to which the farmers of Suye certainly belonged, in contrast to the elite, the relationship between men and women was far less influenced by Confucian ideology. As a consequence, it is said, their relationship was more egalitarian, and women were far more powerful because of their direct contribution to the economic enterprise of the agricultural, fishing, merchant, and artisan household.

The material on the women of Suye forty-five years ago provides us with a unique body of information by means of which we may examine some of these assertions. They are the daughters, sisters, wives, mothers, and grandmothers of farm households, as well as those of small merchants and artisans. The field research was carried out less than forty years after the promulgation of the Civil Code that is said to have transformed their domestic world. Many Japanese have charged that Suye was backward for its time, in part because they were doubtless embarrassed by much of what is reported in the book.[1] Far from the centers of agricultural development

---

1. Others were disturbed by some of its conclusions. In 1937 or 1938 John Embree solicited comments on the preliminary mimeographed version of the manuscript of *Suye Mura* from

of the period and hardly the epitome of imperial Japan as the authorities envisaged it, Suye was at the very least clearly not in the vanguard of the social and technological changes of the period. To the extent that the claim of backwardness is justified, then, we are provided with an even clearer insight into the life of rural women as it was before the central government's alleged transformation of the household and alteration of the social position of women in the early twentieth century.

Because the Embrees lived in one of its hamlets, they were in daily contact with the people of Suye. We shall see them in a perfectly astonishing array of situations, for there was little privacy in the village. Such a wide-open community would surely be the envy of today's ethnographer, struggling to break into an apartment block in Tokyo, where all doors are locked and the privatizing ideology of "my-home-ism" reigns supreme. No conceivable topic of conversation seems to have gone unexplored. Much of it occurs when no men are present, but even when they are, the discussion knows no bounds. Frank to the point of boldness, inquisitive, unrestrained and outspoken, the women of Suye emerge as strongly opinionated, cu-

---

a young Japanese agricultural economist who subsequently became one of that discipline's leading scholars. The closing passage of his response, which for all its indirection reflects some serious concerns, is of relevance. It has been edited slightly.

"About the impressions which may be got by those who read your report and judge rural life in Japan in general from it, let me add a few words. As presented in your manuscript, Suye-mura is rather more old-fashioned than the general run of our villages. Perhaps you also find it so. Generalizations might well be made with this fact in mind.

"About the impact of nationalism on village life, it must be remembered that our country as a centralized state is young, though our nation is very old. Westernization was very rapid (it was necessary to move quickly so as not to become a colony of another country) in all aspects of life, especially the political and industrial. The fact that to foreigners the central government appears somewhat authoritarian toward rural people may be explained from this point of view. As to industrial development plans, as reflected for example in the Economic Reconstruction Program [see Embree, *Suye Mura*, page 44n, and pages 25–26 of this book], therefore, the government always leads paternalistically. Of course it wishes also to enrich the rural people. Their attitude of indifference is one of child-like innocence! The same is true of the political-educational side, as for example the map in the classroom [see Embree, *Suye Mura*, page 67, and page 20 of this book].

"I am afraid that such descriptions will unduly excite those who know little or nothing of our national life. As you know, we all hope that Japan will become a more civilized nation and not justify war only because of the smallness of our land. I hope that your reflections on the nationalism that you observed in Suye-mura will be tempered by your good will toward our nation, which I believe you have, as well as to our rural people."

The major academic review of *Suye Mura* appeared in Japan's principal ethnological journal. Its author was Suzuki Eitarō, a leading rural sociologist. He confesses that he had entertained grave doubts that the Embrees should undertake the study at all, but had changed his mind upon reading the book. He offers some useful criticism and remarks on the backwardness of the place, but his review is important in another sense. Suzuki was persuaded that the approach of social anthropology used by Embree had the potential for revolutionizing Japanese rural sociology. See Suzuki Eitarō, *"Shakai jinruigaku jō no kenkyū to shite no Embree no Suye Mura to nihon nōson shakaigaku"* [Embree's social anthropological study *Suye Mura* and Japanese rural sociology], *Minzokugaku Kenkyū* 6, no. 3 (1940): 353–73.

rious about certain specific aspects of life in the outside world, eager to pass on gossip, and interested in instructing their young foreign visitor in everything from the techniques of raising silkworms to the most intimate details of conjugal life. A considerable number of them come through as quite distinctive personalities, some of amazing strength in adversity, others of hopeless ineffectuality.

On the whole, they were kind, genial, and good-natured, and they ordinarily treated one another with marked civility. Yet close acquaintance with them revealed that the apparent cordiality of many relationships in fact concealed old enmities and even hatred. The men said that such duplicity explains why the snake is one of the symbols of females, for both are wily and tenacious. Girls and young women, especially new brides, exhibited paralyzing degrees of shyness. Older women, far less restrained, engaged in a great deal of teasing of one another and with men about sex, some of it barbed with certain knowledge of past and current infidelities. Unusually outspoken women would often criticize other women to their faces for extravagance, their lack of ability as cooks, and a variety of other shortcomings. Such remarks were generally ignored or dismissed with a light rejoinder, however, and there were few direct confrontations that might have resulted in really bad relations between the two. Women on bad terms simply tried to avoid one another. Men and women alike comment constantly on the prevalence of gossip, and some hamlets of the village were said to be much worse than others in this respect. The tendency to characterize all the women of a given hamlet was very common, and as we shall see the stereotypes reveal a considerable degree of self-awareness.

When pushed too far, an older woman was quite capable of taking on a man in a public dispute. Such colorful confrontation was rare, however, and the women of Suye are far more often seen placating men or trying to deal with them firmly but gently. At one of the many parties where a great deal of liquor was consumed, we find a man pleading with another man's wife to sleep with him. She tries to persuade him to go on home with his own wife, who is also present, and finally slips out with her husband before the situation gets out of hand. There was remarkably little public expression of jealousy, we learn, in part no doubt because of the long-range consequences of its display and in part because there is a very great tolerance of the behavior of people in a drunken state.

The world of the older women was a highly restricted one in many ways. Women over fifty were illiterate, as were many old men, and their knowledge of the world was piecemeal at best. Some of the women had not been more than a few miles from Suye since they had married into the place, and most had only the vaguest notion of where and how far away Korea, China, and Manchuria might be. Several suggested that Manchuria, to which many of their sons had gone as soldiers or laborers, was probably as distant as America. About Korea they had only the most negative views and there was a pervasive dislike of Koreans and Chinese. It was for the Russians, however, that everyone reserved the deepest contempt and fear, and their foreign visitor successfully avoided ever letting it be known that she was Russian-born.

They were, of course, curious about the Embrees and about life in the United States. Upon occasion the journals reveal one of those chasms that opens between the ethnographer and the people on whose good will he or she so completely depends. For the most part the relationship went smoothly, but we shall encounter some marvelous moments when one side finds the other altogether too mysterious to be understood. It is more often the people of Suye to whom it seemed that there simply was no way of accounting for the strange ideas and behavior of foreigners. They did see films that came to the village from time to time, and the younger women often went to movies in town, but until the arrival of the Embrees, most of their information about foreigners, particularly Caucasians, had been obtained primarily from magazines and the few newspapers that villagers subscribed to.

The school teachers and the wives of village office personnel looked down on the wives and daughters of farmers and often expressed their disapproval of the farm women's drunkenness and the impropriety of their public behavior. For the teachers especially, Tokyo was the center of enlightenment and civilization. Suye, by contrast, seemed to them extremely backward although they knew little of village affairs and thought its benighted women crude and unsophisticated. The farm women, for their part, lamented the fact that children no longer feared and respected their teachers as they once had, pointedly suggesting that the current breed of citified women teachers simply could not inspire these desirable sentiments in their charges. Nonetheless, education and learning in general were accorded considerable respect in Suye, as elsewhere in Japan. The two groups of women simply did not mix, except on official or public occasions.

There was a flower-arranging class, the lessons given by a shopkeeper's wife, which for a time included one young farm-wife. She was teased so unmercifully by other farm women that for a time she would not carry flowers through the village on the way to the lessons, but asked someone else to bring them for her. Finally, she stopped coming altogether. There were also *shamisen* (the three-stringed musical instrument) lessons at another house, and all four of the young women who were learning to play it were from nonfarm families. Both of these groups were considered to be very genteel, and neither suitable for the farmers, many of whom could not have afforded the modest fees in any event. Social distinctions were clear, and those who violated rules were subjected to the intensely powerful sanction of gossip.

It was the young women, particularly the unmarried, who chafed most under the restrictions and limitations of village life. Almost all of them with any education looked for ways to leave. Their dreams were modest—factory work, employment as a bus-girl, or perhaps office work as an accountant if they were especially skillful with the abacus. Many went as maids to houses in town, sent often in the hope that they would learn from their betters. The work was considered hard, and one such girl back in Suye on a rare visit confided that she would much rather have gone into a factory where one could make many friends and had only one job to do. She had no idea what her wages were because the money was sent directly to her father, but she did receive gifts of clothing and bedding at the New Year and the midsummer's holiday of *o-bon*, the Festival of the Dead. She was given a ten-day holiday at the lunar New Year, but no other time off, and said ruefully that her employer often struck her when he was displeased. There were other dangers as well. One fifteen-year-old farm girl resisted her parents' insistent requests that she take a job as a maid in another house in the village on the grounds that there was too much drinking there and she'd not feel safe from the men. Everyone had stories of a number of premarital pregnancies that had come about under just such circumstances. Those who went as maids were in some respects better off than many of their contemporaries, for girls were sometimes sold to houses of prostitution, some rather thinly disguised as restaurants or hotels. Curiously, many of Suye's women were extremely censorious of these unfortunate women, an attitude that Ella Wiswell found quite indefensible, since no girl ever went into prostitution of her own accord, but rather was always sold into it by her parents.

Given these grim alternatives, and the universal assumption that farm work was so hard that city girls could not possibly do it and that anyone would choose to escape it if given the chance, it is no wonder that the labor contractors were so successful in their recruiting efforts in Suye. They came through offering work in the spinning mills of Himeji and Osaka, and they found ready takers. From the perspective of forty-five years it is easy enough to denounce the factory system of the period, but it is quite clear that these young women considered such work a decided improvement over what their mothers and older sisters were required to do on the farms. The young men had long been subject to the conscription system and so had gained some experience of the outside world, but for the young women of Suye such opportunities were new. The combination of universal education for both sexes and Japan's industrial growth had opened up to them a world unknown to the older village women.

PROLOGUE

Suye Mura in Retrospect

Ella Lury Wiswell

It was a fortunate set of circumstances that led to my meeting with Robert Smith and my decision to turn over all the Suye materials to him. I had made some use of my notes during the war years when John Embree and I worked in Washington, and I was occasionally asked to lecture on Japan. Later, however, the notes were put aside and forgotten. In 1951, shortly after John's sudden death, I was offered a position at the University of Hawaii and returned to my original profession of teaching European languages. At that time I felt that I would never be able to do anything with the Suye material and I was happy to find a home for it. Hence, it came as a complete surprise when Robert Smith informed me of his interest in using my notes for a book about the women of Suye Mura. I am indebted to him for rescuing these notes from oblivion.

When asked to provide some background information in preparation for this book I found that after forty-five years many details had grown dim. But as I reread the notes things began to fall into place, and I recalled the excitement I had felt when the possibility of doing field work in Japan was first suggested. John had applied for a grant to conduct research in Japan, not only because he was interested in the country from his earlier studies and previous visits there, but to a great extent because Japan was "home" to me and I was anxious to return. Furthermore, I spoke Japanese fluently. Parenthetically, it may interest young anthropologists applying for research money today to know that the grant, which seemed so fabulous to us, was exactly $3000. Eventually, an additional $880 was added for our return fares. The total sum paid for our travel (including our two-year-old daughter), our living expenses for one year in Japan, and the salaries for John's assistant and two young housemaids. We did not splurge, needless to say, and always had to use the cheapest transportation and stay at the cheapest Japanese inns, but we did not starve and, by village standards, we were considered exceptionally wealthy.

As we made our plans it all seemed so simple and interesting, and in my anticipation of going back it somehow did not occur to me that the Japan I knew was very different from the Japan we were to study. I had lived in Japan from 1918 until 1927 when I went away to the University of California at Berkeley and later to Paris to study at the Sorbonne. My father had moved to Japan from the Russian Far East, where I was born, because of his business interests, and we did not return to Russia because of the disturbances following the 1917 Revolution. During those years in Japan, my only close contact with the Japanese people was in Hakodate in 1918–20. There, as a child, I played with Japanese children, visited their homes, and took part in local festivals with them. Of all the places we were to live only Hakodate had the feel of real Japan—the smells and noises that were also a part of Suye. But even there in later years, the small foreign community— mostly Russian—became a kind of island, and as I grew older I became a part of it.

In Yokohama, where we lived from 1920 to 1923, the foreigners on the Bluff had limited social contact with the Japanese. We lived in foreign-style houses, built either by foreigners or by Japanese specifically for foreign rentals. All of the houses had central heating, fireplaces (especially those planned by the British), or stoves. The last were also particularly popular in Hakodate because of the winters. Some parts of Yokohama around the theater section and the Benten-dōri shopping area were Japanese. There we went to movie houses where American silent pictures were shown, accompanied by a *benshi* (narrator) for the Japanese audience. But the Moto-machi shopping district was for foreigners only, as were the British shops downtown, the Oriental and Grand Hotels on the Bund and the Gaiety Theatre on the Bluff. A Russian opera troupe from Vladivostok came there, and a Russian chamber music group performed at the Oriental Hotel. There must have been Japanese in the audience, but they were certainly in the minority. It was a strange colonial life in an independent country, where foreigners were tolerated but always watched very carefully. The Russians were regarded with particular suspicion.

The same was true of Kobe, where we moved in 1924, as did many others after the 1923 earthquake that devastated Yokohama and Tokyo. Fortunately, we were away spending that summer in Hakodate and did not suffer the effects of the earthquake personally, although we lost many friends and our house on the Bluff completely disappeared. Kobe, too, had a large foreign community and there was a certain rivalry among the different nationalities. The British were accorded the highest rank. Here, as in Yokohama, children of foreign fathers and Japanese mothers were a separate group, associating occasionally with the people of the nationalities of their fathers. I remember the consternation caused by the Prince of Wales, later Edward VIII, who at an official reception in Kobe in 1922 selected a beautiful Eurasian girl as his dancing partner. Social life was centered around the exclusive Kobe Regatta and Athletic Club and the popular Oriental Hotel, where the tea dances and American movies were attended almost exclusively by foreigners.

Vacations were spent in resorts catering to foreigners, around Kobe, in Kamakura, Miyanoshita, Nikkō, and Karuizawa, although this last was largely patronized by missionaries in those early days. Occasionally during the summer vacations we stayed at Japanese inns when no European-style hotel was available. I remember particularly an inn in Yunokawa near Hakodate, where we stayed before our own summer house was built. It was a hot-spring resort, and the hotel had three large baths side by side, without partitions—one for men, one for women, and the other for children. Therefore, as a child I took it for granted that mixed bathing was acceptable, providing one used the towel strategically. I spent a lot of time with the maids of that hotel and would sit fascinated, watching the geisha being groomed for the numerous banquets at which they entertained. The elaborate hairdresses, seen only at weddings in Suye, were worn routinely by these women. I also became quite accustomed to the loud drinking parties, although in those days I heard and observed them only at a distance.

Of course, no matter where we lived, we were surrounded by Japanese and had to communicate with shopkeepers and other casual contacts. Our occasional social contacts with Japanese were limited to my father's business associates. All foreign children went to foreign schools: the American School in Tokyo, the Catholic missionary schools for boys and girls in Yokohama, or the Canadian Academy, a Protestant missionary school in Kobe, from which I graduated in 1926. The Japanese language was not taught in the foreign schools in those days. While I learned English and French from private tutors in early childhood, I acquired colloquial Japanese from playmates and servants. I studied the language more systematically later at the Ecole des Langues Orientales in Paris. As I said earlier, my knowledge of the language was a great help in Suye, but I did have to get accustomed to the very special Kuma-*ben*, the local dialect of the region.

In 1931, when I returned from college, my family was back in Tokyo, living once more in a kind of foreign enclave, although there was more exposure to "things Japanese." But establishing contact with the Japanese socially was difficult because they themselves did not particularly want to associate with foreigners. Shortly after my return I made an effort to visit the Japanese student quarter in Tokyo hoping to get to know some students, just as I had done in Paris, but I was made to feel most unwelcome. During my last year at the Sorbonne one of the students in our group was a Japanese from Tokyo. He had been one of us, spoke good French, and we saw him frequently. When I tried to get in touch with him back in Tokyo I found it very difficult to arrange a meeting. He finally came to call, but that was the end of it and there was no further contact. Of course, the problem of isolation simply did not exist in Suye, since there was no choice and the villagers were just as curious about us, the first foreigners they had ever seen, as we were about them, which certainly facilitated our getting about and obtaining information. Because of this close contact, in my one year in the village I learned more about Japan and the Japanese people than I had in the many years before that.

So much for my life in Japan in pre-Suye days. This has been a long preamble, but I have written at length about that early life because I wanted to recapture the feeling I had when I was suddenly plunged into a farming community almost as strange to me as California had been when I first landed there in 1927 after spending most of my life as a foreign resident of Japan. Despite all the isolation, there was a clear feeling that one lived in Japan, albeit as a guest. It was home to me, I loved the country, and was desperately homesick while I was away. But life in Suye was quite different from anything I had known.

Suye Mura is about sixty miles south of Kumamoto City, capital of Kumamoto Prefecture, in Kuma County in the southeast corner of the prefecture. The county takes its name from the Kuma River, which originates on Mount Ichifusa, the sacred mountain of the region. From Kuma County the river runs north through the city of Yatsushiro to the western coast of Kyushu.

Our selection of Suye for the study was largely adventitious. We had spent more than two discouraging months looking for a community small enough for us to handle that would be representative of the majority of Japanese villages. That is, we wanted a rice-growing community rather than a fishing village or one in a remote mountain area. We were also determined to avoid the "model villages" that at the time were being promoted by the government as ideal rural communities, for they seemed rather artificial to us. It was also essential to find a house to live in. After visiting twenty-one places in various parts of the islands of Honshu and Kyushu, we still had not located a community that met these requirements. It was just at that point that a government official in the Kumamoto Prefectural Office suggested that we come along with him on a business trip to Suye. The small peaceful community, nestled in the beautiful Kuma River valley, surrounded by impressive mountains, appealed to us immediately. When we found that there was a house for rent, a rarity in rural areas in those days, we decided that we had found the right place at last.

We returned to Tokyo, where we had left our baby daughter with my family, and packed up for the trip to Suye. In 1935 it was a time-consuming and complicated undertaking. The train ride to Shimonoseki took sixteen hours. From there we crossed the straits to Moji by ferry and took another eight-hour train ride through Kumamoto City to Yatsushiro, where we transferred to a local train for Hitoyoshi, the capital of Kuma County. This two-hour trip along the Kuma River was spectacular, but the bus ride covering the last twelve miles between Hitoyoshi and Suye was bumpy and tiring. The bus's last stop was in the center of the village,

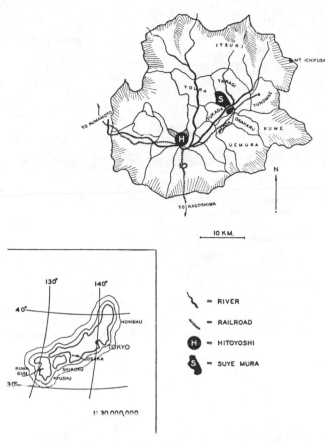

KUMA COUNTY

almost directly in front of the house where we were to live. For all the difficulty in getting there, Suye was not an isolated community, for it was one of a cluster of villages in the valley. Furthermore, the nearby towns of Taragi and Menda, where the villagers shopped, went for entertainment, and marketed products such as vegetables and firewood, were accessible by bicycle and on foot.

At the time of our study the population of Suye was 1,663 persons, consisting of 285 households scattered through the paddies, uplands, and wooded mountain area. Administratively the village was divided into eight units called *ku,* in most of which there were two or more hamlets *(buraku).* These administrative *ku* and their constituent hamlets, the basic units of social life and cooperative labor, were:

SUYE AND NEIGHBORING TOWNS

Ku	Constituent *buraku*
Oade	Ishizaka, Oade, Kamo
Kakui	Kakui
Imamura	Imamura, Tontokoro
Aso	Kami Aso, Naka Aso, Suwanoharu, Yunoharu
Hirayama	Hirayama, Nakanotani, Funeno
Hamanoue	Hamanoue, Tashiroda
Nakashima	Nakashima, Kojo
Kawaze	Kawaze

The Kuma River divided the village into two parts. The only crossing was by means of a very precarious, extremely narrow foot-bridge built of wood and bamboo bound together with twine and straw rope. It swayed with each step and there were gaps in the flooring of bamboo strips that made each trip across it something of an adventure. This bridge was rebuilt by communal labor every autumn, for it almost invariably was washed away in the heavy flooding of early June. Thus, for about a month the only way to get across the river was by a small boat manned by villagers who took turns at the task.

Kawaze and Nakashima, the paddy hamlets, lay on the plain to the south of the river. All of their residents were farmers who grew rice, the main cash crop. In the winter months the drained paddies were planted in secondary cash crops of wheat, rye, and barley. Oade, Imamura, and Hamanoue were upland hamlets, whose farm land was unsuitable for rice cultivation. The farmers there did tend some paddies down on the plain, but were primarily engaged in growing sweet potato, taro, corn, and other vegetables. Some grew millet in drained paddies and in dry fields in the uplands, and used it solely for domestic consumption, mixed with rice for economy. There were also fields of tea and mulberry in the uplands and on the hillsides. The tea leaves were processed and sold; the mulberry leaves were food for the silkworms. Both of these crops, which were attended to almost exclusively by women, were important sources of cash income. Aso and Hirayama were the mountain hamlets, the latter the most isolated of all the *buraku* of Suye. Farmers there grew many of the same crops cultivated in the upland hamlets on tiny plots of land and supplemented their incomes by growing mushrooms and making charcoal. The mountain area was the source of firewood for all of Suye.

Kakui was the main shopkeepers' hamlet. Very few of its residents were fulltime farmers, although some raised silkworms and grew tea. Several small shops sold candy, canned goods, and sundries, and there was a cake-maker, a lantern-maker, and a dressmaker. A few households made bean curd for sale and used the waste to feed pigs consigned to them by butchers in the towns. One large general store sold rice, sugar and salt, a few household items, wooden clogs, cigarettes and pipe tobacco, canned goods, and candy. The *shochu* distillery was in Kakui, which was in effect the village center. At one end of the hamlet's main road was the village office and at the other, on the border with Imamura, was the primary school.

In all of the hamlets most people grew their own vegetables, producing enough for their daily use and a year's supply of pickles. Any surplus was marketed in the neighboring towns. From the soybeans grown on the ridges dividing the paddies, they made soy sauce and the fermented bean-paste used as a base for *miso-shiru,* a soup that was a staple of the diet. In season the fruit trees provided peaches, pears, plums, and persimmons, and there were chestnut trees as well. Fish and small shellfish were taken from the river and the flooded paddies, but for special occasions the villagers patronized the fishmonger who came to Suye from Taragi. Meat, eaten only rarely, was always purchased in town. Eggs, however, could be bought from the several households that raised chickens. Hair oil, used lavishly by women and men alike, was pressed by the women from the nuts of the camellia tree, whose beautiful blossoms were one of the glories of Suye.

In the autumn the village was aglow with changing foliage and bright orange persimmons, and in the spring clouds of white peach

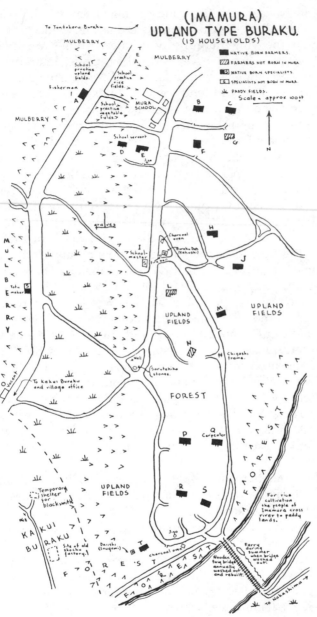

(IMAMURA)
UPLAND TYPE BURAKU.
(19 HOUSEHOLDS)

blossoms gave it a festive appearance. In summer the paddies were an intense green and the surface of the river shimmered in the hot sun. But the winter was bleak, and there were occasional snow flurries. Bundled in layer upon layer of warm clothing, the villagers' invariable greeting at that season was, "It is cold!"

For us the two great problems of living in Suye were the lack of privacy and housing conditions. Our house was on the main road in Kakui. It was not a typical farmer's house, for it had been a country inn at one time. Thus, the toilet and bath were attached to the house instead of being outdoors away from the building. Still, it was rustic. The kitchen was a lean-to with a dirt floor and a built-in wood-burning stove. There was no running water and no heat. Water had to be brought from the nearby well in buckets suspended from a yoke over the shoulder. In the interest of personal comfort we had to make many changes. Lack of plumbing was not new to me, but the Japanese toilet, which in this house was only a hole in the floor, is a nuisance on a permanent basis, so we had a seat built, which was something every villager had to see to believe. It required numerous trips to and from the well to fill the wooden bath-tub, and the water was heated by a wood stove built into the tub itself. Bath water heated to what seemed almost the boiling point proved a blessing in the winter months, but keeping warm otherwise was very difficult and we just about grew into our woolen underwear. At night we used the tub in turn; following custom John, the head of the house, took his bath first, I followed him, and the maids went last. The winter in Suye was mild compared to many other parts of Japan, but sliding paper doors do not keep out the cold air and charcoal braziers do not provide much heat. We tried to improve the situation by using the small portable stoves popular in the cities, which used *rentan* (compressed coal briquets), but our visitors complained that the fumes gave them headaches and insisted on leaving the sliding doors wide open. At night, after the hot bath, we could stay warm by putting on quilted and padded kimono and getting inside the thick padded bedding spread over the *tatami*. In the morning, it was always a trial to abandon these warm robes and get into our clothes in a cold, unheated room. In the winter everybody in the village suffered from chilblains. In the summer there were the heat, mosquitoes, and the pervasive smell of "night soil" fertilizer used on the rice fields a few paces away from the back of our house. Like everyone else, we slept on the floor under a huge mosquito net suspended from the ceiling. One night, to my great consternation, I found a field mouse inside the netting.

Downstairs we had two large rooms separated by sliding paper doors that provided a bedroom and a dining area. We sat on the floor and had only two chairs, which were outside on the little wooden balcony. A narrow stairway led upstairs where sliding doors divided the area into three small rooms. This made it possible to provide rooms for our maids, our assistant, and for our daughter's crib.

Taking care of the house was too difficult for me to do by myself because I could not balance the water buckets over my shoulder and did not know how to manage the wood-burning stoves. I knew that I would have to hire help, and a school teacher with whom we had become friendly from the start recommended one of his former pupils. The idea of having a housemaid was not unusual because all farmers had hired help to assist them with work on the farm and with the household chores. But the young girl who came to work for us almost immediately decided that taking care of a foreign household was much too complicated and insisted that we get additional help. This we did and the two girls lived with us, as did the servants in other households. They received a small wage and the usual gifts twice a year. Keeping the rooms warm did not seem essential to them because one kept warm by putting on extra layers of clothing to be worn inside or outside the house. Housecleaning was another stumbling block. All over Japan, the national health regulations required a thorough house-cleaning twice a year when the *tatami* had to be taken out and the entire house cleaned in preparation for government inspection. This procedure was followed in the village, and the farm households saw no necessity for additional housecleaning in between.

Cooking was a challenge, for I simply could not get the hang of the wood-burning stove, and had to depend on the maids to light and tend it. One great help was a kind of improvised oven, a square metal box that fitted onto a large charcoal brazier. In it we managed to make muffins and biscuits, and a few other baked dishes. There was no bread to be had in the village and we could only get it in the nearby town where a few items of Western food were also available. Meat was a rarity, but fresh fish was brought into the village by a fishmonger almost daily. Since John did not take to Japanese food, I tried to improvise with available products and facilities. I have never been much of a cook and in those days did not know enough to teach the maids, nor did I have the time to experiment with cooking myself. So we worked out a few simple menus that they could handle and stuck with them all the time. One meal was scrambled eggs with muffins made with millet, which at first was a treat. By the end of the year I could hardly bear to eat them and avoided both for years after-ward. I was familiar with Japanese food and very fond of many dishes, but in the village everything was coarser, saltier, and less palatable than city food. I did get to love *rakkyō*, a pungent pickled onion. At first, it seemed strange to have pickles rather than sweet things with tea, but there was no avoiding it because tea was served all the time and as soon as you sat down for a cup, the hostess expected you to extend your hand to receive some of the pickled vegetables then in season. You ate them right off your hand. Some of the vegetables and pickles were very good, as for instance spinach with sesame seed or Japanese radish early in the season, and I became very fond of *mazumeshi*, a dish prepared with steamed rice and diced vegetables, which was served whenever there was a large gathering.

Occasionally it contained barley in addition to rice. Poor farmers mixed barley with rice to economize because upland-field barley, unlike rice, was not a commercial crop. We drank Japanese tea almost all day long, but at home a cup of black tea was a real treat. For all the *shōchū* (a low-grade rice distillate) we drank, we did enjoy a scotch and soda before dinner when there was time for it. While we tried to maintain a semblance of Western diet, the girls working for us prepared Japanese meals for themselves and found the smell of our tinned butter repulsive. From them I learned some Japanese cooking and a method of steaming rice that I follow to this day.

The total lack of privacy was very difficult to accept, but we had to tolerate it since every contact was potentially useful. Because our house was centrally located the villagers were always passing by and frequently would stop in. As they got to know us better, they would feel free to come at any hour, often arriving in a group after attending some drunken gathering. We never turned anyone away because we knew that to carry on our work effectively we had to be accepted. That did not take long. It seemed to me that the people of Suye understood our goal better than the Japanese anthropologists we met, who never did quite grasp what we were after. Maybe the farmers were flattered that a couple of foreigners wanted to know all about them and, as I said earlier, they were curious about us and it amused them to have us around. Fortunately for us, from the very beginning the headman was very friendly and helped us in renting the house. When we moved into the house our things had not arrived from Kumamoto, where we had purchased our bedding and some utensils, so he loaned us everything that we needed. His nephew, who occupied a very important position in the village, became our friend right away and helped us in being accepted by the rest of the villagers. We were also supported by a school teacher who lived in the headman's house.

Being accepted made it possible to participate in village life. The farmers never prevented us from attending any public event. Weddings, of course, were family affairs, and we had to have special invitations. When he was a go-between, the headman arranged for us to be present as guests of honor and on that occasion the women even helped me to dress in a formal kimono. Funerals were more accessible. As a matter of fact, it was after I had attended my first funeral of an elderly woman whose family I often visited, that my presence was taken for granted. It was mostly a matter of learning by observation what one should do in specific circumstances, and what gifts were appropriate for what occasion. Eventually, we became more or less members of the community, taking part in special events, contributing our share of rice, *shōchū*, or money along with the others. I even helped with rice-transplanting to the amusement of the farmers, who let me take my turn and patiently corrected my work.

In spite of the increasing tension between Japan and the United States in the mid-thirties, the villagers always treated us as friends and did not show any suspicion. There was one unpleasant incident instigated by a very nationalistically-minded school teacher—not a native of Suye—and a local friend of his who had just returned from doing military service in Manchuria. The trouble started during a drunken party when our motives for being in the village were questioned, but even then the other men took our side and there were many apologies later.

The extent of our acceptance was clearly demonstrated to me when I returned to Suye for the first time in 1951 after John's death. I was visiting my family in Tokyo and, after some hesitation, decided at the last minute to go to Suye. In spite of the short notice everything was organized for my reception. The members of the village delegation who met me at the Hitoyoshi station when I got off the train had been selected very carefully. The official representatives of the village were the incumbent headman and the head of the village Women's Association. Each hamlet of Suye was represented by someone I knew or had some connection with. Our best friend, who had died after we left the village, was represented by members of his family. The wife of the man who was headman in 1935–36 was there as a representative of her hamlet and because we were such good friends. She spent the night with me in Hitoyoshi at the hotel where a room had been reserved for me. We went to the public bath together that night and slept in the first foreign-style bed she had ever slept in. The following day I was taken to their home where I was to stay. There, a Buddhist memorial service was held for John and Clare just as it would have been for any member of any family in the village, followed by the traditional banquet and a party. Their photographs were placed in the *butsudan* (the family Buddhist altar) next to that of their younger son, who had been killed in the war (see p. vi). I was treated exactly as a member of the family would have been. Furthermore, the pictures remained in the *butsudan* and memorial services on the date of their death continued to be held even though I could not be there.

There was one other touching incident that revealed how this feeling of friendly sympathy spread even beyond the village. After the war Suye became well known in Japan and now and again some new story about it would appear in the Japanese press. One article in 1954 described in detail our stay in the village and mentioned that John was particularly fond of the Itsuki cradle song.[1] It also described my visit to Suye in 1951.

---

1. The words of this haunting lullaby are given in Isaku (1981, p. 41):

odoma kwanjin kwanjin	We're the beggars, the beggars!
an shototachi'a yokashi	they're the nice people.
yokashi'a yoka obi	Nice people have fine sashes,
yoka kimon	fine clothes.
odon ga utchinneba	If I should drop dead,
michibachi'a ikero	bury me by the roadside!
tōru shitogochi	I'll give a flower
hana agyū	to everyone who passes.
hana wa nan no hana	What kind of flower?
tsu-tsu-tsubaki	the cam-cam-camellia
mizu wa ten kara	watered by Heaven
morai mizu	alms-water

This story so moved a certain toy manufacturer in Nagano Prefecture that he sent me a very special gift through the American embassy in Tokyo. It was a music box in the shape of a farmer's house that plays the song. I have treasured this memento along with some other very personal gifts that I received from my friends in Suye.

Before we started our work we decided that as soon as John could find an interpreter-assistant I would collect material on my own, concentrating on women and children. It was not easy to find an assistant, although the publicity about our study resulted in many letters of application. Here again we were lucky. On my trip to Tokyo in November of 1935 I went to the School of Foreign Languages and interviewed several graduating students. Sano-san seemed the most promising. His English was very good and my offer appealed to him. He was a native of Shikoku, a shy young man in his early twenties, who had never lived in a village community. He was easily shocked by the farmers' ribald behavior and at parties occasionally was teased unmercifully by the men. But eventually he learned to get along with everyone and was accepted into the community just as we were. At home he was part of the family. After we left the village we corresponded with him for some time, getting news of Suye through him. Our communication was cut off by the outbreak of the war, and when I returned to Suye in 1951 I was told that he had died during the war.

As soon as Sano-san arrived I began to work on my own. We had discussed different methods of collecting information and had concluded that observation and participation would be more effective than direct questioning. In the end, I had to do what seemed best to suit particular situations, and occasionally direct questioning was essential. I must note that I was not a trained anthropologist. My university training was in French language and literature, and the only formal anthropology I had taken were a couple of introductory courses at Berkeley with Robert Lowie. That was before I met John, and anthropology was just another required course. After 1931, under John's influence, it became a way of life, but I absorbed most of it through osmosis. I managed to participate in the seminars at the University of Toronto where John was working on his Master's degree, and in Chicago I audited lectures by Radcliffe-Brown, Malinowski, and Redfield. It was there that Margaret Mead presented the first exciting reports of her work, which was an inspiration and served as a kind of guideline for my fieldwork.

To obtain information, I always tried to find out whether some special event was taking place. Otherwise, I simply walked about the village, visiting a different section every day. I would drop in to see someone, stop by to observe work going on, watch the children at play, noting their games and songs, and was always on the lookout for some unusual activity. I tried to witness everything, the routine jobs as well as special tasks that differed with each season. I watched the preparation of everyday and seasonal food, such as making of bean curd, fermented bean-paste, and soy sauce, as well as the process of silkworm raising. The women of the village were extremely cooperative. They never failed to let me know about events or activities in the farming routine. The only special event I was never allowed to witness was childbirth. Understandably, it was a very private affair and the midwife, whom I knew well, could not notify me of an impending delivery without the permission of the woman. Even when I knew that a woman was giving birth and waited outside the house, I never heard a sound because, I was told, no Japanese woman ever cries out during labor. One woman told me that she delivered the baby by herself without waking her husband. I was always notified as soon as a baby was born, however, and the women were not reticent in describing the details of childbirth. As a matter of accepted procedure, I attended every naming ceremony and the first visit to the local shrine to introduce the baby to the deity.

Some of this constant wandering about the village was fun. On a cold day it was pleasant to sit by the fire-pit and have tea and pickles and smoke the tiny pipe that all older women used, while listening to gossip. On the other hand, much of it was exhausting because I was constantly on the go. Obtaining information about the remote hamlets up in the highlands was difficult because I found it too far to walk, even though the children from those hamlets managed to get to school every day in our part of the village. Frequently I had to use the bicycle, which was a problem since the narrow paths were bumpy and there was always the danger of falling into a ditch. (By 1968 most of these rugged paths had been paved over.) I very seldom got up to one of those remoter hamlets, and finally we had to spend a few nights with a farmer's family there, which even the villagers thought a hardship.

One of the big problems was the constant drinking. *Shōchū*, which in Suye was distilled from rice rather than from the sweet potato or barley as in other parts of Japan, looks like vodka and is much stronger than sake. Like sake, it is served hot, poured through a long spout of a very attractive jar called *gara* into miniscule thimble-shaped cups. One consumes a great number of these tiny cups because each person present at a gathering must make the rounds of the entire group exchanging drinks, first pouring a drink for the other person and then accepting one from him. It was served on all occasions and even when I accompanied some elderly women on a pilgrimage to a shrine outside the village, we took along some *shōchū* with a cold lunch, and all of us came back staggering. The relaxed atmosphere that followed drinking was a help in getting to know people and observing their behavior, but it often interfered with writing coherent notes. Note-taking was a difficult task. I carried a notebook with me at all times, but it was not possible to take detailed notes at a gathering or even during the informal discussion. So, no matter how tired I was at the end of the day, no matter how much *shōchū* I had been compelled to drink at a party, I would not go to bed before recording the day's events. (Today, a portable tape recorder would probably solve the problem!) Only on reading over my notes today do I realize how sketchy and inadequate they are. Sometimes I was too weary, sometimes too much in a hurry, and at the same time I never doubted that I would always remember what happened and who the people were. I was wrong.

It was a strain not to show irritation and always to be pleasant to everyone, whatever the situation. I do remember that toward the end of the year my patience was running out and I very much wanted to get away. The few trips to Tokyo and Kumamoto during the year provided pleasant breaks, and even going to the nearby towns of Hitoyoshi and Menda was a treat, although there was one trip to the neighboring town of Yatushiro that turned out to be painful. The men in the village invited John to take part in an outing to that resort town, which involved boating, a geisha party, and a night at the hotel. Japanese wives never participate in such outings, but I stupidly insisted on being included. As the only woman present, except for the geisha and the very accommodating hotel serving girls, I felt very uncomfortable and did indeed regret that I had not stayed home.

I was certainly a less efficient fieldworker when our two-year-old daughter Clare was with us because I worried about her and was always concerned about making sure that her food was fresh and the room kept warm enough. There was a problem with milk, for instance, since it was not available in the village. We planned to have her with us because we thought that it would be helpful to our work if we lived as a normal family, so that we could more easily find out what the villagers thought about child care and family relations. Well, they found my ideas very strange and were critical of our ways. The women wondered why the baby did not sleep with us, and could not understand why I was so concerned about her diet and so upset when she got lice from other children. I soon found that I could learn about their attitudes about child rearing without having my own child there, and it became evident that her presence curtailed my mobility and limited my effectiveness, for with regard to these matters, I could not remain objective. My intention was to observe and to find out what behavior patterns the villagers considered right and not to interject my own opinions as to what I considered right or wrong. So we took her to Tokyo to be with my parents who looked after her for the rest of our stay in Suye. I regretted having to do it, but at least I knew that she would be well taken care of. I often thought later that my ideas at the time were too rigid, for surely the village children grew up strong and healthy on the local diet without the benefit of milk and in spite of runny noses all winter long and the ever-present lice. (All children had lice and their mothers were not immune. In fact, it took me a long time to get rid of the lice in my long hair—another irritating inconvenience—and even my poor mother in Tokyo had trouble after I left the baby with her.)

Was the Suye of 1935 typical of villages throughout the country?[2] It was a remote farming village that appeared rustic by comparison with the nearby small towns. (These physical differences disappeared with post-war modernization. I was astounded to find modern plumbing, flush toilets, and electrical gadgets there on my 1968 visit.) Obviously, no single farming community can be typical of an entire country, but I think that basic food habits, child training, and family relationships were pretty much the same everywhere, as was, of course, the national school system. There were other universal traits that were surely common to most villages. Social stratification, for instance, was quite rigid, and its persistence was obvious during my last two visits. Certain people were invited to the welcome party given by the headman, but others had to stay in the kitchen when they came to see me and were not invited into the formal living room. Even those poorer people who had become more prosperous remained in the same social position they had occupied earlier. Only the leading families were invited to the memorial service and the banquet. The others were asked to come to the party after the ceremony. Another universal trait was the use of go-betweens in any situation where personal confrontation might cause embarrassment. Time and again, the headman or a school teacher would be called upon to settle a dispute between different factions in the village or to solve a problem, in our case such as the rent the owner of the house was to charge us and the wages we were to pay to our housemaids.

2. There is some information touching on this question in Jones (1926). Between 1917 and 1924, this American social scientist conducted surveys in five Japanese communities that were geographically isolated or had only recently been opened up to close contact with towns and cities. They were Namase village in Ibaragi Prefecture, Tatekoshi village in Niigata, Shirakawa village in Gifu, Maki (two villages) in Shimane, and Gokanosho district in Kumamoto. While he was concerned with a variety of issues, there is material relevant to the question of Suye's representativeness with regard to what Jones was pleased to call immorality—premarital sexual activity, illegitimacy, abortion, and infanticide. His repeated references to the *Bon* dance, held in mid-August at the time of the Festival of the Dead, reveal clearly its association with sexual license, of which the authorities strongly disapproved.

In Maki, he reports, the *Bon* dance was dying out. The "sexual irregularity" that usually accompanied this occasion was less conspicuous here than in the other four places, possibly because Maki was only twenty miles from the city of Matsue, which provided men with all they required by way of restaurants, bars, houses of prostitution, and local geisha. He further reports that the age at marriage for women had recently risen from seventeen to twenty-one, and that the size of the dowry had increased tenfold (Jones 1926, p. 83).

In both Namase and Shirakawa, the *Bon* dance was still practiced, although it was opposed by "leading citizens," who disapproved of the sexual misconduct that went with it. A careful family was said to prohibit its daughters from attending unless they were accompanied by their mother. In Shirakawa, in a population of 300, the record revealed an average of four illegitimate births per year. In Namase, the head of the Young Men's Association estimated that no more than two percent of the women reached maturity as virgins. In both places, in the past twenty years, the age at marriage for men had gone up two years and that for women three (Jones 1926, p. 88).

In Namase, the police knew of no abortions, but had arrested one man who admitted to practicing infanticide three times in as many years. Until ten to fifteen years before the survey,

In observing the official Shinto religion, the village followed the prescribed national rituals, and, as all over Japan, every household had a domestic Buddhist altar where ancestor tablets were kept. On the other hand, the real living religion in the village was the popular or folk Shinto, with its worship of numerous deities and complex beliefs and superstitions.

One aspect of life in Suye that may well be exceptional is the behavior of the women. Officially, as all over Japan, they occupied a subordinate position, but they did not always act as if they did. It is true that women had no role in village administrative affairs and that at home they followed the standard pattern of subservience to the husband, but in day-to-day contact with men, in their sharing of labor, in their role at social gatherings, their drinking, and their outspokenness, they certainly acted with much greater freedom than any Japanese female citydweller. One noticed this contrast immediately in observing the behavior of the village women and that of the school teachers or the wives of school teachers, who were usually city-bred women. The latter were frequently shocked by the uninhibited farmers' wives, whom they considered strange and uncouth. And yet, it is precisely these traits that made the women of Suye so remarkable, and Suye perhaps not quite so typical of Japanese villages.

the first of the hamlets of the village to open up to outside contact had been notorious for its immorality. It was said that there had been illegitimate children in every house and that every girl had premarital sexual relations. At the time of the study, the most isolated of the three hamlets was said to be the most moral. The *Bon* dance, which had been practiced until six or seven years before, was blamed for promoting immoral relations, desertion, runaways, illegitimate births, and quarrels. It was therefore banned. "In some cases boys take up the responsibility for their illegitimate children, but in most the trouble is that the father is not identified as the mother had relations with a number of boys. The usual practice is to report the child as born to the daughter's mother" (Jones 1926, pp. 92–93).

In Tatekoshi and Gokanosho, he found sexual relations even more loosely regulated than in the other three places. The *Bon* dance was dying out in the former village, while it had never caught on in the latter, where the *kagura* was still performed. It was estimated that only one or two percent of girls in Tatekoshi were virgins at marriage, and Jones remarks that the wife of a village headman in Gokanosho told him that all girls had sexual relations before they married. In both places, illegitimate children were cared for by their mother unless a third party could persuade the father to assume responsibility for them. In Gokanosho, nine percent of the males and eight percent of the females were technically illegitimate. The age at marriage for men was twenty-three, and for women seventeen or eighteen (Jones 1926, pp. 94–96).

As for children, Jones makes the laconic observation that in Gokanosho, "children are allowed to do pretty much as they please. Disease and undernourishment carry away many under one year of age and numbers die later." In one hamlet in Tatekoshi, he found that of twenty children, only three had lived to the age of twelve (Jones 1926, p. 96).

The reader will discover that none of this information about these other communities at a period slightly earlier than the study of Suye is in any way contradicted by the evidence collected by the Embrees.

Three sisters, dressed up for Girls' Day, with their elder brother.

Two elderly women, wandering musician-beggars. The one in the rear is blind.

Rest period during rice transplanting. A young mother nurses her baby.

Granddaughter pulling her grandmother and baby sister in a two-wheeled cart.

Women in work-dress.

Mother holding baby who has just been taken on its first visit to a Shinto shrine.

Little girls delousing one another at the Kannon *dō*.

Waitresses and geisha from Menda at the Inari shrine.

Woman on the way to the fields, carrying farm implements.

Dōnen (same-age) group of boys in school dress.

Young women dressed up for a concert of music and dance.

Members of the Women's Association in "patriotic" aprons.

Elderly woman who lives alone in a one-room house.

A couple serving as go-betweens at a wedding, in formal dress.

Elderly woman processing damaged silkworm cocoons.

Celebrating the day of the wind god (4 April) so that the crops will not be damaged. Ella Wiswell is seated left of center.

The Nature of Women and Their World

Throughout most of our account of the women and girls of Suye we shall see them in action, dealing with their friends, families, and neighbors. In this chapter, therefore, we have tried to provide more general information about them, which we intend to serve as a context for what follows.

The women and men of Suye alike entertained quite specific notions about the virtues and faults of women. Among the former was the ability to endure the hardship of the very heavy labor required of farm women. In the view of adults of both sexes the primary responsibility of women was to marry and become good wives and mothers. They were expected to be faithful to their husbands, although we shall see that some were not, and to serve men on all occasions. By and large, the women did as they were required, but not without complaining about the inequities they suffered. When a domestic situation became too hard to bear, however, they often left their husbands to seek a more satisfactory one. They recognized their penchant for gossip for the dangerous habit it was, and feared its consequences in the form of bad feelings and feuds within the village.

Within the very narrow range of experience of most of them, the married women of Suye led lives clearly dominated by domestic concerns. They knew little of the national scene and even less about their country's involvement in international affairs. Their interest in both was largely limited to concern for their conscripted sons. Many of the younger women and girls, however, dreamed of escaping the village and yearned to find work in the cities; many more of the young men actually did so. Despite their preoccupation with their domestic roles, we shall encounter many older women and some younger married ones of considerable independence of mind who often flouted convention and frequently engaged in behavior almost universally condemned as inappropriate to their sex. It is against the background materials of this first chapter, then, that we shall subsequently take up the specifics of the daily lives of the women of Suye.

The view of women held by village men was less than flattering in all its details, and the women themselves frequently commented on what they interpreted as the frailties peculiar to their sex. In John Embree's journal there occurs the following passage: "Hayashi Fumio says that the word for women's gossiping is 'well-side conferences' (*ido bata kaigi*). He wanted to know if we have gossiping, loose-tongued women in America. He says that he does not like to talk about other people because if you do you are bound to say bad things about them, which one should not do behind another's back." There can be no doubt, on the basis of the evidence, that gossip was one of the chief pleasures of the women of Suye, and a powerful weapon in their hands.

They were charged with other vices as well. "Although one of the songs definitely refers to a snake as a male sex organ, Sato says that he has never heard it used that way in conversation. Rather, he says, the word snake is used in reference to women because both are so wily and tenacious. There is an old story about a man who had two wives. Everything seemed to be going well, but one day while he slept two snakes coiled around his neck and choked him to death."

Many of the older women in Suye still blackened their teeth, in keeping with the old custom of doing so at marriage. Of the practice, one man said, " 'It is much like the *tsuno kakushi* (horn cover) headdress worn by brides at weddings. Both indicate the sinfulness of women. Because she is sinful, woman must be deprived of the possibility of biting others, and the concoction used to blacken the teeth serves much the same function as the bit in a horse's mouth.' [He did not mention it, but one woman claimed that she had been 'bitten' by the woman she suspected of bewitching her. Unfortunately for this theory, the witch in question had blackened teeth.] He went on to say that the bride's horn-cover is more of a decorative remnant and today, like the shaving of a woman's eyebrows, serves only to indicate her marital state."

Younger women, particularly those not yet married, are characterized as both stubborn and shy. "Stubbornness is an outstanding trait, the direct result of up-bringing, I should say. If a girl is against something, giving her orders, no matter how forcefully, is a lost cause." And of shyness, or being embarrassed by practically everything, "*Hazukashī* is an indispensable part of the young lady's vocabulary. One is shy to go places alone and one is shy to discuss personal matters. When a girlfriend says, 'You like that man,' you become *hazukashī* and exclaim, 'I hate him!' So when girls get together they usually confine their conversations to clothes and things they have been doing lately."

Some women of the village, however, were considered to be especially strong characters. "The women were discussing domestic relations. Mrs. Tanimoto says that when her husband returns home from work he does odd jobs around the place, but not much. Then she said of Sato Shichihei that he has not much to say at home and is not very good at his work. 'The women there are boss (*taishō*), especially the daughter.' They are considered the richest family in their hamlet, with much land and money. 'She always carries two or three ten-yen bills with her when she comes to a *kōgin*' [see pages 38–42], they said."

Older women, especially widows, were particularly likely to exhibit behavior that younger women would not dare to engage in publicly. A good example is that of the confrontation between the widow Matsumoto Shima and a man named Toride. The cause of their dispute was the gathering of some bamboo shoots, as we learn from John Embree's journal. "She claimed that he was taking them from her land. He said that he was not, and that he had gathered only a few from his own land. Later, after their quarrel was over, he charged that it was she who had been poaching. Neither brought up the matter again, so it rests there. Their lands are adjacent and there is a complicated history of buying, selling, and exchanging."

There was at least one colorful public exchange between the two. "Matsumoto Shima claims that Toride has been cutting wood and gathering bamboo shoots on her land, so she told his young son to stay off it. His father arrived this morning in a rage and to the amusement of the villagers, who assembled at once, proceeded to say what he thought. When Shima grew too impertinent, he made a gesture as if to strike her in the face. She yelled, 'If you hit me, I'll hit back,' and picked up a *geta* [wooden clog] with which she did strike him. [To strike another with a piece of footgear is a grievous insult.] They called each other *baka* [literally, fool, but the most insulting word in ordinary discourse] a couple of times. He said that he would go to the village office about this, and she said that she will write to her older brother, which she did after he left. 'He takes advantage of women,' she grumbled. After a long argument, he started off, turning around now and then to tell her that she had no right calling him such things, that she was a liar, that he will go to the village office, and that he will beat her up if she says that again. When he turned away from her, he would smile, then make a fierce face again and add a few more imprecations. She followed him verbally all the way down the street with her protests."

Among the strong-willed there were younger women as well. "At Makinos today Otome and her sister-in-law were sewing the newly laundered bedding. Otome [the daughter of the house whose husband is adopted] was very polite to her. 'Pardon me for turning my back,' she would say, and, 'No, you are not at all in my way,' but made it quite clear that she considers herself a much better and faster worker than her sister-in-law. When she asked Otome to help smooth out the padding for the comforter, Otome started to do it all by herself. 'Oh, it is very simple to spread it out alone,' she said, 'I am quite used to it,' with a little laugh, as if to imply, 'You are so clumsy.' The sister-in-law was also very polite, and said only nice things, but one could feel the tension in their relationship.

"In fact, Otome runs the whole show. While Hiroshi and the maid were planning to go out to finish cutting millet this afternoon, she insisted that they stay here so that he could fix the shed and the maid clean the house. She said that she was too busy with the bedding to do anything else, for it had to be ready by nightfall. Hiroshi said that any delay in bringing in the millet would mean that the maid could not attend the Hachiman [the god of war] festival, on which her heart was set. He had teased her about it earlier in the day, saying, 'She will cry if she cannot go.' Said his wife sternly, 'Well, if there is millet to harvest, there is nothing to be done about Hachiman-san.' She would not relent and they followed her orders.

"Where there is only the mother-in-law to deal with, the situation in a house is likely to be less strained, because the duties of the women are more or less set and are assigned by age and rank. But here, where there are two young women, and the duties are not clearly specified, things are more complicated. The sister-in-law is chronologically older and so is called elder sister, yet Otome has the prestige of being the daughter of the house and of longer residence there, and it is she who calls the tune."

Indeed, so completely did she call the tune that the young female servant in the house "says that she wants to leave and go to work in a company in Hakata, but they asked her to stay because the old lady is so ill. She does not know how much she is paid a year because the money goes directly to her father. She will have a ten-day holiday at lunar new year's. She says that the old lady is very kind and the old man not so bad. Otome is very hard to get along with, she reported with a grimace, and sends you here and there all the time and is hard to please. Hiroshi is also very bad, she claimed, and will hit you if he is displeased. I protested that they seem to be quite kind, but she said, 'You cannot trust a face.'

"She went on to say that ordinarily Otome does nothing but nurse the baby, but that now she will have to fix the pickles, for the old lady is far too ill to do it. As I went by she was discussing the matter with some of the Oade women. (Otome's husband was adopted into the family because her elder brother is sickly and not expected to live. The sister-in-law referred to above is the sickly elder brother's wife. The first child born to Otome and her adopted husband was a boy, who is greatly pampered by all the family. It is this exceptional position that gives Otome the domestic authority she would otherwise lack.)" It is highly unusual for married siblings to remain in the same house, and no other case is reported in Suye.

Most women drank, some of them to excess and on any occasion that presented itself. [The drink was shōchū, which was made and sold locally.] They also smoked cigarettes and a Japanese pipe sometimes jokingly referred to as a "one-puff" because of its tiny bowl. "Smoking is a great habit among the women. Mrs. Matsumoto told me that she had a dreadful time trying to quit when her doctor told her she must stop on account of her 'brain disease,' but just could not. So now she still smokes, but only a little. For smoker's hack she recommends fermented bean paste soup or a salt gargle. Eda Shizu said that she did not smoke at all until her most recent pregnancy. She says that she started during her last period of morning sickness and now cannot do without her pipe. On the way to the night-market in Menda the other day she asked me for a cigarette because she had forgot to bring her pipe and needed a smoke badly. The women asked if her husband minded when he saw her smoking for the first time. She said he was surprised, but did not seem to mind. 'When both husband and wife smoke,' said Mrs. Matsumoto, 'the husband does not object.' "

The hamlets that made up Suye were not always on good terms. The women frequently commented on the characteristics of their own and other hamlets, attributing some of the problems of hamlet interrelations to personality conflicts. "The women of Kawaze think that Kakui women have vicious tongues (*kuchi ga warui*) and are always fighting and gossiping about one another. This morning Mrs. Uchida spent hours gossiping with old lady Mori. The gist of it all was that Kakui is a very bad place because everyone there is on such bad terms. 'It's terrible! It's really awful!' they kept saying. This last was in reference to someone in Kakui having accused someone else of witchery. Mrs. Uchida said that she never repeats anything among those people because it always causes trouble. The other day, when I was trying to get away from the Sato naming ceremony to get to the farewell party for Mrs. Soeshima on time, the Kawaze women told me not to hurry. 'Kakui women are always late,' they said."

"Oade is also said to be in a bad way because people gossip so much, and in this respect Kawaze is said to be the best place of all. They are quite right. While anyone here in Kakui will discuss Koyo-chan's pregnancy [see pages 131–34] with me, in Kawaze all I can get for an answer is, 'They did not tell us where she went.' " Indeed, there is much evidence of friction in Oade. "The Oade women came in a little later [to the party], having first attended an Ise-kō (Ise Society) at Amano's. Mrs. Kawabe was not with them, and when I asked after her, the women at once voiced their disapproval of her behavior. 'She went to Menda to an athletic meeting to take her grandchild. As if athletic meetings were not held every year, and now for that she will miss your farewell party.' (Because she does not work as the rest do, and occasionally differs with their opinions, they often express disapproval of her behind her back.) Before they had finished their tea, she went by the house on her way back from Menda, and was surprised to find that they had not waited for her in Oade before coming here. She came later with Mrs. Hayashi of Tontokoro."

"The Nakashima women say of themselves exactly what is said of them in other hamlets—they do not drink much and are not good at dancing. They seldom go out anywhere as a group, and there is always much less dirty talk among them—in fact, practically none—as there is in Oade and Kakui."

It may have been that the Kawaze women were more restrained in their gossip about affairs in their own hamlet, but they were always ready to talk about Kakui. "The three Kawaze women talked about our last party and Mrs. Wauchi said that there are no *shamisen* in Kakui. Mrs. Irie objected. 'That's not true. There are many. I cannot tell you exactly how many, but the point is that Kakui people never lend them out. They just keep them in their boxes, even though everyone knows that *shamisen* go out of tune if they are not used regularly. In Kawaze we are always telling people to use ours so they will keep in tune, but Kakui people are stingy.' Someone warned that we might be overheard. 'That's fine. Let them hear,' said Mrs. Irie, and raised her voice. (The reference is to our last party when we had trouble getting a *shamisen*, but the accusation is not very fair. The only Kakui person present on that occasion who owns one was Matsumoto Shima, who went right home to fetch hers.)

"But no matter, it was decided that Kawaze is a better place than Kakui anyhow. I said, 'Kawaze is number one.' 'Yes,' said Mrs. Wauchi, 'but not in everything. No one in Kawaze gossips, while in Kakui they do nothing but, all of them. In Kawaze, there is just one such person.' She gestured with her head in the direction of the offending house. 'Here they all go *gucha-gucha*,' and she made a motion with her hand in front of her mouth to imitate someone who talks all the time. 'In Kawaze we just get together and have good times and sing and dance at the women's gatherings, but here, gossip starts at once.' Mrs. Wauchi and Mrs. Shimoda did all the talking, while Mrs. Sato, as is her custom, just sat smiling on the scene."

Some time later, "Mrs. Kato was having tea at Mrs. Uchida's. They agreed that Kawaze and Kakui are not on good terms, although things have been better recently. They said that only Kawaze women and Mrs. Tanimoto in Kakui like to make after-party *(ato iwai)* calls unannounced and bring uninvited guests, and will come to any house if they hear a party going on there. Some people, they said, are loud and too fond of drink."

Bad feelings between hamlets were not the only instances of group antipathy, which extended to the two sericulture groups organized by the Katakura and Kanebo companies.[1] "When I told Mrs. Tanimoto about some of the sharp remarks made at the party last night, she said that the women of the Katakura silkworm raising group *(kumiai)* hate those who belong to the Kanebo group to which she belongs. Formerly there was only one, but some fight had led to a split. Some people had remained with Kanebo, but others had paid five yen each to join up with the new one formed by Katakura. Their worms are not always good, and there are fewer members, so fewer cocoons are produced. New members entering the Kanebo *kumiai*

1. Katakura and Kanebo, two of Japan's largest spinning companies, organized the production of silk throughout the country. They formed local sericulture groups of the kind described here, sold them silkworm eggs, and purchased the cocoons. See Embree 1939, pp. 39–40.

pay only a one-yen entrance fee. There is great rivalry between them and neither will tell the other about its affairs. (At the party last night she was joking with old lady Tamaki [a member of the Katakura group], who said, 'We are number one!' and Mrs. Tanimoto had replied agreeably, 'Yes, yes. You have more of everything and do everything better than we do.' But the rivalry is bitter, nonetheless.)"

THE OUTSIDERS' VIEW OF SUYE

The wives of teachers, female teachers themselves, wives of village officials, and other outsiders who were resident in Suye viewed the farmers with a mixture of incredulity and condescension. Many were highly censorious of the women's heavy drinking, and clearly regarded the farmers as backward and primitive. Topics of conversation among young men and women are sometimes a surprise. "Speaking of pickled onions, Fumio said that they make you fart all the time, and Aki said it is true. She used to eat a great deal of them, but it became impossible to sit in the same room with her, so she stopped. She did confide that it is easy to get a good seat in a movie if you fart, so that while others are moving away you can grab a seat. The freedom with which anything is discussed in Suye is very similar to that affected by the ultra-modern, 'uninhibited generation' back home, and the system of bringing up small children reminds me of the permissiveness becoming so popular today. The in-between group, 'civilized' beyond village standards, but still not 'modern'—like the teachers— are shocked by local behavior. Witness poor Sano [John's assistant], a well brought up young man who is shocked every time the villagers get going with their jokes and songs and dances."

The nonfarm women were also scandalized by what farm families ate, which they took as one more indication of their benighted condition. "The other day this group of women were discussing the economic situation of Suye farmers. In Oade the Nagata family is said to be able to save a little money now, and no longer runs out of rice before the next harvest, but all of this has been accomplished at the expense of a very low standard of living. Mrs. Tanimoto thought the entire Nagata family's upkeep costs as much as she and her husband spend for just the two of them. The Nagata live on potatoes and sweet-potatoes, and eat other things these women would not consider fit to serve. Equally poor are the Eda. ('Even though we are friends, I cannot help saying it,' said Mrs. Amano.) They used to eat with their shutters closed so that no one could see, but now leave them open, although the food is still poor. These women just could not live on such stuff, they said. The worst of all is that old man in Nakashima who eats boiled barley ('Barley alone! Can you imagine?'), which he crushes first with a hand grinder. 'Oh, how awful!' exclaimed Mrs. Kato, who was taking this all in. 'I can see that some people have to economize, but they could at least try to make their food appetizing.' There is another family in Nakashima, they said, which is well off, but because they have ten mouths to feed, the women economize by cooking lots of soup which, eaten in great quantities, reduces the amount of rice consumed.

"None of these three comes from a farm family, and they have no use for farmers' ways. They find the local soy sauce inedible. Fermented bean-paste, they said, should be made with a preponderance of wheat malt and tastes better when prepared that way. Since it is expensive, however, local people use more wheat and claim that their bean-paste has a superior flavor. Farmers use too much salt in both soy sauce and the bean-paste, to keep it from going bad. Someone had brought some dried fish, which had to be soaked before cooking. They skinned it and broke it into small pieces before putting it in a pan of soy sauce and sugar. It was a hard job and they complained while doing it, joking when they discarded the skin that it should be cooked too, as farmers would do because they do not like to throw anything away."

There was, however, one striking case of a town woman who had made every effort to become a "village" woman. "Mrs. Kawabe does sewing for a lot of people and on rainy days, if it is a holiday, many girls come to take lessons from her. She is a town girl who became a village woman. Although not a farmer's wife, she is among the women all the time and does farm work, such as growing vegetables and raising chickens. When she first came she says she spoke with a town accent, but now is beginning to 'talk Suye.' She is self-conscious about it, however, and occasionally will repeat something she has just said in a local manner, as if making fun of herself.

"Among the genteel ladies of the flower-arranging class she is a social equal, but is not up to them in elegance, because she is so rapidly getting to be a part of Suye. She does try to cater to the opinion of the village women. Taking flower-arranging bothered her a bit because the other women laughed at it and often talked about the expense involved. 'What? Twenty-five sen for these wild flowers?' they would exclaim. 'Why, you can pick them free right here in the woods!' The hamlet women teased her so much that at one time she refused to carry her flowers through the village on her way from school [where the lessons were given] and would leave them at my house so that she could come back and pick them up later in the evening. Eventually, using the hot weather and her pregnancy as excuses, she stopped coming to the lessons altogether." The pressures to conform to accepted standards of behavior are nicely illustrated by Mrs. Kawabe's trials, as is the marked tendency of the local women to draw sharp distinctions between themselves and outsiders in terms of what was deemed fitting behavior.

The women from the towns and cities were also shocked by what they knew of standards of modesty among Suye women, which were quite relaxed by those of Americans of the 1930s. Women, like men, would stop to urinate beside the path, and were accustomed to using the toilets without doors that were found in most farmhouses. Old women often worked stripped to the waist, but young girls tended to keep their breasts covered. [But see Aki and the delivery boys, page 117] "Discussing with the others the picture that John took of her, Mrs. Shiraki demonstrated how she had been naked to the waist by letting down her kimono and then pulling it up in a hurry, as she had done then. All the men and women laughed. There is nothing indecent in the act. Actually, the gesture of pulling up the kimono over one's knees as a man does when he sits cross-legged is considered much more forward and is sometimes done by women as a joke."

Exposure of the body at the bath was relative, depending very much on who was present. Most Suye people bathed every night, but in the interests of economizing, one hot bath would be shared by a number of families in rotation. "When our maid and I went up to bathe at the Makino's—scaring the two nursemaids who were already there—we found the girls sitting in the bathtub scrubbing themselves thoroughly with soapless towels. The feet are washed very carefully while sitting on the edge of the tub. Getting out of the water, they have a technique of bending forward slightly, to cover the vulva, and then promptly tying a towel around their middles until they get on their pants or *koshimaki* [an underskirt worn with kimono]. Mrs. Makino came last 'because she is still bleeding,' they said. This is her first bath after delivering the baby."

Other bathing scenes reveal somewhat less discretion. "Mrs. Fujita and the Mori nursemaid came to bathe at our house. Pro forma they held a towel over the vulva, but it was not kept in place all the time. The little girl was quite bashful, mostly of me. They wash with soap first and then get into the tub together and rub themselves, and then get out to sit on the edge. There they scrub some more and towel off, rinse, and wipe off with the still wet towel, which they then wash and wring out. Next, as recommended by *Ie no Hikari* [The Light of the Home], they wash the face with cold water to prevent wrinkles. (Magazine instructions are much followed.) Then one must make up, putting on lotion first and then powder. Mrs. Fujita demonstrated how to apply the lotion. In the winter, they use a liquid powder or cream, in the summer a lighter concoction. All toilette is performed at night.

"The pimple lotion being used by our maid was discussed, and Mrs. Fujita said that it is not like what they used when she was young. While the others were bathing, Aki in her black bloomers applied her various lotions and powders with considerable modesty. She is bashful about making up while on duty. In spite of the towels, there was little physical modesty in evidence. They all looked at each other's bodies, compared navels, and even showed one another their vulva and the shape of the growth of pubic hair.

"The other day when pulling up her kimono to do the laundry, Mrs. Fujita had been teased by the other women about her long pubic hair, so when she got home she cut most of it off. Today she showed us all how short her hair is. She was told that her vulva is small. 'Not at all. Look,' she said, holding it cupped in her hands. It is, in fact, rather small in area. She wanted to see the girls', and would have had I not happened to come in at that point. The girls are bashful of me, and Mrs. Fujita reprimanded them. 'What will you do if you go to a hot-springs?' she asked." Hot-springs baths are public, and even those that were segregated by sex in the pre-war period required bathing in the presence of many strangers. Indeed, one of the stereotypical exaggerated claims of the hot-springs resort hotels was and remains that they have baths called *senninburo* that will hold a thousand people.

Yet for all this apparent casualness about exposing the body to the gaze of others, a custom which for decades distinguished the Japanese and the Americans, some kinds of immodesty attracted attention. "At Sato Genzo's, his wife was asleep. The women laughed because she was stretched out on her back in the *dai* position [the shape of the character for large or great]. Men sleep this way, but not women, who usually curl up on their sides into a most uncomfortable looking curve [in the shape of the character *ku*]."[2]

THE WORLD OUTSIDE

Most of the women of Suye had very limited experience of the world, and their access to information about it was severely restricted. The women over fifty were functional illiterates, and many younger women had only the most tenuous control over the complex universe of written characters and syllabary. "This morning I called on Mrs. Tanimoto who was gossiping with Mrs. Toride. The latter had come to ask Mrs. Tanimoto to write a letter for her. It was to some big military figure in Manchuria and had to do with her soldier-son's illness. It appears that Mrs. Tanimoto is the village scribe. Mrs. Toride brought her rice in payment for the service and was in turn served *shōchū* and fish, which she took home with a box of matches slipped into her *furoshiki* [a square carrying-cloth in which gifts are brought that should never be returned empty] as a return gift by Mrs. Tanimoto."

"The invitation to the party that came today was mimeographed and read, 'It has become warm. You must be very busy in this season of sericulture. We are pleased to announce that we have adopted a son whom

2. The practice of training boys and girls to sleep in different postures is reported by Etsu Inagaki Sugimoto, *A Daughter of the Samurai* (New York: Doubleday, Page and Company, 1926), p. 24, where she gives the wholly erroneous impression that the custom was limited to the warrior class: "Samurai daughters were taught never to lose control of mind or body—even in sleep. Boys might stretch themselves into the character *dai*, carelessly outspread; but girls must curve into the modest, dignified character *kinoji*, which means 'spirit of control.' " There are many versions of which is the proper character for girls to model their sleeping posture on, among them Sugimoto's *ki*, the *ku* of the Suye women, and the *kana* syllable *sa*.

we want to introduce to you. Please honor us by your visit at three in the afternoon.' Fumie, who finished the sixth grade about five years ago, had trouble reading it because she did not know many of the characters, reading the second part of *yōsan* (sericulture) as *mushi* (worm) and could not even guess at the first. She did not recognize the character for adopted. The younger girl, just out of school, managed better."

"Fumie's literacy really is very low. She could not write the characters *o-iwai* (felicitations) on a gift I was preparing. Be it said that when I asked Mrs. Sato Kazuo to write it, both she and her daughter first said they would get Kazuo to do it, and when they could not find him, the mother wrote it very simply with far less of a flourish than, say, an educated man would. Women are simply not supposed to be accomplished in these matters. The other day, Sato said of a Suye family, 'Those people are fools, educating their children beyond their means. They sent their daughter to girls' school and then to a music school. What is the use of so much education for a girl?' "

"Almost all of the old people here are illiterate, although most old men have as a rule picked up some knowledge of the syllabary. There used to be private schools to which some boys were sent, but few farmers' sons attended and girls were never given an education with the result that women over fifty cannot read. Mrs. Wauchi, who is forty-six, had six years of school just at the time that it first became possible for girls to go. It was not compulsory [or attendance was not enforced], however, and her older sister, Mrs. Shimoda, cannot read at all. Even the women who did attend school seldom remember much of what they were taught. Mrs. Fujita, for example, is never able to read anything. Only with our generation [of people in their twenties] has schooling reached its present universal level, at least in this part of the country."

Nevertheless, many households subscribed to illustrated magazines. The most popular was *Ie no Hikari* [Light of the Home], followed by *Fujin Kurabu* [Women's Club], *Shufu no Tomo* [Housewife's Companion], *Kingu* [King], *Haiyu* [Actors and Actresses], and various other movie magazines bought by young men for the pictures of the women actresses. Few families subscribed to newspapers. Even those young women who could not write were able to read these magazines, and the older ones who could not read could enjoy the pictures. "The women and children were idly looking through an old copy of a magazine. Some pictures of the colonial peoples—Koreans, Formosans, Ainu—looked very strange to them. There were also pictures of the royal children, whose names and ages were discussed, but no one was quite sure of her information. (In fact, the other day when I was at Mrs. Kato's, two other women visitors politely inquired if it was not her grandchild whose photograph was hanging over the godshelf. It was in fact that of the royal heir-apparent.)"

The women's rather inconclusive understanding of the emperor cult being so assiduously promoted by the central government is neatly illustrated by a lengthy conversation with Mrs. Tanimoto, a literate woman much given to relaxing with a magazine in the afternoons. "Having stopped by for a chat, I asked her, 'You worship the Emperor like a god (*kamisama*), don't you?' indicating the hanging scroll portraying the Imperial couple in the *tokonoma* [ceremonial alcove in the main room]. 'Yes, when we make an offering to the gods, we make it to the Emperor too. When we pray in front of the gods, it is also in front of the Emperor, and to him we offer flowers,' she said. 'Why?' I asked. 'Well, I suppose it is because he is head (*taishō*) of the country,' she replied. Then she described the figures in the scroll. 'There on the left is Jimmu-tennō, the very first, very famous Emperor, and on the right is his wife. Then comes Taishō-tennō and the Empress. Below them is the palace, then the three princes, Chichibu, Mikasa, and Takamatsu-sama. Below, there behind the flowers (she had a tall vase in front of the scroll) are the present Emperor and Empress. They are all great people. They have a very beautiful palace. Have you seen it in Tokyo?' I said that I had, but that one cannot get very near it. 'Yes, no one is allowed near. Only very famous people are allowed to attend palace receptions, and even they only present their names, which are taken in to the Emperor. No one can see him because he is a very high personage.' 'And who is that above them all?' I asked. 'That is Amaterasu-ō-mikami, the first, greatest and most famous of the Japanese goddesses. She, with another god coming out of the same waves of the sea, began all the people. She is the number-one goddess.'[3] 'So? But why are they all in the picture together? What is the relationship between Amaterasu and the present Emperor?' 'I don't know, but they are both there most probably because she is the greatest *kamisama* and he is the head of the country, the greatest person in Japan.' 'Then the Emperor is not a *kamisama*?' 'No, he is just worshipped like a god (*kamisama no yō ni shimasu*), but he is not a real god. He is human, a very great man (*erai hito desu*).'

"I admired the scroll a while longer, and then remarked on the amount of decorations and necklaces worn by the Empress, thus preparing her for the next question, since necklaces here are strictly foreign items. 'Why,' I asked, 'does the Empress always wear a dress rather than a kimono?' 'Indeed, she does wear dresses. I wonder why? Her chest sticks out and her neck stretches up. What a long neck she has!' We both laughed. I suggested that foreign clothes had become a kind of uniform after the Meiji Restoration [in 1868]. Only Meiji-tennō and his Empress are wearing Shinto-style garments in the picture.' We decided that it must be a custom

3. This account is interestingly garbled in that it collapses two major female deities into one. The primal couple were Izanagi and his sister Izanami. It was she who gave birth to the world and most of what is in it, dying upon being delivered of fire. Amaterasu-ō-mikami, the sun goddess, is the imperial ancestress, born of the left eye of Izanagi when he bathed to cleanse himself of the pollution of death upon his return from his unsuccessful journey to the Land of Darkness to bring his dead sister-spouse back to earth with him. Here, as on many occasions, it is clear that the official version of ancient Japanese myth-as-history had not yet reached the women of middle age and older.

that was established rather recently and were both convulsed with laughter. 'Look at her hair-do and the open neck. She is dressed just like you,' she exclaimed. I suggested politely that I have no such beautiful jewels. Then I said that we ought not to be talking like this. 'No, no, we shouldn't,' she said, but laughter got the better of her. 'If the policeman were to hear us, he would tie me up and throw me in prison. But he can't hear, can he?' I said I thought we were safe. I left her laughing on the balcony, dusting and drying her lacquer-ware. So much for Emperor worship."

"Mrs. Toyama wanted to know if we have an Emperor in the United States and was amazed at my description of our system of elections. She wondered if they were like their local elections, where rich men get all the votes. She said that in Japan the Emperor holds his position by descent from way back, and is worshipped at the god-shelf like a *kumisama*. She did not know who the first Emperor was. As to why the Empress should wear a foreign dress, she thought it was something for gala occasions, and maybe even just for picture-taking. At home, she thinks, she most likely wears kimono."

In the constricted world of the villagers, popular magazines, like the movies, were a highly valued window on the world of beautiful women, handsome men, and important personages. "Our maid gets absorbed in *Kingu* love stories, which usually feature two girls in love with the same man, who loves only one of them. 'Which will become the bride?' she wonders, and can hardly wait for the next installment. Sometimes it is a story of a husband falling in love with the wife of another man. 'Now the letters are flying back and forth,' she says, 'but it has not yet come to a divorce.' " ·

"All the girls talk about make-up and more becoming ways of fixing the eyebrows. 'Germans have such funny-shaped eyebrows,' I was once told. I discovered that this information comes from an advertisement in *Fujin Kurabu* (The Women's Club) for some facial cream which features pictures of various movie actresses. Each photograph is shown with the name of a country, rather than her own, under it. Thus Germany is Dietrich, Sweden is Garbo, etc. The least attractive of the lot, a commonplace brunet, is America. So, say the girls, Americans look most of all like Japanese girls."

"Mrs. Sato Kazuo subscribes to a magazine called *Shufu no Tomo* (The Housewife's Companion), rather like the *Ladies Home Journal* or the *Woman's Home Companion*. It has illustrated articles on how to care for a baby, resembling the Bundison method,[4] although walkers are recommended. This month also devotes much space to the Dionne quintuplets.

4. A reference that derives its meaning primarily in the context of the sections on child-rearing in the chapter on Suye women and their children. In answer to my query, Ella Wiswell wrote: "Dr. Bundison was the author of a monthly bulletin distributed through some agency of the State of Illinois to parents of all babies born in Chicago, as Clare was. It contained very valuable information on baby-care, and was particularly helpful to young inexperienced mothers. It foretold with amazing accuracy what the baby would do at each stage of its development and how to cope with various problems. It also had very rigid admonitions to

I have no idea why this belated publicity all over the country, with pictures of the children in all the newspapers and magazines."

"Mrs. Wauchi showed me a copy of *Fujin no Tomo* [The Woman's Companion] and was surprised when I said I had seen it somewhere else in Suye. (As a matter of fact, I mistook it for *Shufu no Tomo* [The Housewife's Companion], so was wrong about having seen it elsewhere.) She said that this is a more serious magazine, and stressed the fact. There was an article in it in the form of letters from an American-educated Japanese girl, with accounts of special Danish exercises, experimental schools, directions for sewing, and the like. By way of illustrating that a foreign dress is not at all like the local *kantan* [a kind of shift] there was a photograph of a foreign woman standing near the Imperial Palace in Tokyo. She wanted to know if I thought Japanese look funny in dresses, and what I wear under mine. 'The magazine mentions so many underthings,' she said."

At another house, "Mrs. Irie and I discussed clothing and she wondered if it is cheaper and easier to make foreign clothes or kimono. The newspaper always runs a series of pictures of fabrics, and many women order their material by mail, by the number and date on which it appeared. Popular magazines do the same, usually giving colored reproductions of patterns and designs. Sato's sisters ordered their new *obi* [sashes] from a magazine, and our maid says she will do so too."

The credulity and utter lack of experience, especially of the girls, was often revealed in discussions of the supernatural that occasionally impinged on the lives of the women in Suye in the form of ghosts, mysterious manifestations, demons, and animals in human form. On the way back from the Yakushi festival in Menda with a group of women and girls, "as we went through a dark part of the road everyone suddenly stopped to look at a string of lights in the distance. 'It's the foxes making a train!' Foxes are also known to imitate funeral processions [the fox-fire looks like a string of people, each carrying a lighted lantern]. A skeptic explained that the lights were merely electric bulbs recently put up around the park in Taragi. I was told, however, that many foxes come down from the mountains and before bad weather arrives they may be seen going round and round in a chain, making a sound like a train and turning the lights on and off. I wanted to know what kind of lights these were. They have their own, I was told, made of some kind of grass they know how to use. They can easily be seen from the temple. Aki entertained no trace of doubt.

"People never become foxes, they told me, but foxes can take on human form. For example, the Okada doctor in Taragi once delivered a fox, and this is how it happened: A very beautiful woman, all white and dressed

---

parents to prevent them from spoiling the child and giving in to its whims. For instance, one was told not to pick up the baby every time it cried, to feed it at regular intervals, etc. In other words it was a system completely different from the permissive one that became fashionable later and certainly it was the exact opposite of the way babies were treated in the village."

in a beautiful kimono with a gorgeous headdress, came to ask him to come with her to Kume. He did so and found himself in a very rich, new house. There were clean *tatami* and a pretty woman was lying there on her bedding. He helped her with the delivery of her baby and received ten yen for his services. As it had grown very late, he was offered a place to stay for the night. He went to sleep and when he awoke in the morning he found himself lying on a grass-covered mound of earth instead of the bedding on which he had fallen asleep. Frightened, he hurried home. When he told his wife what had happened, she realized that he had been bewitched by foxes, who had stolen the money from a rich family in Kume. 'Is that true?' asked Nami-chan. 'Of course,' she was told. Then someone told the story of the mountain woman of Gokanoshō, who had been abandoned there when she was a baby. She grew up to be very beautiful, with long flowing hair, and runs from humans. She had a beautiful baby by the man of the mountains (*yama no otoko*).

"Gorillas are considered fearful because they look so much like humans. 'They can take a human bride. It's true,' said Aki. 'I saw it in a movie in Taragi.' She never doubts what she sees in a movie. In fact, the girl believes everything she is told. Discussing the pictures in a book she will refer to the characters as if they were real people: 'This one wrote to that one, and this one is all broken-hearted now.' The mixture of ancient and modern is sometimes astonishing. After the discussion of foxes and their witchery the other night, the girls fell to discussing Shirley Temple, whose picture they had just seen in the current issue of *Kingu*. Things old and new are so mixed up that it is hard to draw a line, as when our maid uses a movie to demonstrate the truth of a local tale."

Few women were at all concerned with national or international events. "Women do not take a great interest in newspapers. 'Here are some war pictures,' said the little boy. His mother denied that there was any war going on anywhere. I mentioned the Spanish trouble, so she said to him, 'It is just like a squabble between brothers.' While he enthusiastically read out the results of the Olympics [in which Japanese athletes were doing very well], she said absentmindedly, 'Really?' but could muster no real interest. In magazines, however, pictures of strange things, bits of world news, and the like do interest the women—things like the Dionne quintuplets or some exceptionally strong man lifting an incredible load. A picture of the Emperor is always looked at and admired. 'What a beautiful horse he rides!' they exclaim."

For these women and girls by far the most thrilling contact with the outside world came through the motion pictures shown occasionally at the school or out of doors in a vacant lot, or perhaps seen at one of the theaters in Menda. There is an account of one of them that offers both an engaging plot summary and an instructive account of the reactions to it.

"The story, concerning one Takeko-*fujin*,[5] ran in some magazine a few years ago. The actress playing the heroine was exceptionally homely. The point was to demonstrate how a woman must practice fortitude and devotion, and how she performs her obligations with a smile and bears her sorrows in silence. (Later Aki said that the men who give talks at school tell them how to be brave and ready to serve.) The story was that of a girl of noble family who grows up without knowing her mother. (Aki did not know why, but thought this a practice of noble families; I think it had to do with a temple connection.) She is taught never to complain.

"Then the war in China was shown, from beginning to end, with poor soldiers starving and fighting to the last, women concealing their tears, making *imonbukuro* [kit bags]. The movie orchestra, never hitting a right note, playing *Koko-wa o-kuni-o nanbyaku ri* [Here, thousands of miles from home . . .]—composed at the time of the war—all through this. After the war, there was much rejoicing and the girl, now twenty-two, is approached for marriage to the younger brother of her elder brother's wife. 'Bashful, happy,' said the *benshi* (narrator), 'hearing such words for the first time, she consented.' During the wedding the *benshi* said, 'Weddings are a source of happiness, and of tears,' and the young men giggled.

"Then for some reason, the husband was no longer around. ('I don't know where he was,' said Aki. 'He was not shown any more.') But the girl sets out on the path of virtue. To a young bride who complained about her husband's coming home late, she told the fable of a married couple who fought over their reflections in the well-water, which they took to be their respective rivals. Their trouble was settled when an old man made them look down the well together. Next she saved a little newspaper vendor girl who worked all day to feed her sick mother and baby because her father had left the mother for another woman. She was finally shown praying, and 'becoming like a *kamisama*,' as the wheel of constant obstacles that she was mounting is shown changing into a sparkling wheel that leads to Paradise.

"People were most impressed by the little girl who sold newspapers. They said it was very sad to see a little child starving, yet hearing the

5. The film dealt with the life of Kujō Takeko. She was the daughter of Ōtani Kōson, chief abbot of the Nishi Honganji, headquarters temple of the Shin sect of Buddhist, in Kyoto. Himself a count, Ōtani arranged the marriage of his then thirteen-year-old daughter to Baron Kujō Yoshitome. The couple went to live in Tokyo and subsequently his firm assigned him to a European post. She went with him, but returned to Japan in 1916 and lived alone until her death in 1928. During those years she became a poet of renown and was actively engaged in social work. She died alone, a tragic figure so famed for her intelligence and beauty that today older women remember hearing it said of a woman that she was "as beautiful as Kujō Takeko." Her poems in the *waka* form are passionate and almost unbearably forlorn, infused with a sense of loss and despair. In my reading they strongly suggest that she had been sent back from Europe by her husband. I have been told by a man who knew him when were both employed by the same firm that Baron Kujō was a strange and isolated man to whom no one was close.

clatter of plates in the restaurant outside which she stands, and giving the last bit of food to her mother. While Aki understood just as much, or as little, as I did, Mrs. Tanimoto has the story and so has young Mrs. Wauchi, with the exception that Mrs. Tanimoto says the husband went off to England, while Mrs. Wauchi says it was Germany. At any rate, being of the samurai class, he went on a mission to a foreign country. Mrs. Wauchi thinks the young woman was adopted, while Mrs. Tanimoto believes that she must have been the man's daughter by a mistress. That is why her mother did not live in the house, while the mother of her older brother and sister did. It seems that it is a true story about a woman who died at the age of forty-two, who was connected with the abbot of Nishi Honganji. At *o-bon* [the Festival of the Dead, held in mid-August] the movie people will come again and show part two of the film.

" 'On the whole,' said Aki, 'the movie was not very interesting,' which opinion was shared by many, but I noticed that she shed tears with the others. One child sobbed so hard that he had to be taken on his mother's lap to be comforted. All made little jokes about the funny looks of Takeko-*fujin*, who had a long nose and hair fixed in the foreign style (1922), with hair drawn way down to the middle of the cheek."

Few of the women of Suye had ever seen a Caucasian before the arrival of the Embrees, and most had only the vaguest idea about what life in the United States might be like. Their curiosity led them to pose many questions, and there are several entertaining examples of the efforts of these women to explain and understand the inexplicable and mysterious ways of their foreign guests. "When I told some women that we never carry babies on our backs, they were amazed and asked, 'But if you always carry children in your arms, how do you carry an umbrella?' "

"I said that in America we offer flowers, but no rice, to the gods. The Kuwagiri woman said, 'Ah, it must be a water god (*ike no kamisama darō*).' "

"Asking various questions about America, the women were shocked to learn that all night-soil is disposed of. 'Such good stuff wasted,' they said. 'Take us to America.' (Nothing is ever wasted. The bean-curd maker serves scrapings from the boiler, left at the bottom when the bean curd burns, mixed with soy sauce. It is called *kogare*; burned rice is eaten this way, too, or with salt.)"

"Mrs. Tanimoto was shocked at the idea that in America a man might live to be fifty or older and never marry. 'Don't they like women?' she asked, with a slight implication. The existence of old maids sounded implausible to her. 'Here everyone gets married,' she said. When I said that I would have to be getting back to the house soon, she asked me to stay unless I am busy. 'Foreigners always do everything on the hour, so perhaps it is that you have something you must do right now?' I stayed."

Men, too, were curious. "At Uchida's today I ran into an out-of-town wagoneer, who questioned me at length on America, its inhabitants

('What nationality is the majority of the population?') and passed at once to questions of military service, war, and the American navy in Hawaii. 'Is it true that Americans dislike Japanese?' he wanted to know."

The issue of militarism and portents of impending conflict were much on the minds of the Embrees. At a military review at the village school, a deliberate snub by a visiting army officer and her being asked to leave the auditorium during his speech led to this observation: "Most of these people do not know where foreign countries are located, nor will they ever know why a war occurred if one does. But were there a war tomorrow, they will go and kill because that is what they are taught they must do, and they will believe any newspaper trash dished out by the authorities. Yet they are the most peaceful people in the world. When I mentioned that we have no compulsory military service in America, the women asked, 'What will you do if war comes?' " On the other hand, at least one couple thought that a unification of America and Japan would be a good idea, for it would balance trade and production.

The authorities were more than a little interested in the Embrees and their activities. Toward the end of their stay, "when I arrived at the school, people had already begun to gather. The police arrived, the one from Fukada and our 'friend' Omura. They asked such important questions as when we are leaving, why we have advanced our departure date, is John's assistant going with us, and whether or not we will stop over in Kumamoto. The Fukada policeman did not like it when I observed that they will be glad to see us go, but Omura laughed and said, 'No, we shall be lonely.' He treats us as personal friends, but neither responded when I said that the police here bother entirely too much with foreigners.

"They were talking to the principal when someone put on a record of foreign songs done by a famous Japanese soprano. All three agreed that such music is not enjoyable, that Japanese songs are best, and *naniwabushi* [a kind of long ballad] best of all."

For the most part, the women were more interested in the details of everyday life. "Her family moved to Suye from Amakusa long ago. She was quite surprised when I said that we do not eat much rice in America. She had thought that we ate a superior kind of rice. [The word for America is *Beikoku*, 'rice country.'] She was also astonished to learn that all American women, even old ones, wear dresses. 'They are so expensive here!' she exclaimed."

At the Shiraki naming ceremony, "everyone was very gay, and one of the women told of the customs in Yamaguchi where she comes from. Women sit differently there, she said, tailor fashion, like men. This discussion of sitting arose because someone had asked me if people live longer here or in America. I said I thought it was about the same, and said that we do not have many people over eighty. They said that there are many eighty-year-olds in Japan, and decided that it is the way of sitting (making it possible for them to relax) that makes for longer life as opposed to the stiff position foreigners use in sitting in chairs. (The favored sitting position for women here is with one leg folded under, with the other upright with one arm resting on the knee.)

"The woman from Yamaguchi told us about the strange American women she had seen in Moji, who all wore hats with nets over their faces and held on to the men when they walked. Shiraki said, 'America is a big country. Perhaps these women come from a part of it where the customs are different.' [This to explain the difference between Moji women and Ella Wiswell's appearance and behavior.]"

"The teachers from the girls' school in Taragi arrived. Very nice young ladies, they wanted to know about foreign cooking and sewing. It always surprises Japanese women that we do not make our own clothes, and that bread is not something eaten as a substitute for rice. They wanted to know if foreign women have to sit in the kitchen and serve like maids when there are guests, or if they can actually sit and eat with the company. When told, they thought it would be so much nicer to be able to sit with the guests rather than having to act like maids. (In the kinds of urban families these young women were raised in, a wife never eats with the company, but sits by serving everyone, pouring drinks, and making herself both as useful and inconspicuous as possible. She is seldom offered a drink or her presence acknowledged in any way.)"

And predictably, the most common mirror stereotype of all came up one afternoon. "Looking through an issue of Time magazine with us, Otome said, 'All Americans look alike. See, here is the man who came to visit you, and here is your baby. Do all Japanese look alike to you?' "

The man who had visited the Embrees was none other than Archibald MacLeish, who came to Suye with his wife. Their brief sojourn created a sensation. "The MacLeishes still come up in conversation. The other day, Suzuki, seeing an advertisement in Time, noticed the beret and wanted to know why MacLeish wore such a hat. 'It is a very funny hat. It has no brim.' I agreed that a brimmed hat was more practical. 'Well, yes, for the sun, of course,' he said, 'but otherwise is this kind of hat considered better?' I ventured that it was *haikara*—stylish. 'Why does he wear it?' he insisted. I suppose that a serious-minded person should not be accused of being *haikara*. He seemed partially satisfied when I explained several practical advantages of the beret for traveling and finally hit upon calling it a 'travel hat.'

"The MacLeishes turned up again in conversation at Sato Kazuo's. They said that he is not as tall as John and looks very much like the people here. 'He differs only in color.' The women broke in, 'As for her, she is a real bourgeois type, real bourgeois.' [A compliment, meaning that she is a lady.] The women were all interested in Mrs. MacLeish's age and tried to guess at it. They were obviously trying to guess more than her age, but said less than they were thinking. They've become used to us and our utilitarian outfits adapted to life in the village, but foreigners in stylish clothes looked strange indeed."

Then there was the position of Japan in the world. "Mrs. Tamaki observed, looking at a map during the conversation about emigration to Korea and Manchuria, how small Japan was compared with other countries. She said that it had become a bit larger with Korea and Manchuria added, 'And if we get a part of this'—pointing to the vast area of China—'it will be much, much bigger.' "

"Maps bother people. Down to the smallest child, they remark on the smallness of Japan, and how nice it would be if at least a section of adjoining territories could be acquired. Tremendous colored maps hang in the classrooms, and the children read out Russia (always mentioned first), China ('There, that big space in green.'), and then they look for Manchuria (Manshū-koku), and Korea (Chōsen), which they are always glad to find. Next to the map hangs a painting of the Japanese flag, with an inscription attached. 'Rising in the morning the sun becomes brighter. Japan must become stronger.' "

China, Korea, and Manchuria came up frequently in conversation. "Tonight two young men back from military service dropped in to tease our maid about her boyfriends, embarrassing her terrifically. One reminisced about Manchuria, the other about Taiwan, mimicking local speech and ways of talking. Both liked native women, even though those on Taiwan are black, said one. They praised the beauty of the Japanese girls who have gone out to work in the cafés, and agreed that by comparison the Menda girls are frightful."

"Mrs. Sato was the only one to mention recent events in China. She asked me if I had ever been there and whether the Chinese people were the same as the Japanese. She thought the recent murders were dreadful, especially since some of the victims had been tortured. Mrs. Toyama had heard nothing of all this, but thought it awful, too. When Mrs. Sato asked, 'Why is it they enjoy torturing others, and make a game of killing?' Mrs. Toyama said, 'So does the cat.' "

Sometimes the assessment of the behavior of foreigners took an unexpected twist. "Old lady Tanno was surprised to learn that we do not observe o-bon [the Festival of the Dead, when the ancestral spirits return to earth] in America. We then discussed other weird customs she has heard of, such as female infanticide and bride-purchase in Manchuria. She thought the latter particularly dreadful because it must mean that a poor man cannot get married."

"In the evening the children were playing outside. They said that they could already see the rabbit in the moon. [The 'man in the moon' is a rabbit wearing a headband, holding a pestle with which he pounds glutinous rice in a mortar.] Another said that the Chinese believe it is a girl, and the Indians think it is a man and woman copulating. Speaking of India, Mrs. Fujita was talking about the origin of Buddhism in India the other day, and said that Shaka was a prince there." This was almost the only informed remark about such matters made by a Suye woman.

Other countries came up from time to time. "The men thought that Spanish women are very beautiful, much prettier than Japanese. Then the doctor made the radical statement that Japanese women are *kitanai* ['dirty' but here meaning ugly], with poor figures and short legs, all due to squatting. I think it is something polite to say that he must have read in a book. I assured him that all our men fall in love with Japanese girls, 'because they are so modest and shy compared to shameless foreign women.' To which he replied, 'Your men must be attracted by modest glances.' "

"At Ariyoshi's, where I sat for a while in the afternoon, the conversation was about America, and I was showered with the usual questions about climate, the school system, and the alphabet. Said the older girl, a fifth-year student, 'In Russia they kill people,' but volunteered no further information. Since Russia had not even come up in the conversation until then, she apparently just came out with something she had learned about a foreign country at school. She said that she has never been to Menda or Taragi [the closest town in walking distance], let alone Tokyo, and thinks that the village is the best place of all."

The limitations of the world of experience of the village women were evidenced when John Embree went off on a walking trip to a remote district called Gokanoshō.[6] "When told that John is gone to Goka, as it is called locally, all are astounded. Take assured me that the people there are very bad. They used to sleep with knives under their pillows and watch for people with money, whom they would kill and rob before throwing their bodies into the fields. She said they were still like that until about ten years ago, and that going there alone even now would be dangerous. No one has been there, but everyone has something to say about the place. People there give you a wonderful reception, some say, and put out their best and most beautiful bedding, so that you feel as if you had come to stay in an old warrior-class house. Someone else says, people in Goka never give their guests anything to eat. It is much colder there than in Suye. And the Toride nursemaid outshone them all by asking, 'Are the people there like people here?' "

It was for the Koreans, however, that the greatest contempt was expressed. "Craziness—madness—is used as an excuse for many strange deeds, and if an older child reproaches a younger one for boisterous behavior or being untidy, she will say, '*Shinke!*' (Crazy); or 'You look like a Korean, with your clothes all hanging down!' "

The people of Suye had some direct experience of both Koreans and Chinese. "A Korean woman selling junk and buying rags came to Tanno's while I was there. They felt her clothing and discussed the strange

6. He wrote an account of this trip (Embree 1944d).

habits of Koreans, all of whom, even the old women, wear white garments. Everyone here considers Koreans to be very dirty, although one of the young men who was there on military service told me the other night that Japanese think Koreans are dirty only because all the no-goods come here. They are really very beautiful, he said."

"Any stranger creates a stir. A Korean passed through the other day. 'Who is he? What is he doing?' and so on. Today a Korean man came through buying junk to resell in Taragi. He picks it up as he passes through the villages—old wheels, pots and pans, and so on. He lives alone in Youra, but has a wife and child in Menda as well as a wife in Korea. He is a friendly soul who speaks good Japanese with a typical Korean accent, which the children mimic." The Chinese from Menda who came through selling piglets spoke "a pidgin Japanese which the villagers find amusing."

By far the most colorful of the Koreans who passed through was the medicine vendor. His interaction with the village women is a study in the reinforcement of stereotypes. "Because of the heat, he had removed his coat and trousers and was marching along in his white underwear, shirttails hanging out. He called his medicine Canton carrot (*kanton no nijin*—for '*ninjin*') and claims that it grows exclusively in Korea, where it is sold at the exorbitant price of fifteen to sixty yen a root. He would consent to sell the fifteen-yen one for only ten, but had nothing in the box for less than 7.50 yen. He says that his stock is worth about 600 yen. 'This is not a small business,' he boasted, producing testimonials from various notables of the region who have bought from him. It is, of course, a cure-all for everything from headaches to colds to female complaints. Sato says that it is just plain Korean carrot [being sold as ginseng]."[7]

7. *Ninjin* means both "carrot" and "ginseng," and it is not clear from the context whether Sato was saying that it was plain Korean carrot or Korean ginseng, but the implication is that he regarded it as inferior to the Canton variety.

Women's Formal Associations

The women of Suye belonged to several different associations of a more or less formally organized character. Some were units of national organizations, like the Women's Association (*fujinkai*); others were of a religious character; and the silkworm raising groups were the creations of private enterprise.

"I asked Mrs. Mori about the Women's Association here. She said there is one in each hamlet in Suye. Mrs. Sato Tami is head of the one here, and Mrs. Sato Ine of Kawaze is head of the one there. [Actually she proved to be head of the *fujinkai* for the entire village.] Mrs. Mori did not know much about their functions. There is another society of women who belong to the Shinshū Buddhist sect, which includes members from eight hamlets. It is called the *Shinshū-kai*. Sato Ine is its head, she said, and told me to go there to ask for details. I said, 'You come with me,' but she only laughed and replied, 'No, I can't.' She assured me, however, that Mrs. Sato is very nice. Now this is interesting, for Mrs. Mori drops in on Mrs. Tanimoto any time, and this morning Mrs. Tanimoto spent a couple of hours at the Mori's. Is it a clique?"

This rather unsatisfactory introduction to the topic led to a follow-up conversation with Mrs. Sato Tami, head of the Women's Association in Kakui, the hamlet where the Embrees lived. "She is not sure who is head of the others. She suggested that I see Sato Ine of Kawaze, for she herself knows little about the details of the organization. She did complain, however, that the Women's Association here has no real aim, does nothing for the good of the country, etc. 'They just meet and collect money. They've no heads for anything better.' She always complains a bit about this village into which she has married."

Mrs. Sato provided more information about the Shinshū-kai, the Buddhist women's group, and the village Women's Association. "She says that the Shinshū-kai was organized in 1927. Before that there was a united Buddhist group, which met only occasionally. The women decided to organize a separate one for members of the Shin sect. It meets twice a year in December and February, but if everyone is too busy, the meetings are postponed. She notifies two or three people in each of the eight hamlets about the date of the meeting, and they spread the word. All the meetings are held in her house. Each person donates five or ten sen, one yen of which goes to the priest and about ten yen are sent to the headquarters temple in Kyoto. The rest is deposited in the group's savings account in the cooperative's credit association. In the case of a death of a member, some of this money will be used to buy a banner, flowers, incense and candles, and two or three of the members are designated representatives of the group at the funeral. She has been its head since its founding and says she was chosen by consensus. Some women also belong to another Buddhist group called the Kannon-kō [Kannon Society; Kannon is the goddess of mercy].

"Mrs. Tanimoto belongs to two women's Buddhist associations, the Shin and a Zen one. The former has forty-two members now, she thinks, and they meet at the temple three times a year—at New Year's, in April and in October. Each member donates twenty sen, ten for the savings account and ten for entertainment. The savings are used to buy things for the temple. She and Mrs. Sato, the head of the Shin association, go to the Hitoyoshi temple as representatives of the village. Every year they get an invitation by letter. When I asked how they had been selected, she said, 'I don't know. They like my face, I guess, for they invite me every time.' "

It will be noted that there is some confusion in the foregoing, for these women are unclear about which group is being discussed. It is the Kannon Society that has about forty-five members, and the amount of money contributed by each woman is given differently by Mrs. Tanimoto and Mrs. Sato. Furthermore, Mrs. Sato is not only head of the Shinshū-kai, as Mrs. Mori thought, she is also head of the Suye village Women's Association, about which we have much more information. By way of introduction to the subject, the following account of a meeting of this organization at the school is invaluable, for it helps explain why the women appeared ill-informed about its affairs.

"About thirty women attended. First the headman made a speech. It has been four years since the *fujinkai* was organized, he said. Until now it has been headed by Sato Ine, but she is too busy with the Shinshū-kai. Then he said that it has been suggested that the principal of the school [a man, of course] become the head of the village Women's Association. Is that acceptable? There being no objection the matter was settled. The school principal is now the overall head of the village Women's Association.

"Following the singing of the national anthem, the principal read the Imperial Rescript of 1923,[1] and all bowed. He then made a speech

1. This appears to be the rescript issued in the aftermath of the great Kantō earthquake that devastated Tokyo and Yokohama. Its title is *Kokumin seishin sakkō ni kansuru shōsho* [Concerning the Arousal of the People's Spirit]. *Sakkō* also means enhancement, promotion, awakening.

directed primarily at the members of the Young Women's Association (*sho-jokai*) about how they can contribute to the life of their village. Then he addressed some remarks to the women and spoke of work and the program for economic reconstruction (*keizai kōsei*). Men cannot accomplish it alone; women must help. He read a series of resolutions about economic planning, each beginning with the words, 'We resolve to. . . .' The 'we' in this case are the women who had never even seen these resolutions until they were passed out to them later. (Many could not read them anyway.) He then gave a report of past events and expenses of the Women's Association: the cost of kit-bags for the soldiers in Manchuria [of which more later], the money sent to the victims of the fire in Hakodate, and so on. He then fixed a date for a visit to Kume to see the model kitchens there [see pages 31–37] and told them to come to a demonstration of how to prepare soy-sauce and fermented bean-paste at the school.

"The principal then introduced the next speaker, a teacher named Matsuda. He told us that he had come to Kuma-*gun*[2] on a visit ten years ago and notices that there have been great improvements in Suye since then. He visits many regions at the request of the prefectural office and thinks that the people in Kuma-*gun* are the nicest he has met, so he is happy to come here again. He then discussed the economic reconstruction program in terms understandable to women. It was inaugurated in 1932. He wrote out the characters for *keizai kōsei* on the blackboard and analyzed them by writing each one out in *kana* syllabary as well [a form of writing that village women could read]. One meaning for one part of *kosei* is to reconstruct, he said. He then told a story about a man who was ready to die, but whose life was spared. This is just like *kōsei*, for the country will be saved through the work and strength of its farmers. So all the men and women of Suye must unite to work for the program. The character was further explained by reference to the characters meaning one's own strength (*jibun-no chikara* or *jiriki*). The following practices will improve the economy and make the children healthy:

"1. Prenatal care and calling the midwife when necessary. Bringing up the children in a healthy and economical manner. Avoiding intermarriage, which produces deformed children. He said that everyone knows that even cows have bad offspring if they are allowed to interbreed. Avoiding too much drinking, which makes for abnormal births—witness the effects of alcohol on the children of geisha, he said.

"2. Plan food consumption carefully and use a little of everything in the diet—rice, wheat, vegetables, eggs, fruit—and sell some of one's own produce to get money with which to buy other food for more variety.

"3. Since expenses are always high, to avoid over-spending one should make out a budget for the whole year's income and expenditures.

2. *Gun* is usually translated as "county." Suye is located in Kuma-*gun*, Kumamoto Prefecture, and the local dialect is known as Kuma-*ben*. The most popular songs were the Kuma *rokuchōshi* (Embree 1944, pp. 13–26), and the *shōchū* made in Suye, considered the best in the region, was known as Kuma-*shōchū*.

If both are the same, he explained, the result is zero, so the income should be increased. The business of handling accounts should fall to the younger daughter of the house, for the father is likely to be less angry if it is she who shows him that his *shōchū* bills are too high.

"4. Making and storing pickles, bean-paste and soy sauce in the proper way will prevent spoilage and waste. This is an economy.

"5. One should learn how to make use of material that would otherwise be wasted.

"By observing all these rules, women can contribute to economic reconstruction—making *keizai kōsei* through *jiriki kōsei* (self-help). He then told the story of the granddaughter of a hero of the Russo-Japanese War who at the age of forty-two began studying in order to become a teacher at a girls' school. That is true self-help, he said. After this speech came one of thanks by the principal. It was very earnest and something of a letdown after Matsuda's witty—if excessively uplifting—talk. Following this we all went home."

This altogether remarkable meeting scarcely needs extended analysis. Called by men and addressed exclusively by men, it produced not only a plan for women's taking a role in economizing that was written by men, but also featured the appointment of a man, the school principal, as the head of the Women's Association of Suye. "Among the women later there was some talk about the necessity of organizing the *fujinkai* better and having occasional meetings. In each hamlet there is to be a branch head. Kakui is to elect one now. 'One of the younger women should be elected,' says Mrs. Sato. Mrs. Fujita is considered a younger woman, and thus eligible, but she refuses to take on the responsibility. At the mention of the appointment of the school principal as the new head of the organization, she laughed and pointed down, 'A bit different here, don't you think?' She has heard that the same thing was done in Taragi," probably reflecting official despair of the women's ever getting the association moving.

"They were discussing the last meeting of the *fujinkai* at Kato's house, which Mrs. Hayashi had missed. It was quite an affair, said Mrs. Tanimoto. Sato Ine, who had been head of the entire village *fujinkai*, has been replaced by the principal, of course. Mrs. Kato has long been the head of the hamlet association. The meeting was about that, for she had resigned. Even though the other women urged her to stay on, she refused. Then all the fights came out. She brought up some old trouble, and Mrs. Tanimoto told her that if she brought personal fights into village affairs, things would not work at all. After much discussion and tossing the issue back and forth, new officers were chosen, but it all caused much amusement. The women agreed that the hamlet is a hard place to manage."

"Later, when I went to talk to her about it, Mrs. Kato said that running the hamlet *fujinkai* is a hard job. The new head is Mrs. Tanimoto, a fact that the latter did not mention to us yesterday. Yesterday, in fact, the women were amused because there had been an argument between Mrs. Sato and Mrs. Suzuki, Mrs. Tanimoto had not even reported to me that her name had been put up for office. So yesterday I asked Mrs. Tanimoto if she is the assistant head of the hamlet *fujinkai*, as I had been told. She denied it vigorously, and said that it is Mrs. Shimosaka. Today Mrs. Shimosaka said that Mrs. Tanimoto is, and that she lied when she denied it to me. I wonder what this is all about?" To compound the mystery, "I have just been told that when the hamlet *fujinkai* met at Mrs. Kato's two nights ago, after much discussion they elected Mrs. Sato Shichihei and Suzuki Seiichi's wife as head and assistant head, respectively." But it turned out that neither had been elected to any post. What, indeed, was the mystery all about?

It was all about bad relationships among the women of the hamlet, as one might have predicted, and began to clear up as a result of the affair of the aprons. "Yesterday morning, after a visit from an official of the village office, Mrs. Tanimoto announced that she had agreed 'just this once' to take on the job of head of the hamlet *fujinkai*, replacing Mrs. Kato. She thereupon began bustling about, for today the aprons will arrive."

The issue of the aprons came up in John Embree's account of yet another meeting of the village *fujinkai* called at the school. "Each hamlet branch of the association has two officers, but only about half of them attended. All of the teachers were there, including the principal, and the headman was there as well. The latter spoke on the formation [in 1932] of the National Defense Women's Association (*kokubō fujinkai*) as follows: Although we already have the Women's Patriotic Association (*aikoku fujinkai*), it is not meaningless to form this new association in view of the present grave international situation. Not satisfied with merely paying our respects to the families of soldiers who are stationed in Manchuria—the men who have gone out to war—we must help them more positively. It is also necessary that you have a clearer picture of our national defense. The details of this association, he said, are still unknown to him, but he believes this to be its aim.

"He then encouraged the activities of women by relating how some leader of the Women's Patriotic Association who came from Kumamoto was keenly impressed with the fact that its members in Suye had prepared *sekihan* [glutinous rice with red beans, a congratulatory and auspicious dish served on ritual occasions] and served it to the soldiers on the day of the last reservists' muster, with the establishment of the nursery school this summer, and with its many other activities. This official was so moved, the headman said, that he had given twenty-five yen as a subsidy to the Suye association, although he had given only fifteen or twenty to those in some other villages. He was also ready to help sponsor the showing of a film in Suye. On entertaining soldiers on the day of the coming muster, the mayor told them that it will not be necessary to prepare *sekihan* this time. Ice water would be enough, for it will be hot. What is more important, he has heard, is that all the members of the Women's Association should join in the review rather than just entertaining the soldiers. He believes that the men will be made more attentive and serious if they are being observed by their mothers and acquaintances.

"The principal then announced that it had been decided that an instruction session in manners will be held in August, one on cooking in September, and one on making pickles and using things that would otherwise be wasted, as well as dyeing material, in October. He reminded them that in the near future, there will be one on the preparation of bean-paste and soy sauce. He added that women have an important role to play in economic reconstruction, and that they will be made to join in the activities of the association and given marks for attendance at the various meetings, which will be a kind of competition among the hamlets to see which performs best.

"The headman then wanted the opinions of the women concerning the newly established nursery school, but none was ventured. He said that there are six such institutions in Taragi, and it would be good if more could be set up in Suye. There will be another one set up for the harvest season." As before, no woman spoke, even to offer an opinion on the care given their small children while they were busy with rice transplanting.

"Then the headman spoke of the aprons and cloth bands to be worn by members of the Women's Patriotic Association. They are not so necessary on ordinary occasions, but for those such as the muster and the grand army maneuvres which are attended by the Emperor and other members of the Imperial Household, they are essential. (These aprons actually are sleeved smocks with elasticized cuffs that fit over the entire front of the kimono and tie in the back, thus presenting a uniform appearance and presumably serving a sanitary function.) The price of a cloth band is seven sen. As to the aprons, there are three kinds, costing sixty sen, forty-seven sen, and one still cheaper. Then a merchant dealing in them came in and showed samples. After some discussion it was decided that the hamlet association heads should consult the women in their respective communities about which they would buy and make a report before July 28. The inaugural ceremony will be held on the day of the reservists' muster on August 6, when all the women will wear the aprons." Once again all the initiative had come from men and from above, but the women got busy following the instructions at once.

"A meeting of the hamlet *fujinkai* has been called and everyone has promised to attend. Today Mrs. Kato called on Mrs. Tanimoto to consult about the money, for the aprons must be paid for today. The two of them finally decided to put up the money themselves, half each, and collect individual payments from the others at the meeting. Then they had a chat about the aprons, because wearing them amuses the women, who do not consider it a dress-up costume at all. Indeed, if they are wearing an apron when a caller comes, they usually lower the top. A man who visited us from Konose a while ago said that the girls there and in some other places put on the aprons to dress up for photographs, I presume because it is an innovation and therefore considered something fancy. Here again we have a bit of regulation coming from the central government that makes little sense. What it amounts to is simply that all women must wear aprons to demonstrate their patriotism. So all, except those who manage to get out of it because they are alone in the house or have small children to look after, and therefore will not attend, will have to wear them. All in all they think it stupid."

"All the women are talking about the aprons. Oade has decided on the most expensive variety, but Kakui does not know what to do, since no one from there went to the meeting at the school and there has been no hamlet meeting since. Mrs. Tanimoto expressed the opinion that the aprons were all right for younger women, but that the older ones would look funny in white. She hates the aprons anyway because they are so hot. The women agree that no older woman should be asked to hold the position of hamlet head of the *fujinkai* because most of them don't really care about the organization and don't bother to arrange things properly. 'It's a hard job,' said one of them, 'because you have to know how to write.' "

Seizing the opportunity afforded by a gathering of women at the store, "I brought up the question of aprons, since Mrs. Shimosaka and young Mrs. Suzuki were there. This set them off on a long discussion of Kakui affairs. They said it was not fair to appoint an old lady like Mrs. Suzuki to the position of head, that Sato Tami does not do her duty, and that Mrs. Tanimoto was without doubt the woman for the job, with the help of Mrs. Ouchi. Later on, when I raised the question with Mrs. Tanimoto she said that she had not wanted the job, and that Sato Tami could manage it alone if she only put herself out a bit and called the women together. Once assembled they could talk over the matter and make a decision at once. It had, after all, taken them only a half-hour to get together on the preparation of the food for the flood victims in Nakashima."

It was not so easily done but the decision was finally made. "Mrs. Kato went to school today to pick up the aprons, and has been distributing them ever since, even to Mrs. Horie, who said she did not want one. So far I have heard no talk of any objections from Sato Tami of whom it is said that she resigned her position as head of the hamlet *fujinkai*." Even so, the matter was not to be so easily resolved. "The reservists' muster was held today. The women, true to form, began to gather about eight, although it had been called for seven. Almost all wore their aprons and the bands, which turn out to be very handsome, and felt very silly. Some came without them and worried about it. Mrs. Nagata was trying to buy one, but there were none left, so finally Mrs. Kato, who was responsible for her not having one, gave her her own to wear. When the review started the women were all lined up together and told to bow when the military officers passed

by. The officers gave them only a casual glance and passed on. With the
ranks of men, they were more thorough."

To add insult to injury, "the women were assembled after the
inspection was over to hear an address by the school principal, which was
fervently patriotic. Then one of the male teachers read the resolutions of
the *fujinkai* to them. The absurdity of it all struck me when he came to the
passage, 'We shall keep the kitchen clean and in order.' A woman's organization formed and promoted by men for nationalistic purposes. Even
when it comes to leadership of the hamlet-level units, the women try to
refuse the responsibility, and I have never heard a woman make a speech
at any general meeting of the organization. All organizing, all resolutions,
and all the arrangements are made by men. Women only execute the orders." At the party that followed the muster, "Mrs. Tanimoto discussed
the current *fujinkai* events with Shimosaka. Tomorrow they will have a
meeting to elect new officers. The meeting is called for seven o'clock, she
said, because it is the only way to get things going by ten."

"If you wait long enough, you can get everything explained, like
the apron business with Mrs. Nagata. She had none at the muster and
Mrs. Kato gave her her own, which puzzled me greatly at the time because
they are said to be on very bad terms. Today I learned the reason. It seems
that when Mrs. Tanimoto made the rounds before the inspection, offering
aprons and collecting money for them, Mrs. Nagata had refused to buy
one. That night, Sato Tami decided to try to make peace between Mrs.
Kato and Mrs. Nagata, with the former's consent. She came to Tanimoto's
to ask her to assist her, but Mrs. Tanimoto refused. ('I had a headache.')
Mrs. Shimosaka was summoned instead, and they went off to Nagata's
together. After much talk—until about two in the morning—all three went
to Kato's, where the reconciliation was effected. Mrs. Kato served *shōchū*,
some of which Mrs. Nagata had brought. Cups were exchanged, and no
mention was made of the fight, which is a cardinal rule of such peace-
making meetings. (It went on until four o'clock and at the muster the next
day all the women were sleepy.) To show her good will, therefore, Mrs.
Kato had handed her apron to Mrs. Nagata. The trouble between them
seems to have started over some old *kōgin* [revolving credit association; see
pages 38–42], but no one remembers the details any more."

If the aprons were considered a foolish extravagance, there was at
least one activity of the Women's Patriotic Association that was of great
interest to the women of Suye. This was the preparation of *imonbukuro* (kit-
bags) for the soldiers overseas, which were collected from each hamlet and
sent out from the village office.

"The women met at Toride's. She is the head of the *fujinkai* there.
Papers are sent out by the village office, indicating what things can be sent
to the soldiers, and the women meet to decide on the contents of the kit-
bags. Those things that are approved are tobacco, tooth brushes, towels,
cakes, and practically anything else under the sun, but it is recommended

now that one not include perishable items because of the warm weather. These bags are made up and sent off periodically. After the 1923 earthquake, the women sent them to the destitute of Tokyo and Yokohama.

"After a short discussion it was decided to donate ten sen each, and Mrs. Toride and another woman were commissioned to buy whatever they saw fit with the money collected. Before the fifteenth, the bags are to be at the village office, which will send out all the hamlets' contributions in one bundle at its own expense. A list of donors was made out. I offered my ten sen, and although everyone objected that I belonged to Kakui, they took it finally. Actually, no one was much concerned about the business at hand. It seems that the village headman had reminded them about it and expressed his displeasure at their being so late. There was some talk about how expensive the whole thing was, and the discussion switched to the new austerity policy now being promoted in the name of economic reconstruction. They said they can do little about it because they spend as little as they can as it is."

"Today the Kakui women met to decide what to send, and it was agreed that, like Kawaze, they would put together two kit-bags. They agreed to collect six sen rather than ten from everyone, for as one of them told me later, this is a poor hamlet and people might object if they asked for too much. The instructions come from the Kumamoto branch of the national Women's Association through the village office, which transmits them to each hamlet. All were interested to find out what the other hamlets were contributing, and what they had included in the bags.

"Kawaze sent stationery, tooth powder, *Jintan* [a popular patent medicine in pill form], handkerchiefs, soap, and some candy, as well as *sarumata* [a kind of men's undershorts] at a cost of ninety sen a bag. Kakui will send similar things at seventy-five sen a bag. It was suggested to the Kawaze women by the widow Matsumoto, while they were out shopping for things, that a picture of a beautiful woman (she used the expression *haikara na beppin*) would be much appreciated by the soldiers and they agreed. They also chose perfumed soap because, they said, women like perfumed men, and soldiers surely visit women. One of them said it is a good thing to send out these bags, because the soldiers always send back letters of appreciation. She said that letters also came from the 1923 earthquake victims in the Tokyo-Yokohama area. Today Mrs. Tanimoto made up the Kakui bundle for the soldiers, getting a kick out of it as she does out of everything. She put in much the same things as the other hamlets had, including a couple of pairs of undershorts and a picture of a pretty girl."

One of the great pleasures of the Suye women was going off on a visit to nearby shrines or temples (see chapter 3) and on excursions organized by the Women's Association. On these occasions we see them at their leisure, away from the responsibility of serving the men and looking after their children. One of these trips was an excursion to see the model kitchens in Kume, a trip decided upon, planned, and organized by the men who gave the members of the Women's Association their marching orders. After the announcement that a date would be fixed for visiting Kume to see their model kitchens, "there was much discussion of the plans. To make up for their missing the meeting at the school where the trip was announced, all of Kawaze and Nakashima have decided to go. Kakui, as usual, is still debating, 'It is too hot. It is too far away. We are too busy.' Mrs. Tanimoto was laughed at when she said she was too busy [she is roundly criticized for having nothing to do] and so said that she will go after all. Old lady Irie said that she really wants to go but cannot because they are repairing the roof on their house. In the event she left her daughter in charge at home and came anyway."

"After a preliminary announcement at school and a change of date because of yesterday's rain, the excursion took place today. It was very grey and rain was in the air, which discouraged some people from going. However, Nakashima turned out except for one house where there is a small baby. Kawaze was there, except for four people kept home by babies, and Mrs. Nawahara who could not come because someone is ill. Imamura left behind the poor widow and two or three others held back by babies and pregnancies and equally poor. Hirayama [the isolated mountain hamlet] was almost complete. They attend all such functions and school meetings because they come down very seldom otherwise and it amuses them to get away. Tontokoro and Aso sent a fair number of representatives, as did Ishizaka. Kakui and Oade were noticeably absent, which called for many comments. The Oade women feared rain and said they were busy; only one came from there. But the wrath of all was directed toward Kakui. Even its sole representative, Mrs. Shimosaka, joined in the deprecations. (Did she come because her husband is hamlet head, or as some guessed, because she is number two in the *fujinkai* this year?) 'These Kakui women are always like that. Even when they join in, they are late and have to be coaxed. They never go anywhere where drink is not offered. You tell your friends that we said so—they won't go unless there's drinking, as if they could not have a drink anyhow. We could all have a farewell party [*wakare kai*] at the end, each contributing five or ten sen. Yes, we'll have the party in Kawaze and you come with us since Kakui did not go and they won't get to have a party.' This was repeated all day on and off.

"We gathered at Nakashima by nine. Departure had been set for 8:30, and people got impatient. At nine the alarm bell was rung—two long strokes followed by many short ones—to summon the laggards. Then we started off, meeting some women on the way who had taken a different road and much later some additional ones. The members of the Young Women's Association were almost all there; some of the girls were replaced by their mothers. Most of the women were the older ones in their houses, and had left the brides behind to look after things while they were away. A few older 'brides' with their babies came, leaving the older women at home. The few more recent brides present stood out because of their bright clothes.

"As soon as we left it began to drizzle and a few umbrellas went up. It began to rain harder. 'Shall we open our umbrellas?' asked the teacher politely (we were walking together). It began to pour. All of the kimono skirts went up and suddenly the gray crowd was all blue, and green, gay with flowers and butterflies. All *koshimaki* [kimono underskirts] are bright, except for those of the very old ladies, whose are white. It was an interesting procession of some one hundred women, concealed to their shoulders by umbrellas, bright *koshimaki* showing, feet in white *tabi* and *geta*, stepping out, all alike. Here and there was a bump on the back covered with a brightly colored padded coat. It was the baby fast asleep or munching a cookie. All through the day this crowd did everything the same way— letting down the kimono when entering a house, pulling it up again as soon as we went out, and all looking so much alike. When we reached the school the *tabi* were all wet and dirty and stained by the colors of the *geta* thongs, so that they were removed while in the building and put on again when we left.

"The excursion was headed by the school principal and two teachers, one male and one female. Kume is another of those model experimental villages bursting with pride in its achievements, although the man who showed us through a demonstration kitchen did ask, 'Why show these kitchens to you? Surely yours in Suye are much better.'

"The school where we first went is a tremendous place built three years ago, with an imposing auditorium and a safe for the Imperial portrait outside in the yard. There is a special school for the young men which alone cost 2,000 yen. The total cost of the entire establishment was 40,000 yen. There are 594 pupils and all the classes of primary grades are divided into separate ones for boys and girls, because of the large attendance. (In Suye, because of the small number of pupils, boys and girls are not divided into separate classes.) It is true, apparently, that a village can be judged by its school. We were shown through it. Although it was new, spacious and light, there was no provision for heat in any of the classrooms and the only stove was in a common room. It must be freezing, because the school is right in the mountains. The entire site, like that of an ancient castle, is surrounded by a moat.

"A picturesque stream runs through the village, crossed here and there by bridges—real ones, not the makeshift ones of Suye. The village lies on a broad plain surrounded by mountains. Houses are in groups fairly far apart, and the hamlets are said to be working units. There are 500 houses in all, of which 300 are in the mountains, very inaccessible because of poor roads (a new, better one is hoped for and is being planned). These 300 households are a separate community with its own school. The village is like a small town with a large street running along the canal and many shops, including a fishmonger's, a butcher's and an egg shop. It looks prosperous in every way.

"After a look around, we had speeches. The principal of the Kume school told us how glad he was to see us, even though it was rainy weather, and said that he would be glad to answer any questions. He knew all the teachers who accompanied us, he said, because the Suye principal and he were classmates, he and our male teacher were from the same village, and he had taught our female teacher in the fifth grade. He said that the villagers of Kume realized the importance of cooperating in hard work for attaining success, and how all the hamlets cooperated and worked to accumulate savings. Of course, he went on, all work and no play is bad, so people do meet and have some parties and feast on various occasions, thus making work worthwhile.

"He showed us a chart with vertical lines to indicate the amount each hamlet had saved in 1935. The largest amount was 165 yen. The goal was 500, but very hard to reach. The methods of saving are left to the hamlet to devise. One hamlet has a school (which, incidentally, is located by a house surrounded with a beautiful garden and no trace of farming activity. There are no such residences in Suye). This school is for the making of the frames for keeping cocoons of silkworms. They supply the entire village and many others throughout Kume County. Other hamlets make sacks. Individual savings are made by mixing barley with rice, by reducing the gifts to bereaved families, by spending less on sake and parties for the soldiers, by eating unpolished rice, which is healthy and tasty if one uses special methods of cooking it. He told us about the hamlet meeting hall which we saw later. One of these was built from savings; other hamlets got the money in one way or another. All hamlets of forty households have such a hall. General meetings take place at the school, but hamlets often meet separately. He closed with more friendly words and offered to answer questions. The women only giggled.

"A teacher at the Kume youth school *(seinen gakkō)* then lectured us on experimental mulberry cultivation and silkworm raising, and about raising persimmon and plum trees. Our own principal gave a thank-you speech and we settled down to lunch, forming little groups, each provided with a tea pot and cups by the school. All the women had brought either lunch boxes with rice and pickle, or balls of rice stuffed with pickled plum or the spice called *shiso*. Some had a lunch box and others had brought a separate small package of radish pickled in fermented bean-paste. All were amazed that I had no rice. After lunch we visited the village council meeting-room, where the head of the *sangyō kumiai* [industrial cooperative] presided and we were given another talk. This concerned the size of the village, which is large, with seventy *chō* of dry fields and 515 of paddy fields. [One *chō* = 2.45 acres.] There are twenty-four small cooperative work-groups, and a hamlet savings program.

"Next we were taken to the temple of Dainichi (actually Kōbōdaishi)[3] in the mountain. It is a well-kept Shingon temple, above which a park was built about three years ago. It stands in a small clearing surrounded by stone statues of the eight Buddhas, the originals of which were brought from China by Kōbōdaishi to Koya-san.[4] Benten[5] is also there. (When I asked what the temple's sect was, before I had been told by our guide, some of the Suye women said Shin, others Zen. Finally Mrs. Wauchi of Ishizaka settled that it must be Zen, for she had lived in Kume. Only when I got up there did I discover the truth.) The statues are very poor artistically, but, judging from the incense and candle stubs, draw worshippers. There are many lanterns, Jizō, and various small shrines in the precincts. All the women prayed and one old lady lit a candle and had brought *o-miki*. We were served tea and cakes there; the priest was away so his wife entertained us and explained the meaning of the eight statues. The women, much as they do at our house, grabbed handfuls of *senbei* [rice crackers or cookies]. Why they feel they have to take handfuls of cookies and candy served in a common dish, when it is the custom to serve only dainty portions on individual dishes, is a mystery.

"Next came the inspection of the place that makes the silkworm frames and the new village hall, all white and blue and clean inside. Tea, pickles and cakes were served. Next we went to the Maibara hamlet and a talk was given there. This particular hall is the one built with hamlet savings, but it turns out that other hamlets have used prefectural or village funds. It serves many functions but is above all a place to meet to discuss local affairs. General committee meetings of the Shōwa-kai[6] are held here, and members are appointed to various committees, such as the sanitation committee. Women, who are apparently encouraged to meet regularly, get together here. They seem to have a definite place in the village. There is a women's general meeting twice a year and on the twenty-second of each month, a regular meeting when a teacher gives a talk to the women and instructs them in sewing. During the busy seasons the place is used as a nursery for preschool children, with two or three women acting as nurses. The kids bring their lunches from home. For maintaining this place, money is got from the prefectural office, the village office, and once they got a contribution from a newspapers' association and once from the Aikoku

3. The posthumous name by which Kūkai (A.D. 774–835), founder of the Shingon sect of Buddhism, is popularly known. Dainichi, the Cosmic Buddha, is not a historical figure, of course.

4. Mount Koya, on which Kōbōdaishi established what became the great temple and cemetery complex of the Shingon sect.

5. Benten is one of the seven deities of good fortune, often depicted riding on a serpent or a dragon. She is also the goddess of music, in which form she is shown playing a Chinese lute.

6. Shōwa is the reign-name of the present emperor, who has occupied the throne since 1926, but I do not know what the Shōwa-kai (association) was.

Fujinkai of Kumamoto. Each Sunday school children come to clean the place and are given tangerines or pencils as New Year's gifts for this service.

"In 1927, a new idea of savings was introduced. Every day when cooking rice a sake-cup full was put in a separate receptacle. The system is therefore called *sakazuki* (sake-cup). On the first and twentieth of the month the women bring this saved rice to the community meeing hall, where it is measured and recorded by its current value. Later all the rice goes to the *shinyō kumiai* [credit association] and the money is deposited in a savings account. During the past nine years they have saved 1,100 yen in this manner. Another enterprise of Kume is a quarterly mimeographed publication of the Young Women's Association. It contains recipes and culinary advice. The one for last June tells one how to make doughnuts (American style), bake a special sort of bread, cook white potatoes in vinegar, prepare spiced bean curd, pickle eggplant, cook pumpkin, cook unpolished rice, and a couple of others. It is meant to teach the girls to learn to prepare foods that are in season."

"Then the man discussed kitchens, which I remembered was the original purpose of our excursion. Formerly the kitchens were very poor, dark and hard to work in. Along with other improvements, it was decided to change them. All houses are said to have almost identical kitchens, even the smallest and poorest ones, which improved their kitchens at the expense of other things, perhaps. The three main things stressed were light, good ventilation, and cleanliness (i.e., getting rid of stagnant water). Other aims were to get rid of mice, flies, and other insects. All kitchens have sliding glass windows along one wall with an enclosed shelf under them. There are shelves for different objects. The stoves are like those in Suye, with two or three burners, but all have pipes. The barrels of fermented bean-paste, pickles, etc., are kept in the kitchen in easy reach, but it is thought best to keep them separated by a door if possible. (This was not the case where we visited.)

"The five aims of the new kitchens are:

"1. To select implements that are sturdy, and not to be deceived by low prices, which usually mean poor quality.

"2. To have order in the kitchen by having a definite assigned place for each object, which saves wandering around looking for this or that.

"3. To have well-arranged shelves for the purpose of storing seldom-used objects, such as trays for glutinous rice cakes, on top out of the way, things used daily closer to hand (such as the rice bucket), and things used all the time very near by and easy to reach. Heavy things are to be kept low—barrels of food, etc.—and light ones on top because they can easily be handed down. (It is calculated that a woman walks 2,192 *shaku* [one *shaku* = .995 ft.] a day when cooking for a family of ten. Adding another 1,728 steps, the total is 4,320 mostly wasted steps a day. During the twenty years of her cooking career (she becomes a bride at twenty and is replaced by her bride or daughter at forty), she covers 973 *ri* and 12 *chō* (almost 1,000 *ri*) [one *ri* = 2.44 miles] just doing this one job. The aim is to reduce useless labor and give better results.

"4. To get rid of stagnant water by installing a system for running water rather than keeping buckets in the kitchen, where the water easily goes bad. There is no question of true running water—with pipes and faucets, of course—all they mean is an arrangement whereby dish-water runs off through a channel instead of dripping into a bucket which must be emptied occasionally.

"5. To keep fresh air circulating at all times.

"The Suye women were not overly impressed and said the kitchen we saw was dark. They wondered about the rest of the kitchens in the village (we saw only two), but our guide was proud of his achievements. For eating they use a table, placed either in the kitchen or in the adjoining earth-floored room. In the latter case, it is positioned so that people in the house can sit on the step of the room leading to the table, while those doing outside work sit on benches around the other sides. The man said that the new kitchens of Kume 'save women from wandering around in dark kitchens looking for objects in vain.' Whatever the results, the aim is to have a model labor-saving kitchen in order to help women prepare better food with less effort. During his speech we were served more tea and pickles. We saw very few villagers because they were out working, not expecting us to come on this rainy day. After visiting the two kitchens, we started off for home.

"The party broke up gradually as we approached Taragi. The Hirayama women took a short-cut. Some began to talk about going to a movie, but finally only two Nakashima wives went because the others did not want to stay out so late. All talked about a farewell party (so something must have happened later; I did not go). Some went right along toward Suye, but others lagged behind, shopping for tangerines and candy. Kawaze stopped to have some noodles and a smoke. By the time we reached Kawaze, it was dark, and we could not see the boat on the other side when we called out for it to cross over. The river was lovely in the mist, reflecting only a few lights. The boat came across and two Oade women who had been selling rice in Taragi caught up with us and we crossed over together."

A formal organization of another type entirely was the silkworm-raising group. Like the Women's Association, it too was dominated by men, although the whole process of silk production was generally the women's responsibility. "At the meeting of the silk *kumiai* the men and women sat separately. Many of the women brought their babies. I asked some of them what the purpose of the meeting was, but they did not know. Men run the affair and really manage the business end of silk-raising, but all the major work is done by the women." There were many announcements and speeches. "Children were crawling all over the place. No one paid much attention even at the beginning, but by the time the third speaker rose, people had stopped listening altogether. After the formal doings a party followed. I left then, but later a group of women from Oade came to our house late and wanted to come in. All were quite drunk." This was the Kanebo meeting. John Embree reported on the Katakura gathering. "Featured was a lecture by the new teacher and then a very long speech by an officer of the *kumiai* from Taragi, and a shorter one by the village headman. There were about fifty people present, fewer than usual it is said, probably because some members have switched over to Kanebo. The talks lasted from about 3:30 to 7:00. Some of the women said it was too long, and that they couldn't understand what was being said. Toward the end they stopped listening altogether because they were too tired."

A notable feature of the economic and social life of the men of Suye was the *kō* [revolving credit association], which is described in detail in *Suye Mura*, on pages 138–53, where it is mentioned that the women have *kō* as well. John Embree wrote in his journal: "Women's *kō* are almost always for money, but are also useful for promoting friendship among the women [most of whom have moved into their hamlets from other places, of course, and so do not have the long-term associations that characterize the relationship among the men of Suye.] The smallest ones are for fifty sen and the largest up to three yen. Mrs. Tanimoto says that all of them are lottery-type *kō* [that is, there is no bidding, as is commonly the case in men's *kō*]. Most meet three times a year: in the third month, 'when the flowers are in bloom and one can admire them while drinking in the house,' the sixth month, 'when transplanting is over and people want to rest,' and in the twelfth month, 'when people are celebrating the end of the old year'—these are called *shiawase-kō* [good fortune *kō*]."

One common inspiration for their formation was the need to raise cash with which to pay medical bills or meet some other unusual or large expense. A woman would then approach a circle of friends, neighbors, and kinswomen, and invite them to participate in a *kō*. Assuming that she needed forty-five yen, the procedure might be as follows:

1. Needing forty-five yen, she asks fifteen women to contribute three yen each.

2. At the first meeting, the money is collected and it is agreed that there will be fifteen subsequent meetings, so that each member will win the draw.

3. At every meeting, the founder pays in 3.20 yen.

4. Every winner pays in 3.20 yen at subsequent meetings.

5. Lots are drawn at every meeting by those who have not yet won the draw.

6. The winner receives 3 yen from every non-winner, and 3.20 yen from the founder and all previous winners.

7. The last winner, at the sixteenth meeting, receives 48 yen (45 yen plus 3 yen 'interest').

As the schematic outline below shows, the later one draws the winning lot, the greater the amount of money one receives:

Meeting 1. Fifteen members pay 3 yen each to the founder: 45 yen.

Meeting 2. Lots are drawn, and the founder pays 3.20 yen to the winner and the fourteen others pay 3 yen to the winner:

$1 \times 3.20 = 3.20$
$14 \times 3.00 = 42.00$
Total 45.20

Meeting 6. Founder and four previous winners pay 3.20 yen each to the winner and 10 others pay 3 yen each to the winner:

$1 \times 3.20 = 3.20$
$4 \times 3.20 = 12.80$
$10 \times 3.00 = 30.00$
Total 46.00

Meeting 14. Founder and twelve previous winners pay 3.20 yen each to the winner and 2 others pay 3.00 yen each to the winner:

$1 \times 3.20 = 3.20$
$12 \times 3.20 = 38.40$
$2 \times 3.00 = 6.00$
Total 47.60

Meeting 16. At this last meeting, the founder and the fourteen previous winners each pay 3.20 yen to the only woman who has not yet won, making a total of 48.00 yen.

There are sixteen meetings of this fifteen-member *kō* because no lots are drawn at the first pay-in meeting, which is also the occasion for drawing up the rules under which the association will operate.

The aim of the *kō* was usually to raise money for the founder, but they served an almost equally important social purpose, as several journal entries reveal. "Upon returning home I found Mrs. Wauchi, Mrs. Ochiai, Mrs. Suzuki, Mrs. Fujita, and Mrs. Nawahara, all on their way home from a *kōgin* at Mrs. Tanimoto's. The winner, who therefore will be hostess next time, is Mrs. Mori, who was represented today by her daughter. The group stayed to sing and dance, but not very enthusiastically, perhaps due to my own lack of enthusiasm, because I was very tired. It was a family affair, in that two of the women had their small children with them."

And a little later: "Today I learned that Mrs. Fujita, Mrs. Sato Genzo, Mrs. Hayashi, and Mrs. Okochi belong to a very special *kō*, which also includes women from outside the hamlet. These people were on very friendly terms, and liked to give parties for one another, which meant gifts and entertainment expenses, so they decided to form a *kō* for 1.50 yen. Okochi [a man whose side-business is in prepared foods] joined because they wanted him to provide the food. They meet once a year at the winner's house, just for a good time. This is the last year of the *kō*, which was started by Mrs. Fujita for some unexplained economic reason, and because it is fun. She loves parties and just the day before had a grand time in Fukada where she went to visit her mother's grave and had a party with relatives who still live there."

Another group was differently constituted. "This *kō* is made up of Kakui women primarily, but there are members from Tontokoro, Kinoue, and even one from Taragi. Mrs. Fujita told me that the Taragi woman is included because she once lived in Kakui, and that Mrs. Hayashi, the member from Kinoue, also a former Kakui resident, also asked to be included. The *kō* is for 1.50 yen, with an additional fifteen-sen contribution for *shōchū*. Winners pay fifteen sen extra. They met yesterday, and the winner got 37 yen and a few sen."

The scale of all of the women's *kō* was equally small. One that was having its last meeting after many years of existence was for one yen each, and ten sen for food. Previous winners paid 1.10 yen. "Yesterday Mrs. Tanimoto went to a *kō* in Fukada. It costs two yen, ten sen for *shōchū*, and twenty sen extra for winners. It is a *futon kō* (bedding *kō*), and in theory one makes comforters and padded kimono with the proceeds, but they can be used for other things as well. Mrs. Fujita won, and deposited the money in her savings account in the village office."

"There was a woman's *kōgin* last night at Tamaki's in Nakashima. It costs 1.10 yen for previous winners, and five sen for *shōchū*. This means that very little is drunk at these meetings, and as I walked over there was no music coming from the house. When I went in and asked about the music, they fetched a *shamisen* and old lady Haraguchi performed some old-fashioned dances. Because of the big field-day at school tomorrow, most of the women left early." This particular *kō* had a heavy component of sociability. "This group just goes on and on. When all have won, they start again, and have almost finished the second round. No one is sure why it was started, but some thought it had been the idea of the old lady who used to make bean curd for sale. Two of the members are from Kinoue. One had joined originally when she still lived in Nakashima, and the other was a friend of hers from Kinoue who came along to keep her company. At the end of each round, they said, there is often a reshuffling of membership."

A woman might belong to several such groups. "Today there was a woman's *kōgin* at Fujita's. It was started seven years ago when Mrs. Fujita fell ill and needed a lot of money for medical bills. Thirty women joined and there are thirteen years more to go. The *kō* is for two yen (2.20 yen for the winners), and fifteen sen each for *shōchū*. One unusual feature is that the meetings are always held at Mrs. Fujita's house, and the money is collected on the day of the meeting. It is given to one of the co-heads of the *kō* (Mrs. Kato or Mrs. Wauchi), who keeps it until the woman who draws the winning lot signs a receipt for it and receives her winnings.

"Fujita himself was there and passed out small balls of paper containing the 'seating numbers' (*suwaru ban*), which determine the order in which the women take their places in the room. Then he handed around the lots, and they looked to see who had received the winning one. Mrs. Kato, one of the co-heads, served as scribe and accountant, using a book which contains the names of the members and their winnings. Today's winner was Mrs. Shimoda, of whom it is said that she always carries two or three ten–yen notes when she comes to a *kōgin*, indicating how rich the family is. Said old man Eda, who was there to represent his wife who could not attend, 'Money to money.' Food was served, but many people wanted to get away, so the party could not get going. At one point someone began clapping her hands, and all joined in a song or two, but they trailed off. Mrs. Wauchi tried to get everyone to go over to see the Girls' Day dolls [see pages 231–33] at Shimoda's, but she got no takers. Finally she left by herself and eventually the other women went off somewhere. Today's winner got 61.80 yen, which was handed over by the co-head upon obtaining a special kind of receipt made out in the presence of a witness. Of the thirty members, slightly more than half were present, and of these four were represented by their husbands."

The members of at least one *kō* had decided that they could not manage the accounts, and asked a man to join to serve in that capacity. "The woman's *kō* that met today at Wauchi's was started four or five years ago with twenty members, three of whom are not of the hamlet. Shimoda Ichiro handles the accounts because the women say they cannot manage them. It began about one o'clock. The women paid in their money (1.50 yen each, 1.65 for winners) to Shimoda, who counted it up and recorded the sum. A book is kept from the start of a *kōgin* in which names of the members and tallies of the winnings are entered. This book is given to the new winner and kept by her until the next meeting, which is held at her house.

"During the meal, Shimoda was given the seat of honor [as the only male present], and I was put next to him, much to my embarrassment. Everyone ate heartily and *shōchū* flowed throughout the meal, the aim being to get everyone drunk so the dancing would start. Later, one woman made the rounds pouring the liquor directly into everyone's mouth. The new winner was served the first drink, and a special one was served to the present winner and hostess. There was much drinking, smoking, and joking. Finally the *shamisen* was brought out, and the dancing began. Some verses drew laughs, but it is usually the dance itself that causes the most amusement. After considerable excitement, it was decided to go over to the house of the new winner. We went about 5:30 and were served more *shōchū* and pickles. There was more dancing until everyone started off home, I thought, but it turned out that they went back to Wauchi's and danced until around midnight.

"This *kōgin* is a purely social one, and was started by Sakikawa Sen, not because of any need for money, but just so the group could get together. Because no one person can afford to entertain such a large group, each non-winner contributes 1.50 yen and each winner 1.65 yen to defray the expenses of the food and drink, with what is left over going to the winner. Of the twenty members, fourteen attended."

The amounts paid into this *kō*, originally somewhat larger, had been reduced in the interest of economy. Upon occasion, a woman would find that she could not maintain her membership. One such case was that of "the widow Sakikawa who cannot afford to stay in the bedding *kō* [mentioned above]. After talking it over, it was decided some days later to accept her request to be allowed to withdraw. The head of the *kō* arranged to collect from each previous winner, and give her the money right away, without having to wait for the drawing of the lots."

THREE

Interpersonal Relations

The literature on Japanese rural communities, filled with detailed analyses of cooperative work groups, exchange labor groups, and the like, is for the most part silent on the subject of friendship. It is worthwhile, therefore, to consider the many passing references to the topic of friendships among the women of Suye. Men have friends, too, and there are many accounts of *dōnen kō* (same-age group) meetings and parties that bring men together without regard to structural considerations. Of this phenomenon, one man said that after fifty, one's same-age mates become more important than one's wife.

"Last night there was a party of *dōnen* for women between the ages of twenty-five and twenty-seven. Six of them came early and fixed the meal. Mrs. Kawabe, the hostess, boiled the rice for all the guests. At each meeting they draw lots [much as at women's *kōgin*] and the one who gets the lot with a circle drawn on it must entertain the group next time. A girl came over to play the *shamisen* and they collected five sen from each woman and gave it to her."

There was yet another, somewhat older group. "Mrs. Wauchi and Mrs. Fujita met at Hayashi's about a week ago for a small *dōnen kō*. They choose some convenient date once a year and meet at each other's houses in turn. There is no money involved, and each brings *shōchū* and the hostess supplies the food. Last year they were joined by some men (not their husbands) and reported that they had a wonderful time."

"There is a special *dōnen* group that was supposed to meet yesterday, but the party did not come off for reasons I do not understand. It is Mrs. Tanimoto's same-age group, eleven in all, and includes Mrs. Toyama and others of the hamlet. The group was organized just for fun, they say. It has some savings and this time they were planning to use them to have a party with their husbands. Said Mrs. Toyama, 'It is called *hanami* (flower viewing) but since the cherry blossoms are gone, we will look at the violets in the fields.' "

One group of *dōnen* women went off on an excursion to Aoshima, and returned very pleased. "They reported that there was a huge crowd, and that they had walked the five miles from the Hitoyoshi station to the shrine, 'gossiping all the way.' Yesterday they had a party to celebrate their return and send back the god. It was at Matsumoto Shima's and two of the husbands came as guests and poured *shōchū* for the women, saying they must be tired from the journey. One always has this sort of party, for the god has been brought down from his shrine to visit, and now offerings are made at the household shrine to effect his return. It is believed that the sooner after one's return this party is held the better."

Not all friendships were formalized, of course, that being the nature of friendships. "There was a party in Tontokoro last night, given by Hashida. Looking for the house, I came across a small gathering of old ladies, among them the Arasaki grandmother. 'Just old ladies celebrating the holiday,' she said, when I asked what they were doing. They were having tea and toasted rice cake that one of them had just made."

"Yesterday Ochiai Teru had to attend a memorial service in Oade. She, Tawaji Harumi and Matsumoto Shima are said to be very good friends, and they make camellia oil together. (It is this group that went on the pilgrimage to Aoshima.) Today they met for that purpose. They make the hair oil for sale, keeping some of it for themselves. To them our unoiled hair looks very strange, and they also claim that the application of oil prevents headaches. They make it in groups of three to five people who form a kind of cooperative work-group *(kumi)*. The group that met today actually includes women from two hamlets and has been together for five years now. They said there was no particular reason for joining—they just make the arrangements, and they are all old friends. Each brings her own camellia seed and receives a corresponding amount of oil. The labor is communal, but the work is usually done at the house of the member who has the necessary equipment. At the end of the work the women have a party for themselves, each contributing two *gō* [one *gō* = .384 pints; .18 liter] of rice to make *sushi* [vinegared rice with diced vegetables] and five sen for *shōchū*. They say that in the summer the cemetery is very cool and they go up there to have a good time, eat, drink, and dance."

"Some of the guests at the Ochiai naming ceremony were relatives, but mostly they were women from the hamlet, who are not related, but are the women she likes and wanted to invite. Mrs. Ochiai was there, the midwife, Mrs. Kawabe, and Mrs. Toyama. Very often when I am in the area, I see Mrs. Ochiai visiting at Mrs. Kawabe's on her way to or from the fields or town."

"On sunny days [in early March] the women bring out straw mats and sit in front of the houses gossiping or playing with babies. In Fukada one woman brought out her *shamisen* the other day and was teaching the others how to play."

"Early September is a slack season on the farms and women drop in on one another all the time. Mrs. Shimoda was at Mrs. Sato's and Mrs. Maeno at Mrs. Nawahara's, where they were joined by old lady Wauchi. Just now Mrs. Nawahara and Mrs. Takayama went over to see old lady Tanno. At Kawabe's there was a woman from Shoya who was just being served tea. She had bicycled over to discuss something about raising chickens. Mrs. Ouchi was there, too, and later a child was sent to fetch Mrs. Maeno who was not far away gathering persimmons. There was much chatter and laughter. Mrs. Tomokawa was passing by some distance down the street, and they called to her to come join them. She went on to her house and shortly reappeared with some dumplings, which were enjoyed by all."

"An old lady was calling today at Mrs. Amano's. She comes from Nagamune. It seems that once she picked some mulberry leaves for Mrs. Amano, and the latter had wound up with a surplus and so had taken a basket of them to the old lady, not expecting anything in return. 'I never thought about it at all,' she told me later. The old lady now came with a return gift, in the form of a towel and a package of sugar. Mrs. Amano was absolutely shocked, and kept saying, 'Why did you spend so much money? You should not have done it.' Before the old lady left, Mrs. Amano asked her to be sure to come with her somewhere to *sakamukai* [a party given for someone returning from a pilgrimage]. The old lady said she would, because she goes to that house every day. (This party, I found out, will be for Mrs. Amano's sister who lives in Nagamune, who will be back from a Kannon pilgrimage soon.)"

"The *nijūsanya* [Jizō Eve, the night of the twenty-third day of the sixth lunar month] is not going to be celebrated, although Mrs. Kawabe says she will make the special dumplings that day. Mrs. Fujita said that September is not *nijūsanya* anyway, but *nijūrokuya* [the night of the twenty-sixth day of the seventh lunar month, for moon-viewing], and is not observed nowadays. At one time, she and her friends would all go up to the Inari shrine and watch the moon rise about three in the morning. They would drink, have a good time, and often sleep over. But now all the old ladies she used to go with are too ill or have died, so it all stopped."

But another moon-viewing group was formed that year. "Mrs. Tanimoto read in the newspaper that tonight is *nijūrokuya*, which had jogged her memory, and she said she thought it would be fun to sit up and watch the moon rise, which on this night looks as though it has three horns. She invited old man Ishibashi to come along, as he was just passing by on his way back from Tawaji's." So it was arranged. "Mrs. Tanimoto had said that I should call for her at one in the morning, but when I went there everything was quiet, so I came back home and went to bed again. At two she woke me up. It seems that she had gone all the way to Funaba and not finding me there had come back to fetch me. Ishibashi and Hirano were there and had been playing *ken* [a gambling game] since nine o'clock.

We all brought *shōchū*, cakes and candy. Around moon-rise they became concerned that we might miss it from the shrine where we were gathered, so we took some *shōchū* along to the bridge, which afforded us a perfect view. Mrs. Tanimoto had brought along a candle to offer. She lit it right away, sticking it to the railing, and filled a cup of *o-miki* [sacred wine]. But then she extinguished the candle, so we could see the moon better.

"As the moon began to appear, after much waiting, everyone adopted a position of prayer, clapped their hands and repeated, '*Arigatai, arigatai, arigatō gozaimashita* [Thanks, thanks, thank you very much].' Mrs. Tanimoto just said, 'I do not know how to pray, so please accept my thanks for coming out and making us feel so good.' As it rose higher the moon emerged from behind a cloud in its full beauty. All gasped and repeated their thanks. It did indeed look three-horned, because the disc stood out so darkly, as if framed by the glittering crescent of the moon in its last quarter. No one knew the reason for this strange effect, but Hirano said, 'I know, it is to suggest to married couples that they have a baby—a third member of the family.' After admiring the moon, we went to the Inari shrine for a parting drink and then home. (The women had gone to bed for an hour or so before leaving for Funaba, but did not retire again because they had to be up at five anyway.)"

The core of more formal associations often turned out to be a group of friends. "On April 15 the women met at the *dō* [small Buddhist chapel] for a Kannon-*kō*. There are said to be forty-nine members, but as a rule few attend. All of Kawaze missed this one, some saying they had to attend a memorial service in Taragi, others a *dōnen kō* in Ishizaka, and others were just too busy. About fifteen women did gather, however, and agreed that this was just the right number for a good time, but they did not sound very convinced and kept forcing one another to drink. The food was not good and everyone complained that it was improperly prepared. About six o'clock most had left, but Mrs. Fujita, Mrs. Hayashi, old lady Sato, and Mrs. Uemura were well along. On their way home, the Uemura and Hayashi women stopped in here for some *shamisen* playing and more *shōchū*. Some of the songs were new to me, and very free."

"Last night [August 4] was Kannon-*goya* [Kannon Eve]. No group takes responsibility for the *dō* there, but old lady Mori considers herself more or less in charge of serving those who come. 'I have sat here every year, for how many years, I wonder?' she mused. Many people came, but eventually Irie, Mrs. Mori, Mrs. Sato Shichihei, old lady Sato, Mrs. Hirano and Mrs. Hirano Tamezo, and Mrs. Ochiai were the only ones left. They made jokes, asking Irie how old he is and whether he can still copulate. The conversation became very free and old lady Mori turned to the image of Kannon and said, 'Just listen, Kannon-sama, this is the only kind of talk they make here.' Kannon is said to be very good for easy deliveries. A little singing broke out, but no one could be persuaded to dance. I have been told that this used to be a big occasion for song and dance, led by old lady Mori, but that she is not up to it any more."

Young women also had friendships, of course. "The Ouchi girl and Aki are on very friendly terms. When we were out the other night, she came here and had gone to bed, but her father came home drunk quite late and demanded that she return. He came to fetch her himself, despite her mother's having given her permission to stay over." School friends of the same class often got together as well. "Harue belongs to the Young Women's Association and says that they meet occasionally to sew or some similar thing. She and Sato's younger sister and the Wauchi's middle daughter are great friends, and have been from the first to the last year of school. She brought a photograph of the group to show to me."

"A group of young men was standing about near our house for a while, and later I saw them carrying cakes and candy to Sato Shichihei's house, where they held a *dōkyūkai* [same-class association] of boys the same age and school class as Sato's son. The girls are meeting today for the same purpose. They will go to the school, with cakes for refreshment. (They meet twice a year, on lunar New Year and again in the spring.) Today another group of girls also went to the school for a meeting of the Young Women's Association, which began with much giggling and chattering. When the teacher asked the names of some of the girls who came late (she is new and does not know them all) they just giggled and she had to try to recall them on her own. One group went upstairs to sew, but were told they were making too much noise, as there was a lecture in the hall below. So they spent most of their time talking and looking out of the windows. Another group stayed downstairs for a cooking lesson, but spent a great deal of time doing nothing while the teacher vainly tried to locate this or that and consulted with the custodian."

Nevertheless, hamlet affiliation sometimes overrode friendship. At the all-day athletic meeting at the school, "girls tended to stick together by hamlet. Aki walked over with her friend Taeko, but when they reached the school each joined her hamlet group." The same was true for the older women. "At a big party women move in groups. They arrive by hamlet or by large sections thereof, and occasionally when two hamlets are sparsely represented, they will combine forces. To our party came Mrs. Hayashi with the Nakashima group, but she was a bit late and refused to go into the main room alone, so waited in the kitchen until a second group arrived and went in with them. She looked quite lost, probably because she is so young, although it is equally true that older women will try not to have to go in alone. Early arrivals invariably waited until some group came before going in."

Without question the most remarkable scene involving a group of friends having a good time is found in John Embree's journal. "About noontime I heard some drumming from the Kitadake shrine, so went to investigate. A group of five women, all but one from Suye, were eating, drinking and making merry. They said they were beating the drum and dancing, 'to please the god.' (Actually they said it is a goddess of crops who also gives children if prayed to.) The non-Suye woman, a brazen wench from Menda, sat before the shrine with her hands up in imitation of the mudra of a deity, and the others made as if rubbing their rosary beads and praying before her amid general laughter. Even my jaded senses got something of a jolt."

Groups of women did participate in more routine religious activities. While they were not the only ones who attended the lectures given by a visiting Buddhist priest who came to Suye from Saga and lectured at the temple, they were far better represented than the men. "Such priests come two or three times a year. This is his second visit to Suye, and from here he goes on to Taragi, Uemura, and finally to Nagasaki. Since his last visit here, he told me, Suye has not changed much because 'villages do not change.' About fifty people attended the first talk given at night. They were mostly young and middle-aged women who came with children of all ages who spread over the floor and had to be awakened when it was time to go home. The next talk, delivered at noon the next day, was attended by older women, and the second evening talk by young men (who were sent there by the teacher), young girls, and women of all ages. The fourth and final talk was again at night. There were few adult males at any of the lectures, although the Shinto priest was at this last one, as was the curing priest. When asked why the men do not come, the women say, 'His talks are mostly for women—for mothers.'

"The first night he talked about what makes for a good marriage, and then switched to complaining that Japanese do not go to the temples to worship often enough. 'When do you go?' he asked rhetorically. 'Once a year—twice if you are good. You think you are doing well if you attend a New Year's service, but you are never too busy to visit a geisha or go to a restaurant in town. Now look at America. What does Sunday mean there? It is not, like here, just a day of rest with no school and no work, but it is a day of prayer. Everybody in America goes to church on Sunday morning.' He gave this and further examples of American behavior because John and I were present. (Little did he know that we never go near a church.) Then he talked about mothers and babies, and how children must be trained to be obedient. He told a sad story about a man who had three children, which featured a heart-breaking dialogue between his wife and their young son. Many women wept."

"Last night's talk was attended by a multitude, so that many had to stand outside all around the temple. Most of the standees were young women and a few older ones, and the members of the Young Men's Association, there only because they had been sent by the teacher. They paid little attention. The talk was moral and uplifting, with the following general points: international relations are poor; the League of Nations is a problem; the Americans are accusing the Japanese of dumping. When I came in, he had said, 'Since Mrs. Embree is here, let us talk about America.' He also discussed China, Manchuria, and the bravery of Japanese soldiers at length. The danger of Russia was referred to. He made many wisecracks—when talking about young men paying too much attention to their appearance, he said he understands they put some stuff on their hair, 'some bottled stuff. I don't know what it is, for I have no hair.' [Buddhist priests are tonsured.] At the end he talked about his village, where he is encouraging economic reconstruction."

"Yesterday afternoon was the last talk. By 2:30 the place was pretty full. The crowd was older, with all the men on the right in the seats of honor and many more older women. The talk was again uplifting and very touching, for the women sobbed and sniffled vigorously now and then. There was a story of a sick mother and medicine got for her by a self-sacrificing child, and another of a man who prayed to the Buddhas whose intervention demonstrated their power. Only a few old ladies paid much attention, and even the local priest kept leaning over to read the inscription on a bag of rice that had been donated to the temple. These proceedings were followed by a banquet."

In addition to their pilgrimages to shrines and temples [see pages 50–57] and their involvement in the Buddhist associations [see pages 23–24], women frequently resorted to one or another of the curing priests and other practitioners in search of easy childbirth, health for their children and husbands, and the exorcism of spirits placed in their bodies by witches.

"Last night as I started for the market in Menda, I met all of Kawaze on the path. The women, with babies and children, were on their way to the night-market, too. On the way someone suggested that we stop at Konkō-sama [Konkō-kyō is a sect of Shinto]. It was decided that having no rice to offer would not matter, since they would just stop to worship this time and offer money. Mrs. Ouchi has been a follower of Konkō-sama the longest, and when we got there she put some money in an envelope and was given an amulet in return. All the other women are new converts, and it was one of them who had suggested going up. Mrs. Matsumoto also offered some money and sought advice about the silkworms. The man running the place is evidently a curing priest. It is just a private home with one room done up in imitation of a sacred room of Shinto design. Many people gather there every night, and he delivers talks on virtue, health, or some other subject. He is said to be good at treating the ills of the body, and at advice on raising silkworms, which is why Mrs. Matsumoto wanted to go. He asked us to stay, but we went on to the market because it was getting late."

Pilgrimages to more distant places, to an even greater extent than excursions such as the one organized by the Women's Association, gave Suye women the opportunity to go off for a day with friends and neighbors. Three such occasions are reported in detail and they afford a rare view of women on their own and having a good time.

The Yakushi Pilgrimage[1]

"Mrs. Wauchi, old lady Wauchi, and Mrs. Sato started out about 7:30 in the morning. Earlier they had told me that they would leave between six and seven to avoid the great heat. [It was July 27.] But at 6:30 no one was ready. Finally, all dressed up, we started off. The women wore their *koshimaki* of serge, which looks like pure silk and is used because it does not cling, and georgette kimono, with *obi* actually tied in the back. They wore their good *geta* and carried their good *tabi*. Each had a fan and umbrella. Despite my protestations, I was given both to carry. On the way, the women picked up their kimono skirts, and at the worst stretches, picked up the good *koshimaki* as well and took off their *geta*, which they occasionally washed in a stream. Just before reaching the shrine they put on their *tabi* and kept them on for the rest of the day. At the shrine they also let down the skirts of their kimono.

"They decided to take a short cut through Kodonbaru where the road turned out to be abominable. Parts of it had become a running brook, which had to be waded upstream. Kodonbaru was much discussed, the large fields admired, the water reservoir observed. As we went by this or that crop in a field, it would be named and discussed. 'They have so many sweet potatoes here,' or 'Just planting millet.'

"We stopped for a smoke in Uemura, washed our feet, and went on to the shrine. Some distance before Yakushi there is another shrine, evidently popular, judging by all the banners there, but the women were not sure whether it was Kōbōdaishi or what. We did not stop, but inside we could see a life-size statue. (While washing our feet in Uemura, they mentioned the muddy water in the river and sympathized with a local woman that the place would not do for laundry.)

"When we arrived at the shrine, some rang the bell, others did not. Inside, candles are lit first of all in front of all three shrines, and then an offering is made. (Either *o-miki* poured into a large red lacquer cup, or rice in a small bag.) Then coins are dropped in the offering box and hands clapped, and *namanda* [a short form of the Buddhist mantra, *namu amida butsu*] repeated reverentially with closed eyes. I have never heard a person offer a prayer, nor do they admit ever praying silently before or after reciting *namanda*. They say that a different mantra should be spoken in front of different temples and shrines, but no one knows them, so even to the Shinto deities they say *namanda* [which means 'Hail, Amida-buddha'].[2] After this, each one took a bit of special healing water standing in a bowl in front of the Yakushi, drank some, and put some on the face. Then they sat down by the charcoal brazier in the back and had a smoke. Some bought

1. Yakushi, popularly regarded as the god of medicine and hence of healing, is one of the Gochi-nyorai, the five deities of wisdom and contemplation.
2. Amida, the merciful Buddha of the Western Paradise, is the chief object of veneration of the Jōdo sect.

o-fuda [amulets] at one sen each, while others dropped in a coin and got a folded piece of paper with a fortune written on it. They had to take these *o-mikuji* back home to have them read for them.

"By the time we had finished all this it was ten o'clock, and we sat down on a mat outside to eat our lunch which each had brought. A couple at the shrine kept hot water and served us tea. They also sold canned fish and snails at high prices, and the woman was making *manju* [cakes stuffed with sweet bean-paste]. One kind, made with wheat and baking soda, was like that served at the houses of Suye yesterday, and was ready to eat. The other was made of rice-flour, which she cooked on the spot and sold very rapidly. We bought a can of snails and a cake. The women explained that all river food is healthful during the dog days and is especially good for the stomach.

"After food and drink we started out again. Mrs. Wauchi had not brought her pipe, so had to wait to borrow one from another woman. I heard her ask her husband before we left if he had seen hers anywhere and say to Mrs. Sato later, 'He says he doesn't know where it is, but I think he does.' This confirms the story that he objects to her smoking and that she does it in secret. He was sour yesterday anyway. So she had no pipe and later bought a package of Bat cigarettes.

"A little way down we stopped at a stream and a little further down at a well. Then we stopped at a shrine which had been rebuilt last year. It is a very large and impressive building, with three tremendous gateways leading to it. They tossed in coins and said *namanda* again. Then it was mentioned that Tawaji Seisuke's house is next to the shrine. They said it is a very fine place. Other houses were pointed out, as had been done all along the way. One was that of the family into which Mrs. Sato's daughter is married, but she said we need not call. Then we stopped in a store across the street from the school. From there we were thinking of taking the bus, but were told that it was not running. So we had tea, much talk, more smokes, and the women bought some cakes. We left about 11:30 and walked only a few paces until we came to a shop that sells ice-cakes [popsicles]. There we had more tea, listened to a long *naniwabushi* on six records played for us on the shop's victrola. When the ballad was finished, the man turned on the radio to a baseball game of which no one understood anything, but they would not let me turn it off. Each woman ate four ice-cakes and then settled down for a nap, which lasted until about two o'clock.

"On our way again, we emerged finally into Menda, where they shopped for various things for the family and stopped again at an eating place run by a very fat woman where they specialize in *inarizushi* [vinegared rice wrapped in fried bean curd]. We had tea and the old lady bought herself a bottle of cider. Usually Mrs. Wauchi pays for everything, but not this time. We gossiped some more. About four o'clock we started out and, wading through fields badly damaged by the flood and deposits of sand in place of a path, we got to the Wauchi's by five. There I had to drink some Calpis—a weird liquid—served with water by the son of the house."

THE PILGRIMAGE TO ŌTAKE-SAN

"Yesterday, September 23, was the middle day of *higan* [the autumnal equinox]. Early in the morning we left for Ōtake-san. I left our house at five o'clock; the stores were still shut, no one was up, and it was quite dark. As I stood waiting for the Kawaze women at Ishizaka it became lighter and I heard some doors opening here and there. Twenty minutes later at Shoya the silkworms were getting their first mulberry leaves and some kitchen fires had been lit. While I stood there alone a white-clad pilgrim came out of the dark and gave a startled cry as she saw me move.

"At Shoya we met a group of ten or fifteen old people just starting out after a night's stop. They gave us a message to deliver to two others of their group should we see them in Menda. We did see one of them, as a matter of fact, but my companions did not consider it worthwhile delivering the message.

"Both the Sato daughters and Mrs. Wauchi were all dressed up for this pilgrimage. One of the girls had on a lovely homespun kimono, and all had white *tabi* and dressy *geta*. We made the 6:12 train from Menda. In Yunomae a bus was just leaving, supposedly bound only for Iwano, but as enough people wanted to go to Yuyama, where the climb to the shrine begins, the bus driver decided to go up there, and we were all packed in like sardines. By seven we reached Yuyama, where pilgrims usually take hot-spring baths, and started on our hike. It was still awfully cold and we shivered all along because when the sun came out we were still in the shadow of the mountain.

"Alighting from the bus, we asked the way. One old lady pointed out one path, a man suggested a different and wider road. As one group from the bus had already taken that road, we followed after them. We progressed very slowly, because we stopped here and there to ask for straw sandals for the girls (there were none to be had, leading Mrs. Wauchi to comment, 'Well, in the city you cannot find such things'), and at a farmer's house to buy some candles, which we had forgotten to bring, we were overtaken by a school teacher who knew one of Sato's daughters from a class. He called out to us to ask if we knew where we were going. It turned out that we were on the road built by the forestry department for its use, which leads to the peak of the mountain by very hard paths and would bring us to the shrine about three hours later than if we took the real path that leads directly to the shrine. This teacher and a forestry man were out collecting specimens of something for the school. We turned off and had a child show us the way to the path to the shrine. Mrs. Wauchi gave him a ten-sen tip, saying 'Here, buy some pencils.' By wandering through fields and uncultivated upland, we finally reached the right road. Indeed, the group who had gone on ahead of us and did not get redirected came along about an hour later, having had to find another side track. On the way up we stopped to have a rest and some food. A very old lady caught up with us, and Mrs. Wauchi invited her to rest with us and later we went on up together. She lives in one of the villages near the mountain, and although she had gone up many times before, she said this was her first pilgrimage in five years.

"Up to the beginning of the shrine premises the road was not bad, much better and wider than it was in the old days, they said. The young men from neighboring villages were cutting underbrush and pruning and bracing some young cherry trees that grow along the road. After a time we came to a rapid stream spanned by a wooden bridge with sacred straw rope, hung with paper streamers, stretched across it. This was the beginning of the real ascent. A Sato daughter took off her *tabi* and *geta* here and went on barefooted, but the other two went up all the way in *geta*. The ascent was very steep, with rock steps several feet high in some places. The trek is divided into five parts, and little white poles indicate the distance covered. The shrine is, I think, 1,400 meters high. One can go further above it, but few people do so. At the very top, they say, is a small shrine, not a real one like Ōtake. About half-way between the bridge and the shrine is the wooden gateway. People stop there to toss up stones, trying to make them land on the cross-bar. They told me it is just a custom, but when Junko's stone lodged there, all said, 'That is very good.'

"The shrine itself is high up on an elevation, but people do not go there. Instead they go to a long building which leads to the shrine, so that when they kneel to light the candles they face the steps leading up to the shrine. This long building has a wooden shrine. People light a candle, offer *o-miki* into a special clay jar, kneel, toss a coin into the collection box, clap their hands and bow their heads in prayer. Then they go to the back of the room and are offered tea and toasted glutinous rice cake by an attendant. No one liked the rice cakes very much and the tea was horrible. (The walls of the room are decorated with pictures of guns, cannon, and military men on horseback. The state religion here is militarism, and Shinto is being transformed into worship of gods and soldiers.)

"It is said that in the old days all married couples went up there on the first sixteenth of March after their wedding, but that only some do today. It is the god of marital felicity, and helps one find a good husband or wife, for a happy marriage. (Mrs. Tanimoto, hearing that the Sato girls went along, said to me and Mrs. Kato later, 'Kawaze people go a lot to Ōtake-san, I wonder why? What is he a god of—is it not happy marriage?' To which Mrs. Kato replied, 'Yes indeed.' Both of them love to make such apparently innocent remarks, which in this case actually meant, 'The older Sato girl is still not married, hence the trip.')

"There is a side room with *tatami* and a fire-pit in the center where we went to have our lunch. Before going in we had some of the *o-miki* sake that Mrs. Wauchi had brought. (She said her husband had just returned from a trip to visit their married daughter, and Tomokawa had come over with a *sakamukai* gift of sake, which she brought along for *o-miki*.) The old lady had bought some *shōchū* for *o-miki*, which Junko had carried in a flask. Then we went in to eat and polished off the *o-miki* sake. The old lady who had joined us on the way up was offered a drink of *shōchū*. It surprised me that until then nothing else had been offered her, although she sat waiting for us to finish eating and the women had bought candy and *manju* in Yunomae, which they were eating themselves.

"The people who had taken the wrong road ahead of us and who now turned up proved to be relatives of some of the Kawaze women. We only gathered this from the conversation between the priest and the man who was with them, at which the Sato daughters remembered having seen him once at a Suye wedding. (The man's wife was a paternal aunt of Shimoda Ichiro's wife.) Later this group exchanged greetings as they caught up with us on our way down, but no relationship was acknowledged.

"On the way up we had seen a young couple and an older woman—the women barefoot. Once there, after the first obeisance, the women made ten trips to the shrine and back, each time depositing a leaf of a tree at the shrine. These trips are called *hyaku do mairi* [100 shrine visits] or whatever, depending on the number of trips made. It is a *gan*— a pledge made in atonement or in gratitude for some good fortune. They were doing it because some family member's disease had been cured. Mrs. Wauchi said that many women did this during the Russo-Japanese War to guarantee the safe return of their men.

"Although the sun was out now and was very hot, up at the shrine it was still very cold. On the way back, we rested many times. The descent was much easier, although one has to jump down from one high rock to another. Back at Yuyama, we were going to take a hot bath, but skipped it because we just caught a car returning to Yunomae. It was a touring car and so crowded that three men had to stand on the running boards. In Yunomae we made a good connection, and on the train met Sato Kazuo's younger brother's wife with her children. They were on their way to Taragi, and would walk to Kume from there to visit relatives. After much discussion, the women decided to get off the train in Taragi. At once I suggested taking a bus to Tsuiji and walking home from there. On all previous occasions my suggestions had been overruled, and this time, too, the women thought it would be a good idea to rest a while in Taragi until the heat subsided (it was now around three o'clock) and then walk all the way home through Nakashima. As I have already had the experience of sitting around for hours, then trailing along the dusty Taragi road on several previous occasions, I said that they should stay but that I would take the bus, which had just arrived.

"They inquired about fares, and decided they would go to Furu-Taragi for ten sen rather than to Tsuiji for fifteen. The train cost 16 sen to Yunomae and eight from Yunomae to Taragi. The bus was sixty sen each way. The other expenses were the cakes and candy taken up to the shrine, and bought to eat while we waited in Yunomae and some purchased to be taken home as presents. They had spent money on candy and on this and that, but this bus fare seemed just a waste. I said I would go to Tsuiji by bus anyhow, and I am afraid I forced the issue. They all went with me, but getting off the bus all made remarks such as, 'Well, you certainly do get here fast for fifteen sen.' We still had to squat a little ways along for them to rest and eat the remaining rice balls and for Junko to finish her tin of snails, bought at the shrine. This girl, at the age of thirteen, is still the baby and acts like a small child. In Yunomae she wanted ice-cakes, but because her mother would not go with her, she refused to buy them. Getting off the train she still wanted ice-cakes, but since the bus was about to leave, she got none. Getting off the bus she still wanted some, by now quite offended. Her mother said, 'We'll wait here. You go up the road and get them yourself,' but of course she would not do that, but moaned all the way, 'I want ice-cakes.' However, once home, she gave her grandmother one of the cakes bought for her, which she had not eaten, and a fortune-telling slip got at the shrine. We were in Kawaze by 4:30. Mrs. Sato had prepared *sushi* and arranged a welcoming party for us."

The Suyama Kannon Pilgrimage[3]

"On October 14 the trip to Suyama Kannon finally came through. A little after seven this morning Mrs. Fujita, Maki-san and Mrs. Kato and I started off. Mrs. Fujita apologized for being late, saying that she had gone to a party yesterday and still had a headache. It was very cold and the mist did not rise until about ten o'clock.

"These women, like the ones from Kawaze when out on an excursion, discuss each house they pass in a whisper. 'This one has been bought by so and so. This is where so and so lives. This must be the doctor's house—it has so many flowers around it and looks like a rich man's place.' But their capacity for gossip is much higher than Kawaze. It was interesting that Maki-san, herself the object of so much gossip, joined them in discussing the irregular lives of other women. At first current events were discussed. Ochiai is having his roof fixed today and Shichihei tried to get Torao to come and help out, but he refused. Evidently there is some old feud there. Indeed, they said that Shichihei had trouble getting anyone to come because no one is on very friendly terms with Ochiai. They all consider his wife to be a bad gossip. The women said that his first wife had been a good woman. Only Tomekuni's wife came to help. Then the sale of the house that the Sasakis lived in was discussed. They say he got only 100 of the 350 yen that old lady Serizawa sold it for. As we walked along, they spoke of previous trips to shrines. Mrs. Kato has not been to Suyama for thirty-three years. The other two went many years ago, visiting

3. Kannon is the Buddhist goddess of mercy.

all the local shrines when there was an epidemic raging, taking *sekihan* to them all. So, gossiping, they found the road there and back very short.

"After climbing up the very steep and numerous steps, we came to a stone commemorating the building of the stairway and a sign reading: Kannon-san to the right; Inari-san[4] to the left. They decided to visit the Inari shrine first, offer *o-miki* there, and then go on to the Kannon. Since they had one candle each (Maki-san had forgotten to bring any at all), they divided up, lighting one candle at each of the shrines. The Inari shrine was the usual red building behind three red gateways. On the doors, which were shut, was a sign that read: please drop offerings inside. Behind it there was another large structure, about the size of our *dō*, in which there were two deities unknown to the women. They gave them the usual Shinto handclap. They were small winged figures much like Bishamonten,[5] one holding a spear and the other a shell. Between them stood a small spear, all of which puzzled the women. Outside the shrine on the shelf stood two wooden lions, at once pronounced to be the male and female guardians of the place, but they did not know which was which because both had protuberances between their hind legs. However, it was decided that the one with the horn was the female and that the two were the *hi no kamisama* (the fire god) and the *mizu no kamisama* (the water god). All gods in pairs are said to be a male and female couple.

"Much pleased they proceeded to the Kannon temple. There they lit the candle and poured out *o-miki*. Mrs. Fujita deposited a couple of cookies that she had bought on the way up. As one of them fell behind the statue of Kannon, she was worried, but Mrs. Kato reassured her, saying, 'That's all right. It means that Kannon-sama accepted your offering directly.' This sort of personification goes on all the time. Says Mrs. Fujita, washing her hands at a well, 'Pardon me, Suijin-sama [the god of water], for dirtying the water.'

"Then we settled down for a party. *O-miki* bottles were taken down and many cups drunk, although the *shōchū* that had been poured into a cup at the shrine was left there. Before leaving the village two tins of fish and beef mixed with bamboo shoots had been purchased at the shop. These were opened. Each woman produced some special things that she had brought—chestnuts, cookies, candy. My apples were eaten at once. Maki-san had brought nothing extra, and she did not seem to have much money to spare throughout the trip. She also said half apologetically later, 'I have only balls of millet—rather than rice,' but was assured by the others that new millet is very tasty indeed. They had discussed rice mixed with

---

4. Inari is the Shinto goddess of crops, especially rice, the entrance to whose shrines is flanked by two fox-images.

5. Bishamonten is a Buddhist deity of many identities in Japan. He is one of the three gods of war (San-senjin), who holds a spear aloft in one hand and a pagoda balanced on the other; under the name Tamon-ten he is also one of the four guardian deities (Shi-dai-tennō) who watches over the north; and is one of the seven deities of good fortune.

barley or millet before, and had agreed that this dish is very good for the stomach.

"We drank a lot, finishing two bottles of *o-miki* and half of Mrs. Fujita's huge flask. When I began to eat my rice, they said it was wrong to eat rice so early, for after rice they do not feel like drinking, and leave it to the last. Mrs. Kato and Maki-san did much singing, following which we looked over the Kannon carefully, counted the hands, of which there are thirty-three, discussed its qualities, wondered why it is called *yatsude-Kannon* (eight-armed Kannon). Each hand holds a different object—a lotus bud, a lotus seed, a priest's baton, a gong for funeral music, a square box, and many other things. One hand held a sword, another an axe, and on one was suspended what looked like a mask. By its side stood another image of Kannon in the more usual seated posture, and on either side were two large Bishamonten. The head of the Kannon is surrounded by smaller heads forming a halo, and there is an Amida in the center.

"They said that formerly people would break branches from trees in the precincts of this temple to take home to plant in order to make for easier childbirth. (Suzuki Iwa later told me that she went up there before her son was born because she had not given birth to a child for some years and was frightened.) The women decided that Kannon-sama must indeed be very happy to see us having such a good time for her benefit. Before leaving, they asked me to photograph them. At first they were worried about having three in the picture [it is believed that the middle person will be the first to die], but decided that Kannon could be the fourth. Nevertheless, since it is the person who stands in the middle who dies, it was agreed that Mrs. Kato, the oldest, would take that position. (On the way up when she said that this would be her last trip, the others had said, 'No, you won't get up here again, but we might, just once more.')

"All food consumed, all *shōchū* drunk, we started back. Upon our return, Mrs. Kato invited us in and gave us a real party. They had originally planned it as a farewell party for me, but decided to have it later because 'that loud Kawaze bunch will surely burst in today [if they hear a party] and spoil it.' "

GOSSIP AND BAD FEELINGS

One of the consequences of the prevalence of gossip was that upon occasion the women and many of the men of Suye had reason to conceive very strong likes and dislikes for one another. By and large, however, some care was taken to maintain a surface air of amiability and a pleasant demeanor, masking the contrast between the real feelings of individuals and their behavior toward others.

"Mrs. Tomokawa is often at Mrs. Fujita's. Although she always appears to be on the very best of terms with Mrs. Tomokawa, she has revealed to me that she hates the woman. On her way home the other day, Mrs. Fujita stopped in for a chat with Mrs. Tanimoto. They had tea and pickles and much gossip. Mrs. Tomokawa's name came up, and they really let go. 'She is completely mad. I can't feel a bit sorry for her.' Mrs. Tanimoto said this several times. She said she'd like to knock the woman's head off, and swung her fly swatter about vigorously for emphasis. Mrs. Tomokawa, they said, mistreats the old lady who lives with them (she is her husband's older brother's widow), and is unpleasant to the adopted daughter when she comes to visit."

One of the outstanding examples of bad relations was that between the old lady Mori and the whole Hayashi family. "Mrs. Tanimoto confirms my suspicion that old lady Mori dislikes the Hayashis intensely. She says it is just an old trouble, but I think she did not want to tell me about it. She says that the old lady is very bad and dislikes many people, says bad things about them, and gets into many fights. 'She is glad that Shoko [Mrs. Hayashi Fumio] is sick because she dislikes her so.' Because of this situation, Mrs. Tanimoto goes to visit Shoko only at night because otherwise old lady Mori will start saying things about her. She does not like people to be nice to anyone but herself. (It's true that when she knows that I have been to Hayashi's, she always makes some remark about them to me later.) She is also on bad terms with old lady Kato. That fight started during the young Mrs. Kato's divorce, when Mori said something that displeased the Katos, and now they avoid one another on the street. 'Watch for it,' she said, 'It's really interesting!' Old lady Kato herself is said to be very hard to get along with. Her former son-in-law always used to say, 'I can't stand that old woman.' It is she who made so much trouble that he finally left her daughter and got married again." (For more on this affair see pages 161–63.)

"On the way back, I stopped at Mori's. The old lady was making more nasty cracks about Hayashi Fumio. 'Their behavior toward us old people is very wrong,' she said, but Ishibashi, who was there when I arrived, paid no attention. To me she said that Hayashis are now on bad terms with twenty-four households, and that even Shimosaka Seisuke got angry with them the other day. It seems that there is a bit of village property near Fumio's house. Seisuke went there to cut some bamboo for a drain, and Fumio got mad, saying the land was his. Angered in turn, Seisuke told him that his attitude and his behavior are all wrong. (What exactly it is about Fumio, I do not know, but it is true that he does not cooperate with the others.)"

The Hayashis were very conscious of the Mori's ill-will. "Hayashi Shoko was having tea with Mrs. Tanimoto, and Mrs. Eda Mina dropped in with some freshly cooked pumpkin. Mrs. Kuwagiri, on her way back from the fields where she had been gleaning, stopped in too. Said Shoko, 'How nice it is to look out of one's door into a vacant field,' referring to the contrast with her own house, where the old lady Mori lives practically on the doorstep. That set off the gossip. They all agreed that the old lady is awful, mostly because her gossip is false. It seems that the other day she was worried that I might be mad at her for not visiting me for a long time. They said that the younger Mrs. Mori and her husband are just like the old lady. It seems that he was upset because 'only set people' were chosen for the race at the school field-day. He had an argument with one of the teachers, another with Uemura, and finally got into a big fight at Uchida's. Shoko said that she and Suzuki Iwa have the worst time because they are under the old lady's constant observation. Iwa cried the other day because some gossip had got back to her. Shoko said that if they can possibly manage it, they will use the money from this year's harvest to rebuild their house for privacy. They talked about a woman in Shoya who was on such bad terms with everyone there that nobody felt sorry when she died. It was considered an apposite example."

Upon occasion, some women were openly critical of one another or made cutting remarks of remarkable tactlessness. "In the evening, Mrs. Kato, Mrs. Tanimoto, Mrs. Uchida, and Tamaki Take gave us a farewell party of their own. Only Mrs. Tanimoto went to spend all afternoon at Kato's helping with the preparations; Take was out harvesting. This event probably will start new trouble because although the party was to be kept secret, those who were left out found out about it. Some have already made remarks.

"Mrs. Tanimoto kept saying, 'We have nothing, please forgive us,' but was unable to control herself and said, 'But we did our best and we prepared everything very nicely, so please enjoy it. Of course, we cannot do it as nicely as you have it at home, but even in Tokyo it would be hard to find such a tasty meal. If we had proper ingredients, we could have done much better.' The meal was indeed grand, served on the flower-decorated table. But even on this occasion, the women could not do without talk behind one another's backs. First they complained that the raw fish needed more soy sauce and disapproved of the way Mrs. Kato had prepared it. So the minute she went out, they went to fetch some soy sauce, but finding none came and took some from the dish at Sano's place. When she returned, the dish had to be refilled. Then they mumbled something about the *shōchū* being much too thin. [It was sometimes diluted to make it less potent or to economize.] Mrs. Tanimoto announced in a loud voice that she cannot abide thin *shōchū*, and that there was not enough of it. While she was out of the room, the others made several cracks about her in turn, and even when she came back in and was sitting right there they made remarks that she pretended not to notice. The music and dancing did not go well because Take could not sing the songs that Mrs. Kato knew how to dance to. Mrs. Tanimoto was expected to do *dodoitsu* [a kind of short ballad] which they started to play just as she was leaving the room, whereupon she came back but decided to do something else instead. Everyone was surprised and openly very disapproving of her behavior."

A similar situation developed at a Kannon Society party for men, with wives only substituting if their husbands could not attend. "It was held at Uchida's. There used to be a more formal organization of this *kō*, but now they just let Sato take care of the money. This is typical of Kakui, which is always said to be unable to run its affairs properly. The question of food caused a minor disturbance. Mrs. Uchida did not want to make so much bean curd, and decided instead to order dried fish from the fish-monger. He was late in making his delivery, and in the meantime Mrs. Tanimoto, Mrs. Kato and Mrs. Hayashi arrived in high spirits, and at once began to complain about the plans for the food. They did not want the dried fish and asked why the women couldn't have cakes instead. The men objected to the idea of the cakes, which do not go well with *shōchū*. The women then wanted to know why there was no bean curd, and suggested buying some.

"Mrs. Uchida continued to talk in her plaintive, high-pitched voice, and was clearly peeved. As the fish had not yet arrived, she asked the men to buy some. They came back with it just as the fishmonger arrived with the order. At once Mrs. Uchida told them to return the bean curd, whereupon the men refused, saying that she had told them to buy it and it would be a shame to return it to the store. The women thought she should keep it and sell it later. Much confusion. I said that I would take it and exchange it for something else. To this she agreed, and then collected the standard donation of thirty-five sen from me anyway, which enraged the other women, who thought she could at least credit it to my account. Mrs. Kato, reputedly Mrs. Uchida's good friend, appeared to side with the others against her today.

"When all the company food and drink arrived, better spirits prevailed, but the hostess was sour on Mrs. Kato and Mrs. Tanimoto, who made the most noise. The women left first, Mrs. Tanimoto wrapping up her food and mine, making it abundantly clear that she was taking it for her cat. All in all it was not a loving meeting, though everyone was most polite. The gossip at this gathering centered around the Makinos, whose gift to Mrs. Tanimoto for her services at the wedding was much criticized and displayed with a smirk. At one point Mrs. Tanimoto picked it up and flung it across the room, so great was her wrath. To the Makinos she had, of course, said nothing."

Sex: Public and Private

One of the aspects of village life that by turns amused, startled, and exasperated the Embrees was the amount of sexual joking and play. The women and men of Suye were considerably less inhibited in these matters than the schoolteachers, who were scandalized by what they considered to be their extreme vulgarity, and there is no doubt that her life in Japan up to the time of the study had scarcely prepared Ella Wiswell for the earthy humor and candid discussions of sex that she encountered. Among other things, many people were anxious to instruct her in the vocabulary of sexual references and very curious to learn about how Americans dealt with this ever-absorbing topic.

Such instruction went on all the time. "Mrs. Tanimoto informed me that the thumb thrust between the second and third fingers stands for vagina, while the equivalent male sign is the forefinger stretched out, as if pointing. A forefinger thrust between the second and third fingers of the other hand is one of the signs for copulation. At once the conversation turned a bit free. They wanted to know how Americans make love. Mrs. Fujita assured me that at her age people use their tongues because they can do nothing else. She concluded that at my age we still make love and so are too bashful to discuss it. When she was my age, she said, they had intercourse at least twice every night, but now they do not do it even once."

"*Kara-imo* [sweet potato] is a current term for penis. People make jokes like, "How big is your husband's *kara-imo?*' and 'Do you like *kara-imo?*' All such remarks cause much laughter. When the pickles were served at Makino's, Hiroshi, with a glance in her direction, asked me if our maid makes good pickles. A woman who does is 'good here,' he said, pointing to his genitals. So, when he called on his wife's family before their marriage was arranged, he said that he had been careful to make sure that it was she who had made the delicious pickles he was served. 'How do you tell about men?' I asked. 'By how they urinate,' he replied. If a man urinates straight out and far, it means that he has a long (gesture) and thick (another gesture) penis. He also confided that people who are fond of pickles also like to copulate. Further jokes were made about young men calling on our maid when we were asleep, and they wanted to know if John's assistant sleeps with her. Hiroshi, with another glance in her direction, said that she likes him. She was flustered and protested, but took her revenge by saying that Hiroshi likes me. All this amidst gales of laughter. They did not want me to go home because it was so interesting and I was asked to come again soon because it is so amusing to have me there."

Frankness was common, and back-biting only somewhat less so. "Old lady Arasaki said that she stopped 'working' with her old man after their first grandchild was born. She cut her hair long ago, she said, even though she is not a widow. It was some disease of the scalp." On another occasion, "as soon as Mrs. Tomokawa went off, she became the topic of conversation. 'Why does she claim to be younger than she is? She is very upset about her husband's illness. She still wants a man, you know. Yes, she still wants a man all right.' The other day (this from Mrs. Tanimoto) she complained that she has not slept with her husband for fifty-seven days now. There was much laughter but the visitor from Shoya was indignant. 'What? Fifty days! Why at her age husband and wife don't make love that much anyhow.' "

"Mrs. Tanimoto went on to describe intercourse. The position is usually the same, with the woman underneath. Most certainly you clean up afterwards, otherwise it is so dirty that one might drip forever. One uses a kind of paper that with two wipings does a very good job. It is so much more pleasant if you clean up afterwards. If I do not do so now, she strongly recommended that I try the Japanese method. Men also wipe. Having intercourse twice in one night is quite usual, especially on long evenings when you go to bed early and if you are still young. Three times is not really unusual, but once at night and once again in the morning is very good.

"When he was young, she says, old man Eda had a sweetheart with whom he hit the record of eight times in one night. His penis got all red and actually bled at the end. He would do it every time he lay down to rest for an afternoon nap. As for herself, she only does it once in ten days now. (I, being at the very prime of life now, should have intercourse at least three times a night, she thinks.) Is it true, she wanted to know, that it takes an hour for Americans to come to climax. I said I did not think so. 'Then it is just the same as here,' she said. 'Five minutes only.'

"At her age, she went on, they just do 'mouth work' and look at the goods (shinamono), which is quite satisfactory. She calls kissing igisu and demonstrated how to do it by pursing her lips and making a smacking sound. Not everyone in the village knows how to do it, she said, only those who have been around, visited geisha, and have had some experience. Young people would not know about it, she thinks, which would explain Fumie's ignorance of the matter. (While we were discussing Koyo-chan's pregnancy the other day, Fumie had professed complete ignorance of kissing. She did not know the word *seppun* [then the common word for kiss], and has never seen kissing. She laughed at my description of it.) In kissing, she assured me, they have become very accomplished, so it replaces intercourse at times. 'Very interesting, this business,' she said. 'I wonder who invented it?' My suggestion that it was Amaterasu-ō-mikami [the sun goddess, but more likely Izanami, the female of the primal couple] was accepted, and she told me about the sacred Shinto dance done here at the shrines. She said that people cannot help laughing because it is so suggestive of intercourse in all its movements."

When she finally got to see the dance performed, it proved to be interesting enough, "if somewhat drawn out and repetitious, like all other programs here. The dances with the lion's mane were most suggestive. I was reminded of Mrs. Tanimoto's account, but even they were not very explicit. She must have seen a special dance, or was just making up things."

Some time later this woman and some others, along with old man Ishibashi, went out moon-viewing. "He entertained us with songs. All were very heavy on the *double entendre*, and he had to explain them all. One was a short verse which he had sung before I arrived, and the woman demanded that he explain it to them again. It had to do with *mame* (beans) and the straight meaning was simple enough, for it described a walk along a narrow path between paddies where the beans are planted in a row. He said that it also referred to the line down the center of a woman's stomach that leads to the clitoris. 'You know, that small thing in the center,' he said. The women loved it. 'You know so many of these songs,' they said. 'That is because I like this so much,' was his reply, and he made the sign for vagina with his fingers. They teased him about his visits to the widow. The song goes as follows:[1]

Nagai aze michi	By the long path between the fields
yoi kite kureta	thank you for coming to me
suso ga nuretarō	your hem must be wet
mame no ha de	from the leaves of the bean plants

The instruction continued, "Mrs. Tanimoto assured me that women enjoy intercourse just as much as men. 'Why would they bother otherwise? They'd just get tired out.' She thinks that it is best after one turns thirty, which is when women get the most enjoyment out of it. Girls seldom come as virgin brides, and the grooms do not mind, for it is just as well to get it all prepared by someone else rather than having to do it yourself. Still 'fixing' the hymen is also a great pleasure, and people become very attached over it (*kawaiku narimasu*)." [Presumably a reference to a special affection between a newly wed couple where the virginal bride's hymen has been penetrated by the groom.] As for conception, she thinks that if a woman does not reach climax, she cannot conceive because her womb remains

1. Given also in Embree (1944a, p. 35). *Suso* refers to the hem of a kimono.

shut. She demonstrated with her hands how the womb opens up when receptive. So, she thinks that the widows just 'rent the place' to men, without participating much in the activity because they are fearful of having a child. But of one of the widows she said, 'Maybe she uses something.' "

The subject of this widow arose again a few days later in a group. "The women were admiring the fancy mulberry roots that Ishibashi has collected for their decorative value. He told us all about the phallic stones he saw on a trip to Miyazaki. Mrs. Tanimoto stuck her hand inside an oblong cavity in a tree trunk and asked, 'How about this?' Ishibashi said it was too large. He was teased about his past affairs, and then they quite openly discussed the widow Matsumoto Shima and wondered if she does something to prevent pregnancy. (Later, Mrs. Fujita said to her face that she entertains men at her house, whereupon Shima replied, 'And how about you, with your old man being no use now?')"

"As we were having tea, the conversation was not without pep. There was much talk about making babies, and Mrs. Kuwagiri brought up our previous conversation with Matsumoto Shima. Mrs. Fujita thereupon told us more about bulls and their habits, and it was clear that Shoko was definitely embarrassed by all this kind of talk (as the younger wives often are). Mrs. Kuwagiri said, 'No more intercourse for me after the fourth month of pregnancy! You just try it with that lump sticking out in front of you.' Mrs. Fujita recommended trying it from the back. All laughed at such heresy."

Speculating on why the dirtiest and poorest families had the most children, Mrs. Toyama wondered, " 'Is it because the goods are so well made [that these women always have their bellies sticking out]?' She thinks maybe that it is that such people give themselves up so much during intercourse that they always make babies. (I recalled Noguchi's remark that these people have no other pleasure than having children. He should have said 'than making babies.')"

"At the naming ceremony for the Eda baby, the conversation soon turned into its usual channel. Mrs. Amano said that she had tried everything to conceive. She had even carried a stone from the river in her bosom, having first offered it to the gods, but it did not help. Said one of the women, 'It takes a man, not a rock.' They fell to discussing Eda's ability at making babies. When someone remarked that I had only one child, he offered his assistance, as did Makino. I joked that he was not very good, having only two children of his own. 'Yes, but the first was a boy, and the second a girl. If that is not skill. . . . If you want just any kind of job, call on Eda. For a really good job, call on me!' "

While they were sorting mulberry leaves, "Mrs. Shibata was talking about people having too many children. 'You shouldn't work so hard at night. In the daytime you get sleepy and wonder why. It's because of all that night work, which is why you have so many children.' Mrs. Amano suggested that I lend John to her, for he apparently has better seed than her husband [they are childless]."

And at a farewell party given by one of the hamlets, "after singing the verse *otoko daite kara senya* [It's been a long time since I held a man in my arms], they asked me how many times a night Americans have intercourse. 'Four,' they guessed, when I refused to answer, and deaf-and-dumb Setsuko raised four fingers and pointed to her stomach, making it stick out. All thought that once was not enough." Lest it be thought that discussion of such matters was limited to conversation where only women were present, it should be noted that after this same party, which was attended by men and women alike, John Embree wrote: "With typical Suye humor two of the women said that I should leave my *kintama* (testicles), one to each of them, and as a souvenir *(kinen)* they said they would give me *mame* [beans, but here meaning vagina]. This is a joke that combines the usual sexual references with a comment on the way they had been asking for and been given all sorts of our household effects, now that we are leaving."

The children of Suye hung around the parties, eavesdropped when they could, and listened in on adult conversations. Sometimes they were part of the audience for stories of sexual innuendo. "Late in the afternoon a group of colorfully attired people arrived at the store. They are *chindonya* [musicians hired to advertise a business] for the Marukiya in Menda. They distributed handbills, set up their banners, played the *shamisen* and drum, and danced. They will be on their circuit for five days, going from Menda to Kume, down through here to Taragi and back. They are actually advertising for the main Marukiya store, but mention all the branches as well.

"Everyone came out to watch the show and enjoyed it greatly, asking for more dances, and joking with the man who was the leader. After a few dances, he told stories which raised much laughter, especially one which was a parody of a Buddhist priest offering prayers and reciting the sutras. Another favored one was about a girl he said he had once met in Suye. She was carrying a parcel, and when he asked what it contained, she said, 'Food for the god of thunder.' This had frightened him, and he wanted to know what the god eats. After much argument she let him peek in the parcel which contained a two-tiered box. In the top one were belly-buttons, 'which is why all the children of Suye have none,' whereupon all the kids gathered around clutched their stomachs. [The god of thunder is thought to steal navels.] Then the man had wanted to know what was in the lower box. The girl positively refused to show him, although he kept pleading. 'Why can't I see the side-dishes, since I have already seen the rice?' She only wept, and finally said through her tears, 'You have seen the belly-buttons, but I cannot show you what is below them.' This was all told very vividly, with many asides. (What is below the navel, of course, is the vagina.)"

"When the Korean with the Canton ginseng roots came again this afternoon, all the children gathered at the store to listen, but when he patted the younger Ouchi girl on the head the second daughter motioned her away, evidently suspicious of this foreigner. He repeated the pitch he had given the other day. Mrs. Matsumoto was considering buying a piece. Mrs. Ochiai said that I should buy one so that I would have a baby, and Mrs. Matsumoto said that she is afraid to take it because it will make her too wild and scare her husband. Old lady Ochiai said that she is no good any more anyway, so there is no point in taking any medicine.

"All of this talk started the Korean up. He broke in with, 'There are many different kinds of vagina, just as there are many kinds of penis. Now, there are small vaginas (a circle made with two fingers) and big ones (a sign with the forefingers and thumbs of both hands joined).' 'And do you like big ones?' inquired Mrs. Ochiai. 'No, too big is no good. You can't tell if you are in or out,' he replied. He thereupon proceeded to tell about how at the age of eleven he was raped by an older woman and how small his penis was (more gestures) at the time, and how surprised he was. 'Well, I never!' exclaimed Mrs. Ochiai, 'And did you have any juice? Where could it be kept at eleven?' She said that she had never heard of such goings on, but he assured her that in Japan, too, some older women like younger men. He cited the case of the owner of a restaurant in Menda who has a young lover whom she takes everywhere she goes. Throughout this conversation, Mori's little girl Kei-chan stood open-mouthed, catching only a few familiar words like penis and vagina."

"The last time he stopped by, the Korean had a conversation with Makino Otone, who asked him about his wife. He said that he actually dislikes women, but later mentioned his wife and children in Korea. 'Then you must have liked women just a little bit at one time,' said Otome. When he asked for some candy at the store—a kind called *tama* (balls)—he called them *kintama* (testicles). The whole family roared with laughter. They are a family with Rabelaisian humor and always enjoy a joke like that."

At a farewell party, Suzuki recommended to John Embree "that I sleep with a Japanese woman before I leave, 'to show that you are a man.' He pointed to all the men present and said that all have slept with women other than their wives. At one time he slapped Sasaki's daughter on the rump good naturedly as she bowed and served *shōchū* to someone else."

At a party at a women's *kō*, to which many husbands had been invited, the topic of old lady Mori's illness came up. "Mrs. Tanimoto suggested that her old man's penis was too large, and that it's what had caused her sickness. Then, to everyone's amusement, she went on to describe the long, thick, curved penis the old man had. She had seen it once when he was outside urinating. (Old lady Mori's disease is some sort of female complaint, as are most of the diseases of women here.) When they offered me some *shōchū*, and then were persuading me to have still more, the women said it is good for 'aches and pains' and pointed down, in case I had not understood."

Following the party for the Ise-kō, with only women present, talk turned to sexual intercourse. "All agreed that copulation takes place lying down, the woman underneath, but Mrs. Suzuki Tamezo suggested that if it does not work the man sometimes has to raise himself. They wanted to know if our men also 'do this'—illustrating with a jerking motion of the wrist—'because here one cannot do without it.' They were also very curious to know why we do not bathe together. Said Mrs. Tanimoto, 'Their tub is too small. Anyway, it's not good to do it in the tub.' (Evidently some people here made good use of the bathtub!)"

One afternoon at the Wauchi's, "I found the old lady alone sorting some sesame seed. She said that Mrs. Wauchi was away with the two Mrs. Satos, who are her sisters, to visit a relative in Nakashima who has chestnut trees. She did not expect them back for lunch, because they had taken along some food and a bottle of shōchū. Just as we sat down for supper at home, they appeared, all very gay, carrying tremendous baskets of chestnuts on their backs. Mrs. Wauchi produced a bobura [in Kyushu, a pumpkin], announcing that it was really a very large mattake [matsutake is the standard Japanese word], a kind of mushroom, by which she meant penis because mushrooms are a sex symbol. 'Such a large one. Look, Embree-san, this is bigger even than yours, so I brought it to you. We went mushroom gathering. There are many to be found there.' They sang a song about mushrooms, with many improvised verses, led mostly by Mrs. Wauchi. They were so drunk that they refused more shōchū, and had tea instead."

It is worth pointing out that none of this material comes from private, whispered conversations—as is the case with a very small amount of the gossip about fellow villagers that is omitted from this book—on the contrary, it is open, unsubtle, and certainly direct. When a group came in for tea after a stretch of hard work in the heat, "the women laughed a lot when an old man sat down and his red loin-cloth clearly revealed the outlines of his genitals. 'It is no different from being naked,' they kept saying, and laughingly urged me to take his picture." From John Embree's journal: "At the dō, a group of women were drinking and talking with a man. He sang a song and when he stopped, one of the women made as if to wind him up like a phonograph. He imitated her gesture, putting one hand toward the vulva of the woman sitting next to him, and making as if to wind into it."

Also from his journal comes the following convivial scene: "After everyone left our farewell party, Mrs. Tanimoto, Okochi, and we sat around the fire-pit with the girls who had been helping in the kitchen to have some rice. Mrs. Tanimoto told a story of her cat having copulated three times the previous night, and gave a graphic description of the events. She said that she went to Kannon-sama today to give thanks for having grandchildren. [She is childless; the reference is to the likelihood that the cat impregnated his partner(s).] She wondered why they scream so when they come together. She and her husband do not—do we? Everyone was in hysterics before she was finished."

"No chance to make an indecent gesture or joke is ever passed up. Youngsters in the last two years of school are going about today collecting horse manure for the school gardens. They went in pairs carrying a sort of straw stretcher to load the stuff onto. The manure was picked up by hand whenever they saw it. As a group of girls went by Makino Hiroshi, he bent over, calling out, 'Here is some! Hurry up!' which made the girls giggle."

"Mrs. Nagata of Tontokoro came in the shop to buy some material for an apron. As she was stretched out on her stomach on the mats, chatting with the owner, old man Eda came in and stuck a battery coil under her. Shortly after this a woman who came in with some salt buckets stuck the end of the carrying pole between Mrs. Nagata's buttocks. In Menda the other night when we asked Ouchi where umbrellas (kasa) were being sold in the market, he asked, 'Fujin kasa desu ka? [Women's umbrellas?].' This is a pun on hizen-gasa, a term applied to eruptions of the skin caused by venereal disease, and is always used in connection with prostitutes."

"This morning Fumio turned up at Makino's house. He made jokes with Otome, who is very pregnant, and made a couple of passes at her."

And at a wedding party where such humor was one of the favorite ways of tormenting the new bride: "Many jokes were made. Said the go-between, 'This bride has a large vagina. I know from experience.' "

On several occasions, very young children were the object of sexual teasing and play. "There was some reference to pickled onion (rakkyō) as a symbol for penis and seaweed (konbu) for vagina. The little Shimosaka girl asked for some konbu with her rice, and her mother said, 'Want this?' making the three-fingered sign for copulation. All laughed when the little girl pointed to the seaweed and said, 'No, this.' (The other night at the Eda house little Mitchan was running around naked. They played with her and grabbed her genitals, asking, 'What's this?')"

"As I went over to Sato's with a group of men and women, Mrs. Suzuki stopped off at her house to pick up the baby. Her six-year-old son, who had been running along ahead, dropped back and asked where his mother was. 'She's gone to have intercourse,' said his uncle and Mrs. Tanimoto, whereupon the youngster's eyes widened and he dashed back to his house to see. (It was shown by gestures that the word they used, choppai, means intercourse. Not in the dictionary.)"

The general attitude toward children playing with their genitals was quite relaxed, and indeed, "a mother often plays with her baby's genitals, especially if it is a boy. The other day at Kawabe's, the little boy, who is such a healthy baby, was much admired. His mother let him crawl around naked and Harumi remarked how much cuter naked boys are than girl babies."

"The penis is called *chin-chin* in baby talk. Mothers are constantly drawing a child's attention to it. 'What is that I see? Is it your *chin-chin?*' 'Don't run around here naked showing your *chin-chin.*' 'Sit down and cover your *chin-chin.*' These admonitions are repeated constantly. If a baby pulls up its kimono, as it often does, the mother will say, '*Ara, chin-chin ga deta*' (Oh! Your *chin-chin* is out.)' Yesterday, one of the mothers who was playing a hand-clapping game with her baby made him grab his penis, an action the kids hardly have to be taught."

"While the midwife was bathing the baby, Taro-chan watched with much interest. 'Does Tae-chan have a *chin-chin?*' the midwife asked him. 'No,' he replied, 'She has a *memejo* [vagina].' This answer caused much laughter, for this term is not used by children. The embarrassed little boy would not say at first where he had learned it, but after some coaxing said that his father had taught it to him. 'Which do you like best?' 'Don't like either one,' was his logical answer. The midwife's boy, who is four, did not know what *memejo* meant, but was embarrassed anyway. He was much around, and practically got into the bathtub. His mother went through her standard routine, which I have heard before. 'Yukio-chan, shall mother have a *yaya* [baby]? No? You don't want one? What shall we do with the *yaya* when it comes?' Yukio exhibited all the reactions of a pampered only child who is still being babied." Another little boy, whose mother was pregnant, was asked what he will do when the baby comes. He replied that the new baby can sleep in the back of the house. (It was, as we shall see, the custom for the last child to sleep with the mother until displaced by the arrival of a baby. He would then go to sleep with his father.) However, "All youngsters are very fond of the babies in their families. At Tamaki Giichi's the younger boy only giggled incredulously when his mother suggested that I take the new baby home with me [a common form of teasing]. The Sawara girl was disappointed that the baby was a boy, while at Tamaki's the little boy kept asking, 'Why are you putting a girl's kimono on the baby?' When told that the baby was a girl (she is four months old and he apparently had not thought about the matter for all that time), he announced, 'I don't like girls!' But giving her to me was not acceptable."

Young children were, of course, often around to watch the baby being fed, cleaned up, clothed, bathed, and cared for. "The baby was lying peacefully, but once it had been picked up, refused to be put down again. The mother gave him a breast, but the nursing was interrupted because her twelve-year-old demanded that she get him a shirt. She passed the baby to him and while she looked for the shirt, he bounced and rocked the baby as everyone here does. It is the fattest baby going. 'Look at his balls,' the mother said. 'They are all behind instead of being up front.' Suddenly very concerned, the older boy pushed them toward the front, but the baby is so fat there is no room for them."

"Children, especially boys, are always playing with their genitals. No one says anything to them about it, although occasionally a person will make a joke: 'Your *chin-chin* is sticking out.' As they grow older they are never seen doing it, but I have never noticed any severe scolding, nor do I know of any strict taboo on masturbation. At the *dō* Yao-chan stuck his penis between his legs and sat there much amused at the peculiar flatness in front. Some of the kids noticed and laughed uproariously, but one of the nursemaids said, 'That's dirty. Stop that kind of play.' "

"A group of four-year-old boys was gathered at the *dō*, demonstrating their penises to one another. They scattered as I went by, but teased Taro-chan by shouting, 'Look! There is his penis!' A bunch of older boys nearby only laughed. The other day one of these boys stuck his hand under Mitchan's kimono and was reprimanded by an older girl standing by. The threat of being laughed at is made frequently. The nursemaid will say to her charge, who is playing with its genitals, 'Stop that. People will laugh at you.' "

"The little boy who is staying with the Ochiai's seems to have been left there for a few days by his father. The kids bother him a lot, asking about the school he goes to in the city. They tease him mercilessly, but he has a come-back—he goes after the girls and grabs their genitals—a habit they frown upon but do not oppose very violently. He also keeps letting his pants down all the time, intrigued by an intricate suspender clasp. The small Hirano child picked up with him at once."

"At Tamaki Heihachi's house the husband was away cutting wood and his wife was sitting in the sun sewing her younger child's kimono. The child, a girl of six, was playing near the house with two boys from next door. One of the boys disappeared and the girl went after him. Then the second boy followed, and after a while they all returned. The older boy disappeared once more into a sort of shed adjoining the toilet. He was opening his pants as he went in and stayed there a long time. The girl followed him inside and they were very quiet for some time. Then she came out again and stood beside the shed, and after a while he emerged calling to her, his pants still open. This is the first time in more than four months that I have noticed anything like sex-play among the children. The boy looks slightly retarded and is always playing with his genitals."

"Little boys playing out of doors will occasionally show signs of exhibitionism. They pull up their kimono and strut about sticking their penises forward, sometimes humming a tune or singing an especially racy verse of a song they heard at a party. The Ouchi youngster [the older boy of the scene above] runs around with his hand on his penis all the time. He is one of the three or four boys given to this habit, and likes to run up to another boy and thrust his hand into the folds of the other's kimono."

There was, not surprisingly, sexual joking among the children as well. "After a while the little nursemaids began to ask riddles. 'What is this?' asked Yaeko. 'Only six inches long. Not used in daylight. Used at night. White liquid comes out. *(Go sun bakkari. Hiru tamenaran. Ban ni ta-menaru. Shiroi shiru deru mono.)'* Before she got halfway through Fumie began jumping around and yelling. 'It's that! *(Sono koto da!)'* Said Yaeko, after a few moments' excitement, 'It's a candle—there! *(Rōsoku desu—hora)'* Then Fumie went over to her and whispered what she thought it was. 'Well!' said Yaeko, 'Fumie thought it was a penis!' There was much laughter."

"While the adults were talking about the silkworms' progress, the little Hirano girl came up with the older Eda boy. At her instigation they decided to make a toy of Genzo's penis. [He is a man in his early sixties.] It was a pretty strange game. 'Ha! Penis, penis! *(chinpo, chinpo),'* said the little girl, poking her finger between his legs. The little boy imitated her. Everyone simply went on with the conversation. Then the girl picked up a stone and after poking him with it a few times, decided to shove it into his fly. He gently pushed them away, and for a while sat with his hands over his groin and they were distracted.

" 'Where is yours?' she asked the little boy. He produced it for a while, then put it back in his pants. His father and the others continued the conversation. Then the little girl started off again, saying, 'Come along.' He went after her, touching her buttocks and then reaching his hand around in front of her. In the ensuing struggle they both fell down and his father said, 'Hey! What are you two doing there?' They got up and went back to Genzo. She found two sticks and handed one to the boy. Chanting *'chinpo, chinpo,'* they began poking at him. At last, pushing them away gently, he said, 'What are you doing, anyway? Huh? What is it?' This made them laugh even harder, and his wife said, 'Such things these children do!' After a while he started off and they followed him poking at him from behind with the sticks. No one else commented."

"When the little Irie boy started playing with his penis, his grand-mother stopped him and told him not to touch it. Mrs. Ochiai asked me, 'What do Americans do when little boys play with their *chin-chin?'* They thought that children do it because of *kan* (alas, a word of many meanings, but here it is probably 'feeling' or 'sensation'). They also discussed his habit of sucking his thumb and forefinger, and told him a story about a little boy whose finger dropped off as a result of the habit."

During a session of the kindergarten for preschoolers at the school, "the kids were told to lie down if they wanted to. A few did. Instead of cool, loose kimono, these poor children get bundled into ill fitting, ugly foreign school uniforms. The pants bother the little boys and suspenders alternately bother or intrigue them. Since buckles are a novelty they are constantly being fiddled with, resulting in repeated opening up or letting down of pants and preoccupation with one's own and other boys' genitals. Modesty is certainly an imported school influence. Nowadays no children are allowed to run around naked outside, and all the girls in school wear bloomers.

"The Ouchi boy is exactly the same at school as he is at home. He discovered a nude figure in a glass case in one of the classrooms. It is used for anatomy lessons, and he promptly collected a bunch of kids around him with yells of, 'Vagina, vagina!' "

"Today Yukio-chan and Tatchan came up to me and asked, 'Do Americans have children, too?' They answered the question themselves evidently recalling that we had Clare with us when we first came here. (They must have heard some conversation about Americans having fewer children than Japanese.) Then later I heard Tatchan going on with the Eda boy about childbirth. 'First you have morning sickness,' she said, 'and then the baby comes.' There was some inconclusive talk about women and men."

"A bunch of little boys are outside our back porch. First they amused themselves by yelling, 'Teacher! Goodby! (Sensei, sainara.)' But soon they became obscene and took up a chant of 'chinpo kudai, kintama kudai, bobo-manju' (Penis, please; balls, please; vagina—vagina). One of the older boys then started doing a trick with his fingers that was taken up by the rest. It went, 'Nippon—Amerika—Igirisu—ippon' (Japan—America—England—one finger), and first he held two fingers apart, folded them into the sign for vagina, pushed at the thumb, and finally forced his forefinger through the hole. They ended up this performance by asking me to give them money for popsicles. It is impossible to get them to repeat anything verbatim, but they are full of little verses on this order or modifications of standard songs. Hyotabura—bottom or buttocks—is a 'bad word.' A youngster made up a little song about them as he rocked his small sister to sleep at the dō, patting her and using the word over and over. 'That's a fine song,' said an older girl, and told him to stop."

"Suzuki Tamezo's small son who was here last time with the women and laughed at their jokes said to me today, 'Amerika-jin chinpo kudai.' (Give me an American penis, please.) Everyone found this thoroughly amusing." On a visit to a house at Hirayama, "The first thing the boys asked me to write in roman letters was kintao tsukijinashi. I did so, which made some of them laugh very hard, because, as was explained to me, it means chinpo-manju (penis-vagina).[2] Boys and girls mix much more in games in this hamlet than in our part of Suye, perhaps because there are so few children and maybe because the girls are more roughneck. They do have to carry the babies on their backs, but this does not keep them from joining in the most strenuous games."

"Sato's dog is pregnant, and her belly intrigues all the kids, who are constantly feeling for puppies inside it when the poor animal lies down. The other day two little boys came up to pet her, calling her by name. Then they examined her very closely, as kids here usually do examine pets, wanting to see how she was made. 'There's the chinpo,' said one, mistaking

2. At least half of this off-color joke is unclear. Tsukiji is a low earthen wall and nashi means to lack, hence a place without a barrier is a plausible reference to a vagina. I can make nothing of kintao, although it may have something to do with kintama (testicles).

the drooping nipple for a penis. The other explained that the dog is a girl, hence has no *chinpo*. 'Girls have babies,' said the other, but lifted her leg again to make sure there was no penis. Satisfied, they departed."

The people of Suye were always ready for a party, and one cannot but be impressed by their seemingly limitless capacity to find occasions for them. Most parties, whether attended by both women and men, or by men or women only, involved dancing, singing, eating, and heavy drinking, and almost invariably considerable sexual joking and play. There were parties given to mark the naming of a new baby, returning from a visit to a shrine or temple, celebrating a variety of festivals and holidays, sending off conscripts and welcoming them back, dedicating new buildings, and marking the end of rice transplanting and harvest, the completion of the silk-producing cycle, and almost every other enterprise involving more than two or three people. There were as well *ad hoc* party groups, got together on short notice for no other purpose than to have a good time.

And there were parties held after other parties. "Hosts (*tessu*) always have a kind of after-party, and groups of guests often go off somewhere for one of their own. At the one we gave, the Kakui women said they were the hosts [because they were from the same hamlet], and therefore could stay later than the others. The women from Imamura went off and had an after-party at Kato's. Mrs. Fujita, who stayed here very late that night, found a party of men at her house when she got there and joined them, staying up until two in the morning."

"Mrs. Amano is a member of a women's *kōgin* and yesterday gave the winner's party at her house. After the group had left her place, instead of going to the house of the next winner, whose husband is ill, they went to Harada's and then to Makino's and finally to Sato's for a series of after-parties, breaking up about ten o'clock."

On February 1, Yakushi Day, "at about five-thirty some women came over to our place with *shōchū* and *shamisen*. They had gone up to the Yakushi shrine, then to the widow Matsumoto's. The group were Mrs. Sato Shichihei, Mrs. Tanimoto, Mrs. Suzuki Tamezo, young Mrs. Matsumoto, Mrs. Sakikawa, and the widow Tamaki. Matsumoto's mother played the *shamisen*. Kids gathered around and practically fell into the house trying to see and hear what was going on."

What was going on at this and most other parties was the subject of the stern disapproval of the mostly town- and city-bred outsiders. "The women at the school know nothing of what goes on here, mix with the village women very little, and are somewhat critical of the way some of the women behave at parties when they are drunk. A week ago the new school principal's wife gave her *kao mishiri* [a party given by a new resident for the people of the hamlet into which she has moved] for the Imamura women. She does not drink at all and once asked me what *shōchū* tastes like. She says that she will not start drinking because it would be hard to refuse later, and she remarked that she had found the *shamisen* playing and the dancing quite surprising. The drinking simply amazes her. She says that where she comes from people drink only occasionally, and women very little."

"At the Eda baby's naming party everyone got very drunk. The old grandmother became very playful with Masakichi, and Ichiro's father was pawing one of his sisters-in-law. Mrs. Wauchi was very far gone, and the two of us must have made a funny sight coming home huddled under her shawl, as I was without a coat. We stumbled along, talking loudly, and she kept telling me how good it felt to be so drunk."

"Mrs. Hayashi stopped by, completely drunk, saying how sorry she was that she had not left the party when I did. Her husband will be angry at being kept waiting, she said, but she does love to drink, and just could not tear herself away any sooner. She was sure her husband will divorce her, she laughed, for coming home late and drunk again. Today the women were discussing the Kawaze women's escapade of the night before [which we do not learn more of] and how drunk they were here and where they finally went for their after-party."

When the Archibald MacLeishes [see pages 19–20] came to visit the Embrees early in their stay they gave a party for them. "The MacLeishes were a great sensation, she with her blond hair and nail polish, and he with his dancing. We invited some of the women from Kawaze and Kakui to our party. Mrs. Tanimoto did her best by sitting opposite MacLeish and putting her bare legs on his lap. (He wondered, as I once did, where such advances actually lead. Considering the number of local bastards, it would seem that they do occasionally lead somewhere. You often hear it said that so and so likes men and goes after them as soon as she gets drunk.) Our guests outdid themselves, and dancing reached its peak when Mrs. Shimoda brought out a sake bottle, which she held in front of herself, stretching a towel over it and letting it drip slightly. At about six all the babies were brought in to be nursed and all the children looking after them came in too. At one point before that they had pushed in the sliding doors, trying to see what was happening."

Few parties ended without general drunkenness, much dancing and ribald songs, however formal their beginnings. Early accounts are rather mild. "About 7:30 in the evening a group of women arrived at our house, having just left the big party in Oade. They were soon followed by three men. Mrs. Kato played the *shamisen*. Her daughter came later. Mrs. Kawabe was there, Mrs. Irie with her baby on her back, and Tamaki Maki, a very amusing old lady who called herself an old-fashioned girl (*mukashi no shojo*) [perhaps she meant 'a former maiden']. She made many funny jokes. The two other women were Mrs. Toyama and Mrs. Ariyoshi, but it was Mrs. Tamaki and Mrs. Kawabe who danced the most. No one drank very much."

"Indeed all the women entered dancing, as they later did at Kato's. On such occasions it is customary to arrive as if coming on stage. The old lady is a very good dancer, and improvised a costume by taking off her kimono and wrapping a towel around her head. After a while they decided to move on to the Kato's and asked us to come along with them. There food was served, and Mrs. Kato sang some comical songs, made the more amusing by their use of broad colloquial language. One was about Yamada River, which runs black because the girls wash their underskirts in it."

Things soon pick up. "At the naming party, where everyone got so drunk, the songs were very risqué indeed and the dances even more so. To one refrain a cushion was folded and held in front of the dancer in imitation of a penis. The Amano woman performed a special dance that represented preparations for the act of intercourse. First she examined a cushion lying on the floor, peeking under it. Then she picked up another, made a tremendous penis of it and wiggled it about. Spreading herself over the cushion on the floor, she made motions to simulate intercourse. Her violent jerking raised great laughter. There was no *double entendre* in this dance. Her daughter performed a similar one, using a bottle for a penis rather than a cushion. Occasionally she struck it with a chopstick, called it her *chin-chin* [penis in baby talk] in a loving tone, stroked it, shook it and passed her hand over the end of it, and so on."

"Yesterday Mrs. Sato gave a farewell party for Mrs. Soeshima who will soon be leaving the village to move into town. Almost all the hamlet women came. No men were present. The dancing was exuberant, especially that done by the guest of honor. She wore *Otafuku* mask-like make-up [Otafuku is a comic mask of a jolly country girl] and stuffed a cushion under her kimono to make her look pregnant. She was impersonating a geisha who is disgusted with her fate and is willing to throw the baby away anywhere to avoid the consequences of her embarrassing condition. The words for male and female genitals cropped up in almost every song. The children are always amused at this and run around outside repeating the improvised verses. Each woman brought eleven sen and a small measure of rice. The guest of honor got special food, and the party went on until after midnight. The women were not very drunk, but just as with the school dance programs, there was no thought of stopping."

Not everyone approved of such behavior. "Sakakida says of himself that he is crazy (*kichigai*) and has many peculiar tastes and dislikes. For instance, he does not like the dancing at parties. (This reminded me of the comment by Tamaki Take of the wild reputation, 'I hate those obscene dances done by the old ladies from Nakashima.')"

But the dances were a fixture of every party, as we have seen. John Embree records another instance: "At the party in Hirayama, there were many good dances. One was done by Mrs. Suzuki, who used a stick of wood as a penis, held it to her vagina and jerked it up and down to the rhythm of the *shamisen*. This called forth much laughter." Not to be outdone, others joined in. "The young woman who had nursed her 'secret baby' throughout most of the party, got up to dance. She took a small broom and held it to her front like a penis, doing a jerky dance, and attacking half the company with it. When she retired, two women got up and simulated copulation by violently bumping together to the rhythm of the dance. Several younger people did a few of the indecent dances, which one almost never sees in other hamlets of Suye, where they usually just sit by and watch, often obviously embarrassed by the goings on."

He also wrote of an informal party held after a wedding: "After the food and drinks had been consumed, the bride and groom disappeared. A little later the girls and women who had been working in the kitchen came in and drank with the rest of us. The dances were explicit. Mrs. Sato Eiji removed her kimono, bared her front, lifted her skirts and did violent hip jerks, all to roars of approval from the assembled multitude, who sang and clapped to the rhythm. Mrs. Suzuki Iwa sang an impromptu song about my long nose and being lonesome for my wife who is away in Tokyo. Mrs. Tanimoto came over to exchange drinks with me, and when I filled the cup and returned it to her, some of the liquor spilled on the edge. Finding it warm and sticky she said, 'Oh, it's sticky—just like after intercourse!' Later on she and others made many jokes about my being lonely, and when Mrs. Uchida got up to dance, they said that since she is a widow I should marry her."

When the dancing was not sexually explicit, the accompanying songs often were. John Embree wrote of a party on Kannon-*goya* [Kannon Eve]: "At the Oade *dō*, I found mostly women. Here there was singing and dancing, without about fifteen or twenty people present and the young men standing about outside. Mrs. Fujita did a weeding dance by getting down on all fours, rubbing her fists over the floor in a ridiculous, frenzied parody of the movements of actual weeding. There was much laughter, and the dance was accompanied by several indecent verses."

There were also parties at temples and shrines. "The Kannon-*kō* was started in 1925. The Buddhist priest presides at its January and March meetings. There are about forty-five members—the priest is uncertain of the number because so many women have died since it started—from eight hamlets. Each member donates rice for *sushi* and twenty sen, ten for the expenses of the entertainment and ten for the temple. The woman presents her rice upon arriving at the temple and the priest registers her name. Then each pays her dues, bows to the image of Kannon at the altar, and throws a one-sen coin into the collection box. The order of activities turned out to be sutra-reading by the priest, followed by eating, drinking, and dancing by all. First tea is served. When everyone is assembled, the priest reads a sutra, while some bow their heads, some are silent, others entertain the children, and still others whisper to each other. At the close of the service the priest read out the list of names of members and then excused himself, saying that he had business elsewhere. He urged them to enjoy themselves for this is the New Year [it was January 2].

"*Shōchū* cups were passed round and round. Mrs. Hayashi complained that the *shōchū* was bad, which means that it must have come from Taragi. Mrs. Tanimoto said that the Kawaze women were guests and the Kakui woman hosts. *Sushi* was served from a wooden tub, dished out by one or another of the women. Mrs. Wauchi served one round. Everyone ate a lot and made jokes about the prices at restaurants where a plateful of *sushi* would cost ten sen. Here, they said, it costs only three, so one can have as much as one wants. Boxes were filled with the left-over *sushi*, to be taken home. Then there was more tea, served with pickles, and much *shōchū* was consumed. I refused to drink, saying that I was not feeling well, and pointing vaguely toward my abdomen. 'Ah!' said Mrs. Tanimoto, thrusting her thumb between her second and third fingers in the standard gesture for vagina, 'It is getting too big.' When I asked what she meant she said, 'You have too many of these,' making a circle with two fingers. All this caused much laughter because she was insinuating that I had too many eggs, hence was pregnant and so could not drink. Then the dancing began. They sang a great many songs, most with marked sexual overtones, and in one dance a woman followed another around making jerking motions in imitation of copulating from behind." It was just as well, one might think, that the priest had been called away on other business.

On yet another occasion, following the series of sermons by the visiting priest from Saga, there was a banquet and party for the men and women who had gathered at the temple. "It is said to take place every year at this time, which is the end of the season when all members of the community donate rice and money to the temple and get a feast in return. Local women prepare most of the food, which is supplemented by special cakes bought from a shop in Taragi. The same group of women forms the core every year, it is said. They were Mrs. Fujita, Mrs. Kawabe, Mrs. Ochiai, Mrs. Kato, and four others. All drank a good deal, and when the meal was finished brought out a *shamisen* and the fun began. One woman played the instrument while the others danced in turn. The first and perhaps the best was Mrs. Kawabe, who danced very well with a fan and then a towel. Mrs. Hayashi, who calls herself Hayashi *baba* [old lady or grandmother Hayashi] was by far the liveliest and least modest. One of her dances was quite erotic and she was very proud of it. It consists of putting the hands on the hips, legs apart, and lowering the trunk while jerking in an imitation of a man copulating. Another was done by Mrs. Kawabe, disguised in the teacher's clothing, with a piece of cloth over her face. Another woman performed with her, wearing somebody's bowler hat over her masked face. The priest also danced a special number, and John and I were forced to join in. Then Mrs. Fujita did a drunkard's dance, which was very realistic owing to the fact that she was very drunk herself."

John Embree noted that "the general pattern of religious seriousness followed by copious drinking occurred on this occasion as it does at the shrine festivals. In this case, however, the party participants in the afternoon were the ordinary people who had brought donations to the temple, rather than just the priest and some friends as is often the case. Later in the evening, when the guests had gone home, the women who had been working in the kitchen held their own party from about seven to ten. Mrs. Tanimoto, quite tight, made the visiting priest drink *shōchū* until he finally ran away. All the drinking, erotic dancing and general hilarity took place in the central room of the temple right before the image of the Buddha, where earlier in the day the priest had made the women weep with his sad stories of the fate of those who do not trust in the mercy of the Buddha, and where they had thrown coins and offered prayers."

One of the favorite party activities of the women was tossing men and sometimes other women in the air. The practice is called *dō age*. John Embree wrote of his visit to a ground-breaking ceremony for a mill in Fukada. "Members of the Women's Association of Fukada were pounding in the foundation stones. They were hired by the carpenter who paid them about seventy sen each for the day's work, and will put their earnings in their savings account. As they worked they sang and took occasional rests. During one of these they suddenly grabbed me by the legs and shoulders and gave me many a hearty swing into the air to the accompaniment of a song. They did the same to Sano, and later to other young men at the site. They would huddle and without warning attack a man, lay him out and swing him into the air. This stunt is general at celebrations, and may have other purposes as well. Although it was a very hot day, everyone was having a good time at their work."

On the occasion of a farewell party given for the Embrees by one of the Suye hamlets, "the men received us in the main room of the house, where we were ushered right away. The women had prepared all the food, gone home to change, and come back to serve us. After the trays had been brought in, each came in and greeted us formally. Later all the women moved into the room and had a grand time. There were ten couples in all. After the meal, Hayashi, the host, came to exchange drinks with us and after he had returned to his place the other men followed his lead. Then the free-for-all moving about began. We were seated at the head of the room, with Hayashi on our left at the *tokonoma* and the older men down the line. The women sat at the far end of the room in a semi-circle—the lowest seats. The party became very lively, but there were no special dances or songs. But they could not forego the *dō age*, and all of us were tossed into the air in turn. Nonomiya, after pulling me into the group for that purpose, became rather affectionate, but there was much less dirty talk than goes on in either Kawaze or Kakui."

Perhaps the most surprising context for a party is found in the following note: "Today, April 25, was vaccination day at the school. Mothers came from all directions, and the school room looked like a nursery, with babies crawling all over the place. People are notified of the vaccination date by the head of the village sanitation association, who was around helping the doctor. When I left all the older children had got their vaccinations and the doctor was well through the babies. On my way down the stairs I met the custodian with a barrel of *shōchū* and bottles of beer. 'The drinking is starting,' he said. It had not occurred to me, after all these months, that even a vaccination clinic calls for drinking afterwards."

Major celebrations were held in connection with seeing off the conscripts and welcoming back returning soldiers. "Today [January 8] the conscripts left the village. I am sure that to the people of Suye the idea of militarism is very foreign, but sending off a native son to be a soldier has become a big event. Indeed, it has become a tradition, and the celebration is much bigger than those held for weddings and childbirth. Everyone is up bright and early, the women standing around with bottles of *shōchū* and cups, waiting for the procession to pass. They offer drinks to all who come along, and when the procession itself arrives they rush up to the new soldier and make him take a drink.

"Each family arrives in style. First comes the soldier, with a young man carrying the willow tree above his head. Two or three other young men carry the national flag, attached to a bamboo pole, and banners. Brothers and other male relatives are also in the van, followed by other relatives and friends. The whole school was there, each teacher leading his or her class, with the school band and crowds of little kids tagging along. Each such group proceeded to the Ishizaka bridge where they waited for the late-comers to catch up. Some of the people were already thoroughly drunk, for they had been to a party at Hamanoue and another at Imamura until very late last night. There must have been an all-night affair in Hirayama, too, for the women from there were quite tipsy. These women from Hirayama throw their scarves like men, nonchalantly around their necks, instead of wearing them hanging down as women usually do.

"At the bridge the soldiers and the school principal made speeches, while the women continued pouring drinks down people's throats and the young women played their *shamisen*. Two of them, from Imamura, looked like professional geisha, with powder and lipstick. Hirayama went them all one better by supplying a drum, played by the irrepressible Mrs. Fujiwara. Speech-making concluded, the soldiers proceeded to Menda, followed by the young men, their brothers, and some friends. Some even went as far as Hitoyoshi to see them off on the train, but most returned to the homes of the conscripts for the after-parties. Most people of each hamlet went to the house of the soldier from that hamlet. So the guests at Watanabe's were mostly from Imamura and those at Takayama's from Kawaze, but relatives came from all over. There must have been at least fifty people at Watanabe's, counting the young men who returned from Menda carrying the willow tree, which was placed in the *tokonoma*. (It will be planted later, and care must be taken that it thrive, because the manner in which the willow branches reach for the roots of the tree is symbolic of the safe return of the soldier to his home.)

"The Hayashi Masao couple were there, the Kawabes, the Iries, and old lady Tamaki. The Uemuras came too, and he later got very drunk. His wife tried to restrain him when he insisted on making me dance. Sato Genzo's wife was also present, and had apparently been there the night before as well. Mrs. Uemura, the Kawabe daughter, and the Watanabe bride served the food, while the older women of the house did the kitchen chores. The dancing started when the young men returned from Menda. About that time, people began to wander into the kitchen for rice, soup, pickles and tea. I left at noon. When I went back about four o'clock most of the family and a few men were sitting around the fire-pit. Suzuki Seiichi, quite drunk, had just called in on his way home. He insisted on telling me that he cannot 'do this' any more, and kept thrusting his forefinger through a circle made with the thumb and forefinger of the other hand, which means intercourse. More drinks were brought to him."

A soldier's return was marked by equally colorful doings. "After lunch the hamlet women gathered in several different houses to dress up. They wore school girls' skirts and middies, kimono turned inside out, soldiers' uniforms, firemen's uniforms, and all kinds of men's clothing—pants, coats and hats. Mrs. Shibata was dressed in formal kimono and a hat, and sported a false nose with a moustache and beard. She also carried a walking stick, and acted very much the gentleman, making a welcoming speech to the soldier and another to his mother when we got back to the house for the after-party. Several women wore masks, and all had their faces covered in some way. Later, when people tried to guess who they were, they denied their identity. At the shop the woman came out with shōchū, full of admiration for their costumes. Children, on the other hand, went into fits of frightened screaming and clung to their mothers.

"Some of the old women dressed in men's clothing ran about and danced like youngsters. They generally acted in complete accordance with their assumed sex, making passes at all the girls and women. The girls squealed loudly and jumped off the road into the fields to avoid being pinched on the buttocks. One old lady got hold of a young woman, and later a man, and held them against the wall, imitating the movements of intercourse. The crowd roared with laughter, while the poor victims ran away as fast as they could when released.

"Mrs. Shibata made everyone laugh by stopping in front of a shop in Shoya, removing all her outer garments and raising her kimono as if to urinate. (It occurred to me once that if women had to reveal more of their bodies when urinating, they might be more reticent about it. As it is they only have to hike their kimono slightly.) Today, dressed in trousers, they all went off to concealed spots, but not without making everyone in the road laugh by stopping first and making as if to extract their penis from their pants.

"They went only as far as the Shoya shop, where they encountered the crowd of officials accompanying the soldier from the train station.

When he went up to the school for the formal greeting ceremony, the women danced up to his house, delivered a short speech, and quickly left. Gathering for a minute they decided to meet at another house later and come back to Toride's again, each with fifteen sen. [It was a son of Toride's who was being greeted on his return.] So they went back home, took off their costumes, and attended to household duties for a while—spinning, carrying water, preparing the evening meal—until it was time to go to Toride's. Then they changed into more festive (women's) kimono. In about an hour they met at Sakikawa's, all so dressed up as to be almost unrecognizable, to collect the money. One of the younger ones was made to draw up a list of names and contributions. (Younger women are often given such jobs because most of the middle aged and older ones cannot write at all.) They then started for Toride's, stopping here and there to pick up the few tardy ones.

"At the Toride party the house was so full that the guests had to sit in four rows in the main room. The entire village was represented, and some people had come all the way from Menda. (When I got back home, I had found some Kawaze women at Sato's having tea. They said they did not want to go to Toride's yet because they had not been drinking. They said they would be embarrassed to arrive sober, and would go home and have a starter before going there later. They never showed up, and it is quite possible that they had not been invited.)" We do not know the basis for this example of hamlet feuding and bad feelings.

Another occasion for partying and feasting was the athletic field-day held at the school. "October 8 was the big day. 'We farmers have little pleasure in life,' said Suzuki Taketo, 'so we enjoy this one day a year very much. It is our only pleasure (*tanoshimi*).' And enjoy it they did. By nine the entire village was out at the school getting settled. The grounds had been decorated the night before, and places allotted to each hamlet. People brought along mats to sit on, and some, like Hirayama, brought straw as well, which they spread under the mats with blankets on top, to make quite a comfortable seat. Kakui did not bother with any of this and sat on rocks all day, which did not seem to trouble them particularly. They generally sat by hamlet groups, but some joined their families from their original hamlets. Mrs. Shimosaka and young Mrs. Wauchi sat with Oade, for instance, and Makino Otome went there too for a while, while Mrs. Eda sat with Kawaze.

"Everyone was dressed up, especially the younger women, who were displaying their new light-colored kimono and bright sashes. The food supply was tremendous. Some had brought special tiered lunch boxes in various kinds of lacquer finish. *Shōchū* was brought in special containers, some of them very elegant. Drinks were exchanged liberally, and each person treated the other to some of his fish. By the afternoon all were very gay indeed. When the returned Toride soldier was presented with a medal in a special ceremony, he was given drinks by Kakui as he passed by. He was then sent to fetch his mother and she was feasted by first one Kakui group and then another. They all said that it must have been a great pleasure to raise him, for he is such a good son.

"The men of Kakui, having come in second in the men's relay race, also feasted one another, and as for the joy over the young men coming in first in their race, there was no limit. When all was over and everyone else had left, the Kakui men were still sitting there drinking.

"*Konnyaku* [a gelatinous paste made from the devil's-tongue root], several different kinds of bean-curd, omelettes, cuttlefish, cooked and salted small fish—there was no end to the supply of food and everyone brought bags of pears and persimmons and chestnuts, which they began eating the moment they arrived. The capacity to consume food is simply amazing—fish, fruit, candy all eaten together constantly. The children cried for something of everything they saw.

"Everyone had a good time, watching the events or drinking without paying any attention to what was happening on the field. Mrs. Tanimoto was very gay, and as always she ended up sitting with a bunch of men. Mothers watched their children and cheered them on, but did not look especially upset when they lost. Old grandmothers got very excited and cheered their grandchildren. The teachers distributed prizes very liberally. I noticed in one race, for example, where the children are given a list of objects to pick up, that the Suzuki girl was leading at first, but had forgotten to pick up the instruction slip, and ran back to get it. She picked up the object indicated on it, and caught up very well. Having lost her lead, she came in second, but was awarded first prize anyway. People laughed heartily. One race, the *runpen* [from the German *lumpen*: a vagrant], was so funny that Aki laughed so hard that she doubled up and hit her forehead on the lunch box. Everyone agreed that it was the best of the events. Manhunt races were also enjoyed, because the girls had to search out teachers, the headman's wife, and me.

"All the serving was done by young ladies. The old-age group of men and women was seated in a special place in the morning and given special attention. They got *shōchū*, fish, and a box of cakes. Many of the very old left right after they were served, while others went to sit with their hamlet groups. Young ladies were also selling candy and cakes, of which the profits were to go into the Young Women's Association savings account. They passed back and forth all day with trays of the items. All these girls looked beautiful in their dressy kimono, and quite stubby and shapeless when they changed into athletic uniforms for the races.

"The program ran without interruption from nine to five. A few people left early and some, tired of watching, wandered off during the day. At night, there were many parties. Aso celebrated winning one of the races and the Toride servant went back home there for the occasion. He had run for Oade, where he works, but went to his own hamlet for their victory party. The young men from Yunoharu who were not working out elsewhere ran with Aso and celebrated with them. Kakui continued its celebration of winning the relay race and all gathered at Uchida's. This party was attended only by young men, and a similar one was held in Kawaze. The affair in Hirayama was much bigger, and the whole hamlet turned out. The young men were especially honored, receiving fish to eat, but most of them were tired and left early. They were given a bunch of cookies to take with them to make up for the *shōchū* they did not drink. Some houses contributed food and some *shōchū* was purchased with the savings of the Young Men's Association. A few guests contributed cash right at the party—it was acknowledged and called *hana* (flower) just as it is when money is given to dancers after a performance.

"Each did what he could. The poor man who is married to the Makino daughter brought a small serving-bottle of *shōchū*, which donation was announced by the master of ceremonies like all the others. Fujiwara, drunk by then, said contemptuously, 'One whole drink!' Finally the dancing and singing started, rather slowly because all were tired. There was no *shamisen*, which did not discourage the women from going right into their erotic dancing. As we came home at midnight, there was not a sound anywhere, save in Kakui, where a young man was singing."

The reader will have been struck by the behavior of Suye women at the parties and entertainments of the village year. Many of them were accomplished singers and dancers, and most were ready to perform on any and all occasions. Among them the figure of Mrs. Fujiwara, the woman who brought the drum to the celebration of seeing off the conscripts, stands out. Her drunken, libidinous behavior outstrips that of most, and we last see her in a vignette of quite extraordinary power.

"When we arrived, it turned out that they had feared that we would forget to come to the party, and apologized for having nothing but *shōchū* [that is, no sake, as would be more appropriate for a proper farewell party, which this was]. They were, however, very proud of the honey, served fresh from the hive, wax and all. (The honey gave Mrs. Fujiwara the opportunity to make jokes about its sweetness—like a sweetheart—and its stickiness—like semen.) She and Mrs. Miyamori arrived just after we did, with their children. After the first few drinks she settled in on John and had a grand time. 'Let's sleep together tonight,' she said, when all were trying to persuade us to stay over, since it was such a long walk back home. Occasionally she would call out to me, '*Okusan, okusan!* Is it all right if I do this with Embree-san?' She claimed that she had been carrying on with him for the whole year, so they must have a very special leave-taking. She did a couple of dances dressed in borrowed men's clothing, and said somewhat wistfully that she had learned them from an actor in Taragi when she was only sixteen or seventeen."

John Embree's journal picks up the story. "Then the young servant of the house, who had been drinking a good deal by exchanging drinks with others, got up and did a penis dance with a good-size stick. He held it delicately as he danced, singing the refrain while Mrs. Sakakida sang the verses and accompanied him on the *shamisen*. This prompted Mrs. Fujiwara to fall upon him, as though to rape the young man. At another point she danced off into the kitchen, where the old man of the house was dozing, and bumped her midsection vigorously against his head. Her young daughter seemed at times to be annoyed with her mother's behavior, but it was hard to tell. With her hair down her back in a wild tangle, she looked much like the pictures of the goddess who did an erotic dance to make the gods laugh and entice the sun goddess out of the cave in which she had hidden herself. (None of the *o-kagura* dances done at the shrine this year was in the least suggestive, and most certainly would never raise the laughter required to rouse the curiosity of the sun goddess.) When food was served, she wanted some, and made us all feed her with our chopsticks. This by-play was accompanied by much fly-grabbing and affectionate swats here and there that practically took your breath away each time." Their parting is described by Ella Wiswell.

"When we left, she insisted on following us down the path, 'Because I won't be in Kakui to see you off when you leave.' And when all the others who were with the *shamisen*-player had turned back to the house, she followed along for a bit until the Sakakida woman was sent to fetch her. At last she seized my arm in a grip of iron and whispered in a low voice, 'It is lonely here in these mountains. When I first came here, I was so lonely. . . . But I am used to it now. You must come back again before I get grey hair, and too old.' "

The Facts of Life

Girls were told little, if anything, by their mothers about pregnancy and child-bearing, nor did they learn anything of menstruation from them. "At fourteen she is not yet menstruating. When I asked her where she had heard about it if she has not experienced it, she only giggled and said nothing. Tamako says that mothers never tell their daughters anything about menstruation or conception. They learn about such things from older girls at school, and are much too embarrassed to discuss the matter with their parents. Most girls hear that such and such a thing will happen, and so more or less expect it. However, when their first menstrual period arrives, they feel anxious and often run to some young married woman (not their mothers) to ask what to do. She herself went to ask Hayashi Shoko.

"Cotton is used and 'victoria,' a sort of rubber g-string sold in the shops and fitted over cotton to prevent accidents. Many farm women simply use a piece of cloth. She says that a period usually lasts from three to ten days, and there was a girl in her class who menstruated for twenty, to everyone's amusement. Although victoria prevent accidents, she thinks they are a nuisance, 'for you cannot wear them with your good kimono.' "

"The word for menstruation is *gekkei*, the maids say, and women here just keep right on working. They also said that in theory a menstruating woman should not visit [Shinto] shrines, but that they actually do. They seemed a trifle embarrassed when discussing it. Mrs. Mori said that indeed menstruating women cannot go to the *kamisama*, but can visit the Buddhist temples. 'The same is true of people in mourning during the first forty-nine days after a death,' she added." The point is, of course, that both are in a condition of pollution.

"There is a lot of irregularity in menses. Fumie had three periods this month. Hayashi Shoko says that Fumie's first menstruation was signaled by nose-bleed, which is a very common sign. Unlike the maids she did not use the word *gekkei*, but said *tsukiyaku* ('monthlies'). The school girls call it *emu*, and were surprised when I said I did not know what it meant. 'But it is a foreign word,' they protested. Indeed it is—it is the *m* of menstruation."

"The women said that in girlhood they all had monthly menses and that after childbirth they have a continuous flow lasting from ten to thirty days. Then none comes for a period of one to three years. About a month or two before conception, they begin again, and that is how they know they have conceived or may do so. All of these women have had children recently, and those whose baby is less than a year old deny that they experience any menstrual flow. (Otome told me the other day that she did not know she had conceived this last time because she did not menstruate for a full year after the birth of her last baby, and right at the end of that year she got pregnant again.) The midwife says that for some women the flow does not begin for as much as three years after childbirth."

"Mrs. Kuwagiri is pregnant again. Her youngest child is just two this month. After the first child was born she says she had no menses for six months following the first twenty days of uninterrupted flow. After the second child, she did not menstruate for a year, and then had several menses before conceiving the third time. I was curious about the explanation for the long menstrual flow following delivery, but only old lady Tamaki suggested an answer. She thinks that it takes care of the several months during pregnancy when there has been no flow at all. On the other hand, my questions concerning the reason for the stopping of the menses during pregnancy were readily answered by all. They say that the blood is circulating through the baby during that time and so none comes out." One young father had ventured the opinion, however, that babies are made from milk, not blood.

Mrs. Eda, who had recently had a baby, "confirmed the statements of the others about menses. For eight months now she has had none, except for the full week right after delivery. She stopped for three years after the last child, then had five or six periods before conceiving. After she had the older children, she menstruated only once before conceiving again. During girlhood, she said that she was very irregular and often had headaches and pain. Because she was a sickly child, she began when she was seventeen (fifteen or sixteen by our reckoning).

"*Saiki* [return] is the term used for the first menses which occur after the last baby, usually just before the next one. Mrs. Mori said that until now she had menstruated regularly every month, which is very exceptional here, while now [having given birth to her first child] she has had none for eight months. This is attributed to her easy delivery and the fact that she is much stronger than she used to be. (It would seem to me to be the other way around—that working harder and harder she has upset her natural functions, much as the rest of the women have. It should be noted that she does no heavy work of the kind the farm women do.)"

"Mrs. Tanimoto, who is childless, menstruates every month, and reports that her sister has the same peculiarity. Her sister had not known she was pregnant again because she had no *saiki*. As a result, when she got morning sickness she thought at first that she was ill. The women believe that a proper diet produces regular menses and makes them last only a short time after delivery. Mrs. Sato thinks that Otome's twenty-day flow after her last baby came is quite long. She also believes that it is unwise to exert yourself too much during pregnancy, but Otome said that someone had told her that working has no effect at all. In any event, they did agree that only exceptional women menstruate every month."

BIRTH CONTROL

The women of Suye, and some of the men, were convinced that farmers have too many children, but although "the practice of contraception is absolutely denied, in many cases babies are conveniently spaced at intervals of about three years. It makes me wonder about deliberate planning, but Hashida says that people here do not practice it. Even if they do not want children, they have them anyhow, he says, and it is true that I have seen couples upset about a pregnancy, saying that they did not want to have another child yet. I think Hashida would have told me about any devices used if they existed. He says that geisha [prostitutes, in this context] use a quinine douche, and that only about one percent of them are careless and have a child because of the heavy fine imposed by the house that employs them if they do. He also says that abortions are prohibited by law, and that if they do occur around here they are kept very secret. He has never heard of a specific case, but the other day a group of women I was with were discussing just such a case in Taragi, where an infant had been found, just thrown out. They seemed to know the family concerned, but it has no Suye connections."

One of those upset about a pregnancy was Hayashi Shoko. "My suspicions are confirmed. I have been told that Hayashi Shoko is pregnant again. Her youngest child is only eighteen months old. Today, as we sat at the fire-pit, I asked her if it is true. 'You cannot be sure until the child moves, in the fifth month,' she said. She hopes it is not a baby because it is too soon. Lack of menstruation is one of the signs that you have conceived, she went on, but during her first pregnancy she was nauseated and since she is not sick at all now she thinks it may be a false alarm. But her waist is spreading, and she looks very sad. The baby is mostly cared for by the nurse, the orphan girl from Imamura who lives with them now. When I asked her about birth control, she was somewhat embarrassed, and said that nothing like that is done here. Later on she asked me if birth control is practiced in America. When I said it is, she said that most city people in Japan do it too, but not village people. (Mrs. Fujita says that she uses nothing at all, and that people here have so many children because they don't know about birth control.)"

Indeed, shortly after this conversation, she suffered a miscarriage, and several months later she became pregnant again. "Mrs. Tanimoto says that Shoko is pregnant. 'You can tell by her eyes, which always sparkle when she is carrying a baby.' Another sign is the stick in the *yugawa* [well], which always rises when someone in the hamlet is pregnant. Even though you push it down, it stands up again and floats to the top. 'Must be some sign from the water god,' she observed. This happened the other day, and she had wondered who was pregnant. It was then that she noticed Shoko's strange look."

Among the women, the matter of birth control came up frequently in conversation. "Talking of children, Mrs. Tanimoto said she had never had any because 'the seed were bad.' I asked whose. 'My husband's,' she replied. 'The field is good,' pointing to her loins. All laughed, and there was more laughter when I said that my next child would not come for two more years. 'Wouldn't it be nice if we could regulate it?' they said. Only Mrs. Sato whispered that I must 'do something' to prevent pregnancy, but the others expressed no opinion on the matter."

Later, in another gathering of men and women, "I was asked many questions about America. Is it true there is child marriage? The Eda brothers said it is practiced in India. Is it true that ours was a love marriage? There was much wonder when I said that all marriages in America are love matches. Do we have just a set number of children? I said we do. Is it government policy? I explained how it works. And your government does not fine you? I said it does not. Here, they said, the government punishes you for doing such things, so you must have five, ten, twelve—any number of children. That is why people must emigrate to America; there are too many children here, they said. Both the Eda couple and Mrs. Hirano seemed to be very interested in the subject, as if they had seriously looked into the matter. So perhaps birth control could be introduced after all. [Thirteen years later abortion was legalized with stunning success.] Eda often makes remarks about having too many children, who make too much noise. When he does so he is occasionally reproved by old lady Eda who says, 'You made them all,' but on the whole he is full of affection for his kids."

The denials by most women that anyone practiced birth control were belied by hints dropped in a number of conversations. "When Mrs. Amemiya went by I asked Mrs. Fujita why there are no children there. 'They do something,' she said. 'He uses a condom [*sakku*] which you buy in boxes of a dozen. They are used by everyone who has their children well spaced.' But her friend demurred, saying that she thinks there are very few people in Suye who use them, which is why there are so many children. Both think it is a good idea, for three children are quite enough."

It is noteworthy that for the most part men brought up the matter of contraception in connection with their relations with prostitutes, rather than with their wives. During one discussion, at which no other women were present, "the familiar theories were advanced. Geisha are sometimes made barren from sitting too much on cold, hard floors, and do not conceive because they go to the toilet immediately after intercourse. One of the men from town did suggest, however, that condoms and douches are in use. When told about our methods, they were shocked to learn that the tablets are just left to melt. 'No wiping!' exclaimed Sato, and made a face. In their eyes Americans are not very clean, but it is interesting that when they discuss sexual matters they seem always to think only of their relations with geisha."

In point of fact, their concern was less with the prevention of pregnancy than with contracting venereal disease, which was widespread among men and women alike. Both the Embrees were astonished at the lack of knowledge with respect to these matters displayed by younger adult males. "With *shōchū* and later on during supper, conversation turned to a common topic. John's assistant, Sano, asked many questions and was instructed in matters relating to sexual intercourse, including how to prevent getting an infection. If the precautions advised by these men are the only ones taken, it is no wonder that venereal disease is so common. All they recommend is urinating! If you hold your penis and pull the foreskin well down, then release the urine by pulling the skin up three times, all will be well. They are quite sure that you can urinate that much, especially if you are foresighted enough to wait to have intercourse until you want to urinate just a bit and go to the toilet directly after. To our objections, they just smiled and said, 'All the doctors recommend it. It's in the books.' Sano took it all in, and that is how youth goes to the dogs."

Of this same conversation, John Embree wrote: "They also said that if a woman gets up when the man does and walks to the toilet and urinates, she prevents impregnation. When we suggested that urination has nothing to do with it, they hedged by saying that when she walks her womb is opened up and the sperm spills out. When we pointed out that this cannot be very effective for village women, judging from the number of children, Sato said that they are too tired at night to bother getting up. All of this was carefully explained to Sano, who took in all this bosh as gospel. Such is the extent of sexual knowledge held by graduates of higher school in their late twenties!"

Not all Suye men were so naïve, however, as a later conversation recorded by John Embree reveals: "Suzuki, making the sign for vagina behind his hand as they often do to conceal it from the rest of the company, says that he has visited the widow. He knows that urinating after intercourse will not prevent disease, and recommends using a condom or washing the glans of the penis with *shōchū* or sake right after the act."

"The subject of the large number of children often comes up here, and I am asked if we have such large families in the U.S. Today the Komoto brother-in-law said that he has stopped with four, but that may have been a joke. Still, they thought that birth-control measures do percolate down into the countryside, and that it would be a good idea if some people used them. But Noguchi thought that a large family is more fun, and attributed the large size of families in the poorer houses to the fact that they have few of the enjoyments that the rich can afford, so that having children is the only pleasure in life."

Indeed, the knowledge of contraceptive techniques was percolating into the countryside, sometimes in quite unexpected ways. "One must never pass by a group of women talking together. Today three of them were having tea at the shop. They are always ready for a spicy conversation. Said Mrs. Kuwagiri, 'Indeed it would be nice to have no children. You could sleep together with your husband then, while the way things are you have to sleep at opposite ends of the room. Since you get together only once in a while, you make a baby right away and after you get pregnant you bulge out and it's no fun at all, but just a nuisance.' Mrs. Matsumoto laughed and said that at night in the dark, even if the small children are sleeping there, the husband comes over to see his wife anyway. Lack of children suggested the topic of birth control. Shoko told us that a daughter of Aoshima, the girl who works for a company in Yahata, had sent some condoms to her parents, and all mentioned another couple they suspect of using them. She heard the story from Matsumoto Shima [the widow], who heard it from Mrs. Tanikawa. Later Shima told me that the daughter sent the things in a letter which said, 'Use these. You have too many children.' She has no idea if they followed the girl's advice, but thinks that farmers do not use such things because they feel that it is all right to have any number of children, while town people and teachers in the villages use contraceptives."

"It turned out that our maid has also heard this story while helping with the silkworms at Matsumoto's. She maintains that she does not know what a *sakku* is, except that she has heard it can be inflated like a balloon. Later at the Eda's, someone wondered aloud if the widow Matsumoto herself does not use something to prevent pregnancy. Prostitutes and douches were mentioned, and someone said, 'Drinking a lot of water helps,' and turning to the young girls added, 'Now you remember about this, and be sure to drink a lot of water afterwards so as not to make a baby.' "

One of the very few foreign women whose name was familiar to Suye women was Margaret Sanger. "We discussed birth control and she mentioned *Sangā-fujin* (*fujin* is used after the names of married women who are in any way notable or have careers or do independent work). She had heard that birth control is widely practiced in France, and wondered whether too much of it is not harmful. Of course she would not say if she and her husband practiced it, and it is hard for me to judge. Their only child is two years old. When I asked if she is pregnant, she laughed and asked, 'And you?' She is a citified young woman, and the more citified people are the more difficult it is to ask and get answers to personal questions."

"Our maid said that children are not told the truth about where babies come from. They are told that they are born from a black string attached to the mother's navel, which swells until it bursts and the baby pops out. Girls later on learn about such things from their friends—'Never from your parents!'—and in the girls' schools there are textbooks on feminine hygiene. Sato maintains that small children are told only that babies grow from the mother's navel, bursting from the stomach like Momotaro."[1] But when a neighbor's five-year-old son was asked about it, he replied, " 'From the belly!' and explained how the baby comes out of the rectum with a lot of excrement."

"Young Mrs. Kawabe said that no one told her anything before she was married. Her mother never mentioned menstruation or childbirth. When she was fifteen, she went with the other members of the Young Women's Association to hear a talk by some man given at the girls' school in Taragi, but she was too young and did not follow it well. (She began to menstruate only when she was seventeen.) So at eighteen, when she married, she still did not know much although, she admitted, 'at that age you learn things without being told.' At first she did not want to get married. I said, 'You must have been frightened at first,' meaning frightened of sexual intercourse. 'Yes,' she said, 'I knew so little. I could only boil rice and did not even know how to make pickles properly or how to prepare salted plums. So at first I worried, and had to call on my mother to help me the first year.' (So there is no sex education in school, according to her, although our maid says there is some now.) To my question as to why menses stop during pregnancy, young Mrs. Kawabe replied, 'Maybe the blood goes to make up the baby instead,' but she was uncertain and recommended that I ask the midwife. (People talk about the man's seed—tane—being put in the womb, and they say that a sick womb or ovaries causes lack of children, but I am not sure what else they know about the process.)"

There were some ideas about how to predict the sex of the next child. "One way is to look at the creases on the last baby's legs. If there is only one, the next child will be a boy, if two it will be a girl. Another woman said that by adding the ages of the parents at the time of the conception of the child, and adding one if the child is conceived before the lunar New Year (July–January) or two if after, and dividing the total by three, one can predict its sex. If the result is an even number, it will be a girl, if uneven, a boy. Ukichi said that the only way of predetermining

1. The story of Momotaro is one of the most popular and widespread of all Japanese folktales. He was born from a peach that an old man and woman plucked from a stream as it came rolling past. Subsequently he subdued the demons of Onigashima and was rewarded for this exploit by the emperor. See Seki Keigo, ed., *Folktales of Japan* (Chicago: University of Chicago Press, 1963), pp. 40–43.

[rather than predicting] the sex of the child is, 'If you get on from the left it will be a boy, from the right, a girl.' He always gets on from the left. But one of the women remarked that of her eleven children only one was a boy, so she thinks it is something in the seed. The midwife dismisses all this and says there is absolutely no way to tell."

"Makino Otome, Mrs. Kawabe and Mrs. Sato were chatting about how one could not tell what the sex of a baby is 'until the magic box opens.' Both Otome and Mrs. Sato are pregnant, and apparently delighted at the prospect of opening the box soon. Mrs. Maeno came in and embarrassed John's assistant with her talk. First she admired the strength of that man who had fathered quintuplets, and then, becoming interested in the business of predicting the baby's sex, said that there is a method of looking into a horse's insides to see at least if the seed were growing. 'I wonder if the same could not be done for women?' she said. 'Here the midwife cannot even tell if you are pregnant for the first four months, and many women do not even consult one until they are eight months pregnant and sometimes not even until delivery.' "

The course of Otome's pregnancy did not run smoothly. "The midwife came to massage Otome's stomach. I asked her when she stops sleeping with her husband during pregnancy, and she got embarrassed and would not answer. I think she is very much in love with him." The husband was less reticent. "Hiroshi complained the other day that it is getting very difficult because Otome's vagina always swells so late in pregnancy."

Things continued to go so badly that Otome went to Menda to stay with her mother. "She came back here for a day, but returned to Menda. When Mrs. Sato asked Hiroshi about her condition yesterday, he said she is feeling much better, but had gone home because she feels still better when in her mother's house. 'She is still young,' he said, and added that he expects her back soon. 'Here everyone is so healthy,' he sighed. Then they discussed the causes of sickness, and Mrs. Sato said that morning sickness stops at the third month. He said that the trouble with his wife is that she will not eat for fear of getting sick, which is very bad. Of course, the family cannot understand such aberration from the normal course of pregnancy any more than the villagers can realize that hard work might cause miscarriages in some cases."

On the subject of miscarriages, there is the following interesting comment. "Today as Naoko went by, Mrs. Fujita and Mrs. Kato discussed her situation. They said she is a nice girl who gets along well with her husband, but that the grandmother is more or less trying to pressure them into a separation. The grandmother told me one day that since only the woman carries the child, very often a baby will resemble his mother's brother rather than his mother. For the same reason, she said, while cross-cousin marriage [between children of a brother and sister], as in the Uemura case, is all right, that between children of two brothers is not good. However, all the miscarriages I have heard about have been attributed to cross-cousin marriage."

Despite the grandmother's reassurances about cross-cousin marriage, Uemura Naoko's physical troubles during her pregnancy led her, like many young brides, to go to her parents' house. "After ten days, her husband came to fetch her back. When she returned, I found out that she had a miscarriage there, although old lady Tanno had said only that Naoko was not feeling well."

When a woman wished to conceive, she might visit different gods and goddesses. "Mrs. Fujita says that the woman who had ninety-eight children, then had them taken away from her and returned, and was changed into a goddess is especially good."[2] Pregnant women made offerings to various deities as well, the choice being up to the individual. "Makino said, 'My wife went to Kannon-sama.' He apparently goes there, like Eda, to light a candle when the baby is delivered." In a conversation about the taboos on the activities of pregnant women, "I asked Mrs. Arasaki if they were allowed to go on pilgrimages to the shrines [to pray to the Shinto gods, who cannot be approached by anyone in a condition of pollution]. 'Yes,' she said, 'They go to Kannon-sama [who is, of course, a Buddhist deity].' And if a pregnant mother runs out of milk for the child she is still nursing, she would go to Kōjin-sama [a Shinto protective deity], who will soothe the infant." Such divine intervention sometimes was ineffective. "The old lady told me that the younger baby sister of her granddaughter who died last month recently has also died, from a common weaning ailment that occurs when the mother conceives too soon after the birth of her last child."

The women of Suye suffered from a variety of women's diseases, some of them having been infected by their husbands who had picked up a venereal disease in town, others the victims of an almost total absence of prenatal care, poor nutrition, and hard work. Anyone who has ever spent any time in a Japanese village has been impressed by the heavy labor that farm women perform, even in advanced stages of pregnancy and into

2. This is a reference to the Buddhist deity Kishimojin (Hāritī), the Loving Mother, although somewhat garbled. In Japan her story is often told in the form of a homily. She had an enormous number of children—500 or 1,000—yet was a cannibal who devoured the babies of others. The Buddha, heeding the pleas of the bereaved mothers, spirited away and concealed just one of Kishimojin's brood, her youngest son. Discovering the child missing, she searched for him frantically, but without success. Finally, wild with grief, she appealed to the Buddha for help. He admonished her to reflect on her anguish at losing only one of a host of children, and asked if she now realized what a terrible affliction she had visited on the mothers whose children she had eaten. She was stricken with remorse and threw herself on the mercy of the Buddha, pleading with him to assist her. To her great joy he restored the missing child to her and then gave her pomegranates to eat. The fruit's red coloring and sour taste, which the Japanese believe make it resemble raw meat, served to compensate for the human flesh she now abjured. In Japan barren women prayed to her and ate the fruit because of its numerous seeds, which symbolize fertility. She is often conceived to be the protector of children as well.

their later years. For farm women in particular, there was seldom a time for long periods of rest from their labors.

"Today the women were up in the mountains, working just as hard as the men, chopping down trees and carrying the wood in great loads down from the hillsides to the road."

"Nonoyama Tsune was taking time out from the threshing, sitting in the lean-to on the edge of the field nursing her youngest child. She said that she had done the laundry in the morning before starting out with her older son to work in the fields."

"Horizuka Suzue is a girl from Hamanoue, about sixteen years old. She is a maid at Makino's and complains about the work. She says that it is much too hard and that a factory job would be much easier, and you can make friends in such a place. Here she cooks three meals a day, cleans the house, and is required to do a great deal of work in the fields. Today I met her as she was carrying rice bran to the mulberry fields up near the cemetery. The baskets were so heavy that I could hardly lift one on my shoulder. She said that she will make five trips."

"She was cutting some grass for the horses, but when I came up she sat down to chat. Now is a good time for farmers, she said [this is February], but from April on it is hard. First there is the ploughing and then the silkworms to be tended to, and then the sewing and so on. Their older daughter did farming for two years, but said that she did not want to continue because it is just too hard, so they let her go to a job in town. But, she added, at least she has two years' experience at it, and if she marries into a farmer's family, she will not be shamed by not being able to do the work."

"The household, I suppose, is not very different from all other rural houses where income is not large and there are many children. The house is dirty. The mother is constantly calling to one child or another to come to do some job for her, or asking them to look after the younger ones. The kids only vaguely pay attention. One of them tore a leaf from the calendar and ate it, a common practice among children. For lunch they each had a ball of cold rice rolled in chopped soybean and rice bran. She is a hard-working, cheerful person. She made one of the boys pound the *konnyaku* once in a while, but did all the rest of the work, turning the heavy grinder and lifting the big stones to clean them herself. She says that she has not talked to the midwife, yet expects her delivery any time now."

"I shall never stop marveling at the heavy burdens these women carry. I saw the Iries of Oade the other day transporting some wood for charcoal across the shaky little bridge at Nakashima. They were all at it, husband, older boy of fifteen or so, and wife. She is in the last months of pregnancy, and walked carefully over the bridge with a tremendous log balanced on her shoulder. In all, she made six or eight trips. Her son, walking ahead of her each time, would stop occasionally and look back, evidently worried."

"At the house in Hirayama, the daughter-in-law never stopped working, her strong muscular legs bare almost to the buttocks, constantly in motion. She had dried some rice which was spread out on large heavy mats in the sun. She collected it into heaps, and then spread it again with a rake to dry some more. Later, when it was ready, she put it all in a can, which she carried into the shed. The only time she asked one of the younger girls to help her was when she took in the heavy mats. Then she threshed some rice by hand and winnowed it. In between these tasks, she would play with the baby for a few minutes or give it a suck at her breast. She let the baby come to her and pretend to help her, fussing around with the rake and getting in the way. At the end of the long day she helped roast the tea-leaves, first washing the ceramic container and mixing some fresh clay with her feet to spread over some cracks in it, and chopping wood for the fire."

"Everyone laughs a bit because Otome is still resting after her miscarriage, while her sister and the maid work all day because there is a houseful of men to be taken care of. Says the maid, bending over the wash-tub, 'Woman's work is hard and thankless. There is no rest.' "

"Young Mrs. Eda is not feeling well. She has had a bad cold for some time and is in such pain that she is unable to go out to help with the wood-cutting. She says the baby is not due for some time yet, although that is the usual answer here when you ask about the time of delivery. She does not seem thrilled about having another baby just now. 'It is hard to do your work when all of the children are too small to help,' she said. Some neighbor women gathered around told her that she should not work (they were making straw sacks) when she complained about the pain." Not long after this, "Mrs. Eda went out to help her husband in the forest, and today she came home with great loads of wood on her shoulders, her stomach sticking way out."

"This morning I found Mrs. Kawabe washing and putting away the dishes from last night's party. She looks much better these days, but is much thinner. She says that she is taking medicine to cleanse the blood and that her illness has nothing to do with venereal disease. I asked her why she looks so sad these days. She said there is no reason at all for her to worry, and it is only the disease that makes her look thin and sad. She says that things are much better for her now that her husband has got in a servant to help him with work in the fields. She has told him that she does not want to farm any more because it makes her sick."

"The women were talking about one of the teachers who complains how hard her work is and is reported to be quite indifferent to her job, and willing to leave it at any time. Once she had thought it the best occupation, but is very disappointed. Her sister-in-law is said to have told her, 'If you think teaching is hard, you should try farming for a while. I work from dawn to dusk, barefoot in the dirt, carrying heavy loads on my back.' The women, not all of whom are farm wives, are clearly on the side of the sister-in-law."

"While Hirano was in Nakashima tending to some business, his wife went out to see if the millet is ripe enough for cutting. Her husband does farming only when he is not busy with his trade. 'Farming is hard,' she said, 'when there are no children at home big enough to help.' They grow nothing except a small patch of millet for their own use, and some vegetables. Their sons send them rice."

"When the children finished breakfast and went off to school at little after seven, the parents and the old couple ate. The old man prayed in front of the ancestral altar and went to fetch some grass, while the daughter-in-law and daughter went to the mountains to collect fertilizer. They came back at noon and all had a lunch of cold rice and left-over soup. The old lady stayed home and minded the baby, while preparing food for the evening meal. After lunch, the older girl washed the dishes (for the first time since the night before) and went off to pick tea while the old lady straightened up the house. The daughter-in-law filled the bath, carrying the water in buckets from the river below the house, fixed a broken lantern, planted some vegetable seed, and then went off to the fields, leaving the baby and the cooking to the old lady. Presently, to get it out of the way, the baby was tied on the oldest girl's back and sent out. In a few minutes both returned and the baby had to be taken over by the grandmother again."

The consequences of this kind of work schedule seemed obvious enough to some of the women of Suye. "She says she has a female disease, of which there are very many. The doctor's offices are always crowded with women. 'One can never tell what kind of disease they have, though, because they look so clean on the outside and not sick at all.' (I dare say that she herself is the healthiest looking country lass going, just to look at her.) Both she and Aki think that these diseases are caused by too much heavy work during the menstrual periods and pregnancies. She told me that she has had very few menses and has dreadful pains in the back. She is going to the doctor to get medicine and receive injections. She also said that the Shimosaka girl is sick now, and that she started menstruating once, but it has now stopped and she is not well."

"The midwife confirms that there are a great number of female diseases. She thinks that the young girls are usually healthy, but that women do not take care of themselves after childbirth. They get up after only three days, which is much too soon, she says, and complications develop. She also says that venereal diseases brought in by the husband are a great source of trouble. She thinks that syphilis is not too bad because you break out in a rash at an early stage and are compelled to see a doctor. With some care it can be cured completely. But gonorrhea is clean on the outside and reaches a bad stage before it is attended to. With some women it is hopeless, almost incurable."

It was often the case that a young married woman would return to her parents' house when she was ill. One such was the Suzuki daughter Sumiko who had married in Hitoyoshi. "She is visiting here for *o-bon* and yesterday went to the curing priest to see what kind of disease it is she has. Her back aches and her legs pain her, and it is apparent that her ankles are not very steady. When we suggested that she might be pregnant, she laughed. The curing priest told her that she has a female disease. There is something wrong inside, he said, and recommended that she see a doctor in Taragi. This morning she came over to get help with putting on her kimono. She is going to visit the doctor in Taragi for the third time. She does not want people to know that she is getting treatments, so when some women passed by and asked what she was doing, she said she is getting ready to return home. She said that she plans to take a back road, so as not to pass too many houses. Her present schedule is to visit the doctor every three days, and she is also going to a Menda moxabustion specialist. 'It is terribly painful,' she said."

"Sumiko is still going to Menda because she has been promised that she will be all right after two weeks of moxabustion. She says that her back does feel much better, but that the doctor's treatments are very slow, and so far have had no effect at all. She will also go to visit a shrine near Yatsushiro, where some relative of her husband's grandmother once went. This woman could not have children, but after just a week of drinking the medicine at that shrine, she conceived. So, on the first of the month, Sumiko and her husband will go there together.

"Today she stopped on her way back from Menda and talked it over with Mrs. Fujita and Mrs. Goto, with whom I was having tea. At first the women said that the moxa treatment might be good, but when she said it was some female disease, they both told her at once that in such cases a doctor's care is absolutely necessary. However, both also favored the planned shrine visit. They said that in cases of women's complaints one can never tell by appearances, for all such women look healthy enough. Mrs. Goto remarked that in the old days women paid no attention to themselves at all. When she was young, they knew nothing of disinfectants, but now every woman is disinfected daily for a period after childbirth. This amuses these older women."

"It now appears that Sumiko is in a quandary. With the train fare and the doctor's fee of 2.20 yen for every visit—for the medicine, local douche treatment, and injection—she feels it is costing too much. Still, she cannot bring herself to drop it if there is any chance it will help, so she went to consult the curing priest again. (He consulted with the gods the first time she went to him and told her at once what was wrong, correctly guessing where she has pain. He had recommended that she see a doctor.) Today, after consulting the gods again, he said, 'The moxa treatment cannot hurt, but for positive results, you must continue seeing the doctor.' Tomorrow her husband will be here and they will talk it over."

"It has been decided that Sumiko will give up both the moxa treatments and seeing the doctor, and instead will take the baths at Yunoharu, which she has tried and which make her feel much better. I asked why she had not stayed in Taragi and gone from there to the doctor's in Hitoyoshi [since it would be much less expensive to travel that short distance than going all the way from Suye]. She said that when she is in her husband's house in Taragi she feels that she must finish the housework before going to the doctor's, which always made it too late, while here at her parents' home she feels free to come and go as she likes." Whether the baths at Yunoharu proved to be the cure she had sought we do not know.

For many young women, pregnancy was a very dangerous time. "The women thought that Naoko's mother had contracted syphilis or some other venereal disease while she was carrying her, which is why there is something wrong with the girl's body. My suggestion that such problems as Naoko is now having may be the result of pregnant women working too hard was rejected. 'Why just look at all the farmers' wives, and at Mina working so hard right up to the last minute. All their children are all right,' they said, as though no exceptions could be pointed to. This was said even though they had just finished saying that Naoko had started bleeding right in the field during rice transplanting. She had gone at once to Tontokoro and stayed there until she recovered. She had told one of them that the doctor had told her not to work during the final stages of her pregnancy, but the others were not convinced."

"When I stopped by there, Naoko told me that she has gone to Taragi to see the doctor. She said that she is 'no good inside' and therefore has trouble conceiving. I told her that now that she is pregnant, she must avoid hard work, and she confirmed that the doctor had told her the same thing. She said that she was told about childbirth and such things only in her last year in school, and was almost shocked when I asked if her mother had never told her anything. 'Oh no! Mother never mentions such things!' If married late, she said, girls will have found out a little. She was nineteen when she married. The woman is obviously upset about her series of miscarriages. (Of which Fumie said, 'It must have been decided by the gods [kamisama] that she is not to have children.') She said that she had been feeling so well yesterday, and had worked hard, but this morning she felt so sick that she could not speak and had only just got up. We discussed morning sickness, which the women all say is usually relieved about the fourth month. They have a great desire for things they cannot have, but no desire to eat anything served them. 'Every day I stand under the persimmon tree and look at it,' she said, tears coming to her eyes. 'I want persimmons so desperately.' "

She did miscarry, as we have seen, and several weeks later, "On the way to Kinoue I saw Uemura Naoko washing clothes under the bridge and cleaning some vegetables in the water. We had a short chat and she said that she is feeling much better now. She said that she ought to get pregnant right now, 'for the winter, but I always do it in the summer,' and laughed forlornly."

Others were even less fortunate. "Of the daughter there, they say she is insane. The trouble comes from her womb. She was married to one of the Toyamas for a while, but suffered from severe headaches and eventually went back to her parents. Things got worse and she was taken to a doctor. He said that it was womb trouble that had gone to her brain, and recommended that she be kept in bed. She stays there all the time, they say, 'just lying there quietly without doing or saying anything.' "

The most private event in the lives of the women of Suye was that of childbirth.[3] Being very much concerned to observe the delivery of a child, "I mentioned to the Hayashis that I would like to be present when a baby is born. They said it will be difficult because no one is ever allowed to witness a birth. Some women dislike having the midwife present because they are so embarrassed and ashamed. Besides, they added, most babies are born at night."

"The midwife says that I cannot attend a delivery, for even the woman's parents do not go into the room then. She says that I must try to arrange it with the woman having the baby, and cannot go through her. She thinks it possible that some woman might let me sit in the adjoining room. Shoko thinks that I will not be able to see a delivery because people are so shy, and it is a very private thing. Mrs. Ouchi said the same."

Toward the close of the year in Suye, it became obvious that 'I might just as well resign myself to the fact that here absolute privacy is observed during childbirth and let it go at that. Despite many promises, Suzuki did not send for me when the baby came at eight this morning. The midwife says my cause is hopeless. 'They all say yes, yes, but when it comes to delivery they refuse to let anyone in because they are embarrassed. A woman will not let even her husband or mother come near, and if the delivery is an easy one, she will not let the midwife in until the baby is out, and only asks her to wash it. In hospitals, of course, women have to give birth two or three in a room, and these village women do not like hospitals. So it will be impossible to get in, and that is that,' she concluded. The women present agreed, including the pregnant Mrs. Eda, who was my last hope. The midwife did say again that she is quite willing to let me see her part of the job, but she cannot call others in unless the woman herself gives her consent."

It was clear that the midwife and the Suye women actually resented any effort to be present at a delivery, as the following lengthy account of

---

3. For the only detailed historical account available in English, which is useful despite its many shortcomings, see Mary W. Standless, *The Great Pulse: Japanese Midwifery and Obstetrics through the Ages* (Rutland, Vt., and Tokyo: Charles E. Tuttle, 1959). Chapter 9 deals with the period since 1868.

elaborate evasion reveals. "At about ten in the morning I saw the midwife going by in a great hurry. To my question she replied, 'Just over there,' refusing to tell me which house she was bound for. She was obviously relieved when I did not follow her, but turned back toward the boat landing instead. However, in a little while I doubled back and by questioning a fisherman discovered that she must be at Nohara's. Indeed she was there, washing out a pan in the back of the house, but did not so much as acknowledge my presence.

"Mrs. Nakajima was standing outside her house, from which one can see the Nohara porch. As I came away, they asked me, 'Is it a delivery?' and wanted to know if the midwife had arrived. (It later turned out that Nohara himself was away, so the older son had gone to fetch her.) All the Nohara children—three little girls and a small boy—had gathered nearby, along with a few neighbor children. All through the day they would run into the house to have a look and eat some cold rice. When the youngest, about three, tried to peek through the door, the older girls laughed and pulled her away. They obviously knew what was happening, but would say only, 'I don't know,' even to questions such as 'Where is your mother?' When we asked if a baby was being born, the little boy said, 'Not yet.'

"I went back home and after a little while came back to Nohara's. The woman and the midwife were in the sleeping room talking and laughing occasionally. It was about one in the afternoon and the kids were still playing around, running in and out. Suddenly I saw Mrs. Nohara come out and go to the toilet outside. On her way back, she picked up a handful of rice, which she had told the older boy to spread out to dry on the mats, to see how it was coming. Then she asked me if I had any particular business there. I said something about having just got back from Naka-shima. The midwife came out and sat in the main room, looking through some mail. 'Have you some business here?' she asked. I was by now thoroughly embarrassed, because she had once explained to me very carefully that I was not wanted on such occasions. I told her that I was on my way back from Nakashima and stopped in. 'Is Mr. Nohara in?' I asked. She said that he was away and would not be back until evening. I asked why she had come. 'Just to massage the stomach,' she answered. She said nothing about delivery, and it was very obvious that my presence was most unwelcome. I finished my cigarette and withdrew, hoping to get back in time later on.

"But, having been delayed by several things, when I finally returned at 4:30, the baby had arrived an hour before. It had already been washed and the tub was already put away. Only some kids were around. Mrs. Nakajima came along and asked the older boy if the baby was a girl or boy. She knew the child had been born because she had seen the tub from her house. When I had asked him the same question he said he did not know. To her he said that he had not seen which it was. His little sisters only giggled at first, but finally admitted that it was indeed a girl.

"I went over to Mrs. Nakajima's where we were joined by Mrs. Uemura and had a discussion about how many girls Nohara has, and how this delivery had taken longer than she usually does. It seems that she is usually through in the morning, but this one had taken all day. They assured me that no one is admitted at a childbirth, and that Japanese women never cry out at such times. With respect to the large number of daughters at Nohara's, Mrs. Nakajima said that there is a belief that girls are born to women who work in the house and boys to those who work out of doors, but she does not think this is true. 'All of mine are boys,' she said, 'And the farmers have a lot of girls.' So after a while I went home and about an hour or so later the midwife passed by the house on her way from the Nohara's. This was as close as I could get to a delivery."

After a few weeks, "the Makino baby was born yesterday at 5:00 A.M. It is a very cute baby, all white and rosy-cheeked, with much hair, well developed hands and nails. It was about a month overdue. Sato says that all the Makino babies are cute when they are born, implying that later on they change and come to look like their mother. Tamako says that at three o'clock she saw the midwife arrive and thought that most probably Otome had pains. Then, as the doors were kept shut for a long time, she suspected that something was happening, and at five she learned that the baby had come. Apparently there was not a sound. (Says Mrs. Wauchi, 'Why, people would laugh at you if you cry or even moan.' She was greatly amused when I told her that we scream.) At childbirth, she said, women never cry. In Japan it is considered very bad to cry at such a time. No matter how terrible the pain you clench your fists and keep your mouth shut tight, for the neighbors must not know what is happening. Her mother delivered her six children alone, got up to wash them, and then would lie down. People will laugh at you if you cry and will say, 'You were very quiet when the nice things were happening. Why do you cry now?' Delivery is the most secret thing—even one's husband is not allowed in."

"In answer to my question she said that of course women cry with ordinary pain, but that they feel very differently about the pain of delivery and think it is bad to make a sound. Old lady Tamaki dropped in and added that even if the doctor has to cut your belly, you must clench your teeth and keep silent. Tonight, when I told him about this conversation, Sato agreed. 'It is a sign of their strong will,' he said. The woman will grab the midwife's hand and keep quiet, or see it through all by herself."

"Later in the day when we went calling, Makino Hiroshi, the father, asked the midwife if it is all right to keep the baby from nursing for so long. He was assured that the child should not nurse for two or three days. Mrs. Sato and the mother talked about the delivery. Was it hard or easy, did the afterbirth come right out? (It took an hour.) Mrs. Sato kept saying that it was a cute baby and Otome kept demurring, 'No, it's not cute at all,' and saying how much cuter Taro-chan (Mrs. Sato's beloved grandson) had been when he was born. She said it was a great relief to have it all over with."

There were many other visits to houses shortly after the delivery of a baby, naming ceremonies on the third day after birth, and conversations on the subject.

"Going by the Kawabe's the other day, I found young Mrs. Kawabe in bed, and her mother and sister-in-law there from Menda. They insisted that she just had a headache. Shortly afterward the midwife arrived, claiming that the baby was not to be born today, and the neighbor women say that the baby will not come tonight because Mrs. Kawabe is eating her supper. 'With the first baby,' they said, 'the contractions may continue for two or three days.' I had got such a cold reception when I stopped in that I did not dare stay, and went up to Uchida's later on to see what was up.

"At ten last night I went back by Kawabe's and found the shutters closed and could hear no sound. Uchida's doors were also shut, so there was nothing to do but go back home. This morning I arrived at Kawabe's at daybreak—on the pretext of buying some eggs for breakfast—and no one said a word about babies. Mrs. Kawabe's own breakfast was being served. I left and went directly to see the midwife, who told me that the baby had come about midnight, sooner than she had expected. The neighbors report that they heard the baby cry last night, but did not hear a sound from the mother.

"I called again later. The baby is tiny, and the mother seems to be relieved to have it over with. 'Childbearing is very hard,' she told me. 'It hurts so badly and one is so scared.' [The women often mentioned how frightened they are at such times.] While I was there her husband returned from a trip to Kume County. His mother was helping around, some people from the hamlet came by, and neighbors were dropping in. When I got back to Kakui everyone asked me if the baby is cute. They especially admire a lot of jet-black hair."

"Today the Kawabes held the naming ceremony, at one week because the baby's father had been away on the third day after birth. (Evidently not too much store is set by the opinion of some that unless the child is named three days after birth evil may befall it.) I saw him last night at the store and he seemed to be very pleased. He had heard about the baby by telephone, and thinks that maybe it is better to be away during the delivery of one's first child. Mrs. Ouchi agreed with him and said that it is much easier for the woman to deliver when her husband is not present. Later Mrs. Sato came up, and the women told me that there are two kinds of pregnancy. The stomach pregnancy means that the baby is easier to carry and to deliver, but 'back babies' make one's back ache, and although one's stomach does not get so big, they make for a difficult delivery, but the afterbirth comes out much sooner. The old lady said that she has heard that the local midwife makes women deliver lying down. She could never do that, she declared, and had all her children sitting up."

"Yesterday at six in the evening, Mrs. Mori gave birth to a baby girl, who is tiny and has long hair. When the labor pains began early in the afternoon, the midwife was sent for and arrived just before the birth. Unfortunately, I missed it all. This morning when I went there the baby was lying alone in the main room, wrapped in several layers of cloth, and the mother was in a small side room (*nema*, sleeping room). I was told that the mother has taken nothing but milk yet and some medicine of which none knew the name or exact purpose. It looked very much like chamomile tea to me. Later on the room was straightened up a bit and the baby taken in to the mother, after being washed by the midwife. Old lady Mori said that the young Mrs. Mori had severe pains after the delivery. Mrs. Eda, who was calling, said that she too had such pains, but only with her third child and all those who were born after. Mrs. Mori remarked that she prefers to give birth lying prone; Mrs. Eda always does it in a kneeling position."

"There were few callers. 'Nobody special,' I was told, 'just people stopping in on their way by the house.' The husband was away at the time of the delivery and returned only much later. But before he got there, old lady Mori was carrying on at length about men who do nothing but drink and act rough and never do as they are told. (I heard later that things are not going smoothly in the Mori household because of his drinking, which makes the old lady very angry.)"

"On this first day after the birth of the baby, Mrs. Mori is lying on her back with her knees raised. She gets up and goes to the toilet, and when I went over she was sitting up to greet visitors. Food taboos were discussed, and are said to be 'a matter of custom' and no one gives any reasons for observing them. The new mother is not to eat pumpkin, *kon-nyaku*, shrimp, or red fish. White fish is all right, but not black or red. Her rice is cooked very soft, and she is encouraged to drink soup. Mrs. Makino says that she should not take meat or fruit, and that the only sweet that is proper is *ame* [a molasses-like candy]. Old lady Mori said firmly that meat and fruit are perfectly all right, and that the woman can have any kind of sweet cake although it is true that *ame* is the best. They say that all of the taboos are to be observed to protect the health of the mother for the thirty-one or thirty-three days before the infant boy or girl is taken to the shrine to be presented to the gods. Most old women do not allow the mother to drink water immediately after delivery."

"The next day Mrs. Mori was sitting up a good deal, holding the baby in her arms. It will not be carried on the back until it is at least a month old and the ceremony at the shrine (*hiaki*) has been held."

On the third day after the birth, the naming ceremony [*kamitate*] was held at Mori's. "In the sleeping room the midwife washed the baby while the party was getting under way. A straw mat was spread out, and a tub brought in and filled with water. The doors were open right onto the street most of the time, at least into the open hallway, and it was quite cold. She handled the infant adroitly, spreading its arms like wings to grasp her forearm while she held it up and washed it with soap. Then she wanted some water to rinse it with, and some was brought in. It was too cool, she said, but was told that there was no more hot water. She asked that this water be heated up. The doors remain open, the water in the tub cools, but the baby is quiet. The midwife repeats the request for water several times, and each time is told that it will take only a minute. Nothing happens. Children come in from the street and crowd around to look at the new baby. (During the afternoon, only the two older Mori boys were allowed into the room, but now all came.) Finally the midwife gave up, rinsed the baby as best she could, and took it out of the tub. She dried it, changed the dressing on the cord, using alcohol and cotton, and put on the belly-band. Mrs. Mori handed her the baby's clothes—a diaper and the new kimono purchased after it was born. Its face was powdered and rouged, a dot on the forehead and one on each cheek, with a bit on the lower lip. (Boy babies have only the character *dai* [great, big, large] written on the forehead in red, to indicate that they will grow to be big and strong.) Once the father looked in on the scene. When the baby was all ready, she was brought in by the midwife, passed from guest to guest, and back to the midwife at last. Everyone said that the baby is cute and a pleasure to all. The cup that is passed around with the baby has to be full and must be drained to the bottom so that it will not grow up to be a fool. As each person holds the infant for a few minutes, he repeats its name, drinks the cup of *shōchū* and passes the baby to the next person. Drinks were exchanged and the party proceeded. The mother came out only once, bowed to the assembled company, and left."

"The Moris' baby girl's cord came off on the third day. It was wrapped up together with a bit of her hair, the name and date of birth were written on the wrapping paper, and it was put away in a drawer. In the old days, old lady Mori said, they used to stick a needle through the cord. She did not know why, but thought it had something to do with keeping the child free of stomach disease. According to her the cord usually comes off on the fifth day, and attributed the protruding navels of some children to too much crying. (There are some kids around whose navels stick out as much as an inch.)" Inquiries revealed that "no one knows why the umbilical cord is saved. Today Hayashi asked the midwife about it while I was there. 'I don't know,' she said. 'It's an old custom. Maybe people used to do something with it. They say it keeps the child well and safe from stomach ailments, but I don't think that's true.' "

Not long after the birth of the Mori baby, a child was born at Tamaki Giichi's. "Unable to attend the party because we will be away, I went there to apologize and to take a gift. The infant's mother was there, a husky, hard-working woman. She had just come in from somewhere, dressed in her work-clothes. I asked when she had resumed her regular work and she said that today is the first day, since she took the child to the shrine for *hiaki* the day before, a month after delivery. She said that the menstrual flow will continue for a whole month or longer after a child is born. She uses a belt when she works; others use cotton. The midwife had told me also that after *hiaki* it is all right for the couple to resume intercourse, and that it is all right for them to continue to sleep together right up to the end of pregnancy. She recommends not having intercourse late in pregnancy, but there is no customary taboo, she says, and many people do not heed her advice."

The birth of a third child to the Shimoda Ichiros was the occasion for the discovery of more of the practices and beliefs associated with childbirth. "The baby girl was born yesterday. When I called today both the mother and infant were in bed. The baby had already had milk, which is unusual, for they usually are not fed until the second or third day. Old lady Shimoda says that she has become a real grandmother at last, apparently not counting the child born to her son, who went out as an adopted husband.

"I learned that the afterbirth is put in a pot and buried in the cemetery. The father is supposed to then walk over it, to make the child obedient, but Shimoda was away somewhere yesterday and this was not done. They say that the child will fear any creature that steps on the spot before the father does. According to old lady Shimoda the afterbirth used to be put under the house, in order to attach the child to the place, and that some people put it in the toilet to make the interval between this baby and the next one longer. All of these beliefs are recounted with smiles now, but it is obvious that people still observe many of them. Certainly the afterbirth is never simply thrown out, but is always buried somewhere.

"The food taboos observed here are very much the same as those at Mori's. The mother gets soft-cooked rice, soup, fish (*tai, funa* or *iwashi*) [sea bream, roach, or sardine], and a few vegetables. The old lady says the new mother may not eat meat or pumpkin, and agrees that *ame* is the best kind of sweet in such circumstances."

Many of the women took the taboos quite seriously. "Mrs. Kato confirms what old lady Wauchi told me yesterday about taboos on women who have just delivered a baby. They are impure for the period before *hiaki* and should not cook rice [because they should not handle fire]. They should do no heavy work, either, and she thinks that a lot of female diseases are due to women not observing the food and work restrictions for longer than one week."

Some families felt that childbirth should occur in some parts of the house but never in others. "The room next to the main one (*zashiki*) is called *arake*, and next to it is the kitchen (*daidokoro*). Any room off the *zashiki* or the *daidokoro* is called sleeping-room (*nema*) and is used for sleeping and childbirth. When the old lady told me that the room is used for child-bearing (*komotsu*), her older daughter, shocked, asked, 'Why mention such things?' The old lady replied that I am here to learn. In small two-room houses they said that delivery takes place in the *arake*, which in those houses actually serves as the main room, but never in the kitchen, where people eat. (Mori and Shimoda babies were born in the *nema*, Ochiai's in the *arake*. But I notice that the Moris are now eating in the *nema* where the baby was born, so the taboo cannot be very stringent. One may eat in the delivery room, I presume, but not deliver in the eating room.)"

The influence of the midwives on postnatal care of both mother and child was considerable. "Formerly, say old ladies Irie and Ariyoshi, there were no professional midwives, although someone would come to help. A woman just had her children quietly, squatting on her haunches or hanging onto a rope for support during labor. Now they go so far as to call the midwife as early as the fourth month of pregnancy, something unheard of in their day, and no one squats any more except for a very few women, like Mrs. Eda and a couple of others they know about.

"The midwives now insist that the woman be delivered lying down, because it is considered better, but they think it takes away one's strength. Until ten years ago, they said, no one gave birth in such a position. As for post-natal care, there is virtually none. The midwife knows the proper care, but says she cannot make the women here do as she advises. The mother should stay in bed for ten days, for example, but here they get up on the third. For the first ten days or so the midwife comes daily to wash the baby, although some come only every second or third day. After that it is up to the parents to bathe it, and they take it along to the bath when they go. A mother is said to be afraid to wash the baby at home alone unless she is urbane, like Mrs. Sato Kazuo who does it every day by herself."

"When the midwife calls to bathe the baby, she may also massage the mother's stomach, as she does during the contractions at delivery, and if the woman feels unwell the midwife will be sent for. Tomoe has been complaining that she is especially weak after delivery, and unlike the other women cannot do very much work for several days. Today the midwife was there to do the laundry for her and said that after Tomoe's first child was born, she was in bed for fifty days."

As we have seen, some women were said to be so shy that they would not have even the midwife present at their deliveries, but for some the reasons were economic. The midwife "is paid as little as two yen for services and as much as ten. There is no set price, but she seldom gets ten, and considers five a lot. Payments average about three yen." One of the women who did not have a midwife to help her was Mrs. Hayashi. "I saw her doing laundry at the river. I asked her how she had managed, having the baby all by herself. 'It can be done if you make up your mind to do it. Of course, it is not very nice, having to get up at once. If you have money it is better to call a midwife, but we have no money. It costs at least five yen. After the afterbirth came out, I got up to wash the baby.' Her husband was home at the time, but he was asleep and did not know that she had had the baby until it began to cry. She laughed. It was her eighth child. On another occasion I pressed her for more information about her delivery without the services of a midwife, but she does not like to discuss it. 'You do as you find most convenient,' she said, and would not tell me in what position she has her babies."

There were some practices thought to have the effect of insuring easy delivery, but not all the women knew of these beliefs. "For example, Mrs. Kawabe of Oade did not know that the stomach-girdle for pregnant women should be put on first on the day of the dog [in order to make delivery easy, as it is for dogs], but one of the Tawaji women said she had heard of it. So had Tomoe, who said that it was important to put it on on the appropriate day. She says, however, that many farm women do not wear the girdles because they are such a nuisance when you are working. She knew of no medicines given the woman at a difficult delivery—only massaging the stomach and making offerings to Kannon-sama. She always makes an offering there before delivery, and all of hers have been easy. The last time, indeed, her husband had stopped there on the way back from summoning the midwife. She remarked that when her first child was born there was no midwife in Suye, and it took too long for one to come from Menda, so she delivered the baby alone. Mrs. Eda said that she had a white girdle made, about eight feet long, which was put on her by the midwife in her fifth month. They offered *o-miki* on the occasion, but she does none of this any more, 'because I am healthy and don't need to.' "

Not all childbirths are smooth, of course. "Yesterday when I was at Hayashi's, I asked where his wife was, and Fumio said that she was upstairs lying down. It did not occur to me that she has been out of sight for four days now, and that there was an old aunt around helping out in the house. Today I discovered that she had had some stomach trouble which made her deathly ill, and that for those four days she had terrible diarrhea and could take no food. At two o'clock this morning she began having strange pains, and by the time the midwife arrived, she had had a miscarriage. The baby girl was in a caul and was stillborn. It was the seventh month of pregnancy. Fumio said today that she is feeling a trifle better, and was drinking the chamomile tea that is thought to clear out the system.

"Women of the neighborhood began dropping by with rice or sweet cakes, and other miscarriages and premature births were discussed. Mrs. Ouchi told us about her eight-month term baby which had died, even though she had emptied her breasts into a cup and fed it when she found that it could not suck. It lived only fourteen days. Fumio was saying that the whole thing was the fault of the midwife because she had been so late in arriving, but the women said that she could not have helped. Besides, they said, Shoko is still young and can have many more children. Fumio also said that he thinks the child was stillborn because Shoko had not taken

food for four days and had starved it. He said that babies come from milk."
The funeral was held the following day.

Within the week the Ochiai baby arrived, and following the naming
ceremony on the third day, "the women ate and drank and chatted. The
mother lay in the same room, with the baby by her side, smoking her pipe
all along. Once she got up and taking a piece of cotton with her went
outside to the toilet. The next day she was up taking care of the other
children as usual."

"I commented to Hashida later that there are a lot of births recently.
He agreed and said that most of them occur in the winter. His explanation
is that most conceptions take place in early spring because that is when
people's blood runs faster. With everything getting green and blossoming,
he said, the man's spirit rises and he impregnates his wife. This being a
fact, he thought similar findings would be obtained if one looked into the
matter in America. (The midwife says that most babies are born at night,
and almost never in the afternoon. I wondered why, and her husband
promptly suggested that it is because babies are made at night. Then he
made a rather wry joke to the effect that he has no chance to make babies
at night himself because his wife is always out delivering some other
woman's child.)

"My own explanation for the seasonality of childbirth is that while
in the winter (November to March) it is much too cold to have intercourse,
in the summer (June to October) people are much too busy. So the best
time of the year is March to June, when most babies in the village are
conceived. Hence most births occur between December and March, as the
midwife claims. It might be, of course, that people plan it that way, since
this period is the slackest, everyone has leisure time, and lots of celebrations
and parties are held. I fear that both Hashida's and my explanations are
far-fetched. It remains to be seen how many babies are born in summer."
As it happens, few were.

Within days, "Mrs. Eda had her baby about eight this morning.
She had no pains and the baby came so fast that the midwife arrived only
after it was completely out. When I arrived the midwife was washing the
infant in front of an open door in a good draft. One of the old ladies had
taken out the youngest child, while the other was serving visitors tea. She
said that old man Eda had gone to fetch the midwife because the husband
had already left early for work in the forest. When he returned about
eleven, the old man went up to replace him at the wood-cutting. Eda said
that this evening he will take the afterbirth to the cemetery and bury it.
There is no rule, he says, but he prefers to do it after sunset.

"The dressing of the child was very interesting. While the midwife
was putting carbolic acid on the cord, she said to the mother, 'Here is your
medicine. Use it when you go to the toilet.' She put drops in the baby's
eyes, but while bathing it noticed that her own little boy's nose was running, and used the baby's wash-cloth to wipe it.

"As no one could find a bandage for the cord, I went home to fetch some gauze, concerned because the baby was lying naked in the cold while they looked everywhere for a clean rag. (This was not the first snag. When she had asked for some soap, the old man hurried out to buy some, for there was none in the house. While he was gone, one of the old ladies produced some laundry soap, and by the time the old man got back the baby had been washed.) For a diaper the midwife used some old rags she found lying around, lining them with some paper which she first crumpled to make soft, as is the custom here. The baby was then wrapped in an old kimono. Having some rags left over, the midwife bunched them up under the mother's head, for it is thought best to keep the head high. All at once the midwife remembered the stomach-girdle and asked the mother to get up on her knees. They passed an old kimono sash around her waist and the midwife tied it tight 'to get the skin back to normal.' (Many women also wear this girdle during the last months of pregnancy.) After this the midwife was served some rice and dried fish, but ate little and soon left."

The extremely casual attitude toward sanitation exhibited by the villagers and the midwife alike was striking. The latter "is always cheerful, and always smiles. She is right out of a book—a typical midwife, husky, good-natured and efficient. Nothing bothers her, neither her little boy's foul disposition nor the fact that at the last minute at a delivery people never have what is needed. 'Anything will do,' she says, when she really requires a clean towel or some cotton or gauze. Anything is used in bathing the baby. Towels and diapers are really old rags. Only at Sato's is there a large towel to dry the baby, and real gauze always on hand."

Up in the mountain hamlet of Hirayama, widely believed by others in Suye to be backward because so isolated, "there was a birth the night we were visiting there. The midwife did not arrive until the following morning. They say that it is very seldom that she comes on time because it is so far. If the girl's mother lives close by, she is called in 'because the girl is afraid' and her in-laws feel it is a kindness to call her mother to help her through the fearful experience. The mother helps out in many ways and washes the baby. If the mother lives too far off, the mother-in-law or an old neighbor woman will assist. Brides never go to their former homes to deliver because 'then she could not return for thirty-three days.' " The point requires some elaboration, and it is best exemplified in the somewhat unusual circumstances of the naming ceremony held for Sato Kazuo's baby. First it must be understood that there is no easy path into Hirayama that does not require the crossing of at least one stream. "The Satos will have the ceremony tomorrow, but the baby will not be present because before the presentation at the shrine a child cannot be taken across water or the gods will cause trouble." So the location of Hirayama makes it unlikely that women who have married out will return to their mother's houses to have their babies, as many Suye women did, especially when it was their first.

Even in Hirayama, which today we would say was more "traditional" than the rest of the hamlets in Suye, the customs surrounding
childbirth were less than solemnly observed. "They told us that here, too,
the father buries the afterbirth under the house and treads on the spot.
When we called, however, this had not yet been done, and there was much
discussion of the belief about what would happen if a dog or some other
creature stepped on it first. [That is, that the child would fear such a
creature all its life.] Everyone expressed some doubt, saying it was just a
custom. Neither did they see why it was considered necessary to pour
mountain water rather than well water over the afterbirth. 'It's all lies,'
they said. With a smile they said that they wrap up the cord and put it
away 'so that the baby will be able to learn things quickly and well.' At
which one old woman said that might be the reason that she has grown
old without learning anything at all; perhaps her cord was mislaid. Another
said that she had no idea where the cords of her children were, but guessed
that they had been eaten by mice. Although there was a lot of joking about
these matters, all observe the customs."

In the other hamlets of Suye, however, some old customs connected
with childbirth had lapsed completely. "Mrs. Tominaga said that there is
a ceremony on the fifth or seventh day after childbirth, when people are
invited to celebrate. Until that ceremony is held, the mother cannot cross
water. It is for the buddhas, whereas the naming ceremony is for the gods.
No one else confirms this information. None of the other women knows
about it, and they assured me that there is no observance between the
naming ceremony and the baby's first visit to the shrine on the thirty-first
or thirty-third day after birth, when food taboos are lifted and women can
once again cross water. (Later I found that old ladies Mori and Ishibashi
did know about the one-week ceremony for the child, but they said that
although it was current in the past it was no longer observed by anyone.)"

SIX

Young Women and Men: Growing Up

In this society, where for the vast majority of young women and men the first marriage was arranged by their families, there was a great deal of romantic activity on the part of adolescent girls and boys still too young to marry. Some of it was clearly playing at romance, yet the number of illegitimate children strongly suggests that many young couples went further than the exchange of love-letters and clandestine strolls after dark.

The Embrees were early introduced to this world of girls and boys, about which there was constant gossip in Suye, much of it good-humored, some of it vicious and censorious. "There is a certain amount of antagonism in the teasing between little boys and girls. The boys tease the girls, who retaliate by making faces at them. Today I saw a fight which started with a boy chasing a girl. It ended up with their spitting in each other's faces."

By the time they reached their teens, the relationship was somewhat different. "Concerning young men's pastimes during the New Year holidays, he said they *asobi* [this word is not untranslatable; the problem is that it has so many meanings—to play, to have a good time, to go around with others, to relax. Therefore, in the pages that follow it has been left untranslated and the reader is asked to take the meaning from the context.] When I asked for more details, he said, 'Just *asobi*.' They gather at someone's house or go out somewhere as a group. I had just about come to the conclusion that young men and women do not mix at all, and this upsets the idea. So far no young man or woman has ever admitted that they mix at any time, and I have never seen them together as a couple or in groups. The only person I suspect is Harue, because I have seen the same fellow hanging around the well a couple of times. If they actually do mix, it would be interesting to know how love affairs are avoided or handled in view of the system of marriage. If they do not mix, then I wonder how these healthy young women of sixteen to twenty remain so happy and pay no attention to men, when constant reference to sex occurs in songs and dances, and where there are no separate bedrooms (or beds, for that matter)."

Some time later, the sight of a group of young women and men coming back from the mountain where they had been cutting wood and gathering kindling, suggested that things might be otherwise. "It seems to me that such a group might well get into mischief. I asked about that and was rebuked. Nothing happens between boys and girls, I was told. 'Japanese people do not do such things.' Either they are concealing the truth from me, or these young people are different from young people in most other places I have known."

If the adults were at least initially discreet, "the little nursemaids are extremely well informed. As one of the older girls went by, the Yunohara nursemaid at once named the fellow from Taragi, now working in Oade, who is said to be her sweetheart. She even ran up to the girl and asked, 'Where is Takashi-san?' They also spend much time playing with the delivery boys, throwing lassos around them or starting a pinching game, or seeing who can rap his arm the hardest with their knuckles." And there was much teasing among the girls. "While Fumie was telling me who sleeps where in her family, 'the baby with mother, Akira with father,' Aki broke in and said, 'And Fumie-chan with Kazuo.' Fumie got very exercised and chased Aki around the house."

"I met Suzuki going somewhere with a gift this morning. Fumie says that he went to see her family to find out if she can work for them again next year. But her father did not give his consent, and Suzuki said nothing when he came back. She does not know what happened. Said I, 'Maybe you are to be married next year,' at which she blushed, covered her face, and giggled."

Some of the nursemaids were about while a group of women were discussing a recent scandal in Shiba, which had made the newspapers. "A boy of the sixth year in elementary school had intercourse with a second-year girl student, who had conceived. They had been at it for some time, but were only then caught and he had been put in prison in Hitoyoshi. The women were shocked at the girl's age. Said they, in their matter-of-fact way, 'They must have been playing house and gone on from that.' They said that such childish games are common, although one of the women thought the boy must be crazy to take so young a girl. (Madness is used as an excuse for many strange deeds.) Aki and the nursemaids showed great interest in this story, and Jun-chan ran at once to get it first hand at Ishibashi's. Aki wondered how she could conceive if she had no menses yet. The girls told me that when the children play house [*kyaku asobi*] they imitate their mothers not only in bringing out the tiered box of food as if receiving guests, but also imitate intercourse and childbirth."

Many adults firmly insisted that all illicit sexual behavior was limited to the servants. "Sato says there is talk that Koyo-chan [see pages 131–34] used to meet her boyfriend when she came out very early in the morning to fetch water at the well. Maybe, he says, young people meet when cutting grass together in the still-dark early morning, but he knows very little about it all, he claims, because this is all the kind of thing servants do, and he never did such things when he was young. He did recall that Norio used to whistle for his girl to come out under the bridge. When I said that he had been having an affair with the Maeno daughter, he said, 'No, not the daughter. It was the servant.' "

He was quite wrong, it was the daughter, not the servant. Others denied his allegation that the daughters of farm families did not do such things. One of them, whose remarks are found in John Embree's journal, was "the young Suzuki girl, an attractive farmer's daughter of sixteen. She says that although many girls receive letters from young men, she does not. Such letter-writing is not restricted to girls who work as servants (such as Tamako) but includes girls living at home as well. She says that she would put away unread any such letter if one came. She seldom visits the towns and then only on business, and says that she has no special desire to do so. She expects to marry a farmer, and does not care to go to work in a factory. She told me of a girl who came back from such a job with tuberculosis, which frightened many of the girls. For a husband, she wants a good worker, and would prefer one who comes from a different village. She seems to enjoy farm work and thinks that most girls prefer it to factory work." This young woman's attitudes are in sharp contrast, of course, to those of many, and certainly differ from those of Aki and Tamako, as we shall see.

The life she led is surely closer to the norm than the more colorful girl servants. "She went with her friends to the Yakushi festival. They left at 8:30 and were not back until six. She says that they stopped often, talked, visited, and took a siesta at the house of relatives of Shimosaka after lunch in Nakashima. She regards it as a big holiday, although she thinks that *o-bon* and New Year's are even bigger. Her family rises about five o'clock and retires about ten these summer days. During transplanting, they are up at four, home by eight, and to bed by eleven. In winter, it is easier, and they rise at seven and go to bed about nine."

It soon transpired that clandestine meetings and sexual affairs were not, in fact, limited to the servants of Suye families at all. "Yasuo asked me if I had seen Harue lately, and when I said I had not, he remarked that she gets letters from all over the region. [She was a servant, but] she also gets them from one of the teachers, the man so disliked by Aki and her friends." Harue, it developed, was by no means the only young woman who had run into trouble with schoolteachers. "As the girls went by from school, Mrs. Fujita pointed out the girl from Nakashima who was seduced by a teacher when she was a second-year student in higher school. Everyone knew about it, for someone had seen them together, and for a while the girl tells me that Harue had been involved with a teacher, too. When all the girls went home, she always stayed after hours at the school. It is now rumored that her sister 'is the same with all the teachers,' which is a large order, but one man who recently left his post was mentioned by name. As I watched the young teachers massaging the legs of their fourteen- and fifteen-year-old pupils at the athletic meets last year, I did wonder how they maintain a platonic relationship." Gradually, other stories came out. "Yasuo says that Noguchi and his present wife had an affair before they were married. I had to laugh, recalling her vigorous denial of my speculation that young people have affairs."

And, as the year went on, it developed that there were occasions other than festivals and work for young people to meet. "Today there was a *dōkyūkai* (same-class association) at school. Two years after graduation young people begin to hold these meetings—boys and girls together—twice a year, at *o-bon* and New Year. Right after graduation, they are considered too young. Soon they will be considered too old, and some of the girls will be married. The interesting thing is that even before the end of the second year after leaving school, the girls begin to feel shy and embarrassed when around boys. Some groups continue the meetings for three years or more, but usually the group breaks up after the girls turn eighteen.

"While a mixed group from Harue's class were having a good time on the first floor, the slightly older group of boys was upstairs getting drunk. One of them came down and said angrily, 'There are no girls in our group,' and two did go up for a while, but felt out of place and soon came down again. Many girls were either too busy to attend, for *o-bon* is a busy time, or were too shy. Tamako wanted to go, but was kept at home to help entertain callers. She raised many complaints to all the neighbors.

"Each girl contributes fifteen sen, each boy twenty. This is the one occasion on which boys really court girls and try to buy things that will please them. The boys buy *shōchū* for themselves, and cakes for the girls. This time the girls had suggested getting popsicles, which had been ordered by telephone from Menda. It turned out that they would have to place a larger order than they had planned if they wanted them delivered, so more than fifty were ordered with some money left over from a previous meeting. They were eaten up at the rate of five to eight each. Although they were intended only for the girls, only seven showed up, so the boys ate them too. Then they went out and bought some more on their own. It was reported that someone had gotten sick from eating so many.

"Before the popsicles arrived, the girls were sitting on the benches, while the boys gathered around, trying to persuade them to have a drink, and crowding them in general. Harue was very much in evidence, leading the girls, joking with the boys, and going into the teachers' room to talk to the man on duty. Among the boys, young Sato of Oade was the leader. He is a tall, fairly good-looking fellow, quite conceited. When I came along they asked me to take their picture, and sent someone to fetch my camera from the house. The whole idea of these meetings is to have a good time, but there is no real comradeship, because there are no other occasions on which boys and girls mix like this. After leaving school they seldom meet except for chance encounters. All went home about six."

"We asked Yasuo about 'night-life' in Suye, and he proved to know much less current gossip than I do. He tried to question Aki about it, but as usual she denied any knowledge of such matters. She did admit that men will come in at night if a door is left open for them, and said that Tamako meets Masayoshi down by the river, but added promptly, 'It is only to talk.' As to meetings after the bath, Yasuo said that young men used to grab at the girls as they came out because, 'They are still warm down there (gesturing) which is very nice.' "

John Embree provides a glimpse of the night life referred to. "About 10:00 P.M. I went out to watch the activities of the young men who had come to hang around the *dō* on this beautiful early September night. They ensconced themselves there, and soon after Aki went out to talk to them. Up by the Makino house a group of five or six had gathered, and as Tamako closed the shutters they joked with her. She refused to come out, so some of the boys peeked through the knotholes in the shutters to try to watch her prepare for bed, but after an hour or so they all wandered off home. Later Yasuo said that young men don't visit local women as much as they used to, but several go off to the Menda restaurants. If they have no money, they just exchange banter with the girls. One local rendezvous spot is the bridge in Kawaze. He recently saw the Hayashi servant there talking to the Maeno daughter."

John Embree's assistant was routinely suspected of sleeping with their maid, and young men were assumed to have a go at slipping into a house at night with a view to having intercourse with a daughter of the house or a female servant. [The practice is called *yobai*.] Such gossip was not all idle talk. "This morning, Aki told me with a smile that again this morning, about two-thirty, someone had come in the house. He managed to unfasten the kitchen door and came to lie down beside her. She hit him on the head and told him to get out, whereupon he muttered, 'Ouch!' (but she could not identify the voice), and sat up. She put on the light but could not recognize him because of the towel that covered his face. He left unidentified and unsatisfied, or so she says. 'Not big and not small.' She thinks he is from Kakui because all the young men here are small, except Tomio, but he is bigger than her visitor.

"To the young men gathered at the store, I said, 'Who came into our house last night?' They all became interested. 'What did he look like? When? Was he wearing glasses? Was it a thief?' I said that I thought it was not a thief. 'Ah, *mame no dorobō*,' said young Goto. [This is a pun. *Mame no dorobō* means a bean thief, but *mame na dorobō* means a hard-working or dedicated thief. Here *mame*, which also means 'bean,' is a symbol for vagina. Thus a *mame no dorobō* is a vagina thief.] Then Shimosaka Tatsuro said he knew who it was because three young men had stayed with him last night, and the one sleeping at the far end of the room had suddenly grabbed his towel and gone out. It was a fellow from Kawaze, he said, but he would mention no name, although all guessed except myself. Tatsuro went on to say that very few men in the village do such things. He described a similar outing in Imamura (either his or some other fellow's, I am not sure), where he got no further than the kitchen. Said Goto to another young man, 'Let's go out tomorrow night,' but Aki's brother came along just then and they dropped the subject at once. Tatsuro got up to leave and I asked where he was going. 'Home,' he said, 'I don't get along with this,' and held up his little finger, to indicate that he does not get along with girls.

"Aki was very interested in my account of this conversation with the young men and wanted to go over and ask herself, but was too timid to do so with so many people around. She asked me if her brother had heard the story and seemed relieved to learn that he had not. 'It's not that he would be angry, but he'd worry about it,' she said.

"Hayashi Shoko, who knows, absolutely refused to tell me who the fellow was. She maintained that Aki certainly knows, which I think is true. At last I asked, 'Is it the Takayama servant?' and Shoko replied, 'Perhaps so,' which is a sure yes. This evening I saw him go by from work with some other men from Kawaze. While they were exchanging greetings with me and Aki, he went right on with his hat over his face, red as a beet."

But Aki would not admit that she had recognized the young man, and "stoutly maintains that she is a virgin. 'If one is not a virgin at marriage, the husband will be angry.' She laughed when I said that he would not find out. '*Hazukashī*—I'm embarrassed,' she said. Questions about weddings, such as the names of the decorations on the bride's coiffure, embarrass her just as much as questions about sex. She did say, however, that there are many girls who sleep with boys, especially in Aso. 'But they don't do anything,' she maintained. It is so common in that hamlet because there are so many maids there, she explained. A daughter of the house cannot do such things because she sleeps with her mother.

"She refused to make any comment on what is done as a substitute for intercourse, but says that it does not occur. If it does, the girl almost always has a baby, so maybe she is right when she says, 'They don't do that. If they did, they'd have a baby right away.' (The Maeno girl is said to know all about such things. Actually, her sister did not have an affair with her employer, as his wife alleged, but Aki says she had to leave anyway because the woman is so jealous. She says it is a common occurrence for the master of the house to favor the maid and the wife takes it out on her even if the girl is innocent.) Of the Sawara-Amemiya case, she had thought they only went out together *asobi* and had been surprised to learn that they had been sleeping together. The same goes for Harue and her boyfriend Kawagoe. I notice that when she uses this word she never means intercourse. The boy just stays with the girl for a while. She recommended that I ask Reiko [an unmarried pregnant girl who made no secret of her condition; see pages 134–36] about these things."

The social code was, in fact, quite clear about the matter of contact between unmarried young women and men. "Aki says that people laugh if a girl and boy associate in public, so they never do, and in school there are even separate rooms for boys and girls to play in. She says that there is no pairing off and no falling in love. Of course, young Shimosaka is in love with that girl in Taragi, but such cases are quite rare, she says. They have been corresponding for two years now, and he keeps her picture. He asked his parents for permission to marry her, but they refused to take her as a bride because they have picked out someone else. She is willing to marry him, it seems, but he will have to obey his parents. She did remark that there are a lot of bastards in Hirayama, in the mountains. 'They make a lot of babies there,' she said, and thinks that it is because it is such a lonely place. That is also why boys and girls play together more there than they do in any of the other hamlets."

In her protestations, Aki was being more than a little disingenuous. "Some girls were gathered in the kitchen chatting with Aki. As a man went by they said, 'There goes Yuriko's husband.' They have heard that the Horis have been approached about giving their daughter as a bride, but did not know who was carrying on the negotiations. They gossiped on, kidding Aki about the young man who had offered to buy her a gift at the Yakushi festival, she protesting all the while. Later Toride was teasing her about his servant, so apparently she does have her little affairs.

"Some delivery boy is forever in our kitchen having a chat with her. He sprawls on the floor and either exchanges jokes with her or brings the latest news from town. Eventually other girls will gather, and there will be much laughter and mutual teasing. Bashful to open her dress in my presence, she is never bothered by a fellow, and I often find her with the front of her dress open, exposing her breasts to cool off while talking to one of these boys.

"It seems to me that the young men of the village who are so irresistible to the maids and the daughters of the house have a special conceited air about them. They are very dapper when dressed up, have a special self-satisfied smile, and make jokes with the girls. Perhaps they think of themselves as the sheiks of the village."

TAMAKO AND MASAYOSHI

One such young man was Shibata Masayoshi, resident of Taragi, who was involved with a Suye maid named Tamako. Their romance deserves extended presentation for the richness of the detail in which it is recorded, and for the light it throws on the phenomenon of the "love letter" in the society of the young in rural Japan of the time.

"Tonight there was an interesting revelation when Tamako, accompanied by another maid, Kimie, came over to have Aki write a letter for her. It was a love letter. Its object is Shibata Masayoshi, who lives in Taragi. When Tamako went to a festival there she met him, and this is how it happened. (Aki repeated the story with relish, word for word as she had heard it, she said.) While Tamako was watching some acrobats, someone standing behind her moved beside her and stepped on her foot. 'Ouch,!' she exclaimed. 'Excuse me,' said he. 'No, no. It's all right,' she had replied, and the acquaintance was made. After that they went *asobi* for three hours and parted very much in love. He comes from a family that runs a small shop and is a middle-school graduate. ('And Tamako only went through grammar school!' This from Aki.)

"Yesterday came the first letter, which caused considerable excitement. Although it came by mail, the postman had been asked to hand it directly to Tamako. The letter read: 'It has become warm.' ('Just introductory talk,' observed Aki.) 'You must be very busy with the silkworms.' ('More of the same,' said Aki.) Then came the real stuff, about how much he had enjoyed their three hours together, and how he wants to see her again.

"She came here for help with the answer because she cannot write it by herself. 'I have not written anything since I left school,' she said. Nonetheless, she had scribbled out a draft, and Aki, amidst much giggling by all, copied it out for her. Because he had written his name on the envelope in roman letters, she made me write hers that way too. At the end of the letter Aki thought it would be appropriate to close with a song or verse, but Tamako did not know any, and thought it useless anyway. As an alternative, she made me write both their names in roman letters at the bottom of the sheet. After the girls had left, Aki showed me the draft. In it Tamako talks about a sleepless night and the pleasure of their meeting, asks him to visit her when he is free, and to enclose a photograph with his reply. For the closing, Aki had recommended *abayo*, a typical ending for an intimate letter, but Tamako had scratched it out. 'Just write *sayonara*,' she insisted, but Aki had left in the *samishiki* part that means 'in loneliness.' Now, she said, the letters will fly back and forth at a great rate.

"Aki says that she gets no letters from boys, though many come from her girl friends. She showed me some of these, which are not very newsy and rather formal. Other girls do get letters from boys, she said, and named names. The Shimosaka girl hears from a fellow at the place she worked last year, where she made some friends. The Toyama girl, she had just learned, gets letters from the young servant at Takayama's. Children carry these letters and they, of course, spread the news. (I doubt if much comes from all this correspondence, since most of the young people who write to each other never meet. It is said, however, that Tamako plans to see her beau when she goes to town for the night vegetable market. And, to be sure, there are many bastards.)"

Some time later, "I asked Tamako if she had received an answer to her letter. She got all flustered and ran off, calling me *baka*. Later, from across the yard, she said no, and laughed some more. Letter-writing is a mania, and not only between boys and girls. This morning the Suzuki Tamezo nursemaid was painstakingly composing one to Miki-chan, the

Hayashi girl who could not hold a job here and is employed by a family in town. They are friends."

Tamako had heard from Masayoshi and "she told me that he came to Suye *asobi*, but she was too busy with the silkworms and excused herself. He wanted her to go to the movies at the school that night, but she could not. She says, 'He is not a nice man. Drinks a lot. Just a pretty face, but really a no-good.' " But there was more to it than she was willing to let on and the love affair soon became an open secret. "She was teased about it today at Makino's. Tamako was saying that there was nothing between her and Masayoshi. Otome shot back, 'Nothing at all. You're just lovers (*koibito*), that's all.' "

The letters did continue to fly back and forth, as Aki had predicted. "Tamako stopped by tonight with Fumie and they discussed letters with Aki, talking about their own and others. Tamako had one from her young man and another from some fellow in Shimonoseki, which sounded very much like those Mrs. Tanimoto told me about yesterday, when I asked her. 'Of course, we wrote them,' she said. 'Everybody does. Did you not write letters before you married your husband?' She asked this very much as one might say, 'Didn't you go out with other men before you married?' In closing, you wrote, just as Tamako had, 'Please answer,' and usually one came. Or you wrote, 'Please come to see me,' and he came. 'You went to plays together or just *asobi*. If it was a serious case, you would have an affair, but not as a rule.' There were some set phrases, some of which she quoted. 'Your skin is as white as bean curd.' 'On your soft arm to rest and watch the rising of the full moon.' 'No matter what I do, my thoughts are with you.' "

Both the teenage girls and the older women agreed that writing love letters was romantic and exciting. Aki's summation of what it all came down to is therefore all the more touching. "When I asked what young people do when they meet if they do not make love, she said, 'Just talk. It's fun if the talk is interesting.' Writing letters, talking to young men, being in love with someone—all that is fun. It is amusing when you are young, and so you do it, but when the time comes to marry you stop it, discard all the letters, and follow the wishes of your parents. That is quite a different matter. You do not expect to marry the man you correspond with, and love and marriage are not thought of as being related. Of course, she added, marriage is a bit scary, but you expect to marry when the time comes."

Boys were generally under the same constraints, as we see from John Embree's journal. "Last night young Shimosaka read me some love letters, one from a girl in Taragi and a couple from a girl in Shoya. He seems to like the Shoya girl very much. She wrote a letter to him when he was ill, saying how sorry she was. Shimosaka said that if it were not for his father's objections, he would bring the girl into his house and marry her. He approves of big, expensive weddings, and says that without them one feels no change after marriage. He refers to his former sweethearts as girls he liked 'when I was young.' He is now twenty-one. Not only is his father opposed to his marrying the Shoya girl, his mother is now actively searching for a bride for him."

Some time later, "young Shimosaka went to Nakashima to visit one of his relatives and take them some fish. The actual reason for the visit was to see a certain maidservant who works there. It seems that his Shoya girlfriend is no longer so attractive to him. Now, he says, he is more serious, so does not go out with her any more. He met the new girlfriend at the Yakushi festival last year (just as Tamako met her Masayoshi at the Dainichi festival in Tsuiji) and later recommended to the Nakashima relatives that they employ her. They did, and he goes to visit them [and her] as often as he can." It was about this time that people began to say that "Mrs. Shimosaka is getting along with her son rather badly these days because of all his love affairs. She is worried and is actively searching for a bride, but he is adamant in his refusal to marry yet."

Tamako was not yet ready for marriage, either. "There was much whispering among the girls today because Tamako told the other maid with whom she shares a room for sleeping that Masayoshi had been there last night. This sounds implausible, because the house gets shut up very tight—once both girls had to spend the night with us because they came back too late from Menda and could not get in. Masayoshi was by yesterday afternoon with a gift for Tamako, and they spoke at the well. Mrs. Tanimoto suggests that they went off and slept together somewhere else. The matter was further discussed by her and the girls. She assured them that they, too, and especially Fumie, would soon start attracting young men and having affairs.'

Several days later, "the nursemaids and Tamako and young Ouchi gathered in front of the house. Tamako whispered with Aki, and they later disappeared behind the house, where Aki helped her decipher the letter from Masayoshi. It accused her of having another man, since she talked about parting in her last letter, and wanted to know how she can think of going to work in Tontokoro as a maid when she knows that he is jealous of the Hayashi man who lives there. He wishes he could die. Everyone knows about these letters and teases her about them. Asked the Ouchi boy, 'Tamako, did you get another gift from Masayoshi?' She, of course, denied it."

The reference to another gift, however, suggests that the affair between the two was progressing nicely. "Yesterday Tamako went out with Masayoshi again. Evidently theirs is quite an exceptional case. 'It's really very amusing,' said Aki. He asks, 'Tamako, do you want anything? Some water?' and will get her whatever she wants. 'Would you like to have something to eat? I'll get it.' It seems that at their last meeting, he bought her a comb and a jar of face cream, as well as many popsicles. Mrs. Fujita said to Tamako, 'He is your *suichan* (sweetheart),' but she protested, 'No, no. I went alone,' when I asked her with whom she went to the festival. Later she came by Fujita's and told us all about the gifts she had received from him."

More commonly, she denied everything. "While working with the silkworm trays, Tamako complained about something or other. The woman told her that she needs a husband, to which she made her usual protestation, 'I will never marry.' " But on the next holiday, "all the young people went up to Yakushi in Uemura. Many children were taken by their mothers or grandparents, most walking. Before eight in the morning all the girls— daughters of the house, maids, nursemaids—dressed up in their best kimono and were off with their parasols." John Embree wrote, "As we went along, one young man riding by on a bicycle called out as he passed and tried to pull up a young lady's parasol to get a better look at her face. There were many giggles and he was off down the road. For the most part, however, unmarried men and women kept to their own friendship groups. Dates must have been made ahead of time, for Tamako met her Masayoshi and was there with him all day. When I commented on this, some of the women pointed out how attractive Tamako has become and how she suddenly has grown up. 'This is the first year she has been getting love letters and she has gone completely crazy,' said Mrs. Fujita."

They continued to meet. "Tamako told Mrs. Fujita that Masayoshi asked her to come to see the souls off in Hitoyoshi at *o-bon*. He told her that she need bring no money, for he will take care of all the expenses. She replied that her kimono will not be ready for *o-bon*, and he said she could have it made later, it did not matter. He was here for the movie, it seems, and when she went out with the child she was tending the young men called his name, which was a signal for him to go to meet her."

John Embree's journal provides some further information on this meeting. "A great many young men and women were present at the movie last night. Many of the former turned up quite late, about ten-thirty or so. Their purpose was to see the girls rather than the movie, and some picked fights. Tamako left about 11:15 with the Mori nursemaid. They picked up two fellows in the shade of some trees on this bright moonlit night. They laughed and talked together. The two fellows, to avoid being identified, covered their faces with towels as they passed on the path, and then one started playing his harmonica." It was a popular pastime for the young men to hang around the *dō* or outside the house of a young woman and play the flute or the harmonica.

Who were these young men who disguised themselves as they passed? "At the outdoor movie, some men came without their wives, and some women came alone. Tamako came with little Taro-chan on her back, raising much laughter and remarks such as 'My, how fast she has made a baby!' Later on some young men amused themselves by standing at the entrance and calling out, 'Shibata Masayoshi is wanted,' to see her reaction. I had thought that he was not there, but perhaps he was, for there is talk about his getting into a fight with young Irie. As for Tamako, she at first said that he was not there and later slipped and said that he had left early. She also says that she did not see much of the movie and had to leave because Taro-chan cried and bothered other people. But I saw the child sleeping soundly on her back and heard no crying at all. Some say she slipped out, with the excuse that she had to go to the toilet, when Masa-yoshi's name was called."

There had been a fight at the movie, but Masayoshi was not in-volved. Nonetheless, it did have to do with a girl. "The second feature, all about a stolen sword which involved many fights, affected the young men, two of whom began punching each other until they were pulled apart. It is said that they will fight again. Aki got the story out of one of the group of young men who intervened to stop it. Sato Norio had been exchanging letters with a girl from Kakui (presumably the Maeno daughter) and subsequently Irie's son had come between them. The two have been fighting since last year some time. All the boys enjoyed it greatly, and were over at Irie's today, talking about it. Not many people witnessed the fight, having left as soon as the movie ended. I am told that in the old days young men fought a great deal, usually over women. There were fights between hamlets and with groups from other villages. In contrast, said Mrs. Amano, 'Young men and women today are very well behaved (*otona-shiku natte kita*).' "

"Some days later I met Sato Norio at an entertainment at the school and talked to him about the fight. He said, 'Irie accosted me with a big knife, but I won without effort.' Another young man, standing by, wanted to know whether the fight was 'over this' and raised his little finger to indicate a woman."

About a month later Masayoshi did become involved in a serious dispute with some of the young men of Suye. From John Embree's journal: "Last night toward the end of the movie, a row began outside the canvas wall. In no time at all the young men who had been inside watching went out, and others ran up from all directions. It seems that for some reason Hayashi Fumio had hit Shibata Masayoshi with a rock. Masayoshi had retaliated by hitting Fumio on the head with a *geta* and cutting him rather badly. Most of the young men knew only about this latter event. Young Shimosaka went to Fumio's aid; he is always ready for a fight. Then the postman, who like Masayoshi lives in Taragi, came to his aid. The fight soon stopped and Fumio and all the young men of Suye who were present swarmed off down the path by the *dō* saying that Masayoshi must be punished. They determined to gang up on him later and administer a sound thrashing. The mob spirit was very evident as this group of twenty to thirty young men with towels around their heads milled about in the moonlight. They asked Fumio how he was hit, whether he was hurt, etc., and he seemed to expand under all this attention. (He is not well liked, but Suye men rally to the defense of one of their number when he is attacked by an outsider like Masayoshi. Another fact is probably that he has won Tamako's heart, and it is quite possible that the young men of the village resent her picking this outsider. Furthermore, when he comes to visit her, he is very high-hat toward the local young men. Some say that the night of the first movie a month ago he also got into trouble.) Aki says that she did not leave the movie when the fight started, but that Tamako was very worried."

Then, quite suddenly, there was a dramatic change in the Tamako-Masayoshi affair. "Tamako says that her boyfriend has just got married, but in all the flood of stories it is hard to find the truth. Still, that is what she said. 'He wrote to me to say that they have found a bride for him, and that she is not very good looking. He asked me to come to see him, but I have no time for such things.' I asked if she is not sorry. 'No. I don't like that man, and anyway, I am going to Yahata.' Then followed a long story about how her brother has invited her to join him there, and how her aunt wants her to come to her house in Moji, and how she thinks she will accept her aunt's offer, for she was born and raised in Moji. Yes, she will go there and stop this farm work, which makes one's hands so ugly. The next day, it was a different story. She will finish out her contract here and go to her brother in Yahata. Still, she likes Moji, and perhaps she will go visit the family graves there after she has moved to Yahata. Day-dreaming is the girl's favorite pastime, because she so dislikes the heavy work that she has to do constantly, for the Makinos seldom give a holiday. 'I will stop going out now,' she said dramatically. 'No more movies, nothing.' "

"I talked to Tamako yesterday. She was busy writing a letter, supposedly to her brother in Yahata. She says that something is wrong with her and that she does not yet menstruate, even though she is sixteen or seventeen years old. I asked her if she had lost her virginity already, and she laughed and said, 'I don't do that sort of thing.' She continues to insist that she and Masayoshi only talk during their rendezvous, but did not deny that he comes to see her at bath time. She pretends to care nothing for him still, saying, 'I have no use for him. He is no good.' "

AKI AND HER AFFAIRS

We do not directly encounter this couple again, but Tamako is a central figure in a gathering storm of gossip about her good friend Aki, who was about the same age. "I was up at the Makino's, where Aki and other girls were visiting Tamako. They all teased Aki until she blushed and giggled, protesting, 'Arya, arya! Uso bakkari! Iya da yo! [Oh, oh! All lies! Stop it!],' and so on. They made up some songs about her and imaginary conversations with some boy from Menda. They urged her to sing or tell a story (because she is no good at either) and teased her about the Shirayama boy who always brings her home from her trips to town. And letters were discussed. Sato said that he used to write such letters, ending with 'until death,' referring to Tamako's letter, which was mentioned by Mrs. Makino much to Aki's amusement and great embarrassment. They asked me to confirm that she is a good story-teller, but she at once contradicted them, saying, 'At Embree-san's one never talks. Everyone goes off into a separate room by oneself and studies.' They said, 'Then you should be glad to have a chance to talk—tell us a story,' but they could not get her to say anything, amid much laughter."

This good–natured scene increased the suspicions already forming. "I don't know if Aki is above having affairs with young men. Yesterday, as I approached the house, I saw Yasuo give a signal of warning, and Aki darted out of the bath, shutting the door, which did not conceal the presence of two young men inside. Today one of them stopped by to talk to her on his way home from work." She was clearly considered a desirable conquest by some of the young men of the village. "As soon as they found out that Aki and I are alone, with John gone off to Gokanoshō, the young men never left the vicinity of our house, but gathered around, banged on the door, and went behind the house. The Hayashis wanted to know what was up, and offered to come over and spend the night with us. The young men went back to Uchida's and sat around there for a while, but they were soon back. I heard people coming and going late at night, but could see no one when I went out to look. They may only have been the last guests to leave the *kōgin* at Ochiai's."

Nonetheless, it seemed unlikely that Aki could be engaged in any serious romantic affairs. "When discussing letter-writing, she giggles as if she were discussing real love affairs. She also giggles when talking about the three young men for whom brides are being sought just now." But then came direct word from Tamako, who said that "Aki is having a love affair with a boy from Tontokoro. They exchange gifts and last night she met him at the *dō*. To me Aki had explained her absence by saying that she had to see Tamako home, but Tamako says that she returned with Fumie, leaving Aki alone in the *dō*. ('Still waters . . .' it is true. I now recall that she looked very worried the other day when she thought that this same boy had called while she was out.) Said Tamako, 'She told me that just as I love Masayoshi, she loves this man.' "

This warning suggested that something clearly was afoot. "Last night Aki said that she would have to go home for a minute and seemed anxious to get away, not even waiting for the delivery boy to stop by. Later I went past her house on the way to the store and did not see her there. She did not return until midnight, and this morning offered no explanation—both of which are unusual events. Tonight at supper, I casually asked, 'Did you go to Menda?' She blushed and said no. I did not press the point, but think friend Tamako was right."

"Since every time I say a man is good-looking, Aki disagrees, we decided to compare notes last night. She had no hesitation about several men, and said that she does not like the looks of the servant at Tamaki's or the man who made Koyo-chan pregnant. 'I don't like round faces; long ones are better.' Suddenly she laughed and said, 'How about the milkman? I do like that one!' When I accused her of having an affair with the laundryman, she laughed and later I heard her repeating my remark to him. He is forever hanging around."

Several weeks later, when two young men just back from military service in Manchuria and Taiwan were visiting the Embrees, Aki remarked that "she prefers city men to farmers because 'their skin is so white.' Later the men went upstairs to have some cakes, and invited her to come along. The last time they were here she had refused for a while, before finally joining them. Today she went at once," obviously more at ease with young men by this time.

Festivals such as *o-bon* were favorite occasions for rendezvous, for young people were relatively unsupervised on such holiday outings to temples and places of amusement in town. "Earlier in the evening a bunch of young girls gathered on the bridge, singing. Young men in a boat just below them played the harmonica and made jokes. They later came up and joined the girls. If one asks, a girl will say that she went to the bridge 'to cool off.' Aki was not in this group, although she left the house about the time they assembled. She must have been at her home for a while, but what she did later until midnight remains a mystery. 'Went here and there to see the ancestors off,' she said this morning. To my question if she was alone, she replied, 'One does not *asobi* alone.'" On the next evening, "crowds of young men came from all directions, as far away as Shoya and Fukada. They had heard that there is to be a dance at the temple. They just hung around. Aki had a long chat with one of them, a boy from Ishizaka. They were at the *dō*, he sitting down, she standing beside him. Two others were sitting a little way off, discussing the last *dōsōkai* [graduates' association] who had been there, etc."

Within a few days, "I asked Aki who she was writing to. 'To Fumiko-san,' she said, without batting an eyelash. The next morning when Fumie picked up a magazine with the letter in it, Aki grabbed at it at once and refused to show it to anyone, which proves that it is not to her girl friend in Osaka. Either she or Tamako is not telling the truth. Tamako keeps telling me about the numerous letters from many men that come to Aki, and about her relationship with one of them in particular, while Aki just as convincingly denies it all."

And then, as so often happened among the adults, gossip found its way back to its subject. "Tamako, having spread stories to Jun-chan, the Araki girl, is in trouble because Jun repeated them to Aki. Whereupon Aki, very mad, wrote a letter to Tamako telling her to stop spreading lies. Strangely enough, Aki's young man also wrote to Tamako to the same effect. Be it said that he appeared last night at the market, and Aki had known all day that she would be going there with me. In my presence she always likes to pretend that she knows nothing of such doings. If a girl says something about Masayoshi, for example, she asks, 'Which one?' just as if she has no idea that it is Tamako's boyfriend who is referred to every time.

"Said Tamako, 'Why should she be angry with me? All young people talk and spread stories around like I do.' But Aki is really angry, and told me this morning, 'I don't want to talk to her. She tells nothing but lies.' The nurse at Makino's has repeated to her my conversation with Tamako."

Aki's troubles did not end with Tamako's gossip. "When I came home about five, there had been a fight. No one would tell me what was up. Aki said that she knew nothing about it, but I could see she was lying. Kikuko, the Mori nursemaid, was weeping outside, and the other nursemaids were noncommittal. Eventually I figured out that the fight had involved Aki, Jun, and Kikuko. It seems that Kikuko had made some remark about Aki, and Jun had repeated it to her. Aki got mad and scolded Kikuko. Said Mrs. Mori, very justly, 'At her age other girls are married, but Aki still plays with these children and takes them too seriously.' The next day only Jun was in evidence, and in the morning Kikuko came around briefly. A letter that fell from her pocket proved to be a lengthy apology addressed to Aki."

The situation became more complicated and worsened. "The girls are still on fighting terms. Aki does not speak to Tamako (whose Masayoshi still comes to visit her, and did not get married after all), nor to Kikuko. The story is now a little different. It seems that Kikuko said to Jun, while they were doing the laundry, 'Is it true that Aki is having an affair?' Just at that moment, the young man in question happened to pass by and assumed that he was meant to hear the question. Aki was very annoyed when she heard about it. Tonight she admitted that she is not on speaking terms with Kikuko. The Moris are down on her for picking a fight with such a young girl. 'She should be teaching them, not fighting with them,' said Mrs. Mori. Then old lady Mori got going. First she said that she just sits and takes everything in without paying much attention to it or saying anything. But then she hastened to add that it is very bad of Aki to pick a fight with their nursemaid. The Moris and the Uchidas (Aki's family) were both outsiders in Suye once and so had become close friends. The Moris have always been good to Aki. 'Why, if she starts such trouble, it will come to involve the parents,' she continued, and suggested that she knows a thing or two herself. 'Why, that youngest child of Mrs. Uchida's is really Sato's, not her husband's.' After the outburst she subsided."

Despite the gossip, "Aki steadfastly denies having any traffic with young men. When I asked her where young couples go *asobi*, she said she does not know, but thought they might go to the school. She looked surprised when I said, 'Isn't one of the teachers there all the time?', as if to say, why should a teacher interfere? I suggested they might go to the mountains; she did not think so. I brought up the three nights she had been out late. 'To send off the spirits, we all went on the boats and *asobi* together,' was all she would say in answer to that. 'I never go out with a man alone,' she said. I gave up. Yet, both the milkman and the Ariyoshi delivery boy spend hours in the kitchen writing something and then showing it to her."

Eventually, "Aki and Kikuko fixed up their fight, but Tamako is still down on Aki, whom she calls a big liar. She adds, after registering a few more complaints, 'Well, after another year I won't have anything more to do with her, for I am fed up with Suye people anyhow and will go back to my home in Moji.' According to Kimie, Masayoshi came to see Tamako a few days ago during her bath, but she denies having seen him. 'All lies made up by Aki, and those girls must hide the letters they talk so much about, for I haven't seen any!' "

Letters continued to preoccupy Aki, as a matter of fact. "She has finished her kimono. At night she makes up things that she writes down, usually something very poetical. Last time it was about some Kyushu men and women in love. She assured me that none of it had happened, but nevertheless refused to show it to me. She did read it aloud, very confused and almost in a whisper. Then she writes make-believe letters, which she hides away."

"The girls are all excited about the coming Hachiman festival. Every time the fireworks went off, Fumie would exclaim, 'Let's go at once!' They left in the afternoon. The Mori nursemaid, who had been told she could not go, was very annoyed, but at the last minute arrived all joyful because she had secured permission. Aki seemed to have little interest in the girls' plans, and I did not see her leave the house, although she must have done so about five. She had told me that she would be going to visit her aunt in Menda, 'who is not a real aunt, but someone who grew up with my mother.' She had no idea where they had grown up together. I think she was establishing an alibi." And so it seemed, in light of subsequent developments.

"Aki went out again until midnight and as usual refuses to offer any information. Apropos her outings, there was an interesting conversation at Mori's today. Mrs. Mori's mother was visiting there, and the children were all off to Ebisu-san, school being closed at noon today for that purpose. The women were talking about the desire of the young people to go to all the festivals. Old lady Mori repeated what she had told her nursemaid. 'You cannot go out all the time. You have work to do.' Mrs. Uchida [Aki's mother] broke in. 'Yes, it is the same with Aki. When she comes back home next year, she is going to stay put, and there won't be this business of going here and there all the time. When a girl is working outside [that is, in another house, for other people] there is no controlling her. I told her that she could not go to Hachiman-san without the Embrees, but she went off anyway without saying a word. Later no one saw her in Menda.' (This morning a worried Mrs. Uchida stopped me on the road to ask if I were going to Taragi, and if Aki had asked to go with me. At that moment Aki passed by, and her mother called out 'Aki-chan, she says she is not going tonight, so you cannot go either.' Her daughter called back angrily, 'I am not going anyway.' Later she said to me 'That fool!') Mrs. Uchida continued, 'I know what it is like to be talked about, and I won't have her running around like she does.' The other women agreed that girls are a problem, and that the sooner they are married, the better. (The other day some women were saying that before a girl is twenty, any number of people ask for her, but after that they stop, and it is very hard to get a girl a husband if she is too old.)"

For her part, Aki had other plans. "She was talking today of going to Kumamoto, but now says she will go to Osaka. People do not come asking for her as a bride, she says, because they know she will be gone next year. Her mother said, however, that her elder brother considers such a trip a waste of money, so he will not let her go anywhere."

And then, "Aki was out again last night. At first she tried a ruse. Did I not want to take some issues of *Kingu* with me for the train? If so, she would go fetch some copies from home, where she had taken them. I assured her that I did not want them. Then, 'Well, I shall go up there for just a moment then.' This moment lasted until two in the morning, and I am sure she enjoyed the beautiful moonlight. Today I spent most of the day trying to bully her into confessing where she had gone last night, feeling some responsibility for her activities. She made up one fib after another with a straight face, and I still have no idea what she did. At first she said she went home and assured me that she had seen Sano on the way, although he denies it. Finally I said I would ask her mother. 'Ask her,' she said. Later she told me that she had gone to Menda to the movie house called *Kurabu* (Club), but would not say with whom. It was not that delivery boy—she dared me to ask him when he comes here next—nor was it the fellow she had a fight with a couple of days ago. (When the delivery boy arrived this afternoon, both of them looked a little self-conscious, and said nothing, while Fumie began to fidget the minute she saw him coming.) Not long ago the Toride and Makino nursemaids said, 'We hate men, but Fumie loves them. She comes running up as soon as some delivery boy arrives. The Ariyoshi one is her special favorite, not Aki's.' At last Aki said she had gone with some fellow from Shirayama, with whom she had made the date by letter. He brought her home on his bicycle, she said, and denied that they did anything but talk." The mystery of Aki's nights out was never solved.

Premarital Pregnancies

There was good reason for the parents of unmarried girls to worry about the possibility of their becoming pregnant as the result of love affairs. Nonetheless, "Mrs. Kato thinks that the number of bastards is smaller nowadays, although she admits there are some still. It is always known when a child is a bastard, she says, and it is not a good situation. If the father is a good man, he will provide for such a child through school, but some men reject any connection with the woman and the child, which makes everyone very unhappy. The children are branded at school and often teased. City people are more careful about their daughters, she said, but farmers are careless and many accidents happen."

"About illegitimate children, Mrs. Tanimoto made a very interesting comment. She thinks it is very hard for them all, but worse for boys than girls. The boys are more likely to be very embarrassed later in life when they go to school and enter military service. She must be expressing a commonly held opinion, for I remember that a woman in Nakashima said, 'How lucky it is that the Shiraki daughter had a girl.' " [See pages 136–39.]

Within a few months after settling in Suye, it became clear that there were an unusually large number of illegitimate children in Hirayama. "Our maid thinks it is because it is so lonely there [Hirayama is the most isolated of the hamlets of Suye, in the mountains], and that for the same reason girls and boys play together more than they do here. She assumes that the parents reproach the girls who get pregnant, but there is nothing they can do about it. 'Once the baby is in the belly, that's all there is to it.' She knows one eighteen-year-old who has two babies by an unknown father, and she thinks it must be some man from outside who is working for another family in Hirayama. 'They must meet at night and make babies,' she said, but all these cases are exceptions, according to her, and such things should not happen."

But with the continuing reminders that such things do happen, after all, the matter is brought up in several conversations. "Sato was in for a while yesterday. He says that the superior morals of young girls today are explained by their better education, which emphasizes the value of virtue and raises the general level of morality. That is why there are fewer bastards today than there were in the old days. He also thinks that girls have more common sense now, due to the efforts of the schools and the Young Women's Association, where they read books and newspaper articles that explain things to them. As a result it is not so easy to get them into trouble any more.

"In the old days maids, girls of poor education and little common sense, were easy prey for men, but now these girls have learned about the value of chastity and the importance of retaining their virginity until marriage. I remarked that Japanese houses hardly encourage secret assignations, but he said that maids and male servants always occupy separate quarters away from the main house, so it is easy for them to meet."

In John Embree's journal, there is a further conversation with this man, who says that "such affairs are less frequent in Nakashima and Kawaze than in the other hamlets because the young men in those two places are 'more serious.' Of course, servants who come from elsewhere don't count. In all of this social distinctions come out very clearly." Indeed they do, as is revealed in a further conversation he had with the Embrees. "He thinks that such affairs are mostly prevalent among the servants, as I found out when we said that Harue could very well be the next unmarried girl to get pregnant. He was shocked [because she comes from a good family]. But when we mentioned Tamako as a candidate for next year [she comes from a family less well regarded], he laughed and said, 'This year, I think.' He quickly added that his own sisters are still virgins, in response to our suggestion that there may well be none over nineteen years old here."

The viewpoint of this twenty-eight-year-old man is confirmed by a woman of forty-five. "Although she maintains that she married as a virgin and had no love affairs, her accounts of the behavior of girls of her generation differ somewhat from those given by other women. It was then not so desirable that a girl be a virgin at marriage, and all girls lost their virginity about the age of eighteen. 'That is the best age,' she confided, 'for the later one loses it, the worse it is.' Defloration usually happened during some secret meeting, when the young couple wandered off from a gathering or went out strolling at night. But nowadays girls are different, she says, and are told that they must keep their virginity until marriage. As a rule they do. In her day, she says, few babies resulted from such encounters, but sometimes accidents did happen, which was unfortunate. (I wonder how correct this information is, considering the number of local bastards.)"

The lack of importance attached to virginity in the bride in the old days had other ramifications as well. "There used to be a lot of 'secret babies' because the girls were ignorant, but today there are few. In the same way, there were many divorces and remarriages in the old days, but now things have changed. Formerly the marriage ceremony was extremely simple and did not mean much in itself, so if a girl disliked something or other in her new home, she could go back to her family and start over again. Virginity in a bride did not seem important. That is why you find so many old women who have been married so many times. But now weddings have become elaborate affairs, and so girls take them less lightly and do not seek divorce so readily."

Be that as it may, the girl who was about to bear a child out of wedlock was certain to be the object of frantic efforts on the part of the parents to find her a husband. "Sato confirms my suspicions about the Maeno-Kuwagiri union. He says that the girl is not very bright and has a funny eye, but that the chief reason for the marriage was that she had a secret baby by one of the male servants when he was home on leave from the army. Even though the baby died [making it unnecessary to find a man who would take both the girl and her illegitimate child] it was hard for her parents to find a husband for her, so they accepted this low marriage."

Sometimes the young man "does the honorable thing. Everyone agrees that Miyamori's son, who is now in the navy, was married so young because he had an affair with the girl and they were afraid she was pregnant. As it turned out she was not, but they are married anyway. Everyone says it is a mistake to take a bride before you go into military service [because you have to leave her alone for a long time and returned soldiers and sailors are often very dissatisfied with life in the village and with village women]. This girl's older sister also had an affair, and after she got pregnant at eighteen, she married the man and they had three more children."

KOYO-CHAN

One of the liveliest issues for the gossips of Suye was the pregnancy of Koyo-chan, the unmarried Shimoda daughter. "While we were all sitting at the *dō*, one of the girls whispered to Fumio that she had heard for sure that Koyo-chan is pregnant. He does not like to gossip, and it took a long time for me to get the story out of them. It seems that Koyo-chan had gone to Menda to get an abortion, and now she and the young man are going to be married. According to Suzuko the man does not like her so very much, but she likes him and went after him just as she had done with other boys since her elementary school days. Everybody knows about it, for she is four months pregnant and is not around any more. Suzuko does not approve, for she thinks that girls should not chase men. Nevertheless, she said, 'It's too bad for him, though. He will have to marry her now.'

"Mrs. Tanimoto, on the other hand, thinks that it is a very nice arrangement for him, to be able to marry so high, and too bad for Koyo-chan, who is from a good family and has some education. She said that the romance has been going on for three years now. She used to see them talking together very often and knew that something was up. Koyo-chan is so much in love with him that she has rejected three other marriage proposals. I asked who the man was. It turns out to be one of the Sato servants, although they told me only after I had threatened to go to Oade, where Koyo-chan's family lives, and find out for myself."

Later, in Oade, "I got little satisfaction on the subject. To my question, they replied, 'She is at home,' but on my way back I heard old man Harada tell his son not to discuss the matter with others. When I asked Mrs. Tanimoto about it later, she said, 'She is not seen anywhere most probably because she is ashamed to come out.' "

As it happened, however, old lady Tanno was quite willing to discuss the news. "She said that Koyo-chan is pregnant and that she never leaves the house now. Wauchi and Mori have been over to talk to the man who is responsible—he is thirty-three or thirty-four years old—but no definite agreement has been reached. As I stopped at Wauchi's, I found that they were having tea over at the Shimoda's, so I went in, too. The Sawaras have been visiting there since yesterday. Koyo-chan came in with the Sawara baby and promptly left the room again. She is quite distinctly pregnant, which blows up the abortion story I have heard. (Mrs. Tanimoto had even suggested that a relative of Wauchi, an amateur doctor, was to perform it.) Koyo-chan definitely tried to stay out of sight, but the rest of the family did not look very different or depressed. The child's father quite definitely shows no signs of depression either, for I saw him working on the shed the other day.

"Later in the day I saw young Ouchi, who works for Shimoda, on a visit to his family. He says that all know about it and have known for some time, but since it became noticeable she has stopped appearing in public and for a while would not even come out to eat. It is only in the last two or three days that she has resumed eating with the rest of the family. When I asked him if her father is mad, he replied, 'No, not especially angry.' "

In pursuit of news of further developments, "I asked Mrs. Maeno whether it is true about Koyo-chan. She said yes, she has heard about it, but for about a month now Koyo-chan has not been out of the house. No one knows what is going to happen. She thinks that maybe Mori had gone to talk to the man the other day. 'A great pity, isn't it?' she asked. (Least close in this cluster of houses, she was the only person who would commit herself to certain knowledge of Koyo-chan's condition.)

"Old lady Mori says it is very sad about Koyo-chan, but she will not admit that young Mori [her son] went to act as go-between for the girl and the man responsible for her pregnancy. She does think that for some reason the man will not marry. It is hard with girls, she said, and told me a story about two girls who had worked in a factory. Both had got pregnant and had to have abortions. I do not know who they were; it all happened a long time ago when someone else was living at the place that is now a shop."

In one respect at least, old lady Mori was wrong. "Speaking about how unpleasant it is to have sexual relations with a man one dislikes [this is a reference to girls being married to men they have never seen before], Mrs. Tanimoto said that Koyo-chan herself refuses to marry because she is in love with the man who got her pregnant. She quoted the old marriage song:

O-chō me-chō
sakazuki yori mo
suita anata no
chawan-zake
(Instead of exchanging wedding-cups of sake,
I'd rather be drinking it with you from any old cup.)[1]

Then Koyo-chan was gone, some said to Hitoyoshi, others that she had hidden herself even further away from Suye. One young married woman said without qualification that Koyo-chan had gone to Miyazaki to have an abortion. "Sato called last night and we tried to get more

---

1. Given in Embree, *Japanese Peasant Songs*, p. 83. The translation and note accompanying it there seem to me to blunt the point of this plaintive ditty.

information out of him about Koyo-chan. He was willing to discuss the matter, but in the end said that he knows nothing about Miyazaki, insisting that she is in Hitoyoshi at the Sawaras. When I said that she and the man should get married, he said that it is a puritanical idea that a girl should necessarily marry her first lover. He thought they should break off, in fact, because 'he cannot feed her.' As for the baby, he thought there would be none, but when I objected that an abortion in the fifth month of pregnancy is dangerous and asked which hospital she will go to, he replied only that 'She is in Hitoyoshi.' The idea that if a couple is in love they should be allowed to marry did not even arise. Instead, he thought that as a rule such a girl will marry a young widower or a divorced man or a second son [rather than an heir and successor]. He was clearly shocked by the whole business, however, and said that he had really been surprised when he first heard of it."

Even with the girl away and the word of her plight general knowledge, the people of her hamlet would say little about the affair. "While anyone in Kakui discusses Koyo-chan's pregnancy, over where her family lives all I can get for an answer is, 'They did not tell us where she went.' Only this morning I got that very answer from old lady Wauchi, who said she knows nothing about it. And when I brought up Reiko [another unmarried girl who is pregnant; see pages 134–36], she said, 'Yes, she sticks way out now. Do they know who the father is?' She accepted my information on that score and made no further comment.

"Mrs. Uemura said that she has heard that Koyo-chan could not get an abortion after all and is still in Miyazaki. People closer to the family are silent. That morning, when I asked, both Mrs. Sato and Mrs. Wauchi said they do not know where she is. I suspect that only the family is certain of her whereabouts."

But in the end, shortly before the Embrees left Suye, the matter began to clear up. "I asked Sato about Koyo-chan. He said, laughing, that he has no idea where she is. 'You know everything,' was all he would say. Later on, however, he admitted that he has just learned from one of his sisters that Koyo-chan is in Miyazaki with a friend of her brother who is a midwife. She is to have the baby there, then study midwifery, and come back to Suye in a year or two. Her father sends her money. Sato is really sympathetic and thinks it all too bad. He wanted to discharge the servant (who works for his family) at once, but was advised that it would only create more scandal, so he kept him until the end of the year when his contract was up, and let him go in what looked like the normal course of events."

"Now I realize what was going on at the time of the Hayashi child's funeral. Because of the death, Sato thought that the party for the end of transplanting should be put off. In the first place, the Shimodas suddenly refused to participate and said, after the fish had been ordered, 'Let us just eat at home separately.' The Wauchis seemed to resent this decision and decided to have a party together with the Satos anyway. The result was that they all had supper at the Sato's, all the family and the servants, with the exchange of many drinks. I now suspect that Shimoda's refusal to participate was due to the presence of the Sato servant responsible for Koyo-chan's pregnancy, of which I then knew nothing, but which was already known to all. I also recall that Mrs. Sato kept asking all evening where the girls were, as soon as she noticed that any of them left the room."

Somewhat later a brother of Sato's called and we find this report in John Embree's journal: 'The servant in fact would have liked to marry Koyo-chan, the girl he had seduced, but her father refused. The servant thereupon had asked Wauchi Buichi, a relative, and Mori, a very close friend of the girl's father, to intercede on his behalf. They did so, but her father was adamant. Sato says that the girl is now in Hitoyoshi with her elder brother, but would not give much information on the subject. He did agree that usually a girl does not marry the man with whom she has an affair. Such things usually occur between servants, and the Shimoda case is a clear exception to the rule. When a girl goes out as a servant, he explained, she is freer, because less under parental eyes; the same is true of boys."

Koyo-chan's story reaches its unexpected denouement some months after the Embrees left Japan, revealed in a letter from John Embree's assistant. "The most tragic event [to occur in Suye since you left] is the death of Mr. Shimoda's daughter Koyo-chan, which occurred in December 1936. According to Mr. Wauchi, she died in Miyazaki. A big funeral ceremony for her was held in Suye. Mr. Wauchi was informed of her death by telegram, which reported that her baby is alive and in good health."

Reiko

Another young woman in a similar predicament dealt with it in a very different way. "Reiko has reached her fifth month of pregnancy, I learned today. It is assumed that the man is her former boyfriend from Taragi who recently went to Korea and who writes to her often. Our maid says that Reiko got a letter from him only three days ago. Although I had noticed her stomach the other day, I was so far from suspecting that I did not even make inquiries. Unlike Koyo-chan, Reiko is as cheerful as ever, keeps on working, went to the movies the other night, and behaves much as usual. Everyone but me knew about it. Asked Shima, 'How could it have happened? She's working at such a nice house, too.' "

"Reiko looks very cheerful, and told our maid today that she will be going to Korea next year. It is strange to see her pregnant, for she looks so young and still wears the girl's kimono and plain muslin *obi*. Mrs. Kawabe says that her mother is upset about the pregnancy, but that Reiko is not. The women doubt that the man in Korea is really responsible, and say that he no longer writes to her. They all suspect the Hirano boy, but then again because he lives in the same house he is naturally open to suspicion. (So, using Margaret Mead's style: While the mother worried about the fate of the girl and the women shook their heads and gossiped, Reiko went about the village, head high, not in the least embarrassed by her pregnant figure.)"

"Mrs. Tanimoto agreed that girls seldom marry men with whom they have love affairs and babies, but she does not know why. 'Perhaps it is because the parents usually object.' She has heard that Koyo-chan has gone to a Miyazaki hospital for an abortion, and does not know why there is any objection to her marrying the man unless it is the difference in their social statuses. She also remarked that Reiko is not in the least upset. She thinks it is very bad for girls to get pregnant, for afterwards they regret it because they usually get their comeuppance [*buchi kaburu*] and cannot marry well."

As her pregnancy advanced, the girl left service and returned to live with her family. "She has gone back to live at home because the Hiranos got a new maid to replace her, fearing it would be hard to find another later in the year. They say that her mother is worried, but that Reiko keeps getting letters from Korea, so there is hope. The Hirano boy is no longer under suspicion.

"Today Reiko's mother told me that two letters have come from Korea, the last one the day before yesterday. The boy, who is a relative of Tomokawa in Kinoue, said that she should not try to join him now. Since it is not good to travel during pregnancy, especially now that it is turning cold, he thinks it better for her to have the baby at home and for both of them to come to Korea in March. 'We are very relieved,' she admitted. Although Reiko is living at home again, she goes back to Hirano's to help their new servant with the silkworms. They need her help because the Hirano bride, who had planned to stay for some time with her parents, has been called back to town by her husband, who found it hard to get along alone."

A little later, at a *dōsōkai* performance at the school, "the young men sat together, joked and made remarks about the girls, who also stuck together. Reiko was there, not in the least embarrassed by her protruding stomach. When I got back to the house, our maid said that she thinks Reiko is not in the least depressed, but is in fact quite brazen about her situation. She has shaved her eyebrows and now pencils them in. (Shaving eyebrows was formerly a sign that a woman was married.) Not long afterward I saw Reiko out watching the practice for the coming field day, not in the least concerned with the contrast between her appearance and that of her age-mates who were dancing."

And somewhat later: "On my way back I stopped in at Hirano's to find Tamaki there alone having tea before going into town. As Hirano and his wife were both out on errands, Reiko was serving him. I went out to the kitchen with her and asked when the baby is due. She looked down at her stomach, and after a moment's hesitation said, 'In December,' and seemed eager to change the subject."

As the young woman's pregnancy progressed, there was increasing speculation about the affair. "Said Mrs. Taniguchi, 'Look what happens to girls who go out to work alone. It is a pity about Reiko.' (I must say that the only person who seems to feel no pity is the girl herself. Today she was at the Ebisu shrine to have a good time again.) She laughed when I repeated Reiko's mother's story about the fellow in Korea and his letters. 'That is what she says, but how does the mother know? They say she never slept with the Hirano boy, but there were plenty of occasions when they went out to go to work together or could say they were going somewhere but go to some other place instead.' She insisted that the girl had affairs with both fellows—the one in Korea and the Hirano boy—so it is hard to decide who the father really is. (Our maid absolutely denies that Reiko had anything to do with the Hirano boy.)"

Following up, "I asked Mrs. Hirano who had got Reiko pregnant. 'Someone who is now far away,' she replied. 'The baby will be your grandchild?' I asked. She laughed and said it is too soon for her to have a grandchild, and exhibited no sign of concern over the matter.)"

Just before they left Suye, confirmation came at last. "Both men knew the name of the boy from Menda, now in Korea, who had got Reiko pregnant. It seems that this fellow got a job in Korea through some old man in Taragi who runs a string of brothels. It was this young man who later persuaded the Iwasaki son to come over to Korea, and to bring his sister along. They consider this not very safe, and think that young girls should not go off to Korea unprotected and on such a fishy recommendation."

Whether or not she went to join the boy from Menda, we do not know, and if she did, whether they made it back to Suye following the catastrophic collapse of the Japanese empire just nine years later.

THE SHIRAKI PROSTITUTE

The third of the year's premarital pregnancies was that of the elder of two sisters sold into prostitution by their father, who returned to Suye to have her baby. The comments about this young woman and her tragic situation reveal many facets of the village women's attitudes toward this complicated issue.

"In addition to those of Koyo-chan and Reiko, there is another unwanted pregnancy, that of a Shiraki daughter in Oade. She has returned from Kumamoto, where she had been sold to a restaurant, made pregnant by an unknown man. I did not see her, but they say she was tremendous, and this morning was delivered of a baby girl. The midwife, significantly, was from outside the village. I think she comes from Hitoyoshi."

There was much talk, of course, for the young woman, twenty-four years old, actually was working as a prostitute in Kumamoto. "The women did not know which family register the child will be put in, but they did remark how lucky it was that the baby was a girl—and such a lovely, healthy child. Mrs. Hayashi thought that the baby was so healthy because such women just sit all the time [that is, do not perform heavy farm work], but Mrs. Kawabe said that there was no connection. Just as childbirth is easy or hard, children come good or bad, depending on who their parents are and regardless of their way of life. Mrs. Hayashi mentioned that her mother had delivered all eleven of her children alone, without the help of a midwife."

"When I called at Shiraki's earlier in the day, the girl was in bed with the baby, under a mosquito net. I asked if many of the girls had babies. 'Do you mean girls in such places?' she asked. 'Not many, but one had one last year.' When I asked about contraception, she said they use medicines, condoms and douches. I asked what happened to her—was it a mistake? She laughed but said nothing. She did tell me that she worked until the seventh month of pregnancy, rested during the eighth, and then came home at the beginning of this month. She is not paid when laid off like this, but expects to leave the baby here and go back to work when she is able. A nice girl, not very pretty, but pleasant."

On the third day after the child's birth, the naming ceremony was held at the Shiraki house. "Of relatives there were few, but obviously this is not a relatives' affair. It is rather more a formality to which neighbors are invited. The baby's name slip was hanging at the god-shelf and inquiry revealed that the name had been selected by the baby's mother, her mother, and the midwife. Old Mrs. Shiraki said, 'The father wanted a different name, but we thought this was better.' I asked whether she meant her husband or the baby's father, and she said, 'The child's father.' On the assumption that the characters written above the baby's name were the surname of the father, I asked her to read them to me. She could not, and said, 'I wonder what it says?' and asked her husband for help. He muttered something and dropped the matter. [They were, in fact, simply the characters for 'name' which are written on all such slips.]

"They say that the Shiraki girl knows who the father of her child is, as he was a steady customer for a while. He is said to be rich and unmarried (a fact not taken for granted by the women who were discussing the matter). Since he is not a first son, there is hope of marriage, and he is said to have given her money. From the manager of the house where she works, she received a gift of two baby kimono—one pink and one blue, just to be sure." It is not clear when this thoroughly Western notion entered Suye, although it may well have been through one of the many women's magazines.

In a day or two "I called on Shiraki, but the family was out. The daughter was asleep with the child under the mosquito net, but roused herself and came out to greet me. I had brought a gift, and in return she slipped a box of matches into my bag, unable to find a proper piece of paper to wrap them in. I asked if she knows who the child's father is, to which she replied that she has some idea. This contradicts the current story that she knows the man well. She will return to work after the presentation of the baby at the shrine about a month after its birth and leave the baby here with her parents. She denied that she is still menstruating (it has been ten days since the baby came), but it is obvious from her movements that she is. She sat nursing her baby, rubbing her nipples with a moistened finger, as all the young mothers do. She answered all my questions, but did not find it very pleasant discussing the matter. People are saying that the child will be entered in the register of her natal house."

"A few days later, I found the girl sitting inside the house rocking her baby and singing to it, having just finished nursing her. She looks terribly pale all the time, and I always find her sitting inside the house. She was very glad to have the photograph of her taken with the baby. She plans to go back to town in about ten days and said that the baby has been entered in her family's register."

On yet another visit, "she was sitting with the baby tied in front of her on her lap. The child is obviously sickly. Some other women happened by and all came in, recommending that she take the baby to the curing priest (kitōshi). One of them told a story about Hayashi getting cured at the Funaba shrine when the priest there guessed that his trouble was connected with the water god. But then they all said, 'Maybe it's not that. Maybe it's that,' and turned their heads in the general direction of the witch's house. 'What would she want with a small baby?' asked the mother. [See page 268.]

"She plans to leave for Kumamoto in three days, and expects her mother to come along. They will take the baby with them, and her mother will bring it back here when she returns. She did not know how they will feed it then, but thinks perhaps they will use cow's milk. She has heard that the water from boiled rice is just as good, and used by many women. I asked her if she wanted to go back, and she said that it is better here at home, but would not say if this time it is harder to leave than it was the first. The village women are sympathetic."

The Shiraki daughter and her baby did return to Kumamoto, accompanied by the girl's mother. On a subsequent call at the house "I found Mrs. Shiraki cutting the baby's nails. It looked pitiful, for some kind of skin disease has developed around its mouth. They had stayed in Kumamoto for three days, and then she had brought the baby back. 'Yes,' she acknowledged, 'its mother was sad.' They had bought food for the child in Kumamoto. Ironically [for few women understood the metric system being taught in the schools] the bottle, with nipple attached, has gram notation on it for formula feedings. They had bought some powdered milk, but a one-yen supply lasts only ten days. They also bought rakkan ko [a kind of rice flour], which is only forty sen for a bag that lasts much longer. Since they started feeding it the flour, the baby seems to have gained some weight. 'It is made from rice,' she said, 'which is good.' It has to be mixed with sugar, but because too much sugar is bad for the baby's stomach, she mixes in only a bit. In rice and rice-flour they have faith always. Of cow's milk they hear, but refuse to believe in its efficacy. She told me that the baby will be brought up as their own child."

Disapproval of this young woman's father was almost universal, among women and men alike. Shiraki had, in fact, sold two of his daughters, and the circumstances were such to bring down much opprobrium upon him. "I asked why the Shiraki girl had been sold as a prostitute. The women found it hard to say. To my observation that the house is not at all poor, they said that it has been much improved and is kept up with the girl's money. The Shirakis got 500 yen as the first payment for her and later another 250 yen, they think. She has also been sending money home ever since, and they now talk about buying new *tatami* and building a new toilet. 'So she must be making good money.' No wonder the girl felt free to come home to have her baby."

John Embree's journal has more of the story. "Shiraki was heavily in debt to a *kō* to which he belonged, owing ten-yen payments to many of its members. He sold his first daughter permanently to a house of prostitution for 800 yen. He then settled with his creditors at five yen each, half of what he owed them. Then he sold his second daughter on the same terms and with the proceeds bought some paddy fields and made improvements on his house. Seeing this, the creditors raised a fuss, but could do nothing about it. This is all regarded as a sacrifice the girl makes for her family, but in this case (as in others) the cause was not dire poverty at all, so much as the selfishness of the father."

As it turned out the story of the sale was somewhat more complicated. "Of the two daughters sold by Shiraki, the older one is a bastard his wife gave birth to before their marriage, and being over twenty, was sold into a house of prostitution. When he needed to pay off his debts, he decided to sell the second girl. Since she was only sixteen, she could not be sold to a house of prostitution, so went instead to a restaurant. That sale made it possible to finish paying off the debts and improve the house.

"The second girl was sold, people say, because her father felt it unfair to have sold his wife's child and not sell one of his own." If this is true, it shows a concern for equity not generally encountered in the relations between husbands and wives.

GETTING AWAY: WORKING OUTSIDE

For many of the young women of Suye, not yet married, the goal was to escape the village and find work in a town or city. To places like this came the recruiters in search of factory labor. "A man from Taragi, a lantern-maker by profession but now a labor contractor, comes here to collect girls for the factories. He recruited the girl who now works at the Hayashis for a company in Himeji for wages of forty sen a day. He has a good line and easily persuades people that incomes are high for factory work. He was around again yesterday and spent all afternoon trying to persuade the Edas to send their daughter away, but they definitely refused because she is needed to work at home. This girl was taken out of school after finishing only the first year of girls' school because they are short of labor for farm work. All the family, including the girl, seem pleased with the decision."

"The labor recruiter for the Himeji spinning mill was around again. He says that many girls go from here, but in response to my question was able to provide few specific names. He complains that it is hard to find anyone at home [because they are all out working in the fields]. When I mentioned Namiko, he immediately took down the Furuta name. This girl wants desperately to go back to the company where she used to work, making cotton thread. 'It's easy work, after you get used to it,' she told me. Certainly the work is considered lighter than farming, which she dislikes. At the factory, she said, she started work at 5:00 A.M. and worked standing until 2:00 P.M. Then she had sewing lessons in the afternoon and went out *asobi* at night."

"The recruiter says that the girls start at 4.50 yen per month, but can work up to as much as twenty and more. The average wage is ten yen. He gets a percentage for finding the girls, but no salary, so if he can bring in 50 to 100 girls, he does all right. It is his opinion that working in a factory is better than being a maid. Indeed, the Furuta girl's album, which she showed me one day when I was over there, contained photographs of her and other girls having a flower-arranging lesson, and boys and girls in gym suits. It is no wonder she likes it."

It was not only from the blandishments of the recruiters that the girls learned of the attractions of factory work. "The postman stopped in at the shop for some tea and told us about his experiences in Hiroshima where he once worked in a rayon factory. There were about 150 girls from this region there, and he had many girlfriends. 'Not doing anything bad, just *asobi* together,' he assured us. He still keeps up correspondence with some of the girls, he said, and remarked that the most successful workers at the factory were those from Kyushu, while those from Hiroshima were hard to get along with and always ready for a fight."

Unmarried girls who were finished with their schooling spent much time speculating on what kind of work they could find that would take them out of the village. "I stopped in to have some tea. Fumie was there, saying that she is not going to continue as a nursemaid at the Amano's next year. A discussion followed as to where she should go. The Fujita girl suggested going to work in a restaurant in Menda, but Fumie protested. Nonetheless, the discussion of that possibility took place in much the same tone as that of becoming a bus-girl or working in a spinning mill [the girls who go to work in restaurants in town usually slip into prostitution]. It wasn't so bad, thought Mrs. Fujita, for after three to five years on contract the girl can return to the village. The young girl thought that it was possible for geisha to return, but that restaurant girls could not, but her mother said that any serving woman (*shakufu*) can come back if she wishes."

Fumie's negative view of the prospect was shared by other young women. "Tamako was watching the Menda girls at the Inari shrine attentively. I suggested to her that she become a geisha. 'I'd be scared,' she said. 'You are sure to get a disease, and you have to sleep with anyone who comes along, even some big dirty Chinese.' "

"The Ariyoshi girl, a fifth-year student, commented that in Taragi the girls have to paint up and use that dreadful-smelling powder. Mrs. Hayashi said that the powder smelled better than sweat, but the girl looked dubious. She laughed when Mrs. Hayashi said how nice it would be if she went to town all made up and dressed in her best kimono and the young men would make love to her. The nursemaids today spent a great deal of time dressing up like prostitutes, but they think they would not like to go to work in a 'restaurant,' which is scary and hard.

"Tamako is forever talking about how she is going to become a bus-girl and go with the batch that are being recruited now. The problem is that her boyfriend Masayoshi objects. Some days she says that she is going to study the abacus with a teacher and finish the course in a month. Actually, it seems that her father has already arranged for her to do contract farm-work for someone in Oade. 'It's all lies about the bus,' says our maid. 'Young people do nothing but tell lies, because it is interesting and they like to talk about all kinds of things. Now Fumie is talking about becoming a bus-girl, but it is a hard job.' She delivered this tirade just after participating in a lively conversation with Tamako herself about the great advantages of such work."

"Aki-chan has no idea what she will do next year, and goes into the same set of speculations as Tamako. Some days she says she will be married next year in Osaka, or go to work in a company there, or become a bus-girl. She does not want to stay here, for she says that towns are much better places to live than the country. Her brother also dreams of going to Osaka; perhaps they will all move there and leave their mother behind. She denied that anyone has come to ask for her in marriage, but added, 'Well, maybe someone from very far away.' She says wistfully, 'I will never see Tokyo before I die, most likely.' "

One young woman who had tasted the mixed pleasures of city life was the prostitute who came home to have her illegitimate baby. "She said that she had not wanted to go to the house of prostitution at first and was very worried. But she found the work not hard, if unpleasant. 'It is not too different from working in a restaurant.' Each girl has her own room, and they are picked out by the customers from a line-up, sitting in a row, not from photographs as it is sometimes done. In the house where she works there are twenty girls and some nights she has no customers, on other nights there are many. Mostly they are older men, but an occasional young man comes in. The prices are 1.65 yen for forty minutes, 2.20 yen for a full hour, and 5.50 yen for the night. The taxes are, respectively, fifteen, twenty, and fifty sen. The remainder is divided evenly between the house and the girl. She is on a five-year contract [not a permanent one, as some women have alleged], but can leave sooner if she pays it up. She said that she does not know when she will leave, and only laughed when I asked her if she would marry. 'Some do. I don't know yet.' She knew the precise date she started; her second year begins on the twentieth of October. She went at age twenty-two and is now twenty-four. Her sister, now seventeen, was sold into a restaurant last year, but when I brought up the subject she said she did not want to talk about it."

On one occasion while in Taragi, there is an encounter with a girl who has become a geisha. "Before going on to the school for the field day, we stopped in a café where a cute little geisha from Suye waited on us. Very coy, she said ōkini and iya yo [coquettish language] and was as different as can be from her classmates out on the school grounds. Her parents are from Fukuoka, lived for a year in Suye, and then moved to Taragi. She said that when she was in Suye she was shocked by its smallness and by the fact that boys and girls sat in the same classroom."

The prostitutes and restaurant girls, geisha and shakufu of the nearby towns came frequently to Suye, ordinarily to visit the Inari shrine there. [Inari is the patron deity of geisha and prostitutes.] On excursions to town and at pilgrimage sites, the women and girls of Suye often had occasion to observe these women. There was a curious ambivalence in the attitudes held about them.

"The big Inari shrine drew the largest crowd. The restaurant girls from Menda gave a strange touch to the festival. One group, which stayed for a while, got very drunk and reeled all over the road on their way home, followed by a group of village children who thought it was a circus. They grabbed me by the hand, calling me nēsan and obasan, and urging me to accompany them to Menda. The local girls watched them as if they were some kind of strange animal, and looked and listened with surprised expressions to the girls' raucous voices telling men what to do, smoking all the while. They did some singing and dancing at the party."

Later in the year, "all day the Menda restaurant girls were calling at the Inari shrine because it is the first of the month. A group came at three in the morning, which is a customary procedure in the warm season. 'They come as soon as business closes in town,' Mrs. Fujita explained. She was at Ochiai's to buy some grain, and said she had to hurry back to the shrine because the girls were there and she had to serve them tea. She was surprised to see the daughter of a family she knows in the group.

"In the afternoon as another group of Menda restaurant girls was returning from the Inari shrine, Mrs. Tanimoto and Mrs. Hayashi came out to look at them. They criticized the bright kimono, made remarks about their always going by the village office [where they know many of the men, who are regular customers of the establishments where they work], although in fact they did so to avoid the horses that had been brought in for inspection that were blocking the path, referred to the girls as horses, and in general showed much resentment of them. I am always struck by the injustice of this attitude, since no girl here is a prostitute of her own accord, but is sold by her parents. The couple who tend the Inari shrine are much more friendly toward them, but of course they depend on the donations the girls leave there."

"After seeing the girls at the Inari festival, I was talking with a group of women and referred to them as geisha. I was at once corrected by Mrs. Wauchi [whose husband's line of work takes him to restaurants regularly]. 'They are only serving women, not geisha,' she said. None of the rest seemed to be very conscious of this distinction." Yet one or two of the more worldly women reported an extremely interesting reaction to geisha. "While we were at Ochiai's, geisha were discussed. Mrs. Tanimoto said that she once saw some dance in Kumamoto. One was so beautiful that she wanted to have sexual intercourse with her, she said, but being of the same sex could not."

Suye men, on the other hand, tended to display a convenient male rationalization on the subject, when talking about it with John Embree: "Kawabe thinks that most contracts are for four years, and that most of the girls get to like the life. Once girls leave Suye for such work they seldom if ever return. I know of seven cases now, and none of them has come back. The girls in Menda say that they don't like to return to their village, but prefer to go some place where they are not known, and most say that they feel psychologically unfitted for marriage. (It often happens that an ex-prostitute or geisha will open up a restaurant or other business in the town or city.)"

John Embree wrote: "The euphemistic term used for selling a daughter is *azukeru* (to place in the care of). Hayashi Jiro sold two of his daughters as apprentice geisha, one at sixteen or seventeen, the other slightly younger. [A girl could be sold to a licensed house of prostitution only if she were twenty.] It is said that he had to sell them (for about 300 yen each for a period of three years) because he drinks too much and could not work. He himself recently had to get a job in the mines." The sole mitigating circumstance is that this man was a widower and very deeply in debt.

His journal continues: "We were at Tamaki's last night, and it is very clear that they are very poor. The wife is twice married and has had eleven children of whom the last three and one earlier one died. They live in a one-room house with a thatch roof. Their oldest daughter, now twenty-five, was sold through a broker into a house of prostitution in Yahata eight years ago and has since moved many times. She has not been back to Suye once. Her parents do not write to her, but her two younger sisters say they do. The cause of this sale obviously is poverty, yet children are being produced almost annually even though the last three died of what must be congenital syphilis. In this connection, the men say that most of the restaurant girls used to come from outside Kuma County (many of them from Ehime Prefecture in Shikoku], but that there are now more local girls because of the depression and the mounting debt of the farmers. They laughed about it." Nonetheless, as we have seen, in at least two of the Suye cases—the Shiraki and Hayashi—"the cause was not dire poverty as much as the selfishness of the father."

For many young people the lure of the colonies and the mines was very strong, and for most young men, of course, there was military service. The decision on the part of a child to leave for outside work was often the cause of much anguish on the part of their parents and the journal is filled with references to lonely old people, most of them women, who try to keep in touch with their daughters and sons who are away.

"Mrs. Kawabe did not look her old self—very sad and subdued. She said that her son was here a few days ago, went back to Kumamoto to take care of a few things, and is coming here for four days before leaving. The company he works for is sending him to Korea. She is very upset because he will be so much farther away than when he was in Kumamoto. But what really upsets her is her daughter. The girl says that farming is a stupid occupation, and the work too hard. Her brother has been trying to persuade her to leave, and their parents have finally given in. She is going along to keep house for him, and perhaps find a job in a company. It will be three years before he is ready to marry (he is now twenty-three), so brother and sister can be together for a while longer. Tears kept coming to her eyes. Parent-child separations are very hard, she said. (What is happening here is as so many people say. All those with better education and intellect leave if they can.)"

In due course there was a farewell party for the two children at Kawabe's. "At the Kawabe farewell party, much of the conversation was all about people who had gone to Manchuria and Korea, the modern immigration grounds. The daughter joined in from time to time. There were stories of people who were getting high salaries of seventy yen a month and more—100 yen a month was considered very good. There was a definite colonial attitude about it all, with accounts of people, 'Chinese, of course,' standing in line to get any kind of job for three to five sen a day."

On another occasion, "Mrs. Kato discussed her daughter's confinement in Korea. There, it seems, everything has to be done just right, and having children costs a lot of money, so that people put aside special savings from the start. New bedding must be made for the mother, and separate ones for the baby, and guests call from the first day on. At the naming ceremony everyone brings expensive gifts and almost as expensive gifts must be returned (that is, a five-yen gift requires a four-yen return), which makes it better not to get any gifts at all. Medical service is very good, but expensive. It sounded to me very much as if people in the colony try to be very grand, much as Western colonials do."

"There was some talk about an argument between the girl and her father. Old lady Kawabe said, 'Well, a quarrel between a parent and a child is never anything more serious than pissing. They never last.' There was also some talk about café girls and the kind of brides picked out by the men who go to the colonies. Apparently some family squabble is on."

Indeed there was, and there proved to be much more to the affair than at first had been surmised by the ever-watchful women. "When I went up there, Kawabe was out feeding the cow, but came in to join his wife and me for tea. Both were looking at the clock and trying to calculate when the wire from their daughter would arrive if the boat docked in Fusan at ten. They guessed right, for a little later I saw the telegraph man go by on his way to their house. Mrs. Kato thinks that something is wrong there. 'One does not go so far away without a reason,' she said. 'She refused to do farm work, but there must be more to it than that.' Tamaki Take thinks it very strange that the Kawabe son and daughter went off to a distant place like Korea, but assumes that they were attracted by the good money. 'It is hard for her father, because now he has to do all the farm work by himself. His wife is like the daughter and does not like to farm, so she will not help him.' "

Mrs. Kawabe had her own problems. "She had finished the laundry and was preparing food for the evening meal. Now that the older daughter is gone the younger one is being trained to help. She is told to do this or that job—build a fire, stir the pot, roll out the dough. For her blunders she is reproached, good naturedly or otherwise, depending on the mother's mood. Mrs. Kawabe said that she had not slept the night before. Tamaki Takao got drunk at a *kōgin* and quarreled with her husband. 'It is too bad the way he drinks, he always gets hard to handle.' Evidently he had become belligerent and asked Kawabe, 'Why did you send your daughter to Korea?' which led to the fight. They are members of a same-age group."

"Mrs. Toyama thinks that it must be very hard for Kawabe to work all alone, with his daughter away in Korea and his wife dropping farm work. 'If one is a farmer, one should stick to farm work!' she said emphatically."

The fear of losing contact with children who go out for work was very general. "One old woman in the group said her only son disappeared some time last year. Her letters went unanswered, and her inquiries proved fruitless. Then they discussed the disappearances of other young men—three in all. The other women said that they worry when their sons leave the village for fear they will never return. They can give no particular reasons for the disappearance, but the hope is that the men will show up at the reservists' muster."

"They spoke also of unsuccessful sons. There was a young man, son of the woman from Nakashima, who was helping Tanno with the wheat harvest. This came about because she is a widow and the son is no good, and their situation became so grave last winter that she had to ask the Tannos for rice and now she has come to work off her debt because the son has gone off somewhere. Another case is the son of the widow Sakikawa, who, by the way, denies having any children at all. He was a petty thief and left the village finally, although one of the women said she saw him around last spring. His mother is not very well off. The third case is the Suzuki boy, who left for parts unknown after completing his military service. His mother continues to insist that he is a soldier, even though everyone knows that he is not."

It was the case, of course, that many people remained in touch with their absent children, maintaining contact through the mails and—during the Embrees' stay—sending photographs. "The old lady in Tontokoro who once came here asking me to take her picture was delighted to receive the print today. She thought it perfect, although she is almost blind. She will send it to her children working in the Hakata mines. She adopted a daughter, for whom she got a husband, but now both have gone to the mines and she says that she weeps very much. She wanted this picture expressly to send to them. As I sat there a postal card arrived and she listened with tears in her eyes while the postman read it to her. It said how glad the children were to see their grandfather [who was visiting there at the time] and how every night he has his sake, so she is not to worry. She now wants another photograph of herself doing the rice threshing if we are still here then. If not, she can just imitate the process by using some straw. She went on in some detail about how she will have her head towel fixed differently, and will wear a long-sleeved kimono with cords to hold up the sleeves, the traditional work outfit of the old days. The only thing that worried her was that I would not take money for the photograph. 'What can I give you as a gift?' she kept asking, and I finally said that sweet potato would be fine, and she was pleased."

Often the news was not so gratifying. "A woman came into the Shiraki's to have the girl there read a postal card for her. It was from her son, who had sent a wire yesterday. He was writing to say that he is in the hospital because he has developed some disease. The woman commented, 'These mines that they all rave about and are so eager to go to work in are not so good after all. They only make you sick, and you get no pay while you are off the job.' "

"I went up to Tontokoro to answer the request of old lady Sato. She and her husband live in a very poor one-room house. She had asked me to come and take her picture with her cat so that she can send it to their son who is working in the mines."

For girls and boys too young to find employment outside Suye there was the option of taking a job as nursemaid or servant for another Suye family. In mid-April, "after graduation a whole crowd of young nursemaids appeared [they would be twelve or thirteen years old]. Everybody had been waiting for them impatiently for some time [this being just after the majority of births occur]. The Makinos, the Suzukis and the Moris all have new nursemaids and the *dō* is filled with them and the little kids all day."

"The women were discussing the phenomenon one day, and Otome managed to get in some gossip herself. [She was often its subject.] 'Now the Hayashis have a nursemaid,' she said. 'Yes,' said Mrs. Fujita, 'all the rich people have servants,' and enumerated Mori, Ochiai, Sato, and Suzuki. They decided that Mrs. Makino must be pregnant, and talked of her first child, a very beautiful little boy who died at New Year's a year ago from some navel trouble. (As a matter of fact, the Hayashis have no servants. The nursemaid is an orphaned relative who is living with them while they try to find a job for her.)"

The Moris, on the other hand, did have a nursemaid, but had a great deal of trouble finding one. They wanted a girl for two months to do the laundry, cooking and housework, while Mrs. Mori is recovering from childbirth. They first offered the job to a girl in Oade, but she refused on her own, saying there is too much drinking in the house and she would not feel safe. 'She is only fifteen,' says her mother, backing her up. Besides, says everyone, old lady Mori is a terror."

"Even though the idea of women doing independent work is so novel that the people in the village office have decided that I must have a better head than John (this from Kawabe who said, 'We talk about it among ourselves all the time'), there are girls with ideas of their own. One of the girls who shows signs of independence is the daughter-in-law of Hirano Tatsuo, a very charming and attractive girl with thin and delicate hands, unspoilt by farm labor. She tells me that after graduating from girls' school she started work in farming, but just could not do it. She told her family that she was unfit and managed to get away to Kumamoto to a job as a house-maid to a family that had lived in the United States for a long time. From the wife she learned many things about America. Yesterday we discussed clothes—what one should wear in the afternoon, for dinner, and in the evening. She knew the English words for them all. I saw her several times during her New Year's visit to Suye and again yesterday when I dropped in. She was sewing alone, having sent the baby out with its grandmother. She says she likes foreign clothes for comfort, but considers kimono more attractive. [This is the young woman who expressed her admiration for Margaret Sanger.]"

"Another example of an independent girl is our maid's friend from Aso. As an only daughter she was sent—because she wanted to go—to work for a company in Gifu. She did not like it there, so without coming home she switched jobs and went to work for a filling station. From there she moved to another company in Osaka, where she has been promoted from car-washer to pumping gas and earns fifteen yen a month. Our maid says she would like to go away too, but she is pretty sure that this girl will have to come back from Osaka when her family finds an adopted husband for her."

Indeed, such modest dreams of independence and escape from the farm ended for both girls and boys when the time for them to marry came. And it is worth noting that in both these cases, and there are no others reported, the girls of an independent cast of mind can hardly be said to have aimed high and achieved more than a very modest improvement in their lives.

Marriage, Divorce, and Adoption

To an extent not suggested by the literature on Japanese rural society, the women of Suye displayed a remarkable and quite unexpected degree of independence in the matter of marriage and divorce. Many of them had been married more than once, and what is astonishing is that it was not at all uncommon for the woman herself to terminate the marriage, whether it had been formalized or was a common-law one.

"The Mrs. Uemura who called here after the party at the temple is said to be a very difficult person. She left Tamaki Heihachi after 18 years of marriage, and moved out on Sato Mataichi after a few years as his second wife. She and Uemura have been married for the past eight years. She had no children by any of these men. [Which makes the fact that it was she who left her first two husbands all the more remarkable.] As Mataichi's second marriage promptly resulted in three children, old lady Arasaki said, 'It was her fault. If there had been children, she would not have left him.' (It is a common belief that divorces are less frequent when the couple has children. Is there any connection between the high frequency of divorce here and sterility?)"

"Mrs. Goto was married to some relative of Sato's, but left him. When I asked about the reason, she only laughed, but later Mrs. Tanimoto said, 'She did not like him. She likes her present husband.' But Mrs. Goto's present husband, her third, is a man everyone calls Noguchi. She was also married to Goto, who died when he was only thirty-three years old." In a subsequent conversation with Mrs. Goto, she said that her second husband died at the age of thirty-three after the Russo-Japanese War. "Then Noguchi came as her adopted husband, so there was only a small ceremony. All her older children are named Goto because she had them by her second husband. The younger children, all Noguchi's, are registered by that surname, although everyone calls them Goto because it is the name of the house."

"Actually, the whole business turns out to be complicated. Some say that all the children there have the second husband's name, others that the second batch has a different name. No one seems to be sure. This man is either her third husband or her 'guardian.' (Noguchi himself says that the older children are Goto and the younger ones Noguchi.) Today I called there. It seems that the house is Noguchi, according to the present husband, who is the father of the last three children. The second husband was Goto, who also had three children. The older son, who is about to be married, is a Goto.'

The Goto-Noguchi business is something of a puzzle. If she left her first husband and married a man who died young, was she able to take an adopted husband as her third because she had inherited the property of the second? This seems the most likely explanation, but it is not at all clear why the adopted husband Noguchi did not take her surname. One possible answer is that he was a first-born son, who at this period were forbidden to change their names even if they went as adopted husbands without the approval of their family and the courts.

Indeed, there are a surprising number of references to the inability of people to recall the surnames of others or even their own. While it is true that the great majority of Suye families adopted surnames only after the Meiji Restoration of 1868, there would seem to have been enough time for their usage to become firmly established except among the elderly. Yet such clearly was not the case, and the frequency of divorce and remarriage appears to have played no small part in the matter.

"A strange thing happened in Kawaze yesterday. I saw a woman working and asked her name. She did not give it, so I asked some kids who were hanging around. They called her Grandmother Masa, but said they did not know her family name. Then one of them asked her directly, and she said she has none."

"Yesterday the Moris were cleaning the house when a woman from Imamura called to bring some vegetables. She was invited in for tea and they discussed this and that. When she left, no one could tell me her surname, yet all obviously knew her well."

Even young people were sometimes uncertain about the surnames of families they knew well. "I met the Hayashi girl who used to work for Suzuki Tamezo. She left their employ at the New Year, the standard time for changing servants. She had a baby on her back, but did not know the surname of the people she now works for, when I asked her. We finally deduced that it is Hayashi Manzo."

"At the Arasaki place I first thought no one was about. However, the old lady finally appeared and asked me in. I learned that she had no children of her own, so adopted Fumio's uncle-by-adoption, whose sister was married to Genichi and is the mother of Mrs. Soeshima. Characteristically, the old lady could not think of her son's original surname until I reminded her."

"After the party Mrs. Uemura and Hayashi stopped by our house. When I asked her for it, Mrs. Uemura could not recall her surname. Perhaps it is true, as I have heard, that she has been married three times."

REMARRIAGE

John Embree noted early in his journal: "Remarriage is quite common here. A woman in Oade was married once to a man in Hitoyoshi, but left him because she did not like her mother-in-law. Then she married a man in Hamanoue and didn't like her husband—it is said that she would not sleep with him—and finally married a man in Oade by whom she has had six children." Of this case Ella Wiswell wrote, "Today I met Mrs. Maeno. She told me that one of their six children died. Before marrying Maeno, she said with a smile, she had two husbands. The first marriage lasted only six months because she could not stand her mother-in-law's constant criticism, so she left. Her second marriage lasted only a month. She disliked the man and made her bed separately. This third marriage was contracted sight unseen. It is working out fine. Maeno knew about her history but took a chance, she said, and she had decided to start out on a new venture without ever laying eyes on him."

"It seems that the Maeno daughter refused to come here and help serve at our party yesterday, saying, 'I won't do such work.' These girls have a great deal of say-so, which might have some connection with their mother's own strong character, she having left her first two husbands of her own free will."

Unquestionably the record for remarriage was held by old lady Tanno. "She is said to be exceptionally hard to get along with. There is no other like her in Suye. She was once married to someone in Kawaze, but left him and her infant daughter. (This girl eventually married and died without ever seeing her mother again.) Then she married at least ten different men, eventually ending up with Tanno. They say she stays with him because he is so quiet. Said one woman, 'It is seldom that an old woman can have so much to say in a household. I feel sorry for the young wife there. All the children are scared of her because she orders them around so gruffly. It was very hard dealing with her when they were trying to arrange the marriage of the daughter of the house, and she isn't even her real grandmother.' (I have noticed that she always scowls and yells at the kids, and at first thought that she was joking. She is not.)"

"Today I learned that Sasaki's wife was formerly married to Ochiai. She and Ochiai went off to Himeji together, but separated there and returned to Suye at different times. The child was born after they parted, so she kept it. Later I found out that there is talk that Ochiai is going to remarry. When I inquired about the divorce, Mrs. Amano said that his first wife had not wanted to marry him anyway and had left him almost immediately, although she later had his child. Anyhow, it was a cousin-marriage, she said, and they always go bad."

Then, a few weeks later, "at Ochiai's a new room is being added to the house. 'A new room, a new bride,' says Mrs. Shimosaka, which is very true. When she repeated it to the carpenter, he laughed. According to her Sasaki's present wife was Ochiai's first, but she added the information that he married once again to a girl from Menda, who walked out on him six months later. The other woman agreed when she said that a girl's parents do not object to the fact that a man has been married two or three times before."

"Today was the wedding of Arasaki Hamako, eighteen, and Hayashi Goro's son, who is twenty-four. The bride's family is not as well off as the groom's. The marriage may have been arranged because the two families are related. (Old lady Arasaki is the older sister of Mrs. Hayashi's father. The bride and groom are not directly related, however, because her father is an adopted husband.) The groom is said to have been married twice before, at nineteen and again at twenty-one. His second wife is a relative of the Edas. She left last year for some reason that is not clear, although some people say that she got sick and went home to recover. Deciding that she felt better at home, she never returned.

"The groom is said to be a bad lot, crazy about women, and it is widely predicted that this marriage will not last either. (It all sounds to me like a case of a fellow who does not want to be married and who in our society would remain a bachelor. Here he must marry because of family pressure.) The groom's unusual conduct might be the reason for his marriage to a girl of somewhat lower social standing, although it is hard to say that there is actually a very great distinction to be made between the two families."

Because the complexities of the following case reveal so many aspects of marriage and remarriage in Suye, it is given in full, although a second reading may be required to sort out all the relationships. At the center of it all stands an unwed mother. "Not long ago Mrs. Tanimoto made some remark about Toyama's daughter being the bastard of a Menda man. I thought she was referring to Reiko whom I know as Toyama's own daughter. Today I got it straight. She was talking about his son's wife, the beautiful daughter of Sato Mataichi. His wife comes from a Tamura family in Suye, and when she was young she suffered from some disease, perhaps of the lungs, which kept her at home with nothing to do. During that time she had an affair with Mrs. Arasaki's older brother who lives in Menda. He was then already married to Sakikawa Mataji's mother's younger sister. This affair continued for six years and eventually she had a baby daughter.

"Sato Mataichi's first wife died, and his second one left him to marry the man who now lives next door to the Arasakis. Mataichi then took a couple of wives, both of whom left him, and at last Sato of Kakui helped arrange this marriage with Tamura's daughter. Mataichi adopted the bastard child of his new wife and raised her as his own daughter. Some thought apparently was given to marrying this girl to his adopted son, but he decided against it because of the discrepancy in their ages. So she went to Toyama's as a bride. At the time of the marriage, her real father said to Mrs. Tanimoto's niece, who is his neighbor in Menda, 'Isn't it grand? My daughter is getting married today.' Said Mrs. Tanimoto, 'He is a very entertaining man.' "

What is so striking about this and other such accounts is the very narrow geographical range within which so many of these separations and remarriages occur, so that people who were near neighbors turn out to have been married one or more times in a bewildering variety of combinations. "Tamaki Take's sister was first married to Hayashi of Kakui, then to Miyamori, then to a man in Miyazaki. When she left Hayashi, he married Harue's grandmother, who had earlier been married to Sakikawa of Imamura. Sakikawa had left her, taking two of their three children with him. She had gone back to her natal house (Toyama) with her small son and they lived there for a while until she married Hayashi. The boy took the Toyama name and she left him there as successor."

Occasionally there was explicit recognition of the possible complications arising from such proximity. "Old Ishibashi is very worried about his [real] daughter and wants her to stay here with them. She was first married to a Suye man, but when their child died they were divorced. Her second marriage was a love match, and she and the man had three daughters. But when he gave up his work and went into farming, she simply could not do the heavy labor, and her mother-in-law made a lot of trouble, and they too were divorced. Then she married Soeshima, a widower with three daughters himself. The reason for Ishibashi's concern is that her second husband and her daughters by him live in Imamura, and they all fear complications if she goes there to live with Soeshima. She herself is reluctant to go to the place, which is very inconvenient and has no proper medical care for the child they are bringing up, so she plans to stay with Soeshima's natal family in Oade for a while until they can decide what to do."

Older men and women frequently simply made their own arrangements. "Mrs. Tanimoto says that the present Mrs. Shimosaka stayed at home a long time and at last married a man who died shortly thereafter. Then she became the mistress of another man, but he eventually dropped her. So she was at home some more, and Shimosaka married her because he thought she would have no more children."

"This afternoon I heard that the widow from Tontokoro has moved in with the deaf old man in Kinoue. She is the one I met on the road the other day who in answer to my question said that she was 'just moving.' They say that he used to visit her all along, even while his wife was still alive. Mrs. Tanimoto tells this funny story. Every time she went out to gather mulberry leaves for the silkworms, she would see the old man at the widow's place, the two of them whispering about something. She wondered what it could possibly be, since the man is so old. 'They must have been making arrangements,' she laughed."

"The old lady from Tontokoro now says that she has moved in with the old man because he is going to Hakata to visit kinsmen and she is to look after the house while he is away. 'Do people say I came here as a bride (*yomego*)? Bride? Does a man of fifty take a bride?' "

But the gossip continued without let-up. "Had she come as a bride, or was she just living with the old man? She had given no party (*kao mishiri*) to mark her taking up residence in the hamlet, and is said to keep a separate account with the mill. They agreed with my suspicion that she is pregnant. They thought that maybe the old man got her pregnant while he was still going (*yobai*) to her place at night. They explained this word to mean trying out a vagina before marrying a woman; it actually means sneaking into a house to have an illicit meeting with a woman. They decided that humans are really dirty, having intercourse so often. Look at cows, they said, which do it only once a year. This precipitated a graphic discussion of intercourse by cows and horses, and as Fumio came up to the group, they said gaily, 'Come join this *bobo-chinpo* [vagina-penis] talk. We're always at it.' "

A day or two later, when Mrs. Toyama remarked that she had heard that the old lady from Tontokoro is pregnant, "I asked who would bother to go to such a dirty place, and she assured me that it is always to the dirty places that men go. She wondered if I had noticed that the very dirtiest and poorest houses have the most children. Why is it? No sooner is one baby born than another is made. Just look at the Shimodas, the Amanos, and now this old widow—all with their bellies forever sticking out."

Arranging Marriages

In the old days, people said, it was not uncommon for two children to be engaged by their parents, with a view to marrying them when they grew up. Such agreements were kept from the children. "Yasuo thinks this was the case with Hayashi Fumio and Shoko. He knows of another case in Taragi, but is not sure there are others in Suye. The Hayashi case is an interesting one. Shoko came here to live with her aunt when she was sixteen and in her last year of school in Suye. The woman is also Fumio's aunt. When she first came Fumio was away working in Yamaguchi, and she had no idea that they had been engaged since childhood. When she was eighteen, their aunt fell ill, Fumio was sent for at once, and they were married immediately. Our maid says that if parents pick someone a girl does not like, they can be persuaded to change their minds and try to find someone else for the girl, but that true love matches are rare. When they do occur, the couple usually goes out on their own."

The Hayashi couple were cousins, then, and although such marriages were relatively common, most people thought they were very poor prospects for a long happy life together. The case of Uemura Naoko,

Toshio's wife, is instructive. "She came over this afternoon. Yesterday she asked me rather bashfully if she could call. She is twenty-one and has been married to Toshio for two years. They have no children and she says, 'It is very lonely this way.' She is reported to have had four miscarriages. It is her opinion that cousin-marriages like theirs are bad. In her case, however, it could not be helped because the two sets of parents arranged it all. Even the go-between was their uncle. 'All relatives,' she said."

Old lady Tanno of the ten husbands was her grandfather's wife. "She told me that she had been very unwilling for Naoko to marry Toshio. The girl had wept bitterly and said that she would marry anyone else— even a much older man—but not Toshio, because they are cousins and too young. Their uncle, who acted as the real go-between (*naishōkiki*), had to make five or six calls before the formal go-between (*nakaudo*) could come to the house, and even then Naoko refused to serve him tea. 'She is just a child!' said the old lady.

"Naoko had objected to the very last, but her parents would not relent. Old lady Tanno seemed to be on her side, for as she told me this story she kept looking around to make sure that Naoko's mother was out of earshot. It was evidently mostly the mother's doing, for the Uemuras have a tendency to intermarry. In a whisper she confided that she has just learned that another pair of Uemura cousins is also married and that the woman gave birth to a child with no fingers or toes. And Naoko has had so many miscarriages, the most recent in the eighth month of her term. Now she is two months pregnant, they think, and her mother has visited the Inari shrine to ask for a successful delivery this time."

"This morning Naoko came calling at the Tanno's, to rest from transplanting. Both she and her mother deny that Naoko is pregnant. I should think that relations between the mother and daughter would be strained, given the stories about the circumstances surrounding the marriage, particularly since the mother herself has had a baby since Naoko married. Although she blames all the troubles of her unwanted marriage on her mother, there is no outward sign of discord between them."

"This morning Naoko returned from another visit to the doctor in Hitoyoshi. When I arrived there about ten minutes later, she had already changed into her work clothes and was serving the noon meal. Her husband came in from harvesting millet. No special greetings were exchanged, and it seemed to me that he looked rather sad. Aki says that Naoko did not object to the marriage (evidently she is not well informed) but that Toshio did because he felt he was too young, but that now they get along well. They must both have objected to the marriage."

A better-informed source, one who was involved in the negotiations, provided more detail. "Mrs. Kato thinks that the position of the real go-between is even more difficult than that of the formal one and told me of her experience in the Uemura case. According to her, Naoko did not object to the marriage so much, but old lady Tanno had made a dreadful fuss, saying that the girl was too young and had just finished school. She thought that they should wait and find a husband for her who was not a farmer. However, considering Naoko's delicate constitution, it is much better that she married into a family to which she was related, for they are considerate of her. Uemura Toshio would have no one else but Naoko, she said, so Mrs. Kato had to go back and forth and argue. On her second trip she was there from five in the afternoon until three in the morning, and finally won the consent of Naoko's father and grandfather. The old lady never did give in, but was merely overruled."

Family considerations alone frequently determined the course of marriage arrangements, of course. "The women were discussing the Same-shima girl's very early marriage. Old lady Shiraki said it was a pity for a girl of only fifteen to have to marry. I wonder if it is more a pity than to be sold into bondage when just a girl. [The Shirakis are the family whose two daughters were sold to a house of prostitution and a restaurant, re-spectively. See pages 136–39.] It seems that the reason for the Sameshima's haste is that they have only two daughters and were in a hurry to get an adopted husband for their older girl. So while the younger sister is still in girls' school, her older sister already has three children."

Similar considerations of family interest might also delay a young woman's marriage. "Old man Irie was in. He said that their daughter is not yet married, although she is twenty-one, because her brother is younger and they cannot let her go until there is another helper in the house. That is, until they have taken in a bride for the son."

Young women could and did refuse marriages when they were not pleased with the prospective husband. "Kazuo's family proposed to the Hayashi Masaos that they marry their eldest daughter to him. The Hayashis replied that she has no kimono ready yet, whereupon Kazuo himself went to Taragi where she works and asked her point-blank if she would marry him. She said no, probably because he drinks too much and is considered unreliable. The other day, he was using the new telephone at the village office to call up a Menda restaurant. 'This is a certain government official speaking,' he said, to which the woman on the other end apparently re-plied, 'Why, it's Kazuo-san!' This confirms the general theory that he is a frequenter of the restaurants in town. He is said to spend about 100 yen a month there, but his salary is only thirty. The rest he gets from his family. It is no wonder the Hayashi girl refused to marry him, or that her family did not take up the offer."

"Marriages do seem to be arranged in accordance with one's po-sition. Mrs. Uchida, for instance, is married (not really married) to a sort of ne'er-do-well with no money and no standing, and she herself comes of a family of low estate. Her late brother was a public nuisance and the whereabouts of her family are uncertain. According to the family register he was born in Kawaze, and his death is recorded there, too, but about her it is hard to obtain any information. Some say she comes from Imamura, while others claim that her family once rented a house from the Satos, but no one is sure of their name. She does not like to talk about her family." A desire to conceal one's origins, then, may also explain the apparent inability of some individuals to recall their surnames.

Nonetheless, sometimes the differences between the two families were too great to be overcome, even when a woman's family made many concessions, knowing that a marriage would be difficult to arrange. "It seems that the Ochiais tried for the Tawaji girl who has been married once, but has come back home. Even though she is already old, which will make it hard to find a husband for her now, the backgrounds of the two houses are said to be too different to make a match possible."

There were other reasons for social disparity between the families of the bride and groom, or in their ages. "The old grandmother at Hayashi's has been away for a month. She is eighty-one. She went to attend her daughter's husband's funeral. The man was only one year younger than old lady Hayashi herself. He died at the age of eighty, while her daughter is only fifty-six. It seems that she already had an illegitimate child when they were married, hence the discrepancy in ages. He was a widower with children, and the old lady said, 'We wanted her to go to a nice place.' It is quite common for widows and unmarried mothers to marry a widower who is nice but not always as suitable as one would have wished."

The combination of independence of mind and unwed motherhood sometimes produced very complicated situations. "In Shirayama there was a house that died out, leaving only one daughter. Old man Hayashi who, for reasons unknown, was in charge of settling the affairs of the house, took the girl in. She eventually got pregnant by an unidentified man, but most probably one of his servants. Later he gave her as a bride in Fukada; she took her baby son with her. But after a while she divorced the man and married another, who refused to take her child. So he was sent back to the Hayashi's and they say of him, 'He is the child of someone in Fukada, and has become like a son to us.' "

Women often gave up their children for a variety of reasons. In this connection, Mrs. Kawabe's plans for her son's marriage as well as the history of her own are instructive. "I asked Mrs. Kawabe what they will do about selecting a bride for their son, who is going to work in Korea. She said that they will not get a farm girl because he will be employed in town. If they can find a bride from Hakata or some place around there, the wedding will be held in Korea, but if they get someone local, he will have to come back here for a while. But the whole thing is a long way off, she said, because her son refuses to marry until he is twenty-eight.

"Then I got a little more of her story straight. When her baby was only eight months old her first husband went into military service and was killed in the Russo-Japanese War. For the next seven years she stayed with his family, but at last it was decided that she should return to her parents' home. She continued to receive her late husband's pension, but the child was kept as his successor. She had gone home, but was very upset about having to leave the boy behind. 'I could do nothing about it. Of course, his father died for the sake of the country, but it was very hard for me, and very hard for the boy to grow up without having known his father.' She had a portrait made of her late husband, and as the boy began to grow, she would tell him about his father. 'But he always seemed sad and tears would come into his eyes.' Often, when they sit talking together, he says, 'Please don't talk about those old times. It only makes me cry.' Now he calls Kawabe 'father.' In any event, after only twenty-eight days at home, she came as a bride to Kawabe. 'So this is my second home, and it was very hard at first.' It was hard at first mostly because of the old lady who ran the house. She was very difficult to get along with, and died only recently at the age of eighty-two. 'She came from a samurai family,' said Mrs. Kawabe, and it is true that there are swords in the house."

In seeking a bride or groom for one's child, an important consideration was that of 'bad blood.' "Mrs. Tanimoto said that Tsutomu will have a hard time finding a bride. Both his father and grandfather had bad blood, and died of leprosy. (The descriptions sound more like a paralysis of some kind.) His father had to be buried in a long box, she said, because they could not bend him into a sitting position to fit into a regular [cask-shaped] coffin. This sounds fishy to me."

"Today she was still going strong on the subject of bad blood. This time she said that the father of the man we were discussing last time did not have it, but that the grandfather indeed died of leprosy. (No mistake, because she described the symptoms of open sores and pieces of skin sloughing off.) According to her, a grandchild of the old man also died of leprosy. There are few cases now, she said, although she knows of one in Kamo, and remembers seeing Mrs. Shimosaka's father when she was young. He suffered from it, and his daughter's dark skin comes from this bad blood. Bad blood is in the Maeno family, also, which is how she explains the bad matches made for their daughters. 'No one asked for them.' People are afraid to marry such people, for fear that the children will be infected. She does not know what it is, but something is the matter with the blood there, for the idiot girl from Yunoharu is Mrs. Maeno's niece, and her brother has a hare-lip, which is 'something ordained by the gods.' "

"Nothing happens here without drawing comments. Yesterday Mrs. Suzuki Tamezo went to Shoya to her sister's wedding. This girl had been working at home with her family in Oade, but is marrying a clothes dealer in Shoya. One woman asked why she had married so far away. I suggested, with genuine innocence, that perhaps the man had seen her somewhere and taken a liking to her. 'That's what the women are saying,' said Mrs. Tanimoto, meaning the Suzuki women. 'She is a pretty girl and he must have seen her here when he came through selling clothes. They must have had an affair.' (Just another traveling salesman story!) Whatever the reasons, the wedding took place yesterday and today her mother was going there again for a women's gathering for the bride."

THE WATANABE BRIDE

The unhappiness of many young women newly married into Suye families is revealed in its most extreme form by the story of the Watanabe bride. "As we were talking the Watanabe bride was mentioned. The women wondered whether she was getting along with her husband better now. All of this was news to me. They said that she was this and that, she did not know how to say good-day properly, she looked so haughty when pouring *shōchū* for guests, she turned her back on people and never said a word to them, and so on. It seems that the engagement had been arranged two years ago (she is now nineteen), whereupon she had cut her hair and refused to be married to Watanabe. The families agreed to wait a year, but even so she came to the wedding in tears. She has done nothing but weep since, they said. 'Maybe there is some other man,' suggested one of the women. She is said to refuse to sleep with her husband, who has been seeking advice from his friends, for he does not know what to do. 'But maybe it is all right now,' said Mrs. Tanimoto. 'Maybe she tried it once and decided she liked it.' "

"The Makino bride is said to be quite the opposite. She is short, but very nice, and helped serve at her own wedding. She was polite to everyone and has visited the grave of her mother-in-law frequently since the old lady died. Everyone mentioned how grand that wedding had been and how complete the bride's dowry was. Still, I heard Mrs. Tanimoto whisper that nothing had happened on the first night there either because the bride was unwilling or because she just could not do it. Having thoroughly enjoyed all the gossip and singing, they left."

"I can readily believe the stories about the Watanabe bride. The night she came to our house for a party she refused to mix, would not drink, condescended to do one dance only after much pleading, and sat all by herself in a corner with her back turned to everyone for most of the evening. She also stayed away from everyone at the parties for the soldiers. At our house, her husband asked me to offer her a drink because she would not mix. He seemed concerned about her behavior."

John Embree wrote that it may well be that she "wept at the wedding not because of her unwillingness to marry, although she had objected at first, but because of the differences in their ages. He is twenty-nine, she nineteen." Whatever the cause of her tears, her husband was very concerned about her. "He feels sorry for her because she is so inexperienced, and says she probably never exchanged a word with a man before their marriage. She graduated from girls' school this year and is the first of her classmates to marry. He thinks that she has so little experience that she probably had never even stayed at another's house or served food or drink to others before. She was brought up tenderly by her parents, who must feel very troubled about her behavior. Watanabe thinks that both bride and groom should have a few years before they marry to get to understand one another, and has come to believe that love-matches are a good thing. He thinks the problem is that her parents first decided on the marriage and then had to persuade her to go through with it. She was not inclined to come to him, but he says that cannot be helped. For all their current troubles, he hopes that some time in the future they will be able to get along well."

At one of the parties celebrating various victories in the day's athletic meet at the school, the Watanabe bride and two other young women were serving the guests. "The other two left, leaving her to entertain. She is still very reticent and kept her back turned to most of the doings. She served drinks, but looked a bit distracted and did not mix at all. I noticed that when she went to use the toilet she chose the one that has a door as against the open one that faces the house, which was used by all the other women at this party."

Intrigued by the gossip and by the quite unusually reserved behavior of this young woman, "I went to the Watanabe's. The bride, whom I found alone sewing, refused to commit herself about anything much and our chance for a tête-à-tête ended when her mother-in-law came home. She would not tell me how she felt about marrying a man she had seen only once, but did admit that she does not like Suye very much. She sounded less than joyful over the fact that her husband comes home at six o'clock every day. They sleep in a separate room from his parents, she reported, and said that she cooks and cleans the house. Her hair does look short, and may well have been cut off a year ago as the women claim. I left, discouraged at my failure to get any kind of information out of the girl."

"Now the women think the Watanabe bride, who objected to her husband so strongly at first, has changed. They say she fixes his lunch and takes it to him when he is working nearby. She is said to have developed considerable charm (aikyō), but is still young and bashful and won't talk much. Another report has it that the family agreed to excuse her from all farm work until she comes of age (twenty) a year from now. According to one of the teachers who used to teach in the village she is from, the Watanabe bride did not study well and was disobedient. Some people say that she must have had a lover and so objected to marrying Watanabe, whom she did not love, but that now things are all right between them."

The subject came up again one day in the course of a conversation on the standards of physical attractiveness. "I had further proof that our standards are quite different. While I definitely prefer the young Mrs. Toyama, Mrs. Kawabe thought that the Watanabe bride is better looking, although she admitted that she lacks charm, perhaps because she is so young. She said that now she and Watanabe get along quite well, but that for the first two months after they were married she would have nothing to do with him. She always turned away when he spoke, so that they never exchanged so much as a word. His parents were very worried, and it was especially hard for them because one does not like to air such domestic troubles and so they tried not to talk about it."

Our last view of her is less than promising. "On the way up to the bus stop we met Watanabe and his bride going back to Hitoyoshi for four days. She was not more talkative than usual, and while waiting for the bus she hid behind the *dō*, thus avoiding all possibility of conversation." John Embree's journal provides us with a hint that she has at least made the one friend who might help smooth her adjustment to the community: "His younger sister was with them, and they say the bride is friendly with her. She certainly is not friendly with most of the villagers. Last night, while we were all waiting for the bus, he sat alone in the shop while she waited behind the *dō* with his younger sister. Once on the bus she was no more communicative than usual."

THE KATO MARRIAGE

Some marriage arrangements went smoothly, however, and the final outcome appeared to please all parties to the affair. Such was the case with the Kato marriage, or more correctly, remarriage. "Young Mrs. Kato's impending remarriage is an open secret. Her first marriage, which lasted five years, broke up only recently. She left her husband because her mother objected to the way she was treated and to his spending money too freely. It does seem that he was powerfully fond of women, who were attracted to him by his undeniable good looks. Before he and the Kato daughter were married, he used to live in the extra room of a house in Oade and had an affair with his oldest brother's wife, who came by bicycle to see him all the time. Then he dropped her and for a while went around with the Menda girls. All along, he was calling on the Katos and the marriage was arranged. Not long after the wedding he began carrying on again, with one of the teachers and with the younger sister of Shimosaka. Mrs. Kato noticed all this and was very displeased. He, too, was an adopted husband and brought a big dowry, and was very jolly and all, but he was a ladies' man."

"Mrs. Sato says that the Kato daughter was very upset by her first husband's behavior, especially the way he carried on while her mother was away in Osaka for her younger daughter's delivery. Everyone had expected that the man would marry his mistress after the divorce from the Kato daughter, but something happened there and he did not, even though she was pregnant. He said that he could not be sure the baby was his, because she had two other lovers somewhere outside Suye. Besides, she said, he liked women in general, and when he was not with his wife or his mistress he was off with some restaurant girl. She said that he was a very special case."

The household was in a flurry of preparation. "Mrs. Kato said that the wedding will be all at her expense because the groom is an adopted husband. She talks at great length about it and does not conceal the fact that she is greatly relieved that it has all been arranged successfully. 'Shōchū tastes so much better now that I feel so happy. I could not drink while I was worrying,' she said. She discussed the groom and his family with Mrs. Tanimoto, much as if he is some prize animal she is buying. 'He is quite big,' she said, and Mrs. Tanimoto commented that it is indeed a good thing for a groom to be larger than his bride."

"Today Mrs. Kato called to apologize and say that owing to complications with the seamstress, her daughter's wedding will be postponed briefly. Hence the hamlet party for the bride, given by the women, will be put off, and she will let me know the new date. She said that the groom is 'funny-looking' but feels only relief since it was the first husband's good looks that started all the trouble. I suggested that perhaps her daughter feels differently about his funny looks, but the other day Mrs. Tanimoto told me that this is their fourth try at finding a groom, so she has to be satisfied regardless of what he looks like. The first three men they approached probably would not come because they were seeking an adopted husband. Few men will go under those circumstances unless it is a very good bargain. It seems to me that Mrs. Tanimoto once hinted that a man may also object if the bride is not a virgin, an argument that does not hold water, I have discovered, but perhaps she said that the objection is to a woman who has been married before."

"While Tawaji was at the store today I went in to buy something, and the subject of the Kato wedding came up. He insists that he and the groom are the same age, which means that Mrs. Kato has been lying about his age to make people think he is older than the bride. Today the women of the hamlet were invited for their party. In many cases their husbands went instead because the groom is an adopted husband. Most left early, but at nine there was still a small close group gathered about the bride and groom drinking sake. The groom sang, but neither he nor the bride would dance. Tomorrow is *mikka modori* [three-day return], when the couple will visit his parents."

The wedding over, the young couple settled into what is described elsewhere as an enviable season of the romance of early marriage. And "Mrs. Kato behaves as if she has just recovered from a severe illness. She beams as she works, greets everyone effusively, treats all her visitors to tea, and tells everyone how marvelous her daughter's new husband is. She says that he has a good heart and jokes a lot, and always comes home earlier than expected [rather than staying away from the house as long as possible, as many men do]."

"There was much discussion of the Kato marriage. I remarked that she goes to greet him when he comes home, and sees him off when he leaves the house. One of the women recalled that as a new bride she was always hurrying home to cook something nice for her first husband. I suggested that men here are not good because they never see their wives off or greet them when they return home. They agreed at once."

"Mrs. Kato positively throbs with delight these days. I took up the pictures of the wedding we had taken and she insisted that I come in for tea. On the spot she and her daughter decided to send the extra prints to some friends of theirs, while I happen to know from something he said to me that the groom wants to send them to the people in the photographs, who are his relatives. I wonder who will win?"

A few weeks later, "I was talking with Mrs. Fujita, when Mrs. Kato stopped by. She is still raving about her son-in-law, and all her stories are accompanied by her gay laughter. She told us how sorry she is for him because he has to rush between two houses [the one into which he married as an adopted husband and that of his own family]. He said only the other day that he would have his shirt washed at home, and she was amused because she could just imagine his family saying, 'Look, he went as an adopted husband and they won't even do his laundry.' She thinks that her daughter looks better now than she has in all her life, and her body seems just right for having a baby. She hopes it will come soon.

"Mrs. Fujita took it all in, laughed, and made a lot of cracks with double meanings, most of which went right by Mrs. Kato. After she was gone, Mrs. Fujita was very quiet until she was sure the other woman could not hear, and when I said that she certainly looks happy, she caught me right up. She said it was just the same with her daughter's first husband. Mrs. Kato had been just as happy and made just as much fuss over him until she found out what he was really like. But, she said, perhaps it will go better this time, because this man does seem to be better for the daughter and she might have a child. They think this husband is fine, but Mrs. Fujita is of the opinion that he is demanding and bad-tempered. She confided that he drinks a lot, and that he is very loud when he is drunk. The first husband, although he was a ladies' man, did not drink and had a better disposition."

Her enthusiasm undimmed, we last see Mrs. Kato at the autumn field-day at the school. "While exchanging drinks, Mrs. Kato did not miss a chance to discuss her daughter and her marvelous new groom, saying how well the girl looks now and how she has never been so stout. 'It must be that she has no worries on her mind,' she said."

Not all adoptive marriages worked out so well. "She says that she does not think much of Makino Otome, who is very bad-tempered and likes to be the boss (*taishō*). The dispute at the Makino's is about the family property. Hiroshi, Otome's husband, was adopted because her parents, having only two children, did not want to part with either of them. 'Who would ask for her anyway, with her face and her temper?' she asked. Before she died old lady Makino was very worried and would often say, 'We did the wrong thing. You should never take an adopted husband when you have a son of your own.' [See pages 3–4; 154.] Mrs. Fujita agrees with that one hundred percent, and predicts that they will separate within the year. She thinks that Otome and Hiroshi will get the bulk of the property, and that the rest will go to the son, with whom the old man will go to live."

The temper was not all on Otome's side. "This morning I stopped at Makino's and found that the old man has gone to Kumamoto. Hiroshi has a cold and was sitting near the fire-pit looking very sour. Their little boy was playing by his side. Otome, with the baby on her back, was sweeping out the rooms and airing the bedding. When the baby cried for something and she did not respond right away, Hiroshi became very angry, as he often does, and told her to hurry up and see what was the matter."

TRIAL MARRIAGE (MIKKA KASEI)

A very common form of marriage, practiced by poorer families or in cases where there were reasons for haste, involved minimal expense and display. A kind of trial marriage, it was called *mikka kasei* (three days' labor), about which there were many different views. On one thing all were agreed, however, and that was that they had once been more common than they were in 1935. "When I asked old lady Arasaki about the *miai* [marriage interview between prospective bride and groom] of the Hori bride, she did not understand me at first. Then she said, 'Oh *mikiai*. Yes, the groom comes alone and they serve only tea. (Others have also told me that only tea is served at *miai*.) Today they have this fancy business of *mikiai*. In my day we just went to the groom for the first time at the wedding ceremony, but after all they were all *mikka kasei* arrangements.' "

"The bride who went from Fukada to Oade yesterday was a *mikka kasei* bride. According to Mrs. Fujita, the old custom is that the bride spend two nights with the groom and return home on the third day. If she is considered satisfactory, the wedding will take place. If she is not, she simply remains at home. All reports are that it is most embarrassing to be rejected in these circumstances, and rather hard to make another match. Today, however, it seems that few such brides are rejected, and a trial marriage is usually agreed to only if everyone expects a positive outcome. The trial, therefore, is more formal than actual.

"Mrs. Fujita said that in this particular case, the trial occurred because the engagement had already taken place, but there had not been enough time to schedule the wedding before the new year, and weddings should not be held during the first month of the lunar year. So, since the ceremony will be delayed until the second month, the trial took place in order to make sure that the engagement will not be broken. The bride will stay about a week, not three days, hence it is not a real *mikka kasei*, she said, and will divide the rest of the time until the wedding between her home and that of the groom. When she went by, she was not dressed up, and her hair was done in the ordinary way [not the bridal coiffure]. Mrs.

Fujita thinks that such trial marriages are fairly common, but others say that things are done this way only if it is absolutely necessary."

"Another instance of *mikka kasei* marriage is that of the Arasaki daughter, age eighteen. Her grandmother said that weddings are too expensive nowadays, so some people hold simple ceremonies where only *shōchū* is served and no large sake cups are used. [Ceremonial sake cups are larger than ordinary ones. *Shōchū* cups, which are smaller than the ordinary sake cup, are never used on ceremonial occasions, although *shōchū* may be used then and referred to as sake.] The Arasaki bride has been at home since the *mikka kasei* period ended almost two months ago, and the wedding is now scheduled for the twenty-eighth of the lunar month. She spent three days with her husband and returned to her family, and then went back to his house. They both came here to visit at New Year's and she went back with him again, but was called by her parents to come help with the wood-cutting. She will now stay until the wedding. She did not look sad, gay, or otherwise impressed by her recent experience.

"In the meantime the groom has been coming up now and then, and spending an occasional night there. In fact, he called this morning and was greeted joyfully by all save the bride, who was busy spinning. She did not come out to greet him, but as soon as he finished shaving the old man, who was going out to call on Toride, the groom went into the room where she was working and stayed there the whole time. The bride's dowry was all there—the small dressing table and the chest of drawers filled with beautiful homespun kimono which she herself had woven, putting in elaborate designs, and dressy red bedding. The wedding will be in Nakashima but since the groom and the go between will come here to fetch the bride, her father is replacing all the sliding doors in the house with new ones."

The wedding was held in due course, and subsequently we learn something more of this particular *mikka kasei*. "The Arasaki girl slept with the husband when she went to his house, and he came here to sleep with her several times before the wedding itself. Mrs. Arasaki said that the arrangements are sometimes broken off after the initial three-day stay, but that nowadays they usually go through with the wedding. At first her daughter was worried because she felt she knew nothing about the new household, but now she feels better. She came back here a while ago because of a sore back, but after two days her husband came to fetch her and took her home on his bicycle. The man has been married twice before, she said, the second time to his mother's niece. She is the one who fell ill, went home to recover, and decided to stay there. She then remarked that having daughters is a great worry unless you can marry them off early. In her day, she said, the bride saw the groom for the first time at the wedding, but added that they were not particularly worried by this."

The matter of marrying a man one had never seen came up a number of times. "Mrs. Kawabe said that she did not see her husband until their wedding. Unlike Mrs. Arasaki, she said that one did worry about it, but that after the wedding ceremony everything was all right. Yoshie agreed, saying that she had seen her husband only once and was quite concerned before their wedding day. The old lady Sato said that in the old days it did not matter so much, because there was no electric light, and you did not mind because you could not see the man. Of course, on waking up the next morning, you would see this dreadful man beside you and say, 'Iya da! Iya da! What a terrible thing!' But in the dark it was all right. All this greatly amused the unmarried girls present."

Nevertheless, most young unmarried girls were extremely reluctant even to discuss their engagements. "This afternoon I heard that the girl servant at Tawaji's who is Nagata Nobuo's niece from Itsuki, is going away to be married. I went over to Nagata's and found the girl helping make cakes. When I asked what was up tonight, Nobuo said, 'Nothing. Just a village holiday and she has come to help us make cakes.' I asked her directly if she is leaving, and she said no. Later on the young boy of the house came in and said to her, 'When you go tomorrow . . .' which made everyone laugh. She continued to insist that the rumors of her impending marriage are false. But Nobuo's wife told me that the girl had been in Itsuki to visit her family at o-bon and she had seen this fellow, an Itsuki native now working in Hyogo Prefecture, who was also home on holiday. Some Itsuki people were the go-betweens, and tomorrow she is going there to be married. At this, said her cousin, 'Aren't you happy to marry such a good-looking fellow?' 'Not at all,' she replied calmly. Evidently the farewell party for her is tonight, but no one would admit it. She is nineteen."

"At Tawaji's, where I called later, everyone, including the bride, was working much as usual. Mrs. Tawaji was cleaning up the main room. I asked the bride about the coming wedding, and she laughed and said it is not yet, and that this is only a visit (o-cha iri) and she will just go there to see how things are. It should be a mikka kasei, but because the mother of the groom is dead, she will stay there a little longer than is the usual custom. The man she is to marry lives with his father and grandfather. She said that she saw him at New Year's, not o-bon. When I asked if he is a good man, she laughed and said that she is worried about everything concerning the marriage, but she did not look at all depressed. She assured me that they are cleaning the house for the coming festival, not for a wedding."

But it was for a wedding, although it was all done in some secrecy, so that few people knew about it. "Only three people went with the bride, her grandmother, Mrs. Sato Genzo, and the wife of the real go-between. I was told that there would be three women at the groom's house to greet her, two relatives and the wife of the formal go-between. When I arrived at the Tawaji house, the group was about to leave. The girl was all dressed up, but not in a bridal kimono. She was powdered and smiling, and I joked that I had come to say goodby. She said that she will be back in a few days, but I don't think she will, for it is said that she will have to stay longer at her groom's house than is the usual custom, as there are only men there."

The reluctance to discuss the plans for the wedding and the semi-secrecy in which the departure of the bride took place both suggest that the *mikka kasei* arrangement was not one that a family was proud to make. There were in Suye a number of different explanations of the custom. "Sato thinks that the word refers not to the three days of work which the bride gives the groom's house, but the rest-period she is given after her deflow-ering. This is an idiosyncratic view, and the more usual explanation is that the bride does in fact go for three days to help at the groom's house. She may stay longer [as did the Tawaji bride]. Mrs. Tanimoto said, 'I had a real *mikka kasei*, and came home after three days.' It is said to be a trial period, to see how things work out. If all goes well, the bride returns to her home to wait for the wedding day. No formal exchange of ceremonial sake cups (*san san ku do*) takes place, but the sake, which is really *shōchū* in these cases, is poured three times in the usual ceremonial fashion. The guests are only members of the immediate family and the closest relatives who live nearby. The food is fairly typical of ceremonial food, but not elaborate, and no gifts are brought by the guests. Mrs. Tanimoto says that in Japan almost all marriages are *mikka kasei*, but the non-farm women think it an awful custom. Mrs. Nakajima says that it does not exist at all where she is from, and all of them thought it peculiar to this area. It seems that adopted husbands can be brought in on the same basis, and they thought that the recent marriage of young Sato from Kinoue was such an adoptive trial marriage. Tawaji, on the other hand, says that *mikka kasei* is a make-shift arrangement, resorted to only because the dowry is not ready. He says that the three days referred to are those the bride spends at the groom's house. Thus, the 'marriage' has already taken place before the wedding ceremony, which occurs later when the bride's furniture and kimono are prepared."

"Today I met the Goto bride returning from having delivered a heavy load of wood to Suwa and we went up the path together. She says that she does not know when she is going to her husband's house in Hamanoue, but until she does she will continue to work for her family. Hers was a kind of *mikka kasei*, and she was married in a hurry because she was suspected of being pregnant by the Goto boy."

There were weddings of a very simple sort that were not true *mikka kasei*. "The first son of Noguchi was married yesterday. The wedding was very small indeed. The groom works in Miyazaki and the bride, without the fancy headdress, brought only her baggage over. She is a servant of Tawaji Bunzo, and originally comes from Shoya, but she has worked here for many years. The women of the hamlet expect to be invited over to meet her today. It is said that she will now go to join her husband in Miyazaki, and that someone from his family will accompany her there. (She never did leave Suye, but he came here several times to visit and finally moved back to stay.) On the same day, Suzuki took his second daughter to Menda for a marriage that was only slightly less simple. The girl went without the bridal headdress, but it is said that the groom was present and there were more guests."

"The day before yesterday the first fall bride went by from Taragi to Nakashima. At the moment she and the groom are in Tamaki's house, where the wedding ceremony was held. They are not to stay long, however, but will leave the old couple and go to Kumamoto where he has found work. Some people say it was *mikka kasei*, but others claim that it is called that only because the ceremony was so simple. When we called at the Tamaki house, the old woman, her younger sister, and the bride were cleaning up. It seems that there was a small ceremony last night. There will be no greeting party tonight, but the bride is expected to stay. The groom is the son of the old woman's younger sister, the bride is the niece of the old woman's husband, and comes from Hitoyoshi. Answers to my questions were given with a queer smile, so probably there are some peculiarities about the whole affair."

DIVORCE
It was the general opinion, held by women and men alike, that divorce was far less common in 1935 than it had been before. The bases for this point of view were various, however. "Mrs. Kato thinks that divorce is less common now and attributes the change to the fact that nowadays young people always have a chance to meet and talk before the wedding. Formerly, because the bride and groom never met until their wedding, they could not work things out between them in advance. She approves of the new system and in fact had her daughter's new husband come out here to meet the girl. In the old days, she said, there might be as many as seven or eight divorces in a family."

A considerably more pragmatic explanation was offered by a man. "Kubo said that the present elaborate wedding ceremony is more or less an innovation. Formerly they were very simple, and one could get married for five yen. That is why divorce was so frequent, for five yen you could go to a restaurant, visit a whore-house, or get married. As a result, one broke up marriages without too much thought. Now, however, so much money goes into them that one thinks a long time before getting a divorce."

Generally, the women thought that a wife would put up with a lot if the couple had children. "It is hard to believe that it was for the old lady there that Shimoda had made his first wife so miserable that 'she left in tears' in spite of having to leave her two children behind. Said Mrs. Wauchi, 'She must have been really troubled to do that.' "

And of one man it was said that "his first wife left him and later remarried. People say that they might not have been divorced had there been children, for under such circumstances divorces are rare. It is very hard on the youngsters to be left with one parent or the other. Of this,

Mrs. Tanimoto once remarked that the step-parent does not get along with the children of the original couple. As an example, she mentioned Mrs. Shimosaka and her step-son, who do not speak to one another for months on end. She even refuses to do his laundry. 'It must be very hard for his father to see them on such bad terms,' she said."

The role of the go-between, so critical in arranging marriages, was also of great importance in divorce settlements. "All property brought by the bride or the adopted husband is returned, and there is some division of property acquired by the couple since their marriage. This occasionally causes trouble. The person being divorced is also paid compensation, depending on the length of the marriage and how much she (or he) contributed to the income of the family. In the case of straight desertion, when a spouse simply goes off with someone else, no settlement is made. She said that divorce is very unpleasant, and thinks that it is much less frequent today and that settlement has become more difficult because the weddings are now so big and costly. The other women objected, saying that in the old days divorces were much more frequent because of problems with the mother-in-law and because the brides went out at much younger ages—often they were only fourteen or fifteen years old. They said that according to law, a man is not allowed to remarry within six months of a divorce in order to make sure that his ex-wife is not carrying his child, but that it is not observed much. Mrs. Amano said, 'All men forget quickly.' Said Sato, upon hearing of the frequency of divorce and remarriage in Hollywood, 'Easy to warm, easy to cool.' "

The divorce of Kawabe's sister raised both the question of children and the settlement of property. "The genealogy of this house is very complex, as I began to suspect lately whenever someone who was first called a sister or a brother would turn out to be something else. To begin with, Kawabe Tokio was adopted as the husband of the eldest Kawabe daughter, for the house had only girls. This wife died and it would have been the usual thing for him to marry her younger sister, but she was just a bit too young. Instead, he married the present Mrs. Kawabe, herself a widow. Later, the younger sister went to Taragi as the second wife of a widower, who had some children by his first wife. Things did not work out well, so the Kawabe daughter got a divorce and took her own child away with her when she left him. The man who had been go-between for the marriage was asked to pay her 300 yen on the grounds that she could not get along without money. The women said that this is not a common practice, but may be done if the relationship between the go-between and the couple is a good one, and if there is a good reason for the woman's leaving. If it is distinctly the husband's fault, he is supposed to pay 200 to 300 yen as parting money."

One divorce in particular was very much on the minds of the women late in the Embrees' stay. "I learned a bit of gossip while we were sitting having tea, when Misako asked one of the women if Mrs. Ouchi was still there. She said she had heard they had a bad fight which will lead to divorce because he has another woman. Not many seem to have heard about it yet, but old lady Matsumoto confirms that a few nights ago about eleven o'clock she heard loud voices that sounded like a quarrel. She says that he goes to Menda too often [to visit prostitutes]. This is an interesting case because it reveals the influence of the town on the village. Ouchi has many contacts outside Suye and is away a great deal. The couple do very few things together, unlike farm couples who do the work together, which requires that the men be home much of the time. Refusal of either spouse to do his or her share of the work will raise a row in most farm families. With the Ouchi divorce, the causes are quite different. She works very hard, and like most citified men, he has a bad reputation."

A more surprising break-up, because there had been little advance warning, was that of the Abe couple. They lived with her widowed mother and a young female servant. Suddenly it became known that Abe was divorcing his wife, and then only when he went to the village office to make the arrangements. The women said they had heard that he would pay her 300 yen and wanted her out of the house as quickly as possible because he had found another woman. "I went up to the Abe house, but found no one there. At length I discovered the old woman and Mrs. Abe in a small hut not far from the main house. The old woman complained that she had found it very inconvenient here in Suye when she first came and was worried for a while about living without electricity. But, she said, she has got used to it, even though she always lived in the city before. She had visited Suye many times, but moved in permanently only a short time ago because she did not like living alone in Kumamoto. She said, 'My daughter has been married for twenty-five years . . .' whereupon her daughter told her not to go into that and finished the sentence for her, 'So I have moved in here to live with my mother.' The daughter would not commit herself further, but the old woman said, 'Yes, he has divorced her. He does not want his old wife any more. He wants a young bride, so my daughter has moved in with me.' Mrs. Abe has been heard to complain that her husband is always buying gifts for the maid but nothing for her, and was threatening to discharge the maid. (Indeed, the maid was discharged finally and is now back with her family, but Mrs. Abe is leaving, too.) People say that she was ill, and while she was recuperating her husband got out of hand. I asked if a husband supports a wife after they part and they said it depends on the case."

"Old lady Ariyoshi denies the story that Abe tells about the maid, who is her older sister's daughter. She says that girl was discharged because of Mrs. Abe's complaints about her. The girl denies that she has done anything wrong, and says that Mrs. Abe has not left the house once at night, so it hardly seems possible that she was having an affair with the husband. But everyone says that Abe has another wife (*gonsai*) in Hitoyoshi, and Mrs. Uchida reports that she has often seen him coming home early in the morning."

The maid herself not only denied any wrongdoing, but also said that Mrs. Abe's charge that she had been getting too many gifts from her husband was simply untrue. But, as John Embree noted: "The girl is rather pretty, and flirts with the young men as she goes about the village." When asked what she planned to do, "she said that she has been approached for a year's contract work elsewhere. She laughed when I asked her if she found Mrs. Abe hard to get along with. 'A bit,' she said. It is her opinion that there will be no wedding ceremony when the new wife moves in, so that she will become his mistress (*mekake*). 'Maybe there was some ceremony when she became his mistress, but she has just moved in with him now that his real wife (*honsai*) is gone.' "

This conversation occurred after the 'real' Mrs. Abe's departure from Suye, which was not without color. "I heard that Mrs. Abe went to say goodby to the village office people last night, and someone cracked that she really went there because she owns some land in Suye and wants to stay on the good side of one of the officials who will protect her interests against her husband. This morning the old woman was hurrying to the village office to telephone the man who had promised to come for her baggage, but had not shown up. Her daughter was alone in the house and sour as ever. Everything was packed up, and a man from Shirayama came to take away a clay jar he had bought. She said they are going to Hakata to her brother's house. She also said that she does not want to leave, but that her mother insists.

"Sato says that Abe had told her that he would not pay her anything if she did not clear out at once, so she took 360 yen and left that night. From Mrs. Tanimoto I learned that a number of years ago the Abes had separated, and she had gone to work as a serving woman and made some money at the job. When he moved here, she came back to him and gave him 600 yen of her own money. Now, on the occasion of the divorce, she claimed her 600 yen and apparently got the 360 as additional compensation. Everybody says that he will bring in the other woman as soon as this one leaves. This woman, who comes here sometimes by bicycle, is a serving woman in Taragi, and they say is about twenty-seven years old."

John Embree's account is briefer, and based on the remarks of several men. "Old Takayama said that no woman can outwit Abe. His wife got the money which he used to start his business by working in a restaurant (as a prostitute, that is). Now that he is doing well financially and she is getting older, his eyes have turned to more youthful women. Takayama says that she will not get much of a settlement out of him. (His admiring tone itself reveals clearly some of the less attractive aspects of the attitude of men toward women in Suye.)"

Among the many somewhat irregular domestic situations, that of Maehara Kohei, thirty-seven, stands out for its complexity. The early references to this man and his two wives are brief. During one round of gossip among a group of women, "he was represented as a weakling who drinks a lot and then starts weeping, telling everyone how bad he is and how much trouble he has had." Mrs. Maehara was a member of the flower-arranging class. At one of its meetings "I heard her apologizing to Mrs. Wauchi, saying, 'A lot of trouble has been caused by my personal affairs,' referring to the recent quarrel between Mrs. Maehara and her husband." Upon inquiring as to the nature of Mrs. Wauchi's involvement in the affairs of the Maeharas, the complicated story began to come out.

From John Embree's journal: "Mori seems to have got into a fight with Maehara at the party. Since Maehara is generally regarded as the weaker of the two, another man stepped in and stopped the fight. Later, Maehara was blaming his wife for asking the third party to intervene. Evidently she is fed up with him, and went to Wauchi's to pour out her grievances. She wants to leave him permanently. After some talk, Wauchi and the man who had stopped the fight went to Maehara's house and patched things up after several hours of talking and drinking. Maehara felt that he had lost face when the fight was stopped. He has been married once before, and his first wife left him because he was too severe with her. (About the fight, the general feeling is that there is little to choose—Mori is much worse than Maehara, they say, and has cheated far more people.)"

Some weeks later, following up on the gossip, "I went to Aso expecting to renew my acquaintance with Mrs. Maehara. When I got there, however, I found a Mrs. Maehara I have never seen before. She mumbled something about someone being in Hakata [a city in Kyushu] but beyond that I could get no information. When I started to ask, 'Is it you I took the flower-arranging lessons with?' her husband interrupted and said yes, yes, without giving her a chance to say anything. But when I said that John had called there once, she made a slip and said, 'He has not been here since I came,' which allowed me to ask Maehara when she did come here, and it seems that it was only last April.

"So this is the woman he was said to have been keeping in Hakata. She is very pleasant and brought out a chair for me on the earth floor. She keeps cigarettes in a box and offers them to guests, an unheard of thing in farm houses. They have a nice garden with a variety of flowers planted in rows. The house, which is not a typical farmer's residence, is large. After preparing food, she changed kimono, sat with us, and exchanged drinks. The Maehara daughter came home from school, and I took a picture of her with this Mrs. Maehara. (I had always thought that Maehara's daughter was his first wife's child, but she looks very much like this woman and later said that she is her mother.) As she was showing me the way home, I asked if her mother had been here last winter. She smiled and said no. I had heard nothing of this change of wives."

That was precisely what had happened. "Of the Maehara change of wives the women thought favorably. This one is said to be a good worker and not 'an *okusan* type' [by implication a lady] like the one who has left. She gave a *kao mishiri* [a 'face-showing' party given by one who moves into a new community] when she arrived. 'At Maehara's,' they laughed, 'they have to throw such a party because the wives change so often.' (I learned later that his real wife—the first one—is not officially registered as such.)"

Maehara's first wife was a Suye woman, and they had been divorced some years before, but he had insisted on keeping their daughter. People said that she was very upset and missed the girl, and had offered to come back to live with him regardless of his beatings, just to be with her daughter. The divorce had finally come about after many disputes. John Embree's journal provides more details: "She then became the wife or mistress of two or three men in Kume. Meanwhile, Maehara married his second wife, and it was the quarrel between them that Wauchi, with some outside assistance, had settled. Now it appears that the second wife has gone to Miyazaki and the first wife has returned. People expect her to stay this time. It is said that she manages both Maehara and his finances." The women were later to say, however, that "Although the villagers prefer this woman, Maehara does not, because she always fights with him about her being such a good worker and his being so lazy. Mrs. Wauchi says that he really had only one big fight with his second wife, adding, 'But now I am over there all the time trying to settle their troubles.' "

Maehara, as one young man remarked, was probably the only man in Suye who was living with his first wife as his mistress, and that she appears to have been a strong woman. Nevertheless, her stormy marital career clearly reveals the very limited options available to a woman who, for all her strength, could be with her daughter only at great personal cost.

ADOPTION

Closely related to the issues of marriage, divorce, and remarriage is the well-attested tendency of the Japanese to adopt a child (or a husband for a daughter) in order to preserve family property intact and continue the family line. Adoption was seen by the villagers as a course of action not without peril, however. Mrs. Tanimoto made an interesting comment in this regard one day. "She said that little babies are cute, although she does profess to dislike children, but maintained that you could not become as attached to an adopted baby as to one you had carried in your own belly and delivered by yourself. She said that, after all, being alone is the best of all. She had adopted a niece way back, but had sent her home again because there was really nothing for her to do and she was only in the way. She plans to take her back later. As for adopting males as against females, she says it makes no difference, since you have to find a husband or a wife whichever you take in. You adopt whatever is available at the time."

"On the way back from Yunomae the other day we saw a girl whom Mrs. Wauchi identified as the niece once adopted but since sent back by Mrs. Tanimoto. She could not refrain from remarking that Mrs. Tanimoto is very hard to please, which is why she sent the girl back home. At the time the girl's mother said that the situation was quite impossible for the child, and that Mrs. Tanimoto had better get someone when she is very old and will need the child more. One young unmarried woman told me that her aunt had wanted to adopt her, but like many others, she did not want to go as an adopted child, preferring to find work instead."

The process of adoption was almost as complicated—and sometimes more so—as arranging a marriage. "Mrs. Kato says that adoptions are made through a go-between just as marriages are and for the same reasons. Without a go-between it is hard to settle problems when they arise; which they frequently do. A go-between can always be called in to negotiate differences."

"Mrs. Sato of Nakashima was having her afternoon meal, and her husband was out fishing. He goes every day, but seldom gets enough to make any money from their sale. A short while ago I had seen a young girl there. It turned out to be her older sister's son's daughter, whom they are thinking of adopting, and then getting a husband for her. 'But it looks impossible, because we are too poor,' she said. Adoption and marriage, she said, require a lot of money for the go-betweens, the food, and the exchange of gifts. 'It would cost at least twenty or thirty yen right away.' They have a son, but when he was sixteen he left to work in the mines. He never writes or sends money, so they consider him gone for good."

There were many comments on the difficulty of adoption, and the chance events that might spoil even the best-laid plans. "Her brother, now in Nagasaki, lost his first wife when their daughter was only nine months old, so the Hiranos brought up the child and when she was six, they returned her to her father, when he remarried. The agreement was that when his second wife had children of her own, they would take the girl back, but the woman proved to be barren. This accounts for the fact that the girl does not resemble her 'mother' at all. I had wondered about it when they were visiting here at *o-bon*. The girl refers to her aunt's family as her own and calls her aunt's real daughter 'sister.' Speaking of adoptions, Mrs. Hirano said that it is very difficult when the person adopted has grown up in some other house and formed his or her own habits. It cannot possibly work."

Upon occasion, adoptions result in genuinely tangled situations. "Mrs. Awaji had just returned from Taragi when I called about ten o'clock this morning. I tried to get some of her genealogy straight, which was not easy, because neither she nor her husband seems to know much about the family. At any rate, what I got goes like this: Awaji Tomoyasu was a younger brother of an Awaji family in Tontokoro who had established a separate household in Fukada. He was somehow related to Mrs. Amano's mother, who was from Hirayama. This Awaji Tomoyasu adopted her when she was a fifth-year student and brought her to Fukada. Her husband, who came as her adopted husband, had been a servant in Kumamoto, but being an eldest son could not change his surname, even though he had a younger brother in Kumamoto. 'There was a lot of trouble,' she said, 'because we were both adopted.' She refers to Tomoyasu, the man who adopted her, as 'grandfather.' The Awaji household has since died out, but the Amano keep their ancestral tablets, which they worship, even though none of their children was given the name Awaji."

Adoption was often the cause of conflict among family members, as John Embree's journal further attests. "There is disagreement between the two families about plans for an adoption. The two groups of relatives favor different candidates for adoption, so no one has been taken in yet. Yet it is over a year since the husband died and the old lady needs a young man in the house for practical as well as family reasons. She has a son of her own, but he is a bastard born before her marriage. He might have been a good candidate for adoption—his name was entered in another family's register when he was born—but he turned out to be a bad egg and is no longer in Suye. In fact, she routinely denies even having a son."

Another case complicated by adoptions was that of the Kawabe family. "Originally there was a Hayashi house that moved here from Hito-yoshi a long time ago. There had been many separations in the family, so that finally only an old man and his two daughters were left. For the elder daughter, Masao was adopted as a husband, and he came here from Yunomae with his mother and his younger sister. So the whole family was adopted, but since Masao was an only son they kept the name Kawabe. (It was a samurai family, which, they say, is why the old lady is so hard to please.) Masao's sister married a man who lived in Shoya. Then Masao's wife died, and after several other wives, the present one came. Then old Hayashi (who had adopted them all in the first place) died, and the name disappeared and the house became Kawabe, although Masao kept his Hayashi tablets. Mrs. Kato says, 'It sometimes happens that a family dies out, but if there is only one son—as in Masao's case—he cannot change his surname, so there is no help for it. What people do is adopt such a person even though there is the obstacle of the name, because they want a likeable man and it is often very hard to find just the right person.' "

John Embree provides some additional materials. "To keep a family alive, a son may be adopted. However, if the adoptee is an eldest son he cannot change his name except by consent of his kinsmen and the court. In such a case [where his wife takes his name] some of the children may be given the original surname of the adoptive father and some the surname of the family into which he has married. When Tamura was adopted by Kato, he had his name changed legally, but after separation, he resumed his original surname of Tamura. When a person is adopted into another family and appears to be the eldest son, it is very likely that he is not a true first son, but a bastard of the mother's born before her marriage."

Wives and Husbands

The women of Suye often spoke of conjugal relations, a subject about which Ella Wiswell early came to entertain some very definite opinions. On the whole, although there are occasional references to one happy family or another, and a few couples are singled out by the villagers as examples of conjugal bliss, the relations between wives and husbands generally were of such a character as to produce some of her most biting passages. The Embrees themselves were often used by the villagers, women and men alike, as a standard of comparison.

"Noguchi said that he thinks that John and I get along very well, while Japanese couples are forever quarreling because of disagreements about work and various other misunderstandings. Mrs. Sato confirmed that we seem never to fight, and that we do everything together, even visiting places where there will be women [that is, going to restaurants and parties where geisha and *shakufu* are in attendance]. She is always remarking on the fact that John takes me along swimming. A local couple that had got along for twenty-five years without a fight was cited as an outstanding exception."

The relationship between the newlywed young Katos [see pages 161–63] was a very special one. "The Kato couple went off to Hitoyoshi by bus for a few days. The relationship between them is very playful. They constantly exchange little jokes and jocular compliments. 'You know everything, don't you?' she says, smiling when he instructs her in some matter of which she knows nothing. She calls him *anata*, although it is said that most brides are too bashful to use this familiar term for some time after marriage. She started using this affectionate term earlier than most, they say, because it is her second marriage. (Which is also why she served drinks at their wedding party, not overcome by shyness like most of the brides.) She was dressed up and looked very happy. Marriage may bring much romance. The couple takes trips, makes visits here and there together, goes on boat excursions on the river, and the like. An unmarried girl hardly ever goes out like this with a fellow, except for the occasional meeting like the one Tamako had yesterday with her boyfriend. She usually goes with other girls or her parents."

Couples married longer sometimes gave every appearance of congeniality. "At Serizawa's I was given tea and cakes. While I was having these with him in the main room, his wife went out to the kitchen and was apparently taking great pains to prepare some special dish for me. He became concerned because it was taking so long, went out to see how she was doing, and fetched some trays for her. They seem a friendly, cooperative couple." Husbands sometimes helped out with domestic chores, albeit often under exceptional circumstances. "The pouring rain kept many people at home today, but some are still hiring out for transplanting or weeding in Shoya. Suzuki Tamezo sat at home all day and cooked the rice because his wife was out. As a rule women hire out for transplanting because they are good at it and men consider it hard work. On the following day, a village-wide day of rest, I found him giving his wife a shave. She was stretched out on the *tatami*, her eyes blissfully closed, while he carefully shaved her eyebrows, forehead, cheeks, and around the ears and neck."

And one formidable woman, who had no children, was said to be waited on by her husband. She was not highly regarded and it was said of her that "there is not a thing about other people's affairs that she does not know."

On the other hand, "Women do not occupy a very high position here, certainly. While a wife usually speaks to her husband with a certain degree of respect, there is less formality here than in the towns and cities, although they do say 'please.' The husband just demands 'Water!' or 'Rice!' and gets it. Our maid says that it is not customary for a man to say please when talking to a woman, and finds it quite natural that it should be so."

"The position of a Japanese wife is hardly enviable, with the constant necessity to be doing one type of work or another. She does nothing but cook, sew, wash, and wait on the men of the house all day long. For companionship there is left no room, unless it is a case like the Katos, where the mother does all the work. On our way back from a party in Menda we stopped at Wauchi's the other night. Mrs. Wauchi said that she had been working in the fields all day, and had planned to go out again at night with her son, but he would not let her. Said Wauchi, 'See how hard my wife works?' Said she, 'If we farm wives don't work, there will be nothing to eat.' Then she said to me, 'Your husband should have stayed overnight in Menda [that is, with a prostitute].' "

At Wauchi's on another occasion the exchange between the couple was even more pointed. "Wauchi came home later from some business in Menda. He stretched out on the floor and began to complain that there were food spots on the *tatami*. Whereupon she grumbled, 'If you would eat with the rest of the family, you would not notice things like that so much.' I begin to wonder if all is quite well in this family [it was not, as we shall see] since in making a joke this afternoon, Mrs. Wauchi had said that she has nothing but shamefully old clothes to wear and has to smoke a cast-off man's pipe. 'It must be nice to have a husband who buys you new things instead of one who only expects you to work and wait on him.' "

Certainly one of the criteria for a good wife was that she be a good worker. "I have learned that Tamaki Giichi has been married three times. His first wife is now in Hitoyoshi, the second is the sister of Kawabe, and his present wife, say the women, 'Is the best worker of them all.' " It was also agreed that among the chief virtues of a wife were patience and forbearance. "Of young Mrs. Mori, Mrs. Kato said, 'It is a pity about her. She has such a hard time doing the bidding of her husband and the old lady all day long.' "

Never far from the heart of most conversations about conjugal relations are the various professional women of the towns ("geisha," serving women, and prostitutes). Very early in the year, it seemed that "jealousy is not an obvious or current thing here. This morning when I dropped in at a store, I found the owner's wife Yae and Mrs. Shimosaka chatting. Their children were there, the older boys dutifully entertaining the baby. Yae's husband had gone to Hitoyoshi on an outing, so I asked them if they ever accompanied their husbands. Their reply was, 'No. How can we with all these children?' Aren't they ever lonely? No, they never are. Aren't they worried about their husbands going out alone? No, because when he gets back, he will tell you all about the things he did and saw. Do married men ever go to geisha houses? No, they never do. That was that, and said with apparent sincerity. Men and women never go out together. That has always been the custom. Mrs. Kawabe later confirmed their account. She said that she does not mind when her husband goes to geisha parties, as he sometimes must do in connection with business affairs, or is invited over by Mori, where at the New Year geisha are hired to come and entertain him and some of his friends." In a marginal note, written some months later, there appears the following comment: "On the matter of jealousy, see later notes. This information proved to be about the way things ought to be, not as they are."

The matter of geisha came up quite frequently. "Sato, genuinely puzzled, asked, 'But how do you satisfy your sexual urge if men have no geisha to go to in America?' I said that men have wives or sweethearts. 'No,' he said, 'a wife is different.' We went on to discuss prostitution in America, and I do wonder whether theirs is not the more honest attitude, however shocking on first encounter. He said there is no romance in marriage, only affection and certain obligations. All sexual pleasure is got in extramarital relations, they claimed, and on that score the wife simply does not count." For all the bravado displayed in this conversation, it is well to remember that the people of Suye discussed sex with much relish, and that most of them were talking about marital sex.

During their stay, the Embrees went on an excursion with some Suye men and friends from one of the nearby towns in the company of some of the Menda geisha just referred to. "Yae wanted to know all about our excursion, saying that women never get to go on such pleasure trips. They know that their husbands take along geisha, and they know that every time there is a party in town the men sleep with the girls. She said that nothing can be done about it. When a husband comes home from such an occasion, he says nothing at all, but is very reserved, holds his head high, and is asked no questions. Sometimes, however, there are domestic quarrels, and the wife will complain that she does nothing but work while he goes out on pleasure jaunts, but it does not get you anywhere to say such things. Today Mrs. Wauchi asked me whether there had been *shamisen* and geisha on our trip, of which she had heard nothing from her husband. 'It's nice for you. Look at me, working so hard to get ten or fifteen yen for the silk, and even that goes to my husband.'"

And in another group, it developed that "none of the women had ever gone down the river on a pleasure trip. There is no doubt that there is more romance and glamor in taking a moonlight trip on the river with a beautiful geisha rather than with your plain wife whom you see every day, but what do the women get? Mrs. Tanimoto says that it is only the men with money who can afford such outings, which I can readily believe. Our little excursion cost seventy yen." Many Suye families lived on less than that a month.

It is in a long conversation with a group of younger married men, in their thirties, that the most revealing sentiments are recorded. "After much talk about geisha we asked if a man is ever in love with his wife. They said, 'Of course he is, but that is quite a different thing. Married love is not the romantic love of young people. Foreigners have love first and then marry, but Japanese marry first and then love starts.' They proceeded to describe what they mean by married love.

"If you come home late at night drunk from a geisha party and your wife is waiting up for you no matter how late the hour, and greets you nicely, and folds your clothes which you drop on the floor, and covers you up when you lie down—when that happens you are touched to the bottom of your heart and understand what it is to have a good wife. And when you have spent twenty or thirty yen in one night and come home to find your wife mending *tabi* just to save twenty sen, you say, 'Why do you bother? Buy a new pair.' But later you think about it and realize how right she is, so you think hard and feel it to the bottom of your heart. That is a Japanese characteristic, they said. 'When you play, play hard—even going so far as to pawn your wife to meet your expenses. When thinking, think hard.' That, then, is married love, which they explained to John's assistant, who confessed that he did not yet know this higher type of love. (It takes about three years of married life, it seems, to begin to see the beauty of it and to develop this elevated type of love.)

"Yasuo said that tears come into his eyes when he watches his sisters working all day in the house and in the family's fields and then going out to work for others just to earn eighty or ninety sen [roughly a day's wage for field labor]. It's not really necessary for them to do this, but they are so proud of making even this small sum that he feels humility. (He does not think of helping out with the work, however.)

"The man from Kumamoto said that it is best not to bother looking for an intelligent, well-educated girl to marry, for you will find it is all no use once the children start to come. It is best to get some mountain girl who is good to look at but not too beautiful, who works hard, can do your laundry, and take care of the children. 'A man must train his wife to be a good mother,' John's assistant explained to us, quite impressed. Before their first child was born, said the man from Kumamoto, he always thought of buying little things for his wife, but now everything is for the child. A wife need not be educated; she is to be a mother. (Our maid denies such submissiveness in the women here. It cannot be helped when men go out, but wives do get angry and reproach their husbands when they return. But Yasuo did say that it is not reproach that makes for love, but submission.)" It will be remembered that one of the village men said that when a man passes fifty, his age-mates (dōnen) are closer to him than his wife.

The Embrees' maid, as we have seen, denied that Suye women were as submissive as some of the men alleged. There were many reports of quarrels between husband and wife. The principal cause was said to be jealousy, followed closely by money problems and refusal of either spouse to perform some assigned task. There seems little doubt that men retained firm control over family finances, although there is some evidence that women contrived to accumulate some money of their own. "The women were discussing household budgets. Mrs. Fujita says that she gets money from her husband any time she asks for it. She just says, 'Please put it in my bag.' He gives all the money earned from silk to her. But Take says that she does not get money piecemeal, but in lump sums, from the old man. But it is all wheedled out of her by the children, she says. Their son gets no money of his own from his father. Mrs. Fujita thought that her son may be handling the money now that he is grown up, but she is not sure."

"At this gathering there was another bit of gossip about money. Ishibashi gets a lot from his daughters, the women agreed—seven to ten yen a month regularly. When she was here last Fusako gave him seventeen yen, they said. Still, he never has any money with him, because without letting his daughters know he has set up two savings accounts where he deposits the money they send him. Whenever he goes out he has to borrow. Recently he received a letter from Fusako's eldest son, who is out working somewhere, asking for twenty yen, 'since I am your daughter's son and have a wife.' Ishibashi wrote back to say that he had no money to send.''

John Embree was told that "in most families the head of the house takes care of the finances. Other household members are given money when they need it. This includes the married son and his wife. In the case of an adopted husband, the head of the house usually gives him money every so often without being asked, for it is embarrasing to have to ask. Dis-adoption often occurs because of money troubles, he says. He has a younger daughter married in Hitoyoshi, and since she gets no money from her father-in-law, she makes rope and sells it to get money for herself." In another passage, he wrote: "Women evidently do have some private cash. Once Maehara [he of the two wives] was planning to sell some grain without drying it first. (It is sold by weight, and since undried grain is heavier the seller gets more money.) But it is the custom of this region to dry grain before selling it, so one sunny day Mrs. Maehara spread it all out to dry, not knowing her husband's intention. When he found out what she had done, he was very wroth, and demanded that she make up the 'loss' he would incur. So she had to go over to Hayashi's and buy some grain to make up the difference, using her own money for the purchase." This Mrs. Maehara, soon to be divorced, had come to the marriage with money earned working in restaurants and had actually staked her husband to 600 yen to help him establish his business. They were not full-time farmers.

The extent to which women controlled some of the income from household production of silk is demonstrated by the trials gone through in trying to purchase some homespun from Mrs. Harada. "I praised the silk, as did the old man, but Mrs. Harada kept saying it was dirty from weaving, had been bleached improperly, and so on. The knots I had admired were dismissed as defects, although to me they are the chief attraction of homespun. When I got down to business and offered to buy it, we could not get anywhere. She suggested that I buy some new silk thread and she will weave it for me, then said that if I had only spoken up sooner they would have woven me something special, and so on. Of price she knew nothing and could say nothing. But when I suggested that she ask her husband, she objected immediately, saying that her husband has nothing to do with this. It is all her work and he had nothing to do with it and knows nothing about it. The homespun, she said, is the only pleasure you get from raising the worms. The prices are low, and you don't see much money, but making the thread, weaving the cloth, and seeing a new kimono made of the material—those are the real pleasures. It seemed that it was just hard for her to part with the stuff." Clearly it was hers to dispose of.

Another woman who apparently had funds of her own was old lady Tamaki. "Tamaki bought a horse, which was brought from Menda by a broker who got this horse from Aso-gun where the best animals are raised. He produced the certificate and pedigree of the five-year-old mare. With him was another man from Menda, the formal go-between (in this case *sewanin*) for the deal. There were two or three others as well, one of whom was somewhat interested in buying Tamaki's old draught horse, used to pull wagons, which is for sale.

"Old lady Tamaki took an active part. They discussed the price and the rules of Kuma-gun that govern horse sales. Then the dealer and Tamaki clapped hands under a towel, and the dealer and the go-between did the same, mentioning the percentage to be paid the broker. The go-between did most of the talking. Then Tamaki, bringing out thirty yen, said to the old lady, 'Grandmother, you give them the rest.' She produced some bills wrapped in paper. 'Here is seventy yen,' said Tamaki. 'We will pay fifty later, toward the end of the month when we get the money for our last batch of silkworms or sooner if we sell the other horse.' The man said he wanted it in about five days and told them when he would come for it."

Upon occasion the consequences of the strength and financial independence of an older woman proved disastrous for others. "The Sasakis are moving to Kumamoto. He comes from Shoya originally and says that he thinks that Kumamoto is better than Suye. She is young and pretty and has a boy of seven by her first husband. It appears that she does not share her husband's view that the city is superior to the village. She was busy here and there all day, but at night as they started out and stopped to say goodby to Mori, her eyes were red from weeping. Their story is interesting. Her father and one sister are in Taiwan, and her brother works in Osaka. Last year her husband borrowed 100 yen from old lady Serizawa and as security mortgaged the house owned by his wife's now scattered family. The money (100 plus twenty-five yen interest) was due by the end of last year, but he could not pay it on time. Without wasting a moment, the old lady sold the house to someone else. When Sasaki learned what she had done, he protested, and finally managed to persuade her that he was entitled to fifty of the 135 yen she got for the house. So the buyer paid him twenty-five and 110 to her. She is supposed to pay the balance of twenty-five yen to Sasaki. So far he is still waiting. 'I hear the old lady has a new husband,' said Yasuo. The whole situation was being discussed today by the men working on the road. 'That old woman! (*ano baba*)' they would exclaim, describing her doings. Tonight the Sasakis left in pouring rain to walk to Menda to catch the train. Their baggage had been sent on ahead."

One day a family stopped by one of the shops in Kakui on their way back from the fields. There were five of them and all had popsicles. "The woman paid for them, and when I asked about it Mrs. Kawabe said there is no set rule. For instance, at Wauchi's the other day, when we started out on our shrine excursion, her married son gave some change to the old lady, who thanked him politely, and some to his wife, who simply took it. But she spent more than she got from him, so she must have money of her own. Mrs. Tanimoto says that the husband usually takes care of the big expenses, while women have the money to run the household. Around here, however, she said they never get very much, in contrast to the towns, where wives control the purse strings. But Hayashi was at the mill today, bragging that he went to five different houses last night and spent three yen on cider *(saidā)* and *shōchū*. On such occasions, he says, he often buys things on credit and his wife goes about the following morning paying off the debts he incurred the night before."

Other bits of evidence abound. "I saw Mrs. Uchida today and she was saying that if she keeps up all this running around *(asobi)* she will have no money left. She has not been able to sell any fruit for the past several days because of severe headaches. 'What about your husband?' I asked, and was assured that he brings in no money whatever. She is a nice person and does all the work there. He spends most of his time fishing, not always with success, but contrary to her statement, he sometimes sells his catch for a goodly sum."

Some old women learned a skill or two by means of which to make a little extra money. "Mrs. Fujita has a sore neck and stiff shoulders, from which people here often suffer. Whether it is from overwork or rheumatism due to the cold, damp weather, I do not know. She came to old lady Eda for a treatment. The old woman is famous for her skill. First she had the patient sit down, and massaged her. Then she had her stretch out on the floor and pressed her neck where Mrs. Fujita said it was particularly sore. Then she used her needle, which is of metal and blunt at one end. It is put into a bamboo tube about one and one half inches long. She applies the tube to the sore spot and presses the needle well into the flesh, removes the tube, and twists the needle further in. No blood is drawn, and the pain is said to be much relieved by this treatment. In her bag containing her equipment she has a bottle of alcohol, which she rubs on her hands and on the needle. She did not know why she does it, but old lady Mori confidently said that it is a disinfectant. After she puts the alcohol on the needle, she runs it through her oiled hair to make it slide more easily, just as one does when sewing. The old lady said that she learned this trade herself and bought the needle in Taragi. From each patient she collects a few sen 'just from the heart *(kokoro kara)*.' "

There were models of the conjugal relationship available to the villagers, in the form of stories in the newspapers and magazines, books, and film. Few villagers read very much, and it was in the films that they frequently were treated to the instructive examples of good and bad marriages. "The movie last night in Menda made fun of a 'modern' married couple. It was well done and well received. It dealt with a Japanese wife imitating foreign women—fixing her hair when she should have been attending to her husband's wants, and making him wait on her, fetch her things, refusing to help him at all, and causing him to be late to the office. As a contrast, a truly Japanese couple was portrayed. In the end, there was repentance and a happy ending when the bad wife came to understand at last how wrong her attitude was."

Certainly some husbands were extremely tolerant of their wives' shortcomings. Mrs. Fujita, who loved parties, stopped by the Embrees' house one evening, quite drunk. "Her husband does not drink, so she often goes to parties alone. When she comes home, he is always there waiting for her, and she says she feels ashamed and apologizes, but he always says it is all right, even if he does have to wait for his supper."

On the other hand, husbands frequently exercised decisive control over the domestic arrangements at whatever cost to their wives' happiness and peace of mind. "My suspicions about that house are correct. The man has both a wife and a *gonsai* living with him. All three seem to be on good terms, which I am told is unusual. This term is very interesting, for it is used to distinguish the woman from the real wife (*honsai*). The women say it used to be common to keep two women in the same house. For example, Sato Seisuke of Oade once brought home a geisha from Hitoyoshi. His wife did not like it much, but stayed on. When he died the geisha, whom they referred to as his *gonsai*, married a man in Taragi. His widow still lives in the house. Mrs. Fujita said that her father, long since dead, brought a geisha from Hakata home with him and installed her in the house along with his wife. The wife became very unhappy over the situation, so she left him and later married a man in Taragi. This habit of bringing in a concubine was pretty well accepted when she was young, she said, but not all women would put up with it even then." The implication is that even fewer would do so now.

There was considerable coolness between some couples. "I am always struck by his amazing detachment from his family. He was over at Eda's today, and as he sat helping with the work, his wife came in with their baby. She chatted with Mrs. Eda for a while, but he did not exchange a word with her or take note of the baby, nor did the child make any sign of recognition. After a while his wife left with the baby. He stayed on and one would never have suspected that there was any relationship between them." There is no evidence that they were on particularly bad terms, however, but the coolness between them was remarked on by the women.

Another couple provided an even more dramatic example of distance. "Mr. Tomokawa is still very ill. He has purchased all kinds of medicine, but none has had much effect. His wife strikes me as being rather lazy. While we were there she let a visiting kinswoman do all the work of serving the tea. When many callers came to visit when her husband first fell ill, she is said to have complained about having too many guests to look after. She is his second wife, much younger than he, and does not seem especially concerned about him."

Among the villagers there were men known to mistreat their wives physically. "Today Fujie was sent for from her home because her mother was sick. They said that she had been ill for several days, but that today she fell down in a fit and her daughter was needed to help out. Our maid wondered if it might not be a pregnancy attack, but when I went there I found her in a fit quite similar to Mrs. Makino's of a few weeks ago. The women who had gathered there said it seemed to be some kind of disease of the brain, caused by pressure of the blood on it. The doctor had been sent for. Said the women, 'It comes from too much worry.' Later they told me that her husband beats her a lot, so that she worries and gets these attacks after a few days of poor health. The children were playing at the neighbor's house and seemed quite cheerful, but later Fujie, looking very disconsolate, said that she would have to stay the night. Her mother did not move. When I went by the husband, who was working a bit away from the house, he did not speak to me. Later Fujie told me that her parents fight all the time, and that her father occasionally strikes her mother, who will not leave because of the children. She weeps occasionally over the situation at home. (They live off on the far edge of this hamlet and are the only people who do not fit into an otherwise very cooperative place.)"

"As I was standing in the street with Matsumoto Shima and Suzuki Mina there was a loud outcry from the Ochiai house. It was the wife there, shouting, 'That hurts!' There followed loud remonstrations from her son, '*Baka!* What are you doing?' We all turned. It did sound as if she might have been trying to do something she couldn't manage, but there is always the possibility of a fight. Later, when I asked her what had happened, she said, 'I wonder,' and looked a trifle embarrassed."

To the Embrees perhaps the most disturbing aspect of conjugal relations in Suye was the prevalence of venereal disease, contracted by men in their premarital or extramarital sexual relations, and passed on to their wives. "A few days ago Serizawa stopped by and Mrs. Fujita asked him in for tea while I was there. She asked after his wife, who has been ill lately. 'Is it morning sickness?' she asked. His reply was that it would be nice if it were, 'but it is something else.' She wanted to know why they have no children. He said that he does not know for sure, but is afraid it is his fault, because he has been to a doctor who told him that he cannot have any. She joked that he must have got all used up before he married. He seemed quite upset by his sterility, but later remarked that it is best for poor people not to have children anyway. (Since he is said to have led a fast life when still single, he probably has a case of gonorrhea that has rendered him sterile and infected his wife.)" The problem was not uncommon. "Suzuki Taketo has some kind of venereal disease, and makes no particular secret of it. His wife appears to have it as well, and all their young children have skin rashes which disappear when they are five or six years old." Of another man John Embree wrote: "Sasaki said that he visits the restaurants in Taragi, and once asked a girl [prostitute] if she was all right and she told him that she had no disease. But some days later he found that he had picked up gonorrhea. He told his wife about it and went to a doctor and got cured. He regarded it all as a bitter experience. Most men who contract venereal disease do not bother to tell their wives, I think. Suzuki's children almost all show signs of disease when they are young, and his wife is ill. The men think that practically all the girls in Menda and

Taragi are diseased, but that the prostitutes in Kumamoto are all right because they are licensed and regularly examined."

Thus, both wives and children suffered from its effects. "The young man has bad eyes, for which he was treated by doctors in town. Mrs. Amano says that it is the result of venereal disease in the family, and that when he was a child his eyes were always inflamed and full of pus. But it is hard to know if this is true, for any rash on a child is at once attributed to venereal disease, including even cradle-cap *(ushi no kuso)* on a baby's head, which is almost universal here and very vicious-looking.

"Mrs. Tanimoto tried to ascribe Mitchan's boils to venereal disease, too, but Shoko [the child's mother] says that her husband told her that he has never had any such disease. He has, however, had gonorrhea since he came here, a disease that is described as producing inflammation of the tip of the penis and pain during urination. Everyone laughed when I asked if he had got it in Menda, and Shoko said at once that it is not that kind of disease. 'The man at the drugstore in Menda says that Mitchan's boils are the result of too much sun and heat.' But she must have some doubts, for the child is literally bursting with boils all over her head and under her eyes. Possibly it is gonorrhea, but it is evident that their ideas on venereal disease are not very clear. Sato says that not all the diseases children have are from that cause, but that many are. (Interestingly enough, Mrs. Tanimoto did not ask of Shoko, 'Aren't you sick?' but rather 'Isn't your husband sick?')"

Among Suye women, old lady Mori had a firmly established reputation as a very difficult person. "She is always complaining about her son's drinking and is forever praising her daughter-in-law. As a matter of fact, young Mrs. Mori is a good person. She does all the work and has been up and about since the second day after her baby's birth. She takes care of the kids very well and in a truly wifely manner keeps her husband's clothes in order and helps him into his kimono when he dresses to go out. If I have some doubts as to whether Japanese children are good or bad, I have none whatsoever about the absolute goodness of Japanese wives."

In a conversation about marriage, there occurs the following remarkable statement concerning adultery committed by the wife. "Mrs. Fujita thinks that if a husband finds his wife in another man's arms, he will be very angry and beat the man up. It might lead to a separation." It is remarkable chiefly for not saying that the husband would beat up his wife and divorce her, which is more nearly what we would expect, given the common view of the treatment of adulterous women in Japanese society.

Mrs. Fujita's opinion is her own, of course, but it did suggest that the whole matter warranted investigation. Among the members of the class in flower-arranging, attended mostly by the wives of teachers and other nonfarm women, the view of marital infidelity was quite different. "At the flower-arranging lesson today one of the teachers told a story about an unfaithful husband. The women were all much surprised when I said that we have unfaithful husbands in America, too. During the subsequent conversation, the only kind of adultery they mentioned was that committed by married men who visit the restaurant girls. Sleeping with one's neighbor's wife did not seem conceivable, and as for wives committing adultery, there they drew the line. 'That sort of thing does not happen in Japan,' they said. Wives, it appears, disapprove of their husband's adultery, and some are seized by 'hysteria' [*hisuteri*] and third parties have to be called in to settle the matter. Then there was a lot of local gossip that I could not follow, and when I asked for clarification they only laughed and said that such stories were not for me. Women with whom I am not on intimate terms do not like to discuss local gossip with me. Only today, Mrs. Kawabe maintained that local married men do go to the Menda restaurants, while some time ago she had said that such things never occur. Obviously they try to conceal them."

The efforts at concealment were desultory at best, for shortly after this conversation, "there was an after-party [*ato iwai*] at Wauchi's. Suddenly Sonoda became very agitated. I found him sitting opposite Mrs. Wauchi, practically on top of her, trying to persuade her to sleep with him while her husband is away. All the while she was holding his wife's hand and kept trying to get him to go home with his wife. It was half-past three in the morning before most of the guests left. Everyone was reeling."

And at a field-day party at the school, "Mrs. Tanimoto was very gay and as always when drunk she ended up sitting with a bunch of men. There is a tendency here to hold hands when exchanging drinks if one is drunk enough."

The women had gathered for a bit of gossip and some tea, and the group included the widow Matsumoto. "Before we broke up, a couple of the women made jokes about the widow Matsumoto, saying that she entertains men at her house every night. She, smiling in her prim and proper manner, only shook her head in denial."

Struck by these remarks, "I sought out Mrs. Tanimoto, and this afternoon we had a long chat. It appears that her joke about the widow Matsumoto was not a lie. After the party at our house, Ochiai went there 'to have his pants fixed,' which obviously has nothing to do with mending. So I asked if the widow entertains men, and was assured that she does. 'She likes men and they like to go there. Isn't that awful?' she said. Both married and unmarried men go there, and some wives know all about it because, 'In the village there are a lot of evil tongues which will soon report to a wife that her husband was seen going to the widow's house.' When they hear this the wives get angry and jealous. The widow, she said, likes money, which she receives for her services.

"I asked about the risk of pregnancy, and was told that she has had her share of children (four, as a matter of fact), but that maybe she 'does something there.' It seems that there are other such women in Suye—

Ochiai Teru, for example, who lived with Shimosaka for a while. It was a great love, and one of her children is his. That is why he and his wife did not get along for a while, but he doesn't go to Teru any longer. The Ochiai family did not approve, but 'since he is an important man, he is more or less free to do what he likes,' she said."

The widow Matsumoto was mentioned frequently. "The women who are down on Sato Shichihei say that he and Koriyama are now the chief frequenters of the widow Matsumoto. They call the practice dirty, and when I said that I saw nothing dirty about it, they asked, 'Would you like to sleep with such a puny man?' ". Some time later, "all the talk of sex led to references to Tamaki, who is said to have displaced Sato and Koriyama at the widow's. Mrs. Amano said that she heard he was there last night, which may explain why Mrs. Matsumoto was unable to attend the party 'because of a sore back.' I suggested that under the circumstances, love-making was out of the question. 'Maybe they did it upside down, but most probably they did not really do it at all, but just had mouth-play.' I asked how she knew about such comings and goings. She said that I retire too early, and should watch about ten or eleven o'clock, when most people are asleep. (Still, all doors are always shut at night, and I have often been out that late, only to see nothing at all.) While John was away, the young men were hanging around late. When I went out to look, however, I could see no one nor did I see any signs of activity at the widow Matsumoto's. I think that what is significant is not whether anyone actually goes to see her, but that it is a recognized pattern that widows entertain men. Even Mrs. Tanimoto says it must be nice to be a widow, 'For then you can have any number of lovers.' " John Embree's journal is equally inconclusive: "Sato says that Sasatani went by the widow's house and asked for some tea, but she sent him away. The other night when Kawabe and others were drinking, she passed by the house, and Kawabe called out to ask her to give them some of her tea. She said she would, but Sato does not know if he went." Tea is not in fact the topic of this interchange.

"Mrs. Tanimoto said that the widow Matsumoto likes her *choppai*. (Not finding this word in the dictionary I had broached the subject to her. 'Does the word *choppai suru* mean intercourse?' I asked boldly. It does. She thought it the cutest expression, but hastened to tell me that men say *bobo suru*.) She heard some of this at Ishibashi's the other night, and some she has learned from others. She says that Sasatani Ukichi was at the widow's house the night we went moon-viewing, but that the widow told her that she does not like him even though he keeps courting her. One night Ishibashi went out to see who was with her and found her asleep in the arms of the Hirano boy ('The one who got Reiko pregnant. He takes them all!'). Anyone goes there. She suggested that I send John as a test. It seems the widow entertains her visitors upstairs, and so it is hard to see them from the street. (I still have no actual proof of any of this.)"

"The women finished their work, and the talk turned to marital infidelity. They said that while a wife is sent away at once if discovered [*pace*, Mrs. Fujita], the husband can have any number of mistresses, and the richer he is the more he has. An unfaithful husband is called fickle (*uwaki no hito*). In such cases the wife is said to burn with jealousy here, with a gesture to the stomach. They said that men go to visit *goke* (I thought they meant the Menda restaurant girls, but they meant widows). 'Why do married men go to such women?' they wondered. 'Is it that they want a change?' I gathered that Kawabe frequents the houses of widows a lot, as do some of the men in the village office. Said one of the Aso women to Mrs. Kawabe about her husband's activities, 'If he comes home by eleven at night, you have nothing to worry about.' "

"She went on to say that the old lady at Sato Shichihei's was also 'bad' in her youth. She never got married and just had children by different men. People said that she had them all by herself (*hitori de dekimashita*). 'When a widow has a child, that's what people always say,' she snorted. Old lady Sato's daughters followed their mother's bad example. One had a child before leaving Suye and another has had three children by a male servant who works in another house. Since the old woman's voice is very nasal, it is widely believed that she suffers from syphilis. What I cannot understand is how any of these people get any privacy in the houses here."

"She loves to discuss all these affairs, but never fails to register righteous indignation. 'Isn't it awful? It is really shameful for an unmarried woman to bear children.' This reminded her about Mrs. Suzuki Tamezo, who probably did such bad things in her youth, too, because when she married into Suye she brought a little boy with her. (Then she apologizes for gossiping so much.) She thinks that young people today do not go in for free love, although one does hear of a few cases. By and large, young people today are much stricter (*kataku narimashita*) than they were when she was young. Today it is usually unmarried women who carry on affairs, but married women sometimes do so. It is hard, she said, to find out what's going on in such cases."

It was hard, but not really impossible to find out. "I asked her if women were ever untrue to their husbands. She said that such things do occur, but very seldom in Suye. Then, lowering her voice, she said, 'Mrs. Toride and Sawara are like that,' bringing her two fingers together. The rest of the conversation was carried on in whispers. Mrs. Toride's husband does not know about it, for Sawara goes there only when he is away. Then Sawara is around all the time, and just the other day the neighbors saw them having morning rice together. This has been going on for five years now, and everyone thinks the baby is really Sawara's, because their eyes are so alike.

"She went on to talk about the infidelity of young Mrs. Kato's first husband, who fell in love with one of the teachers who used to be here. She is said to have been a very beautiful young woman, and it is well known that she left because she was pregnant, had the baby in secret, and was reassigned to a different school. That affair was the cause of the Kato divorce, and everyone had expected that the lovers would marry, but they could not for some reason, and so parted. Two months after his divorce, Kato married again, to another beautiful girl and she is now expecting a child. They live in Taragi. Later on I asked Fujie about the Kato divorce and she said that she did not know the cause for sure, but that it may have had something to do with another woman. The official explanation given here is simply that he is mad. I think that Fujie, like the rest of them, knows the true story, but does not want to discuss it, so parrots the explanation given the school children."

Other information was not long in coming. "When I asked if this group of women always meets at Tawaji's for their parties, one of them replied that they do because Mrs. Tawaji cannot trust her husband if she goes out. She nodded in the direction of the widow's house. Later on, when I acknowledged that American men are sometimes unfaithful, the widow said, 'The heart of men is the same everywhere,' and so their behavior is the same all over the world."

"The postman came and stayed for tea. He knows all the gossip about who keeps up a correspondence with whom and who is visiting whom. He told us about Uemura Akira of Oade who has three women there, which beats Maehara's two. In addition to his wife, Uemura keeps her younger sister, whom he takes with him everywhere he goes, and the widow at the shop next to Koyama's. The widow had wanted to take in an adopted child [as a means of securing support for her old age] but he would not let her. Uemura's wife worries quite a lot and seems to have lost weight as a result of her unhappiness. The women wanted to know how he manages his night life with the women all so close by, but that the postman could not tell them. He did volunteer the information, however, that in the city of Hakata all men have several women, just as Uemura does.

"I inquired if women ever behave the same way. 'Oh yes, women here often have another man besides their husband. They see him when their husbands are away.' They mentioned a case that sounds like Mrs. Tomokawa [see pages 193–94], and it was said that she has at least four men. Mrs. Maeno was also discussed as being famous for taking lovers. As I had suspected, her daughter left her job in Taragi because of the jealousy of the wife of her employer. So it seems the daughter is often worthy of the mother."

After some discussion of premarital sex in her day, "Mrs. Tanimoto said that in those days married women often—as they still do—had love affairs. As Wauchi Buichi went by, she called out a greeting to him, and said to me, 'Now there is a nice man, and if I were young, I would send him a note saying to come and see me, and he would.' If the husband finds out about such activities, he gets angry, beats up his wife, and may even

get a divorce, but husbands seldom find out. She said that Mrs. Toride is
having an affair with two different men right now."

"Of Mrs. Fujita she said that the woman would not keep her first
two husbands because she always found someone she liked better, and
each of her children is by a different father (the girl is Mori's, the boy is
Shimosaka's). There was a third child, who died, by a man who now lives
in Taragi. (Much later Mrs. Wauchi pointed out a house in Hitoyoshi where
Mrs. Fujita's first husband now lives. 'Is he the father of her children?' I
asked. 'Well, with her it is hard to say to whom the children belong,' was
the answer.) There is a back room in her house, it seems, to which the
men can be admitted directly from the outside."

Having tea one afternoon, "the old relationship between Ishibashi
and Mrs. Hayashi was discussed at length, Mrs. Kato being an authority
on the subject because they both live near her. Old lady Ochiai knows
about it, too, they said. They are pretty sure that Hayashi knows what is
going on, but that he does not mind because she used to get money from
Ishibashi. When their oldest daughter was born, the first girl after two
boys, Hayashi said, 'Since this is female, perhaps there was a different
seed.' The person who really minded was Ishibashi's wife. 'But,' said Mrs.
Kato, 'she did the same thing herself while she was still young and unmarried.' This came as a complete surprise to Mrs. Tanimoto [who is said
to know everything about everybody]. Several of Mrs. Ishibashi's esca-
pades were related, one of which Mrs. Kato remembered with particular
clarity because it happened on the night the Russo-Japanese War started.
As for the Hayashi-Ishibashi affair, it was all sixteen or seventeen years
ago, but they said that even now he always takes cakes when he calls
there."

Somewhat later, we find the following observation. "Of marital
infidelity I do not think there is an overabundance. When I asked Mrs.
Tanimoto whether anything is wrong between the Ouchi couple, she said,
'No, everything is all right now. There was some trouble for a while, but
not now.' Then she asked me who I thought was better, Mrs. Maeno or
Mrs. Ouchi. It seems that Ouchi and Mrs. Maeno had a short romance and
someone told Mrs. Ouchi who got very angry. Ouchi also had a short affair
with Mrs. Kawano, for when he gets drunk he likes women. The affair
was short because Kawano came home and found them and beat his wife.
As for Mrs. Maeno, she likes men, and Shibata was once her lover. (All
these stories get so involved eventually that one can hardly keep track of
who lived with whom and when and how it all got squared around.)"
What is interesting is that so many of the problems did get squared around,
and there was much talk about a woman in Ichibu who hanged herself
because she was found sleeping with her husband's sister's husband. No
such drastic atonement was made by any of the women involved in any
of the adulterous affairs reported to have occurred in Suye.

"There is much gossip concerning the Shimosaka family. The son is said to be far too fond of women, and the father has also been in trouble. Their next-door neighbors will have nothing to do with them because Shimosaka once seduced a sister of the husband of that house. When I asked if Shimosaka had been married before, I learned a great deal. She said that he has been married many times. One of his former wives is now Mrs. Tamura. Another of them remarried and lives in Taragi, but their daughter stayed with him and turns out to be the girl I thought was a servant, from the way he treats her. 'He likes women and had many mistresses, too. He and Sato.' This was a surprise to me, for I had always thought that the late Sato was an upright citizen. It appears that for some twenty years he was a lover of Namiko's mother, even while her husband was still living. Indeed, her youngest child is said to be his. It is true that the boy looks exactly like one of Sato's daughters, and that for a while she refused to go to school because everyone referred to him as her brother. 'It is dangerous to have such affairs, when children so often look like their parents,' said Mrs. Tanimoto, with some justice.

"It seems that Sato would go to her every night after her husband died about ten years ago, and come home after breakfast. Just five days before his fatal illness struck, he was there. Now that he is dead, she has taken up with Tamaki Takao. 'She must be a beauty,' said Mrs. Tanimoto, and when I demurred, she said, 'Maybe down here she is,' and pointed toward her lap. (In the course of this conversation she gave me the paternity of another illegitimate child, but she has it mixed up. It is interesting how people try to trace bastards right to their origins, and how general the knowledge of them is.)"

The parentage of Namiko, for one, was not in doubt. "Old lady Tanno was telling me about how well Namiko was working out as a helper. She lowered her voice and said, 'Her mother and old Sato. . . . She is his child, you know.' She said that it was such a flagrant affair that Mrs. Sato once protested to his face that it takes a lot of money to support two families, and then told some women about the scene that followed. 'Oh, yes, she was his mistress, all right,' she said. 'But then he had women wherever his business took him—Kumamoto, Taragi, Hitoyoshi. When he died, she did not come to the funeral. [A severe breach of etiquette, because they lived in the same hamlet.] Oh yes, there was much trouble in that house. He spent so much money. Do you know, he had four women servants?' "

The women who were parties to such liaisons often put on a bold public face. "At the party, there was one ironic touch when Mrs. Tanimoto started telling the women that I had told her that in America men do not have mistresses, and that if they take one, their wives are sure to divorce them. Said Teru, 'No *honsai* and *gonsai*, then,' and all smiled. 'That is good, because think of all the trouble women have here!' she added. Considering her own history with the Sato house, it was difficult not to laugh. All the women smiled oddly." Much later, a conversation during an excursion revealed that "the capacity for gossip of these women is much greater than that of Kawaze's women. It was very interesting that Teru, herself the object of much gossip, joined them in discussing the irregular lives of other women." Indeed, this woman was never particularly discreet in her behavior. "When we called there last night at nine, the party was about over. The husband was in a drunken sleep and a group of women from Oade was just leaving. Toyama Tokichi was sitting there, looking very much as though he intended to stay the night. Because of all the gossip, I have my suspicions about Teru, who acted as hostess and served us the drinks. She seemed to me to be rather playful with Tokichi."

The story of one of her adulterous affairs unfolded slowly through the year. "It seems I missed a cross-current of bad feeling yesterday at the party between Mrs. Shimosaka and Ochiai Teru who, I was told, never exchange drinks, but just sit silent when facing one another. It has to do with an old love affair between Shimosaka and Teru. [As we have just seen in an earlier conversation.] From Mrs. Tanimoto I learned that during the first year of Shimosaka's second marriage, he still continued his relationship with Teru. But one day her husband found them together—this was told with hand gestures to demonstrate how he had found them, one on top of the other—whereupon he went at Shimosaka and ripped out his kimono sleeve in the struggle. It was shortly after that that Teru and her husband separated. Shimosaka tried to hush the whole thing up, but Teru's husband spread the story and his wife found Shimosaka's torn kimono. Ever since then the two women have not been on speaking terms, and their husbands have severed all connections. She said that there is less bad feeling between Teru and Mrs. Mori because Mori's relationship with Teru, which resulted in the birth of another illegitimate girl, occurred before she and Mori were married."

Then there was the case of Mrs. Tomokawa, whose husband was seriously ill [see page 184]. "Mrs. Fujita assured me that Mrs. Tomokawa is all right 'because she has enough men to make up for it. She loves men and lots go there now.' As we were chatting with Mrs. Tamura, an elderly woman wearing a fairly light grey kimono went by. The two women exchanged glances and said that it was a shame, but that she too liked men and was somewhat mad to boot. It seems that she is Mrs. Tomokawa's elder sister, and dresses much too gaily for her fifty years. Her hair was done up in a kind of *marumage*, a chignon appropriate to a married woman. 'She should wear a kimono of darker color with a smaller pattern at her age,' they said. Her sister, of course, is accused of having the same fondness for men."

"It would appear that the chief offense of Mrs. Tomokawa is that she has gone, or rather has always been man-crazy. 'Crazy here,' said they, pointing to the vagina. While she was still young and married to a man in Hitoyoshi, she slept with her father-in-law, precipitating a divorce. Since she married Tomokawa, she has proceeded to seduce other men. Whenever she drinks, she climbs onto other men, usually married ones, and she is said even to have seduced her adopted daughter's husband. The daughter, being an intelligent woman, pretends not to notice and says nothing, but on the last visit her husband did not come with her (and is unlikely to ever visit there again) for fear of being assaulted by Tomokawa.

"She will take on any man who comes along, but one of the current favorites is Tawaji Ichiro. And finally, the reason for the extreme wrath that Mrs. Tanimoto directs toward Mrs. Tomokawa came out. The woman had gone after Tanimoto seven or so years ago. Whenever Mrs. Tanimoto would leave the house for a bath, Mrs. Tomokawa would come to their house and the two would sit close together, separating only when she returned. The woman is almost fifty now, and still wears a red kimono underskirt," which is much too youthful for her.

Perhaps most colorful and public of all the illicit liaisons was that between Wauchi and Mrs. Fujita. The party held after the memorial service for silkworms sets the stage. "After all the speeches and the priest's homily, the fun began. Food was brought in and spread out. During the preliminaries men and women sat separately, and for the party they took up positions at opposite ends of the room. But soon they started making the rounds to exchange drinks, and by the end were all very much mixed up together. Mori went over to exchange drinks with Mrs. Uchida, and I wonder if it is not the beginning of some new scandal. A few men got thrown to the floor and some were tossed into the air by the women. One of the teachers, anxious to see that all were having a good time, made the rounds with a cider bottle filled with *shōchū*, hurriedly pouring drinks without sitting formally.

"Mrs. Fujita promptly took off. 'I am offering drinks,' she announced and started her rounds. When she got to Wauchi she stuck. She held his hand, patted his knees, and practically sat on his lap. Said the woman with whom I was going around, exchanging drinks with everyone, 'She likes men, so she will be there forever. Let's move on.' Later Mrs. Fujita whispered to me that Wauchi had suggested that he come to visit her tonight. A few women left early, but the majority stayed until there was no more *shōchū*, and just as they were about to go, a new supply was rushed in. The dances were the usual, with much daring jerking of the hips. One woman had a very funny trick of holding her index finger in front of her in a very suggestive manner. Undoubtedly things do happen after these parties, for they get very chummy and flirt a great deal. (On the way home, one of the men put his arm around my shoulders. It was so dark that no one else could see.) In the closing hours of the party, Mrs. Fujita kept sending me and others to go take care of her husband and make him drink. She would press a cup into my hand and say, 'Go drink with my husband.' Before setting off for home with me for an after-party she went to see if he was still around, but otherwise had little to do with him."

Then the plot began to thicken. "Wauchi, who was among those we had left drinking at the school, arrived at our house to join the after-party then in full swing with much drinking and dancing. This morning, his wife was very surprised to hear about it. Her son, who had already got to our house when I arrived, had reported that I was very drunk, she said, but as he had left before his father's arrival, she had not heard of it. This morning, then, when I called there and was telling her about the after-party, she said, 'Oh, so he was at the school. That's why he is still asleep. He came home drunk.' Then she started questioning me. Had he come to our house with all the others or did he arrive later? Did he and Mrs. Fujita leave the party together? Some questions she asked several times and it became very obvious that Mrs. Fujita drinks a lot and likes men. 'Yes, she is always fondling them. There was once a lot of trouble here because of her. When you have a husband, you should not act like that with other men, and she has such a bad tongue. But she has charm and therefore men are attracted to her.' Jealousy is obviously at the bottom of this bad feeling."

Not long after, "while I was at Mrs. Fujita's house, she made a special point of stressing that she had left our house before Wauchi got there. 'I saw him only at a distance. Who was he with?' she asked. (After my conversation with Mrs. Wauchi of the other day, this insistence on the fact that she had left before he arrived is very interesting, for in fact she did not.) Later she said that she had gone right home and went to bed, and that she was in her house when some women stopped by and called out to her to come with them to a continuation of the after-party in Nakashima. She was too tired to join them, so she had not answered."

Still later, after the group of women returned from an excursion and stopped in at the Embree's house for the usual after-party, another group of women "burst into our house. They were from Kawaze, accompanied by many women from Imamura and a few from other hamlets. Shortly thereafter, Wauchi arrived and immediately started saying that although he had been with me at the last party (as though he had done something wrong) without his wife, she was with him this time. She came in, looked around, and insisted that we call Mrs. Fujita to join us. Someone was sent up to fetch her, but returned to say that Mrs. Fujita refused to come. Whereupon Mrs. Wauchi herself went out and soon returned dragging Mrs. Fujita along. She then spent the rest of the evening sitting by her side and offering her drinks, 'because she has just returned from a shrine pilgrimage.' (While she was out getting Mrs. Fujita, her husband had asked me, 'Where is my wife? I am worried.' All of this is more and more interesting.)

"Finally Wauchi came right out into the open. 'Which is prettier?' he asked me, 'my wife or Mrs. Fujita?' I said that his wife was, and he said, 'Of course.' Said Mrs. Toyama, who was sitting nearby, 'But both are his wives. Do you know what *naishin* [true feeling, innermost heart] means?' Wauchi mentioned the earlier party again. Had I told his wife that he had come here with Mrs. Fujita? Did his wife ask me a lot of questions? I tried to get out of it as best I could, but something is up all right. (Another jealous wife at this party behaved quite differently. When Teru arrived much later with a group of women, Mrs. Shimosaka promptly left, saying that she was drunk. The excuse had to be accepted for in fact she had earlier gone out to lie down in the kitchen for a while.)"

John Embree's journal contains this report: "At our party Wauchi tried carefully to avoid sitting next to Mrs. Fujita. Later his wife forced Mrs. Fujita to come over and sit between them, but he soon moved. The women sang a song about how 'once you liked me very much, but now you are so cold.' There were many jokes about *gonsai.*"

"To find out more, I called on Mrs. Fujita to try to get some more information on Mrs. Wauchi's behavior at our party last night. All she would say was, 'She came and dragged me out for *sakamukai*' [for the excursion mentioned above], and showed not the slightest trace of embarrassment. Later, when I told Mrs. Kato what had happened, she was more helpful. She laughed and said, 'Yes, they are not on very good terms!' and when I wondered if there might not be jealousy there, she said, 'Maybe so.' Neither Mrs. Fujita nor Mrs. Kato expressed surprise when I said that Mrs. Shimosaka had left the party when Teru arrived."

For all the public evidence that something might be going on between Wauchi and Mrs. Fujita, however, "Mrs. Kato and Mrs. Uchida said that his wife and she are getting along much better now, and they doubt that anything really happened. They think that it is only that Mrs. Wauchi is jealous and always suspects the worst." It is apparent that she had some reason to distrust Mrs. Fujita. "As usual there was much 'dirty' talk. Mrs. Fujita was saying that the parties of the Young Men's Association are no longer held at their house. Whether in that connection or another, she said that people in Kakui 'like only this' making the sign for vagina with her fingers. Evidently the meetings were discontinued, as she said, but the reason remains obscure. So, meetings used to be held at Fujita's house before they moved to the school. But since the term refers to anyone under forty, Fujita must have been a member too. When I asked him about it, he said that they were discontinued after he became too old for the group. Later when I asked Mrs. Fujita about her earlier remark—she had said that she had put a stop to the meetings at her house because the men misbehaved—she denied having made any such statement, and said that they just stopped automatically."

Despite the obvious tensions, there was a great deal of joking about the subject of adultery. "At our party Mrs. Maeno and a couple of other women were teasing Kawabe, saying that he cannot wait through the month after their baby is born (during which intercourse is prohibited), and so goes out to other women. He, of course, denied it." Their teasing of Kawabe was not unrelated to his reputation. On another occasion, "a man stopped in to ask for directions to a house where medicine for skin disease had been ordered. Said Mrs. Maeno at once 'Maybe it is Kawabe. He went to Menda to see about some rash he has got. It is like a woman taking a chance on getting pregnant. A man always runs the risk of picking up some disease.' Said John's assistant, 'I did not know that Mr. Kawabe goes to Menda so often.' 'Oh, no, that was before he was married,' said Mrs. Maeno, and smiled."

Many others were the target of jokes or made jokes about them-selves. "Tamaki got thoroughly drunk and could not find his way out of the house. Once he started off home and the women worried because he had taken the wrong direction, but one of them said, 'You don't have to worry in such cases. He'll be back.' Sure enough, he turned up again. The women teased him a lot, making jokes about his 'going home in that direction' pointing to Oade. They also joked about his having so many *okusan* [a term that is never used for farmers' wives], including his own."

"Setsuko stopped by and wanted to know where Harada was. Mrs. Harada said, 'I am so old and wrinkled that he won't have me any more. He's off sleeping with a pretty young woman.' Both women laughed."

"Old Goto was working in the mountains. When a man who wanted him to cut bamboo stopped by to fetch him and found him gone, he asked, 'Did he go alone?' They all laughed, 'Yes, yes, alone, alone. Unless he has picked up some grandmother (*baba*—old lady) somewhere, that is. You never can tell.' "

Sometimes, however, the joking turned serious. "In the afternoon, Mrs. Kawabe came over and wept because we will soon part. She brought my parents' pictures out of the other room and wept over them, probably thinking about her own parting with her daughter [who had gone to Korea]. Then Shimosaka and Mori came in drunk and joking. Said Mrs. Kawabe sharply, to Mori, 'It is a sickness with you. You can talk of nothing else.' (She meant other than sex.) 'It is hysteria,' she said, referring to his well-known love of women." There were other men with similar reputations. "Of Ishibashi, she says, 'He still wants women, so satisfies himself by spying on the widow. He used to love women. Just the other night, he told how after one of the moon-viewing parties he did not come home, and how angry his wife was.' When they and the Hayashis used to live close to one another, many years back, she reminded me, Ishibashi carried on an affair with Hayashi's wife, despite their considerable age difference."

A similar case is that of Makino. "Mrs. Hayashi went by on her way back from Kawaze where she had gone to help make *miso* [fermented bean-paste] and spent the night. The women said that she is becoming Makino's mistress (they used the term *yomego*—bride—rather than *mekake*) because she has spent the night there a couple of times before. They remarked that he is still young—fifty-eight or fifty-nine—and it is quite natural that he should want a woman since his wife died."

For women as well as men, the period of life after their sixtieth birthday was in theory one of lessened responsibilities and considerable freedom of action. It was often these old women of Suye whose behavior at parties most severely shocked the outsiders who lived there, and it was they who were thought most likely to be witches. For some of them old age was a pleasant enough period and they aged gracefully. For others illness, family troubles, and poverty were constant concerns.

"Mrs. Sato Eiji wears red flannels, which she says is a prerogative of sixty-one-year-olds, both men and women, who 'have become children again.' This came up when she was telling me that people openly laugh at the way she talks because she is old and uses old-fashioned words. As we sat there, old grandmother Hayashi came in to make a call after a long absence at her daughter's house in Hitoyoshi. 'It has been a long time,' she said, in the standard greeting for such occasions, and then added jokingly, 'You must have been lonely without me.' She is a very gay old lady. At eighty-one, dressed in work clothes and carrying a tremendous parasol, she was out to work in the fields soon after returning from a month's absence."

"At Matsumoto's old lady Eda was calling. The old blind grand-mother Matsumoto sat there, too, looking quite content. Another old woman who lives all alone in the Oade called later to bring a pair of straw sandals she had made for her. Old lady Matsumoto, despite her almost complete deafness and blindness, does all the household chores, including the dishes, and also does a lot of the cooking. When all the others in the house were out gleaning, she went off alone to gather some grass and visit her sister who lives in Nakashima. At the naming party for the Eda baby the other day she played the *shamisen* for a while. Because she is deaf she cannot hear where the sound of a voice comes from, and when given a cup she repeats her standard protestation, 'Oh, just a little, please,' and then returns it politely, often into thin air because she cannot tell if anyone is there or not."

Not all women were so agreeable. "At Tanno's a relative of the old woman was fixing the padded garments that had just been washed. Old lady Tanno is not able to do much now. Her visitor is a pleasant soul and seemed shocked at the old woman's abrupt manner with the children. [See pages 151; 208]. She asked me to come into the room on the mats when the old lady went out for a moment, because I had been left sitting on the boards on the porch. A girl from Tontokoro came to announce that her mother had given birth to a baby last night and to ask old man Tanno to come to the naming ceremony tomorrow. (The girl's mother is the old man's daughter by his first wife.) Old lady Tanno was very sour about the whole thing. 'Another child there,' she grumbled. 'Maybe this will be the last.' She was not very nice to the girl and did not ask her in. When the girl started to leave, the visiting relative looked upset. 'Oh, she is saying goodby,' she called to the old woman, who had gone into the next room again. 'After all, she has come a long way.' (Old lady Tanno refers to all her relatives as 'the old man's grandchild' or 'the old man's nephews,' as if she were no kin to them at all. But of the people in Shoya, where she is from, she says, 'my so and so.')"

They were sometimes on bad terms with their grown children. "This morning old lady Mori went past our house without bothering to say hello and looking very angry. It turned out that when she sat down to have rice with her son this morning he disapproved of her outfit and told her to go eat somewhere else, whereupon she left the house without eating and had tea at Matsumoto Shima's, where she aired her grievances." These grievances included her son's drinking and philandering, but she was on very good terms with her daughter-in-law.

The women in some three-generation households sometimes did not get on at all well. "Mrs. Sato [the wife of the head, so the middle generation here] only sat and talked to her guest, while young Mrs. Sato [the daughter-in-law] did all the work. She had been interrupted at her sewing and seemed a trifle cross. When someone suggested serving persimmons, the old grandmother got up to get them, whereupon the daughter-in-law said, 'Why do you go, grandmother? Mother [*kaka-san*, a term used for the wife of the household head] can go.' She gave Mrs. Sato a funny look, who only said, 'That's all right,' but made no move. The grandmother said, 'It's all right, I can get them.' Later, having put some vegetables on to cook, the daughter-in-law went back to her sewing, saying, '*Kaka-san*, please add the soy sauce and salt later.' As nothing was done, she came out in a little while and put in the seasoning with rather brusque movements. Mrs. Sato then got up and emptied the old rice from the pot, washed it, and left it empty in the kitchen. The daughter-in-law stopped her sewing again, washed the rice, and put the pot on the fire. Mrs. Sato, who had resumed her place, told the younger woman to get some *shōchū* and passed the teapot to her to be refilled with hot water. I left before the food was served, with the strong impression that the two women are not on very good terms." The impression is also very strong that the grandmother was doing her best to maintain harmony between them.

Several old women were unpopular because of their reputation for being vicious gossips (see page 5), and some because they were simply considered nuisances. "When I called at Sameshima's, old lady Irie from next door came over. She was neglected on my account, or perhaps for other reasons. She was not invited into the room where I was being served tea, and as she was not asked to stay left almost at once. I think Mrs. Sameshima may be tired of her because she is always dropping in."

There were, to be sure, occasions on which much solicitude is shown old women. "Since Kawabe has gone to Miyazaki for ten days her relatives stay with the old lady in turn. The grandmother was there during the day, the niece stayed the night. Today old man Uchida was sitting there with her to keep her company, he said."

"In Menda one always sees one or two Suye women selling wood, bamboo shoots, rice or vegetables. They often travel in pairs for company. Today I heard some women in Oade making arrangements to go there together. Tawaji Harumi was going to Tontokoro, where some houses had asked her to bring some particular items they wanted to buy. As she came by she saw an old woman with a pile of firewood sitting at Goto's. She told her to hurry along to get to town ahead of the others. Apparently Harumi is not worried about the competition, and later I did see the old woman coming back empty-handed [having sold her wood]."

Their attendance at the talks given by the Buddhist priests, involvement in temple affairs, and general interest in religious pilgrimages indicated clearly their concern with approaching death. "Said old lady Wauchi, as many others have, 'When you come back here in ten years I shall be sitting up there somewhere like this, looking down at you.' She folded her hands in imitation of a Buddhist image. The old women often say, 'We shall not meet again.' "

However difficult the lot of a wife might be, that of a widow or abandoned woman was undeniably worse, which explains the tendency of women to remarry if they possibly could. "I discovered a very poor woman living in the house next door to Uchida. It is a very mean house, which she rents from Uemura for 2.50 yen a month, and she goes to Uemura's for her bath [because she cannot afford to heat her own]. She says that everybody is rich around here, and sounds as if she is down on them all. This woman has five children, an older girl of seventeen working out somewhere, three in school, and a baby of two. Her husband left her three years ago when she was still carrying the last child. 'He never sent any money and never even came to see the baby. I have no idea where he is.' She cannot work with the baby on her back, so can cut wood only on Sundays when her other children can look after it. She works some upland field for Uemura. Her kimono was torn and her *geta* unmatched. She was doing the laundry when I stopped by, soaking some dirty baby clothes in cold water, taking them out, and putting them back in the same water to rinse. There was a piece of soap lying nearby, but I did not see her use it."

Without doubt the saddest of all were the elderly women who lived alone, having been abandoned by their children. "To indicate that someone is suspected of thieving, you hook your index finger and make a kind of catching motion with it. This I learned today while talking about the son of the Sugeta widow. He is not around and she always says that she has no children, so that many people do not even know that he exists. All sorts of stories are told about him."

"The widow Sakikawa was at home, and apparently had had a couple of drinks. When I offered her a cigarette she said that she does not smoke, but drinks a lot. She told me how lonely she is now, since her husband died in August, and how she has trouble sleeping. She said that one should have a lot of children. They had only two, and both died, so that she is now quite alone. I suggested that she marry again, but she said that she is too old, but that she might try to adopt a son. She does think that she would be happier now if she had some money. (She must be lonely, for she spends a lot of time peeking out through a knot-hole in her shutter watching what is going on along the path that passes right by the house.) She told me that she was born in Kinoue and has a few relatives there, but none here. Apparently she is distantly related to the Tannos, however, for she was helping out at the ridge-pole raising ceremony the other day."

"Old lady Eda sits in the sun and makes sandals out of bamboo skin. Her fingers are so stiff that she can hardly manipulate the material. Yesterday she was trying to patch some clothing, and it was pitiful to see her trying to hold the needle. She is an old widow who came to live with the Edas and is not treated on an equal basis with the other old lady of the house. She is never at their parties."

NINE

Mothers and Fathers

All of the women in Suye became wives and most became mothers. It was the rare woman who openly expressed a dislike for children. "If I tell a woman I have no children she is always sympathetic and says, 'You must be lonely.' " The Embrees were endlessly fascinated by the permissiveness with which the women and most of the men treated their children, and frequently astonished, as most foreigners in Japan have been, by the excessive indulgence shown them. Until they reached school age at least, both little girls and boys usually got what they demanded in the way of attention and care from adults of both sexes.

The people of Suye themselves often remarked on the very strong attachment between children and their mothers in particular. "At the farewell party of Nakashima the women had their babies with them. Mrs. Sato Mataichi's little girl—about five—never left her mother's side. When the woman went around exchanging drinks or doing anything else, the little girl followed her. At one time she got up to dance and the child flew into a tantrum. Hayashi made a remark about 'mother-child love' and said, 'Our children are like that. They do not want to be separated from their mothers for a moment.' The Kayama grandchild was having a fine time running from her grandfather to her grandmother with a towel wrapped around her head. When her father removed the towel to use for a dance, there was a terrible storm which took some time to quiet down." They were quite well aware that the attachment extends far beyond childhood. "A fight was reported to have occurred between the couple showing the movie and the woman had gone off crying. Shimosaka said, 'She was crying 'mother, mother,' because even when you get to be her age, you still cry for your mother when you are hurt.' "

The casual indulgence of small children is treated in some detail in the report of a visit with Mrs. Tawaji, who was busy at her weaving. "The baby got its hands dirty, and came up to have them cleaned, saying *bebe* [baby-talk for 'dirty']. On her way to her mother she stumbled over some *geta* left lying about by her elder sister and raised a yell. The older girl, told to pick her up, acted exactly as her mother does in similar situations, saying in a patronizing tone, 'What's happened? It's all right.' The baby stopped crying. 'Her nose, her nose,' her mother said for the hundredth time, as if the child's running nose was an unusual sight. The nine-year-old took a tiny piece of paper and wiped the baby's nose with it. Every time the baby came near her whimpering, her mother would ask, 'What is it? Oh, your nose,' put her hand into her kimono bosom, fail to find any paper there, and call to the older girl to wipe the baby's nose. She, busy sewing her pebble-bags (like bean-bags), would respond or not according to her mood. It did not much matter to anyone, obviously.

"The baby would yell '*shi-shi*' until she would actually start to wet herself, whereupon her sister would rush over, laughing, pick her up and let her finish. After a while the baby discovered a can of ashes and proceeded to amuse herself by filling up all the high rubber boots standing about, scattering ashes all over the front of the house. She picked up a sweet potato left by one of the boys and mixed it in a basin with some ashes. 'Dirty *(bebeka)*,' said the older girl. This magic word, used both for excreta and anything dirty, always works to make a child drop something it should not touch. The older girl took the ruined potato to the stable for the horses. (Nothing must ever be wasted. In this house they feed the rice from the funeral offerings to the horses, too.)

"No one paid any attention to the ash game, or at least no one minded it, until a neighbor passing through the yard said, 'Look at her, all dirty with ashes!' At once the mother said, 'Take them away from her.' But the older sister decided that there was no place to take them to, so she dragged the baby away instead, much to its distress, followed soon by tears, and tried to cover up the ashes. Then she was hit by a tidying-up spell. She emptied the boots, hung them up, cleaned the *geta*, and swept the front, sending clouds of dust and ash into the baby's face. 'Look, mother, look,' she exclaimed, holding up each ash-covered object. The mother would utter some appropriate exclamation and go on with her weaving. When the baby came over and practically sat on the loom she just said, 'My, my *(ara, ara)*,' and told her sister to take her away. The baby began to cry again and the mother told the girl to find something for it to play with. She repeated the instructions several times, and finally a dilapidated old book was fetched and the baby, much gratified, amused herself with it. The mother finished her weaving, got up and went in to cook the noon meal."

Such chaotic situations were not uncommon. "Looking for the Hayashi house in Kinoue I came to Tawaji's. The three-week-old baby was yelling under the mosquito net, a four-year-old was yelling in the kitchen, wanting her grandmother, who had just gone to the upland fields to take tea to the men harvesting there. The mother was in the kitchen, busy with something, and kept saying, 'Now, don't cry, don't cry.' This four-year-old can say only a few words and wets herself, which is very backward for local children. She was promised that her grandmother would be back soon and distracted with a story about a trip to Yunoharu she is to be taken on, and finally given a pillow to play with. Presently the grandmother returned and the child said, 'Grandma,' but did not jump into her arms as most children here would do. She had in the meantime been further distracted by being allowed to run in and out of the mosquito netting with her older brother, almost stepping on the baby, who never stopped yelling. The mother finally went under the net and attended to its wants."

"Children are a constant source of wonder. All through the day of the baby's funeral at Eda's the children behaved much as usual, running around, fighting, getting in people's way, refusing to go where told, asking for rice on all occasions, bringing food into the just cleaned main room, crying for mother or father, insisting on having their clothes changed, and then refusing to wear the garment produced. And for all that they got only a loud '*yoshi!*' [enough!] or a glare.

"The little girl got in the way only once when she hurt a tooth and wept very bitterly, although her father yelled at her to shut up. She was the only one of the kids who understood that there was a funeral, and cried for that as much as for her tooth. 'They do not know,' said the relatives about the little boys. With the mother sick in bed everything was a mess, because no one knew where anything was, and would wander about pulling one thing or another out of the closets. Occasionally Eda would know where something could be found, and would produce the item with a frown. He scowled at the children, but if something happened—as when the younger boy choked on a piece of glutinous rice cake—he became solicitous and tender, much like a great protective dog growling at the puppies.

"Yesterday they succeeded in getting the youngest boy to go off with the old lady. She carried him around all day, but every time he saw his father he yelled for him because they have been together a great deal during the mother's illness. Today, however, they could not get him to go with his elder sister no matter what they tried. He was making a dreadful noise and playing with the trays, following his older brother around. At length they persuaded the older boy to go outside, on the pretext of going to watch an athletic meet at the school, and told him to carry the little one with him. At one point the father exclaimed, 'What can you do with such a child?' as if he had nothing to do with its existence. They tried everything—something was going on at the school, there was a new machine at the mill, there was an airplane overhead, a sound-truck down the road, a drum-dance—but he seemed to sense that these were all lies or else he was simply determined to have his own way. Finally he fell to crying because he decided that he wanted a cake and none of those that were handed him were the kind he wanted, and anyway he wanted his father to give one to him. He got the one he wanted at last, choked on it, and had to be given water. After more persuading and more tears, his father finally took him on his back and carried him outside." It was of this man that she had earlier written, "Eda is very fond of his children and although he often glares at the oldest, he is always glad to see the youngest come back from a walk, and hugs him. He helps him change his clothes and asks him where he has been, what he did, and so on."

Indeed, many young fathers openly exhibited affection for their children. "Because his wife has not yet recovered from the effects of her miscarriage, the baby is with Fumio all the time. He plays with his son and carries him around and takes him on his back when he has to bicycle to Menda. Fumio said that Shoko has no milk, so the baby eats soft rice. I suggested buying cow's milk, but he said, 'That's no good when the baby's stomach is still upset.' " But he could not manage for long. "Shoko still being sick, Fumio took the baby to her mother's house in Hitoyoshi yesterday. It is said that it is a poor house with many children, but Fumio just could not handle everything here. He cooks the meals and scrubs the pans and is busy around the house all day, looking very cheerful, however."

"At the naming ceremony for the Tamura baby the young father showed much pride in his new son. He looked at the baby with great interest and affection during its bath, and was very helpful in finding various rags that would serve as towels and diapers."

Although the patience of most mothers was not inexhaustible, it seemed nearly so. "Mrs. Uemura was mending a kimono when I stopped in. She asked me to stay 'because I have nothing at all to do.' She has three boys and wants a girl. The baby was wearing a dress and his hair is still cut like an infant's, so that he does in fact look like a little girl. She pets her youngest, but is quite harsh with the middle one, who is the worst behaved and the most ill-tempered. When the youngest hit another baby and its sister said so, she said, 'Liar! You did it yourself.' She will first send a pesky child away, but always gives in and does what he asks. If a child wets the floor she says nothing, but someone will mop up the spot and the other children are amused."

Upon occasion, however, the permissiveness displayed in the above scene seemed to border on neglect and indifference. "While I was over at Amano's the other day, the baby boy threw his rice-ball on the floor. The older child picked it up and handed it to the mother, and when the baby refused to take it back, she absently ate it herself. She pays even less attention to the children than does their father. Even the old man is more attentive to them. When the baby cried for some sugar, she gave him some, but when he cried that it was not enough, she ignored him. The two men tried to soothe him, and in fact he did not cry very much. He whines in a tiny, squeaky voice, but does not yet talk, and his mother mimics him. He squeaked for some water to be put into a cup with his sugar, so she poured some boiling water out of the tea kettle. 'Now, be careful and sit down to drink it,' she admonished him. Since he is too young to understand, he drank it at once, and burning his tongue, set up a howl. When the old man reproached her for giving such hot water to the boy, she said, 'He did it to himself. I warned him.' Then she tried to force him to drink some more when it was cooled, called him *baka* when he refused, and made an effort to lull him to sleep. 'There, there,' she said, 'it will stop hurting soon.' He did not want to sleep, and finally pulled out her breast, but he was still in pain and dropped the breast and began to sob. She gets impatient with the children and snaps at them. To me she talks as if I were a criminal because I have left my baby in Tokyo."

For the most part, however, mothers and fathers were extremely solicitous of all small children. "One of the younger boys cut his hand trying to slice a persimmon. His mother scolded him and fetched some peroxide which she wanted to put on the wound. He made a face, protesting that it would smart, and after a fit of protestations, when he looked ready to cry, she gave up and wiped off the blood with a dirty piece of paper instead. Like most little boys, he knows well the influence of tears."

"Taro-chan created much excitement by catching Tae-chan, his little sister, on the cheek with a fish-hook. All the nursemaids gathered about, yelling at him, but none dared pull it out. The poor baby, who had been napping, yelled. Later she was taken home, and forgetting the pain, went around to show everyone where the scratch was. Her mother insisted that his father take the hooks away from the boy. 'What if he had got her in the eye? What if it had been someone else's baby?' "

"This evening Suzuki Taketo came over to look at some of our photographs while waiting for his little girl to come home from school dance practice. She is afraid to cross the fields alone. He was sitting out back to look at the pictures when the little girl came to the front of the house. She came around the corner weeping, for she had expected to meet him on the road and not finding him there had become very upset. Her father frowned at her for crying, but did not scold her. Soon his wife came over with the baby, as it was raining, and she was worried about the little girl."

Yet for all their affection for the children and all their concern for their well-being, there were a very few occasions on which adults were less than attentive to their needs. "At the woman's *kōgin* in Nakashima one event did surprise me. A little Hayashi boy who was playing in the yard got to crying and fell to the ground in a fit as if he were unconscious. An older boy went over to him, and pounded him on the back to restore his breath. 'Whose child is it?' asked the women, but not one went to have a look, and his mother was not present. Only the kids gathered round."

And at the night festival at the local Suwa shrine, "people began to gather about seven. The children arrived first and made a terrific racket throughout the performance of *o-kagura* [see pages 63; 84]. Some were much too young to attend the affair. The younger Ishikawa girl got a dreadful spell of weeping because she was cold and sleepy and wanted to go to the toilet and there was no one to take her out. Since no one paid any attention, she somehow shoved her way out to the edge of the porch and found an older sister. Kids are always being taken and sent places when they should be home in bed. The Moris tried to send their five-year-old boy to the shrine with some other children who were passing by, when the poor boy was so sleepy he could hardly sit up."

"Women never worry about leaving their babies in the care of young nursemaids for hours on end, but nonetheless most of their time is spent in taking care of the children, with a display of an infinite amount of patience and love. '*A-a-tta,*' a mother will repeat time and time again until the baby catches on to what she is trying to get it to react to, so that the kids begin using baby-talk very early. The words are repeated in a sing-song manner which the baby learns to imitate. Toilet training begins early, too. Babies are picked up any number of times during the day or night and taken out to urinate or defecate, assisted by grunts and hissing sounds from the mother. All this is done very casually, and if the baby protests and fails to perform, it is simply brought in again. So it is that often a child only twelve or fifteen months old who is just finding its legs will look uncomfortable and grunt, a sign to someone to take him outside. Diapers and rubber pants are used only if babies are carried around for any length of time or taken to some public affair such as a meeting at the school. Newborn babies are left strictly alone, lying in a room under a pile of comforters, except for an occasional outing after they are a month old on the back of an older sister or brother who wants to carry the baby. After about two months of age, they are carried everywhere. To put them to sleep, they are rocked on one's back or carried about cradled in one's arms."

"A very small child is never allowed to go to sleep alone. After he reaches school age he just falls asleep anywhere, but until then is usually put to sleep by his mother, father, sister or nursemaid. When still a baby, he is usually strapped on the back and rocked to sleep. As he gets older he is put down and the older person lies next to him, holding him close. If it is the mother, he usually has some milk and falls asleep with her nipple in his mouth. In fact, this is a test. If the child is really asleep the nipple is easily removed and the mother can get up and go about her business; if he is still awake, he will object and hold on."

It was considered very bad to leave a small child unattended, even when everyone in the house was busy. "When Mitchan found herself alone for a moment she started screaming. Everyone got excited. 'Oh, what a shame, leaving her alone like that.' When in the house, someone always sits beside the baby or holds it. Time and again I have found Mrs. Sato Kazuo sitting with her baby on her lap, and except when it sleeps it seems never to be let down. Today she said to Otome, 'It will not do to let him lie alone, for then he will only cry.' To which Otome replied, 'Yes, even when the baby cries at night, I pick her up and walk with her. She is not so heavy and it is no bother at all when it is your own baby.' It was a wonder to them that we let Clare sleep alone at such an early age."

Mothers were concerned that their children study, girls and boys alike. "Mrs. Mori asked the Hirano boy to help her little girl with her arithmetic homework because she herself never learned the metric system in school, and cannot be of much assistance. She is a wonderful mother."

"Along with everything else, mothers have to help children with their school lessons. Little Sato Emiko tugged at her mother's dress and pushed her book in front of her. She could not understand the problem, which was, 'If you buy *geta* for forty-two sen and *zōri* [thonged sandals] for five sen, how much change will you have from one yen?' In the first place she could not read it, so her mother read it for her and told her to sit down and try to figure it out. The fact that *zōri* cost only five sen amused her. 'Only five sen!' she exclaimed, and laughed. They both laughed all through the lesson, because the little girl could not concentrate and her mother was much amused by her."

Not all homework supervisors were so indulgent, however, among them the terrible-tempered old lady Tanno, the woman who had found a satisfactory husband on her tenth try. "She is forever grumbling at the grandchildren and ordering them around. She tells the little girl to study. 'At your age your sister was already studying the *shamisen* and doing her school work too. If you don't study hard you'll never get into girls' school.' Often when she yells at them she laughs, 'That's not the way to do it, you fool! There is not such another fool.' If they took her seriously they would be deathly afraid of her, but they do not seem to pay her much mind. She teaches the oldest girl how to serve tea and occasionally says things like, 'If I were well you would not have to do this,' almost apologetically."

Breast-feeding

All babies were regularly nursed by their mothers if they had enough milk, and when a child was fretful any woman present might give it her breast. Weaning was very late, although the following scene represents the extreme case. "While we were talking the eldest Eda boy came in and sat down beside his mother, playing with the baby she was nursing. Then he began to play with his mother's breasts, squeezing them, pulling on the nipples, and pressing out some milk. No one said anything. He is fourteen years old. (Evidently breasts are quite dissociated from sex.)"

The casual attitude toward breasts and the ease with which women produced them for children of quite advanced age was a constant source of surprise. "Mitchan was being taken care of by her father. Because her mother is ill she is deprived of the care to which she is accustomed and of her mother's milk. When the grandmother came in, she carried the child around for a while and then offered her her breast. Later, when Mrs. Ouchi called, she too gave her breast to the little girl. Even Mrs. Tanimoto, who professes to hate children, will open up her kimono and offer her dry breast to some fretful baby. While Mrs. Ouchi was nursing Mitchan, however, she told her older daughter to take her baby sister away because she usually starts a fuss when she sees her mother giving her breast to some other baby."

During preparation of food for the men of the fire brigade during a minor flood, "there was much joking among the women throughout. Everyone enjoyed the work and kept thanking one another for helping out. At one time I dropped a lighted match and Mrs. Nishi jumped up. The other women laughed, and one said, 'You have burned her vulva!' This set their minds in that direction and all complained that it perspires so much that it dribbles in the hot weather. Mrs. Nishi described it vividly, imitating the dribbling sound. Then Mrs. Sato Genzo picked up little Mitchan, who at once began fumbling for her breast. She produced it, with its tiny pink nipples and kept saying, 'Isn't it cute?' and played with the nipple as if it were a musical instrument, saying 'ping, ping' each time she flipped it with her finger. Mitchan did not drink, but proceeded to play with the nipple, too. As she reached out her arm to Mrs. Fujita, she opened her kimono and produced her breasts with their strangely large nipples. This started a general discussion of nipples, leading everyone to open up and bring out her small or large, long or short nipples for comparison. Old lady Eda's breasts looked so youthful that I asked her if she had ever had any children. She said she had one, but he disappeared last year and she has no idea where he is now."

Breast-feeding was not without its perils for the mother. "Otome has a bad scar on one breast. She says she got it when the older child was a baby and she contracted an infection through the nipple. 'Germs got in,' she says, and it had to be lanced by a doctor. 'It hurt so badly I couldn't speak.' "

"Today most of the people in Imamura were out working in the fields, leaving the old women and children at home. Old ladies Irie and Ariyoshi sat together in the sun watching the small children who kept running off out of sight. One little boy hurt himself and started to cry. He came to his grandmother and started fishing for her breast. 'You want milk, don't you?' said the old lady, whose breasts are so dry that they could not be used even for make-believe nursing. The child went on crying and reaching for her breast but was finally distracted and wandered off. This boy's baby brother died when only one month old and he has gone back to nursing, which is a very common pattern. Even when a child is outgrowing its breast-feeding days, if it is upset it promptly demands consolation in the familiar manner."

"On the way to Imamura I came across young Mrs. Serizawa. She was working on some felled trees, gathering up limbs. Her three-month-old baby was brought to her by the little boy who was looking after it. She fed it, cuddled it for a while, and sent them off. The baby had around its neck a tiny bag containing three small snail shells, brought from the mountain. This was done to stop its crying at night, and she said it had helped."

The usual feeding schedule for nursing babies was nine, twelve, three, and five o'clock, which meant that they often had to be taken out to where their mothers were working in the fields or forest. At rice transplanting time, when the little children were mostly at school with their siblings, "at the breaks in the transplanting, the mothers would look around anxiously to see if their babies have been brought to the fields yet. As it depends entirely on the child in charge of the baby, they are often late and arrive only after the mother has returned to her task."

"Mrs. Irie was working in the fields when I called and stopped to play with her four-year-old boy, who pretended to want milk but only played with her breasts. All mothers take a keen delight in handing their breasts to babies. Some train the babies to say please when asking for milk; others make them open up the kimono and take the breast out themselves."

"The Harada boy is five. He cries when waking up from his midday nap and gets the breast at once. If for some reason he has to be put down, he cries some more. When he gets sleepy, he will get his mother to lie down with him and give him her breast until he drops off. His brother was given the breast until he started school. The little boy at Fujita's is extremely spoiled. He is four or five years old and is the more spoiled because his parents argue in front of him about this and that. He will thereupon set up an obviously forced howl at the least provocation. He is picked up and petted by either parent, usually the one who precipitated the yelling. He still takes the breast, but laughs while at it. Today his mother said, 'You must not laugh while drinking milk.' "

"Very often one sees a woman absently playing with her breast, left hanging out after a child has been nursed. Babies also play with the breast while being nursed or when just sitting near the mother or on her lap."

At one of the many parties, "all the babies were there, crying for milk, asking for sweets, going to sleep. A delightful sight was Mrs. Hirano, both breasts hanging out, politely bowing and exchanging drinks with old man Ishibashi, while her youngest daughter kept whining for more milk. Later on she was smoking her pipe and nursing the baby. On such occasions both her breasts are out and the child absentmindedly pulls at the vacant nipple while nursing at the other."

"Wandering through Kamo, I came across Mrs. Hashida. Her son was running around playing with a bunch of other little boys, but he ran up to her, stood on tiptoe and had a good drink of milk from her breast. She laughed when I took a picture of the scene; he did not mind at all."

"While she was tending the silkworms, her four-year-old boy came in wanting milk. He refused to wait and threw the mulberry leaves around. She had to take him into another room, lie down and let him nurse. She smoked her pipe throughout and he went off to sleep."

"After nursing her own baby, Mrs. Kawabe gave her breast to the baby of the couple who tend the shrine. The two families are very close and she often helps out at shrine festivals."

"The Sameshima grandmother, who lives next door to the Kawabes, came by with the youngest baby in her charge. Mrs. Sameshima is short of milk, and Mrs. Kawabe at once offered her abundant breast. When the old woman said, 'Every day I bother you,' she said, 'What nonsense,' and took the baby to her bosom. Her own baby, a very healthy specimen, is carried around by his older brother, who looks after him like a nursemaid."

"At Suzuki's I found all the women busy with the silkworms. It was time for the baby to have his milk, but Mrs. Suzuki wanted to finish up, so she asked the oldest girl to carry the baby around for a while. She did so, bouncing it and singing to it, and finally took it out into the yard to watch the chickens. She came in every few minutes to ask, 'Mother, aren't you through yet?' The answer was, 'Take it away. It makes too much noise in here.' Finally when all the trays were finished and all went in for tea, she took the baby to her breast."

"When a baby gets older he is given some rice to stop his crying if his mother is not there to nurse him. Food is always used to console or coax or bribe. If a baby refuses to be taken on someone's back he will be given some food and grabbed up while he is absorbed with it."

From all the foregoing it is quite clear that a child was given the breast whenever it wanted to nurse, and until quite advanced ages. "Mrs. Kato says she nursed her younger daughter until the girl was nine years old and in the third grade. The child stopped of her own accord after seeing something about late nursing in a school movie. Otherwise, she always had mother's milk for breakfast and again after she got home from school." Some women strongly disapproved of the practice. "Mrs. Tanimoto [who has little love for children] was quite indignant because her six-year-old niece still is given the breast and yells if she is refused it." Not all mothers were so lenient. "Mrs. Amano says that she stopped nursing her last child when he was eighteen months old. Her children stopped wetting the bed at four years, however, after she began to take them out at night for toilet training."

Toilet Training

It can hardly be said that toilet training was very rigorous, but it did begin quite early. "As early as two months of age babies were held up for bladder training, although of course they wet their diapers often. They are not really trained until they can walk around and even when they are a year or two old they will have accidents if no one is around to watch them. Diapers are used when the baby is put down for a nap, and when they are taken out the skirts of their kimono are tucked up in back so that the garment remains more or less dry. A watchful nursemaid keeps the child dry, but some kids who have been forgotten by those in charge of them will wet on the floor of the *dō* without much fuss being made about it. 'Peeing like that in front of Kannon-sama,' exclaimed one of the nurse-maids, with mild disapproval, but she was not worried because her one-year-old charge is still kept in diapers. Today, however, Tae-chan, who is usually good about asking to be held up for urinating, gave up and just let go on the floor. At once her nursemaid rushed her off to hold her out over the ground, while some other girls mopped up. All cried, 'Dirty child!' and her little brother expressed much pleasure by going around crying, 'Tae peed! Tae peed!' The older children always make a game of looking after babies. If a baby has a bowel movement, the favorite trick is to make it stand on all fours while they run around looking for a stray piece of paper. Usually the baby tires of waiting and sits down, which makes every-one laugh. The other day I was at Tawaji Bunzo's. Their little girl, who is nine, is a perfect devil. She was left to look after the eighteen-month-old baby who was wandering about the yard. The baby has only a few teeth and is not very steady on her legs, so that her *geta* are tied on her feet with cords. She does get about, though, and can say a great many things in baby-talk. She also repeats anything that is said to her and imitates the actions of the older children. When she indicated that she wanted to uri-nate, her mother went right on weaving and asked the nine-year-old to hold her outside. She took her and held her over the cess-pool. When she was put back on the ground, the baby had a small bowel movement. Looking, the girl said, 'There is some left,' and squatted the baby down, raised its kimono and told it to wait while she ran into the house for some paper. The baby went right ahead and relieved herself. The little girl came back, raised the kimono, exclaimed, 'It's gone!' and broke into peals of laughter. Baby, mother, and the brothers all joined in."

The attitude toward cleanliness differed so greatly and some fam-ilies were so casual that it led to the following speculation on the differences among them. "I wonder whether it is early conditioning or living conditions that influence a person more. There is the Kuwagiri woman, Maeno's daughter. Now, the Maeno house is all right, but the Kuwagiri's is really dirty. The tea cups are never clean, she is always a mess, and the kids' faces have dirt on them that is often there for days. When I went over yesterday morning I saw some of the same spots that had been there the day before. The little boy's tail is filthy and his kimono shows signs of having been used to wipe instead of paper. (Often when a small child has a bowel movement, the nursemaid will run to the trash pile to find a piece of paper to wipe it with, but not all do it.)"

"Old lady Mori is forever complaining about the dirt in the Hayashi house. Mitchan's diapers and toilet habits bother her. She says the child's hands are never washed and she is never cleaned up properly. In her own case she says she would put her hand between the child's legs and smell it to make sure that the child was washed thoroughly. There is no doubt that the Mori kids are more pleasant to look at, and the baby there is the only one I have seen this summer without heat rash."

"Mrs. Shimoda came in and Tsune-chan got much attention, as usual. All of her achievements, such as pulling a cup toward her mouth, were discussed. Mrs. Sato favors this baby over her other son's new baby. Already Mrs. Shimoda is holding the child up and urging her to urinate by making the *shi-shi* sound." And on another occasion, "to cool off the women stopped work to have some tea. The Maeno baby created mild excitement by squatting quietly and moving her bowels on the *tatami*. She was snatched up at once and taken outside, but since some had already dropped on the mats, the place was thoroughly scrubbed. She was washed and changed, without any scolding."

"At night kids will huddle up somewhere in a corner and fall asleep. When they are to be put to bed finally, someone—often the grandparents—will call to them, 'Get up. Get up and go to bed, but go urinate first.' They never let a child go to bed without first seeing that it urinates."

"At Suzuki's house, the two-year-old wandered home having followed his grandfather whom he had seen going by as he was playing outside. He raised his kimono to urinate in the yard, but his older sister stopped him and told him to come along to the toilet. She placed him there, warned him against falling in, and went outside to wait. Both of them had a good time because he amused himself with his penis while she stood laughing at him. Later she came into the house to tell us all how funny he was. The whole family is the most good-natured imaginable. Everyone there is always giggling."

WHO SLEEPS BY WHOM?

The emotional and nurturant bonds between parents and their children were greatly strengthened by sleeping arrangements, which commonly paired an adult and a child. In Suye, as elsewhere in Japan,[1] it was the practice for the mother to sleep with the youngest child and the father with the next oldest. "At the Toride's I learned that the last but one child was given the breast until the age of six, when the baby arrived. The baby sleeps with its mother, the father sleeps alone, and the little boys sleep together. Mrs. Toride says that if there are no children, the husband and wife can sleep together, like the Fujitas do. I asked, 'But if you sleep separately, how do you make children?' She laughed."

"In the evening I called at Makino's. They were sitting around the fire-pit keeping warm. Otome had the small baby asleep on her breast and Hiroshi was busy writing something. The elderly Sato couple from Fukada were there, as were Kazuko [the Hayashi maid] and her friend the Ouchi girl who comes over to help her out from time to time. I asked what Kazuko

1. William A. Caudill and David W. Plath, "Who Sleeps by Whom? Parent-Child Involvement in Urban Japanese Families," *Psychiatry* 29, no. 4 (November 1966): 344–66.

was doing there, and that started a lively conversation. Hiroshi said that she had come to sleep with him, to be his number-two wife (*gonsai*), because his wife now has to sleep with the new baby. The Ouchi girl, they said, was to go to sleep with old man Sato, who had grown tired of his old wife. The girls protested violently, laughing. Then old lady Sato suggested that since I had decided to take Clare to leave her in Tokyo I ought to make another baby. (This decision of ours is discussed with some wonder. All the women said, 'We just could not part with our babies!') I said that I could hardly make another baby so quickly, which caused more merriment.

"Old lady Sato said that she never had any children because she preferred to sleep with her husband. To my question as to how she had managed not to have any children if she always sleeps with her husband, she replied, 'We just sleep. Nothing else.' I wondered if women with small children do not get lonely sleeping without their husbands. 'Not at all,' said Otome, 'babies are much nicer.' She said that you do not feel sorry for a husband, as you do for a baby, and that babies are much more lovable (*kawaī*). Hiroshi laughed and joked that she comes begging him to let her in beside him at night, and that he visits her when the baby is asleep. Later Hayashi Shoko said that during menstruation you sleep beside your husband, 'But you only sleep, because you are sick.' "

"At Mori's the nursemaid used to sleep alone, but in the summer, since there are only two mosquito nets, she and the old lady sleep with the little boy and the two little girls, all in a row, while the parents, the other little boy and the baby sleep together in the kitchen. When it is not hot, the parents put two sets of bedding together and sleep with the baby, with the youngest boy nearby."

"The older couple usually sleep in one room with the older children, the younger couple in another with the baby, who is placed in the mother's kimono when it is cold. Servants sleep separately. The *nema* [sleeping room] is often referred to as *komotsu tokoro* [child-bearing place], and is used for sleeping at all other times. To my question, 'What do you do about your husband if you sleep with the baby?' they usually laugh and reply, 'He sleeps alone.' Today, the Makinos told me that Otome sleeps in the *komotsu tokoro* with the new baby, while Hiroshi shares another room with their little daughter Tae-chan. The doctor recommends sexual abstention for forty-five days, but there is no taboo. She laughed when I asked if she is not lonely. 'This is the easiest way (*ichiban raku desu*),' she said, the usual answer when asked if the wife does not miss her husband."

"Mrs. Tanimoto thought that the mother's sleeping with the baby is no problem, since you can have intercourse after it falls asleep. But when the child reaches school age, it gets to be more complicated, because older children only pretend to be asleep and watch the proceedings. She cited her own experience. Nonetheless, she does not think that children go about imitating their parents, although today again I saw the boys shut themselves off in a shed and whisper."

"Our maid says that one hears about conception vaguely in the family when one's mother seems to be worried and says, 'I've made another child *(mata kodomo o tsukutta)*.' People don't want children too close together, she said. As for intercourse, she giggled when I brought it up. When you are small you sleep with mother and when you are much older you may go back to sleeping with her again. But in between parents sleep in one room and the children in another. When you sleep with them, you lie between your father and mother. She giggled again. 'I don't know what happens, because the kids always go to sleep.' "

At the Suzukis, "even though it is the season for feeding the silk-worms, the sleeping arrangements have not changed. The young couple, with one baby each, sleeps in one room; the old couple with the two little boys in another; the younger daughter with her aunt in a third. The servant sleeps in a separate shed in the yard."

"Mrs. Kawabe says that generally young couples share one room, and only go into separate rooms when they become grandparents. She does know of some cases where the young husband and wife sleep apart, however. Toride is one such, where the father sleeps with the boys in the main room and the mother with the baby and the nursemaid in the *inkyo beya* [a room originally added to the house for the retired old man and his wife]. Said the Toride nursemaid, who has been there for almost a year now, 'Not once have they slept together.'

"If there are no children, says Mrs. Kawabe, couples sleep together until they are fifty or older. Otherwise they stop at about forty. In their house, the parents sleep in the same room but with separate bedding. The girls sleep in the main room with their aunt. Later on, Tatchan went to sleep there, too, but her father said that he was lonely sleeping all by himself, so the aunt moved into a tiny room alone and Tatchan, now fifteen, sleeps with her father, 'in his arms.' I asked why she did not go sleep with her husband instead of sending their daughter, if he is so lonely. 'A child is more lovable,' she said. This investment of all affection in the children is quite common; a child is always dearer."

Happy Families and Beloved Children

Like the Fujitas, the Suzukis were a happy family. "They take the greatest pleasure in one another's company, and enjoy looking after each other. The other morning I found the mother and older daughter having a grand time watching the younger girl imitate the dances she had seen and mimicking the professional women who come to the Inari shrine. She pretended to be all dressed up and took polite little steps. When she got through, amidst general laughter, the baby went around imitating her, which everyone found even funnier."

The women and men of Suye very obviously loved their children and took great pride in their accomplishments. They cared about them and they tried to look after their needs as best they could. "Of small babies just learning to crawl, people say, 'The most dangerous time is when they do not know enough to be afraid.' Later they are taught to be afraid, and to be careful." Women took great pride in their babies and were always interested in those of other women. "The six people gathered to watch the hatching silkworms are thoroughly bored. Tamaki Ichiro's wife dropped in to leave the baby with him, saying she was tired of carrying it on her back while doing the laundry. She stayed to show off all its tricks, however—how fast she could crawl, how she could say *yaya* (baby), wave to one to come to her, and play peek-a-boo and other games. She gave the little girl a few sucks at her breast and went off to finish the laundry."

"At Shimoda's when I called this morning Koyo-chan was holding the baby, rocking and singing to it every time it squeaked. Mrs. Shimoda was roasting rice-cake while her daughter-in-law [the baby's mother] was busy with some household job. When Koyo-chan was wanted to fix the tea, the baby's mother was called in to hold it, and later Koyo-chan took it back. The baby is never left alone, but constantly carried about by someone, and cries constantly. The Mori baby, by contrast, is very quiet and is always left lying all by itself except when someone takes it out for an airing."

"The minute a baby cries—because it has hurt itself slightly or is annoyed at something—it is picked up by a nursemaid or someone who until that moment has been engrossed in some other activity. This is why the youngest baby cries so much and the next oldest, who has just been deprived of all the attention, is likely to fly into a tantrum." It seemed sometimes that "babies are not left in peace for a moment. They get put into a sitting or standing position even before they can hold up their heads. Some object will be placed in front of them, so that they have to bend down, maintaining their balance, to pick it up or grab it. Fretful or sleepy babies will often be given their grandmother's dry breast to quiet them. Alternatively, another woman will take them up and try to pacify them. Because it cried while Tamura grandmother had to do the laundry, she asked Mrs. Shibata, who was visiting, to hold it for her."

Despite the reluctance to leave babies unattended, "I did once see Mrs. Hirose fix her baby in a hammock and leave it there while she went out to do some planting in the fields." Other women occasionally did this too, but most disapproved strongly of the practice. "A few days ago at Hayashi Manzo's, Mrs. Kawabe and Mrs. Sato were scolding Mrs. Hayashi because she had gone off to the fields one day and left her youngest child at home alone. '*Baka na!*' they kept saying. She only laughed and assured them that nothing bad could happen. She is much younger than most of the housewives here and they all patronize her a good deal." Ordinarily in such circumstances, the child would be left with an older sibling. "Their mother is out in the fields, so the two little Nagata boys got some water in a basin and carefully washed their baby sister's face, rubbing at the dirty spots and carefully dabbing water here and there with their fingertips. She stood patiently through the operation. Younger children become very attached to their older brothers and sisters, who take care of them a lot. The little Suzuki girl came out in the evening with the new baby on her back, leading the older boy by the hand. He got tired, so she picked him up, too, clasping him to her front, almost disappearing between her two little brothers."

The appearance of babies was often commented on. "The naming ceremony was held today. The ugly baby was pronounced beautiful by all. At these affairs the shape of the baby's head is usually discussed. The ideal is a long head. The mother was up, this being eight days after birth, and greeted the guests. The father drank a lot and obviously was very proud of his new son." A little later, she observed this baby's mother and another woman. "The two of them come out in the afternoon, each holding the baby, and exchange compliments. 'My! What white skin!' To which the reply invariably is, 'No, she is not white at all. Doesn't your Ryo-chan have nice hair, so black and coarse. And look, he has teeth!' They make noises and faces at one another's children and discuss all their good points."

There was a great demand for photographs, especially of the children, and particularly the babies. "Today I took a photograph of the Shimoda baby, amidst much excitement, posing, demands to get as close to it as I could, so the picture would be as large as possible. I am drowned in demands for pictures of babies. The only woman who ever asked me to photograph her older son is Mrs. Nagata; all the others want babies. Earlier I took a picture of the little boy at Toyama Iwaji's. He is their youngest, and it seems they have a lot of photographs of him, taken at different ages, as well as some of the other children when they were infants. Men and women alike are very fond of their babies, and keep them in long hair as long as they can."

"This morning I went to Sakikawa's in Kawaze to take a picture, as I had promised. All the Kawaze women came to have me take pictures of their babies, too. Mrs. Shibata tried to stick her son and his bicycle into every picture. So did everyone else, with the result that all were spoiled by people pushing their babies in and the babies' yelling. Mrs. Shibata had herself photographed with her cat, he with the cow. All of this came about because they want to send a picture to their only daughter in Yahata, where she is studying midwifery."

"Everyone is pleased to get prints of the photographs I take. They are passed from one member of the family to another, old folks put on their glasses, and the kids are shown the pictures, repeating with great glee, 'It's grandpa! It's grandma!' Many are disappointed because the children did not smile for the picture. Many ask for extra prints to send to relatives or children or grandchildren. Old lady Goto wants to have her picture taken for her five-year-old grandson in Fukuoka—the one who was so attached to her, she says, when she was living there. She always tells the same story, about how he would follow her even when she went to the toilet and how if she got up early and left him in bed, he would cry when he woke up. She showed me his picture and looked at it lovingly, pointing out how he drew up his mouth at the corners in a characteristic way when he was being serious."

Baths for the baby were a big occasion for the other children, neighbors, and any adults who happened to be about. "Sato Etsuko bathed the baby. She does it every day, she said, for the midwife came only during the first week. She says that others do not do it every day. The family assembled to watch, and the older daughter waited impatiently to be allowed to hold the baby after its bath. Kazuo [the baby's father] smiled at it and said, 'You're growing fast.' His younger brother, visiting from Hakata, was close by, being helpful and obviously enjoying the child. Earlier he had picked it up when it cried and crooned to it. This is the only house where they use a clean piece of cloth for a wash-rag. Two white undergarments are put inside the regular padded one, each tied separately. Diapers are just wrapped around and allowed to hang loose, but sometimes an inner padding is folded up and tucked between the baby's legs."

Some children were a delight to all. "Tonight at Makino's there was bath-taking in a big way. Taro-chan bathed with his grandfather, his baby sister Tae-chan with the mother. Taro-chan had been awakened from his nap and taken out under great protest, but he soon quieted down in the bath and was brought back across the street wrapped snugly in a small towel to protect him from the chill night air. All clean and pink, he was dressed in the same clothes. The baby, wide awake, was delighted with the idea of a bath and made movements of taking off her clothes when the word was mentioned. While splashing in the water she made a grunting sound and was promptly removed and held out over the ground. Her mother made the standard *shi-shi* sound, which worked. The two children played together for a while, and it was evident that their mother took a keen delight in watching them. Little Tae-chan is growing very rapidly, and now shows her age by holding up three fingers. Her brother can show his age and tell you how old he will be next year, the year after that, and the year he will go to school. Tae-chan will do what she is told and manages her chopsticks pretty well now. She and her brother have a good time together."

"Altogether there are nine people in the Tawaji house, counting the servants. The baby of the house, two years old now, toddles about, talks baby-talk incessantly, and seems to understand everything. She greets visitors by kneeling and bowing quite properly. Rice is *mamma*, water *momo*. There is a special word for sitting down, *chin-shinai*, and for walking, *ambe-ambe*. There are others for falling down and for throwing something away. Dirty is *bebe*. But if she wants more of something to eat, she says *mo itchō*, like any adult. She also sees to it that she gets what she wants. People will sometimes try to ignore a demand for another helping, which is forthcoming every time a child has been given anything, but as a rule the children end up getting what they are after. The Tawaji children came in where the silkworm *kumiai* party was being held, and were given some rice. The baby used her chopsticks quite cleverly to eat pickles between sucks at her mother's breast. The older children settled down quietly to do homework for school. The little Goto girl made a fierce face at the baby, which she thought was funny, but when the adults implied that it was really scary she decided to be frightened and ran away."

"Mrs. Mori says that all her children were toilet trained early and did not wet the bed from an early age. The youngest is now two and is trained day and night. He talks a good deal, understands everything, and plays with a penknife and hammer and nails. He spends most of his time with his grandmother. Everyone uses baby-talk a great deal when speaking to children, and the kids themselves use it when they first begin to talk. Although the Mori children are spoiled, there is a certain amount of discipline, mostly learned through imitation and the mother's constant admonitions. Mrs. Hayashi, too, spends hours with her baby, giving her something to eat or making her understand what to do with the pieces of food. If she grabs at something lying around, her mother will say 'kudai' or 'chōdai' (please), over and over again until the child hands it to her, and each time she is given something, she says 'attō' for thank you."

"At Makino's, all, including the four-year-old boy, were eating at the table in the kitchen. Otome was sitting nearby eating off a tray, still convalescing from the birth of her child. Every time she was served, she would apologize, or if something was done for the baby, she would say, 'This is so much trouble. Please finish your meal first. Hiroshi-san [her husband] will get the water.' Tae-chan, the youngest child, was at first asleep under the mosquito net, but she woke up and came to sit beside her mother. She is only two, but when she was told to bow to me, she did so. She was then given a bowl of soup and rice mixed together, which her mother fed her. She asked for water and drank a glass. She is spoken to in special baby-talk. (The other day, young Sato was carrying the baby around and asked its mother, 'What is the word for rain in Sen-chan's language?' When told, he went off with the baby on his back, satisfied, talking to the baby much as its mother does.)"

"The older girl at Kawabe's is very smart and not a bit bashful. While she and I sat alone in the main room, she told me that the gifts in the corner are for her, but that the kimono being made for her will not be ready until after *o-bon*. When her grandmother came in with sliced watermelon, she wanted some at once, but when told that the first piece would be offered to the ancestors, she agreed to wait. Of the pears her father had brought home, however, she had to have one at once. Then she wanted to go out swimming, and was permitted to do so. The Tawaji child also impresses me as being very bright for her age. Spilling some tea on the mats, she dashed to the doorstep, picked up a foot-rag lying there, wiped up the tea with it, and returned it to the place she had found it. She can barely walk yet."

"The Makino baby, just like the Hayashi child, is just beginning to talk. She repeats words after her mother, using exactly the same intonation, albeit only baby-talk, since that is all that is taught her. *'Aaa-tta'* serves for good-day, goodbye, and thank you, and if told to ask for something, she will hold out her hand in the proper manner and say *'chōdai'* (please). Her older brother babbles away all the time and the other day had a long story about electricity going from the house to the road. He knew that Daikoku-san was in the kitchen. When asked where his grandmother is, he said that she went to the cemetery, and when Mrs. Fujita said that she would be coming back, he said, 'She can't. She's in the ground.' If he does something his mother disapproves of, she calls him *baka*. When he is angry at someone, he does the same."

LORDS AND MASTERS

Which brings us to the issue of male children and their position in the family. "There is nothing to control a little boy's behavior. He is the lord. A tantrum will always work, and it is pitiful to see them when a new baby arrives and gets all the attention, so that their tantrums go unheeded." Nevertheless, "a boy soon learns to order his mother around, much as the father does. Mrs. Sato was alone with the baby and her little son. *'Kaka!'* he said, 'Give me some paper for the toilet. Hurry up!' She left her lunch and went to fetch some newspaper, although she was in no rush and even read an item in it before handing it over to the boy. Later on he said, 'Get me a shirt. Hurry up!' She did, asking him to hold the baby while she looked for it. He is about twelve."

"One cannot say that the children are bad. It's because they never hear 'no' that they behave the way they do. While still babies they are not allowed to cry, for they are promptly picked up and fed or rocked or quieted. When older, if they say anything in baby-talk, everyone praises them. If they ask for something, no matter how busy she is, the mother will usually get it for them. 'Mother, come here!' a kid will yell, and his mother will come in from the kitchen to see what he wants. 'Bring me that, mother,' he says, and she will fetch it. Today, for instance, Mrs. Ouchi was packing a lunch basket and picked up a jar of brown sugar from the shelf and put it in. One of her boys promptly jumped up and demanded some. 'Not now,' she said mildly, because she was busy. 'Please,' he said, over and over. Finally she took out the jar and gave him a lump of sugar, and replaced it and the other things that she had taken out of the basket."

"The young Eda wife called me in today. The two little boys are cute. They came in asking for *mamma* and got a ball of cold rice each, whereupon they at once demanded *kon-kon* (baby-talk for pickled radish— *daikon*—but actually referring to all kinds of pickled vegetable) and ate an awful quantity of it. They are friendly kids. The mothers here have infinite patience."

"Sabu-chan yells for anything he wants. First he went into a tantrum because no one would go fetch him a popsicle. When he finally got one he yelled because he wanted a rice-ball just like his sister's. When she made him one it was not round enough to suit him, so the nursemaid was asked to make a proper one. By the time it was ready he had dropped off to sleep, his feet on the porch, his head drooping on the *tatami*. His mother had suspected he was sleepy but nonetheless gave in to his every whim. He was eased into the room so as not to waken him."

"The next to youngest boy was throwing a tantrum because he was mad at his mother. His father was sent out into the yard to appease him, without much success. Eventually the boy picked up a *geta* and hurled it at his mother. It landed in the charcoal brazier instead. '*Odomo shiran!*' she exclaimed, and moved to another place with the baby. Everyone laughed and after a while she went out with the boy and he calmed down."

"She had her little boy, who is four, with her and carried him all the way, melting with sweat. At a shady spot on the path she persuaded him to get down from her back, which he did reluctantly, following her very slowly. When she urged him to hurry, he stopped dead in his tracks. 'Hurry up or the crazy man who lives in the *dō* will come out,' she said, whereupon he began to cry and ran to her, so that she had to take him on her back again. Scaring children with beggars, crazy people, and snakes is popular."

"Mrs. Kawabe stopped at Ochiai's on her way to buy some stationery. As the Ochiai boy came in from school and did not say the usual '*tadaima*' (I'm back), Mrs. Kawabe reproached him. 'Even a dog growls when it comes home. You must say *tadaima*.' His mother laughed. He said nothing."

"The Wauchi boy came to Tamaki's this afternoon with his mother. He was left outside to play but kept running into the house all the time. He whimpers and screams for anything he wants and is never refused. Nevertheless, he always yells from the outset. The Tamaki boys are better behaved. The younger one bloodied his mouth somehow, tied a dirty towel around his face, and let it go at that."

"Among the many people at the party were Hayashi Masao, his wife and daughter, and small son who had refused to stay at home. He made a nuisance of himself until his mother said, 'This child! He cries when he is here and he cries when he is taken home.' She held him on her lap the whole time."

Such behavior was by no means limited to boys, however. "At school the Kanebo silkworm group held an end-of-season banquet to be attended by two people from each member household. Everyone came, mostly married couples, but in some cases older women came with their sons. There were babies, of course, and those who did not bring theirs with them had them carried in later by older children for feeding. All through the speeches the kids ran around and made so much noise that at one point a teacher got up and asked the people to keep the children quiet. Mrs. Tanimoto just glared at the kids."

The following rather extended account nicely illustrates the socialization of a little boy and girl to their respective roles, as well as the indulgence with which the children were so routinely treated. "Yesterday Mrs. Kawabe took her new baby to present it at the Suwa shrine. Along went the midwife, with her ever-present little boy, who had to be talked to and persuaded to walk faster all the way. She used various tricks. 'Who can walk fastest? It must be Yukio-chan. Just see how he can run, even faster than the bicycle!' He also wanted to eat, and his mother would stop now and again and produce a rice-ball. Between the Kawabe house and the shrine he consumed almost a package of candy, two rice balls, and several slices of konnyaku. Arriving at the shrine, he had another rice-ball and several handfuls of other food, more candy, and some chestnuts given him by the priest.

"Old lady Kawabe joined us on the way up. She had her baby grandson on her back and was leading her little granddaughter Sumi-chan by the hand. This little girl is also a pest, but better behaved than the midwife's child. They raced and amused one another with such lines as 'The baby comes out of the vagina,' and 'Balls come out of the belly.' The midwife did not go all the way up to the shrine, but sent her little boy to throw in the coin for an offering and bow at the entrance. The only time he was quiet was when he was climbing up and down the steps. Old lady Kawabe had brought her rosary along, and the little girl imitated her grandmother, while Yukio-chan jumped about. After the baby was presented to the gods, Mrs. Kawabe came down, but the old lady with the baby boy on her back stayed, saying, 'Now Cho-chan will bow,' and threw in a coin for him.

"On the way back home, old man Kawabe showed up, but walked way ahead of us. Yukio-chan's mother kept saying, 'Hurry along. You are the man. You must walk ahead. Sumi-chan is a woman; she will come behind you.' To me she said, 'With children of this age it is impossible because they never leave your side. One might leave a four-year-old girl at home, but never a boy that age.' "

Dreadful Children

Some children seemed to be totally out of control. "When I stopped at the Soeshima's, she was sewing and apologized for the disorder. The five-year-old boy there is impossible. He cried when I appeared and ran into the house screaming, 'Mrs. Embree is here! Mrs. Embree is here!' as if I were about to eat him up. Then he cried because he saw a piece of rice cake and wanted some. He calls Mrs. Soeshima mother (kaka-chan) although he is really her brother's child. He followed her around yelling, 'Mochi!

Mochi!' After some had been placed over the charcoal to roast, he forgot all about it because by then it had been suggested that he could be taken outside. He began jumping around, crying again because he was not being dressed quickly enough. (He was to be taken out on her back, since it is too cold to run around on his own. He weighs at least forty pounds.) He let out a constant stream of yells without any reason other than to get attention. Most of the time he gets it, but occasionally when she would move about to do something, she would leave him sitting on the floor screaming."

It was for one little girl, however, that the most vehement remarks were reserved. "The worst child in the vicinity is the Toride's baby girl. She has grown very big and much too heavy for her tiny nursemaid to carry, but is still lugged around. She cries for no reason at all and is obstinate and hard to manage. It is impossible to coax a smile out of her. I suppose that being the youngest and an only daughter in the house gets her a fair amount of spoiling. Her mother is devoted to her. I wonder if her illegitimate origin has anything to do with her mother's attachment to her?"

"The Toride's baby girl is just as bad at home as she is in public, and the mother executes all her wishes, so that the child has only to whimper when she wants something. (Children will cry for food, not because they are hungry, but because they are always given anything that elders are offered and insist on getting it first. For instance, the Ouchi boy, also spoiled, will cry when he sees an older sister eating a sweet potato and will whimper until he gets some. When his mother is offered anything, from pickles to foreign candy, she always passes a piece to him. If children are standing outside during a gathering in a house, a kindly woman will pass helpings of food out to them, sometimes at the expense of the guests who consequently get less.)

"Yesterday when I arrived at Toride's, the little girl was lying on the floor kicking her feet and yelling, *'Baka! Baka!'* 'Come here,' said her mother, and when she did, she got a suck at her breast. Then she wanted the coin which her mother had given to the nursemaid to buy a popsicle with. She got it. She also got a baked sweet potato. She wanted it wrapped. Then she wanted both the coin and the potato wrapped in a single piece of paper. Then she wanted the paper torn in half. She wanted the coin wrapped differently. When she finally got up on her nursemaid's back, she wanted her padded coat put over her. She called for her mother when she went out to the toilet. The whole time I was there she never stopped whimpering."

The little girl's behavior represented something rather out of the ordinary. "It is interesting that masturbation and sex play usually comes out in the children who are in general hardest to manage, such as the Ouchi boy and the Toride girl. The only time I saw her smile today was when she was sitting on the *dō* with her legs apart, holding her hand on her genitals while one of the little boys playing there kept peeking in. She was much pleased. Her little nursemaid, very concerned, took her hand away and explained that it was bad to do that."

She was also frequently involved in sex-play with other children. "Today Taro-chan and the Ouchi boy threw the little Toride girl on the floor and while one held her down the other raised her kimono to see how she was made. An older boy going by with his sling-shot stopped to observe this amusing scene and smiled knowingly as if he had done the same thing himself. Then he threw stones in all directions and tried to shoot one up between the legs of one of the little nursemaids."

Several days later, "the nursemaids and their charges are assembled in the *dō* as usual. The Toride girl is thoroughly disliked now, so that she is often provoked to tears by being teased. She sits with a scowl all the time, looking for something that might displease her. Yells come out readily, and at once the nursemaids begin to mock and push at her. Today she bit Tae-chan's finger over a dispute about some colored paper and then cried because she was reprimanded. She is still nursed and eats very little other food, hence the tears. She wants her milk in the middle of the morning and refuses the rice brought to her by the nurse. At noon she gets her mother's breast again, but between feedings she is in a constant tantrum. There is a lot of thumb-sucking among those children who have been taken off the breast because of the arrival of another baby. The thumb is taken from the mouth and sometimes the child is teased or reproved. Even if the baby gets the breast again, as at Irie's, where the new baby died, he still sucks his thumb."

"A child will sometimes start yelling, '*Iya da! Iya da!* (No! No! or I won't! I won't!)' for no good reason and keep it up for hours to the great perplexity of the young nurses. The other afternoon the Ouchi boy kept up his yelling all the way from the bridge to his house. 'What's the matter?' I asked. 'Just crying,' said someone. Today the Toride baby would not stand up so that her nursemaid could get her on her back, and would not lie down either. The nursemaid could not manage her at all, and finally another girl came up and helped put the child on her nurse's back in spite of her yells."

At length, however, it became evident that not all the fault lay with this unfortunate little girl. "Although she is older than the other babies in her group, the Toride child wets herself more often, which is in keeping with the rest of her behavior. Yet there is a complicated situation there. Her child-nurse has become permanently irritated with her, so that she is now always rough on the little girl. She lets her go off by herself to play behind the *dō* and if she finds her wet after having neglected her, she pulls at her and scolds her, provoking still more tears. Today at the *dō* she pulled up her dress and stuck her finger into her vagina. All the nursemaids yelled at her, and called her a dirty child. They complain that all the nursemaids are ashamed of her."

"As I came up to the Toride house about 7:30 in the evening, they were just starting supper. The little girl was running around naked, and in a much better mood than I have ever seen her in at the *dō*. Everyone joked with her and was ready to serve her, which may account for her fits when she is out with the nurse, who is not so eager to gratify her whims."

Certainly the Toride girl, whatever the source of her troubles, was not alone in throwing tantrums. "Children of three or four have tantrums very frequently, and more often than children of any other age, especially if there is a new baby in the house. Until then they are permitted everything and made much of, but when the baby comes they are no longer nursed regularly, are not carried around on mother's back any more, and left more to their own devices. Usually they will join a group of children of their own age in the vicinity and play around all day, moving about in groups and imitating each other and older children. But once in a while one of them will throw a fit. He will want to stay by his mother and follow her when she is going somewhere with the baby, or he may demand something that he cannot have. 'You stay here,' the mother will say sharply, or 'Don't touch that box!' or 'Stop that noise!' or she may call him *baka*. He does not like such treatment and cries all the louder. Instead of being given in to, as would earlier have been the case, he is teased, made fun of, or ignored and the crying goes on until he tires of it. This period lasts about a year, I should say, and the more other children there are around, the sooner he becomes independent. The second oldest boy at Mori's, of course, went over to his grandmother long before the next baby was born, so he does not mind the transition too much. Yet when someone says, as they do to tease him, that the baby is the boss (*taishō*) of the house, his eyes well with tears. At times he is very good, at others a dreadful pest. He is occasionally hit by his father when he is drunk, but is never severely punished."

"The younger they are the worse children behave. Yesterday the little Irie girl got taken to the doctor because she cried so much and they thought it might be her sore eye. She cries all the time and the minute some demand of hers is not met or the person looking after her goes out of sight, she bursts into loud howls. The next oldest girl calls her grandmother *baka*, won't go to sleep when told, and will not go off to school without coaxing. The older children are very well behaved."

The eating habits of Suye's small children drew the following acerbic comment. "The nursery school is much better organized now, although the teacher is not authoritative enough for her charges, who pay little attention to her. The Hiyama child, whose parents are not local farmers, is a good example of the development of eating habits. At ten o'clock, when a sort of dumpling soaked in brown sugar was served to the kids, one on a plate for each child, they all went for it with both hands at the expense of clean faces and clothes. Most came around for a second helping and were all through and outside playing again while this city-bred child was still struggling her way through the first one with a pair of chopsticks."

DISCIPLINE

Physical punishment of children was so rare that the few exceptions stood out. "More than once I have seen Fumie's sister give her kids sound slaps, which shows that Japanese do hit their children when sufficiently provoked." Only Mrs. Tanimoto openly recommended that children be punished when they deserved it, however. It is understandable, then, how striking the following incident must have been. "During the afternoon I saw a little boy punished for the first time in the three months we have been in Suye. I was told that he was too rowdy. Although I did not observe the offense, I did see his father pick him up and carry him bodily into the brush near the house where he tied him to a tree with vines and left him. The yells were more than loud, and never stopped. Finally, all the other men became very sympathetic with his plight, and another boy was sent off to release the offender."

Far more commonly adults resorted to bribery, cajolery, and outright lies when attempting to persuade a child to do something. "Children are just not taught to obey. If they must be got from one place to another, they are bribed with promises of money to be given them later, or by a story about something interesting going on somewhere else. The kids usually know these stories to be lies, and defy the order to leave until they have made up their own minds to go elsewhere." So prevalent was this device that one of the men who had spent some time outside the village remarked that he was "still puzzled by our unusual treatment of Clare. Every time he picks up some baby to play with and talk the usual baby prattle at it, he says, 'You never tease children or tell them lies. Is that considered better now? Is teasing and lying to them a native (he meant primitive) way of bringing up children?' "

The use of these devices is perhaps best exemplified in the following scene. "About two in the afternoon Mrs. Hirano came out with a sickle and carrying-pole, ready to go check the millet field. Her hair was loosely tied up in a towel and her work kimono was hiked up to her knees and open at the breast. At this moment her younger child decided that she wanted some milk, so the mother sat on a stone while the child, standing up, began playing with her breasts and taking an occasional sip. She obviously was not going to stop. 'Finish quickly, it is getting dark,' her mother said. The old lady from next door called to the child, 'Come over here and see what I have.' She is always ready to help with the children. 'Look at obachan ('auntie' - a reference to me). She is laughing at you. See, she even took your picture.' The little girl turned her head to see the camera and then went back to the breast.

"Finally the old lady came over and pulled her away and the mother started off down the path. At once the little girl wanted to follow, and her mother turned. 'No, you stay here and play with all the nice things 'grandmother' will give you. No? All right, then, I am not going.' She turned back and the little girl tried to run up to her. 'No, you go on to the field,' said the old lady, and she made an effort to keep the little girl from following her mother, but she broke away. At once the mother said, 'Oh, what is it in the house? Look! What is it I see?' The child looked suspicious. The trick did not work. But when one of her older sisters pretended to see something down the road, she went to see. Her mother started off for the fields again. This time her next but youngest girl tried to follow her, but was bribed to stay put with a ball of rice from the old lady."

When none of these popular techniques worked, the child might be threatened. "If a kid gets out of hand or tries to run away from his nurse, he is warned that a *kanjin* [beggar] will come and carry him off. It usually works." And, "at Tamaki's, where they were making soy sauce, the kids were under foot the whole time. To keep them quiet or get them out of the way, they were scared with warnings of snakes or dogs or 'a mouse that will come and bite you,' but none of it had much effect. Promises and bribes have little effect either, because the children learn early that they will not be fulfilled."

Far more common is the following scene of ineffectual efforts to keep the children quiet. "The Amano family was just settling down to have some toasted rice-cake. When I arrived I was served some tea and pickles and two pieces of the rice-cake with brown sugar. Then *shōchū* was brought out and served with herring roe and hard-boiled eggs. The two older children ran around without sitting still for a minute. They ran in and out of the next room, making a draft and blowing smoke from the wood-burning fire-pit. Occasionally the father would cry out, 'Hey, you two, sit down! Stop running around!' The mother would say, 'Close the door,' as one of them ran into the next room, leaving the sliding doors wide open. But on the whole no one paid much attention to them. When the boy stopped to poke his finger into the baby's mouth, the baby at once started sucking on it. At first the mother objected, saying that his hands were dirty, but she soon became amused and laughed with him. Occasionally both kids would run up to their mother and talk to the baby, using the same baby-talk she uses to it. The baby is said to be so small because the mother has little milk and little else is fed it."

At a house in Hirayama, "while the old lady was preparing supper, we all sat and talked. The children were playing in the yard, and when the noise got too loud during one game in which all formed a chain with a leader and one boy was trying to break into it, the old man yelled at them. They instantly disappeared into the neighboring yard."

One afternoon, while the women were caring for the silkworms, "the Ouchi baby was brought in by one of the older girls. The boy was there, too, and he and the Eda children were running around. The older girl was helping sort the worms, while the older boy rushed back and forth delivering the sorted ones to the men. Finally Mrs. Eda called a halt and said that all should go in for tea. There was steamed sweet potato, pickles and cold rice. At first the women refused the rice, but the kids all yelled for it. It was a remarkable scene, with the children rushing about the room asking for this or that, eating everything they could lay their hands on, getting in everyone's way, snatching food from one another, and yelling. When Mitchan grabbed food from the Eda baby, she would get a clap from her mother, but Mrs. Eda would pick her up and tell her own child to keep quiet. Babies were taken out to urinate and some were changed. The small Eda boy is a jolly, friendly child, who gets little attention and likes to be petted. He came up to his father and settled in his lap, cuddling up to him. When the father said, 'All right now, I have to go to work,' the little boy got up with a smile. That room, teeming with all the kids and the worms, was a strange place."

As we have seen, grandmothers generally took charge of the youngest child when it was displaced by the arrival of a new baby. "When a baby is born the youngest child is passed on to the grandmother, who sleeps with him and takes care of him thereafter. That is why the little Suzuki boy was told so much about his grandmother's death. Now he spends much of his time with his father, because his mother is busy with the baby. When his father is busy he is carried around by one or another of the little girls (the ones he calls 'aunt') who live there."

"Mrs. Mori no longer looks after the youngest child, as she is expecting a baby any time, and the grandmother has taken over. Still the boy is very grouchy. The old lady says it is because he knows that another child is expected and does not like it. Occasionally she tries to discipline him. If she puts him down after carrying him about on her back he yells. She pays no attention so he yells some more. This may go on for fifteen to twenty minutes, but she always takes him up again finally. Now and again when I see her out with the child on her back she says, 'He cried so much that I decided to take him out.' The mother is never with the children but does all the work around the house."

"At Tamaki Giichi's old lady Tamaki had just come back from the mountains and was having tea with old lady Ariyoshi. The two Ariyoshi little girls and one of the Tamaki boys were raising a rumpus all over the house. They were told once in severe tones to get out, but were given some food every time they came to ask for some. The older Tamaki boy returned from school. 'I want to eat now (Hayo meshi kū),' he announced, and ate his rice standing up. Then, 'Give me some money, please (Zeni kudai).' The old lady protested that she had none, but finally went in the back and brought some to him. He was in a hurry to be off to Menda. Said old lady Ariyoshi, 'All the children come to their grandparents for money.' She said that she gets hers from the head of the house and never has much, but what she does have the school-age children get away from her."

Pets as Surrogates

For the very few childless women pets provided obvious compensation, and even in houses where there were children, the pets were a source of amusement and pleasure, albeit sometimes of a kind that took some getting used to. "When cats bring in their prey, be it bird, mouse, or insect, everyone derives great enjoyment from the scene. The other day the kitten at Amano's brought in a small mouse, which it proceeded to drag all over the room. 'Well, now, where did you get it? So you have a mouse!' they laughed, and no one minded when the cat ate up the creature, leaving a spot of blood on the mat."

"Today Mrs. Tanimoto [the childless woman who professes to hate children] laughed herself sick because I felt uncomfortable when her cat came in with a bird, which it would let flutter away occasionally. 'Let mummy see it, bring it here, good cat, good Mī-chan, go and get another,' and so on, she said. To prevent the bird from escaping she took it from the cat and clipped its wings with a pair of scissors. Then she told me with pride how he brought in a bird yesterday, and how she had helped him catch it when it escaped and flew about the room. She was also proud that the cat brings everything to her first. 'He wakes me at night to tell me he caught a mouse. Why do you dislike mice? They have such nice, clean flesh. They really are cute. I see them sometimes eating the rice on the altar. They always hold it up in their two front paws. It is a pity to have them caught.' I had trouble sitting through the scene, so she obligingly closed the door on the bird's final moments. She does this with any creature the cat brings in, helps him keep it, and praises him always."

"She jumps up at once when her cat yowls, much as a mother does when her child lets out a cry, to see with whom he is fighting, and rushes to his rescue. Yesterday she dashed into the house from the yard, hearing his yowling, and found him standing in front of the mirror looking at his own reflection. She talks to him as if he were a child."

Now this does not necessarily indicate that Mrs. Tanimoto thinks of her cat as a substitute child, but consider the following remarkable scene: "She rubbed her breast. I asked if she had milk. 'Like water,' she said. 'The cats drink it.' She told me how she used to nurse her dog and massage her breasts to make milk for him. She opened her dress and produced a breast. 'That is why it is like this,' she said. Indeed, the nipple is very long and dark, in contrast to the usual girlish and delicate nipples of the other childless women here. She went on. This dog was wonderful. It would offer its paw to be shaken, and could imitate the walk of prostitutes, and danced. One day it suddenly became ill and she sent for the veterinarian. But it was too late, for the dog had intestinal trouble and died within a half hour after the doctor arrived. She wept and fixed him up for the night in front of the Buddhist altar with incense and candles. Her husband read the sutras—both Shin and Zen—and the next day she buried the dog, saying, 'Be reborn a human.' If one does that, she explained, it will be born a man next time. She had another dog, but it died too and so she gave up having dogs at all. One loves them too much and it is too hard to lose them, for they are so cute and clever. Her last cat was a sad case; it got bitten by a dog and the vet had to poison it. The cat died in two minutes, and she put up a monument for it. But it was her dogs she nursed."

Whether others nursed their dogs, we do not know, but Mrs. Tanimoto is not the only woman given to demonstration of extraordinary degrees of affection for pets. "The younger woman is his second wife, and the old woman is his uncle's widow who lives with them because she had no children. There is a dog in the house and the younger woman pets him, talks baby-talk, and cuddles him just as Mrs. Tanimoto does her cat. This dog is small and kept carefully tied up. While I was visiting the other day, she took the dog on her lap, sat it up on its hind legs and asked, 'Penis? Where is your penis? (*Chin-chin wa? Chin-chin wa doko?*)' and played with it, just as mothers often do with their little boys."

The pregnancy of a dog named Mary who belonged to a family in Oade was much on the minds of the people of the neighborhood. "Mrs. Tomokawa, seeing Mary, asked about the puppies. Everyone who sees that dog always makes some remark about her having had puppies and wants to know what happened to them. She told us a story of a pregnant woman who had killed her cat's kittens [as she assumed someone had done with Mary's litter], and when her own baby was born it had only one eye. That reminded her that the male cat they have had for nine years died the other day. She took it as a sign that it had died instead of her ailing husband, so she had it buried at the cemetery, glad to have lost the cat if it was a substitute for the old man." Pets clearly served purposes other than that of surrogates for children.

TEN

Little Girls and Boys

The little girls of Suye were treated to the celebration of Girls' Day, March 3, by the new calendar. "Tomorrow will be the girls' festival, observed only by those to whom a baby girl has been born since the last celebration. Those who already have many girls do not mark the occasion, even if a new girl baby has been born during the year. Thus, the Moris are not observing the day, but the Tamaki Giichis are having a big party because their first daughter was born this year. The Shimodas will celebrate because it is their first baby. Both the Suzuki Tamezos and the Tawajis of Imamura will mark the day, the latter with a very large display of dolls."

Explaining the use of peach blossoms at this festival, old lady Tamaki said, " 'Long ago there lived a big snake which married a young human girl and she conceived a snake offspring. Her mother then gave her some peach sake to drink, which made the snake leave her body. Ever since then, peach sake is taken as *o-miki* on this day to purify one's body. Of course,' she added, 'this is an old tale, and I do not know how true it is.' Everywhere I went they served plain *shōchū* but called it peach sake.

"No one at the Tamaki's knew why Girls' Day is called *Hina matsuri*. As for the display of dolls, the old lady said that in the Tokugawa period there had been some disturbances and to make up for the numerous deaths clay dolls had been made on the third day of the third month. Since then the custom of displaying dolls has been observed. There were peach blossoms in the *shōchū* bottle which had been used to make the offering when setting up the dolls and in the bottle from which the first cup had been poured.

"The doll display at the Tamaki's was very impressive. None of the dolls had been bought by the family, but were gifts from relatives and villagers invited to the party. They were arranged in the display yesterday morning, having been brought by visitors the day before. They were put up in the *tokonoma*, so that the usual hanging scroll of the Emperor was in the background and the two little cups of rice and a vase of *sakaki* [a plant used to decorate Shinto altars] had been moved to the corner. On the top shelf center were two dolls, the old couple who are the symbol of conjugal felicity, sitting under a little black and gold lacquer canopy. The rest were dolls that represented the Yasuki-bushi dancers, the Gonbei Tanemaki dancers, Kintaro, the famous giant baby holding the huge sea bream—a fish served on all auspicious occasions—the three Manchurian soldiers,[1] and several historical figures. There was also a hanging scroll of an elaborate display of dolls. On the lower shelf was the *o-miki* and two cups, one of which was later taken up and used by the old lady. There was also a bowl of parsley, which was handed to people as they came in just for a moment to admire the dolls, as many of the young girls did. There was also a miniature offering-tray, an exact replica of the regular ceremonial ones. Here these trays are used for making offerings to the spirit of the dead on memorial days and any other occasion on which an offering of food is made to the gods or the buddhas. It had the complete set of rice and soup bowls and a small plate in the center holding pickles or a vegetable.

"In addition to the peach blossoms there were many other flowers. Among them was a branch of *higan zakura* [a kind of cherry] from a tree near the Fujitas which always blooms at this time of year, and a kind of flower that looks like a violet. They said that plum blossoms are used because they are auspicious flowers. *Mitsumata*, a very fragrant white and yellow narcissus-like blossom of a tree from which the paper for sliding doors is made, and camellias were also used, because they are in season now and seen everywhere. The festival cake, placed at the center of the display, was very colorful, representing the sea bream, plum-cherry-bamboo, a crane, and a large peach. To my questions about the peach, I was told that it is the peach from which Momotaro was born, but no sexual associations were mentioned. There was also a plate of glutinous rice-cake, two dishes containing green and white ones, and a plate with green and white cakes of glutinous rice cut into diagonal pieces and placed in a design called *hishigata* (a rhombus), which is done only at *Hina matsuri*.

1. The "three Manchurian soldiers" is a reference to the three Japanese soldiers who gave their lives by carrying a land torpedo into a barbed-wire barricade and blasting a way through it in order to facilitate the advance of their unit against fierce Chinese resistance. Although the event occurred at a place called Miao Hang Zhen (J. Byōkōchin) during the Japanese assault on Shanghai, following disturbances there to protest the invasion and conquest of Manchuria, many Japanese believe that it occurred in Manchuria itself. These men were subsequently dubbed *Nikudan san yūshi* (Human Bullets: The Three Brave Warriors) and became celebrated as peerless examples of patriotic self-sacrifice. Until 1945 their story was made known to every Japanese child through textbooks, and statues of the men were erected in hundreds of schoolyards and public parks throughout the country. If any of them remains, I have not seen it. In Fortune Magazine's special issue on Japan of September 1936 (volume 14, number 3: 98–99) there are three photographs relating to the incident. The first shows schoolboys shouting *banzai* before such a statue. The second shows the mothers of the three soldiers bowing to their sons' portraits at a funeral or memorial service. The third shows a land torpedo being carried in army maneuvers.

"First we were served tea and parsley. This grass figured in all the celebrations, and is considered special to the occasion. Another dish served everywhere is a kind of scallion-like onion, served tied in a knot. Burdock was much used, either by itself, or as tempura. The festive meal itself was *sashimi* and tempura, a bowl of hard-boiled egg and taro, bean-curd and mushroom soup, a dish of cold sukiyaki, onion with a sweet bean-paste sauce, and a plate of cakes. Most of the guests were men because the women were busy at home entertaining their own guests or calling somewhere else. Some relatives, like Uemura of Kinoue, could not come at all because they also had a girl born this year. As I was leaving about six o'clock, I met Mrs. Watanabe coming in. Her own guests had just left and she was hurrying. Mrs. Tamaki worked hard and came out late for her sake. After I left more guests arrived and soon the music and dancing started.

"At Suzuki Tamezo's the display was much simpler and less festive. There were no peach blossoms in the *shōchū* bottle and the cake was simpler, but attractively arranged with the character *o-iwai* (felicitations) in the center. There was no meat or *sushi*. At the end of the meal rice was served with a plate of fish and vegetables boiled in soy sauce, squid, raw fish, and a bowl of bean curd and fish. At Mori's the display was modest, with very few flowers and not many dolls. However, much fish was served—there were three raw-fish dishes, squid, onion with whale meat, and a plate of cooked fish and vegetables, with banana and orange."

Boys' Day, the fifth day of the fifth lunar month (May 5 by the new calendar), was also celebrated rather modestly by most houses, partly because the festival fell at a very busy season for the farmers. "This festival is celebrated only by those whose first son was born within the year. Very few houses observe it for second or third sons. As a matter of fact, not all observe it for first sons, as against the girls' festival which very few households fail to celebrate." In fact, Boys' Day was observed more generally in the cities than in places like Suye. "Contrary to custom, it has been officially transferred from the old to the new calendar, but even so the silkworms are spinning and the farmers stick to the old. According to some people the banners [of carp and other flags] are an innovation here—'we have become very fancy *(haikara ni natta)*.' "

PLAY GROUPS

Small children learned to play from one another as well as from slightly older boys and girls. "The little Toride girl invited Taro-chan to play today. She is just a baby, but started the paper-rock-scissors game called *jan-ken-po* [the standard term is *jan-ken-pon*], which she can do, but whose principles (who wins and loses) she does not know. He soon sees that she does not understand, so he calls out 'you lose' every time and is thus the winner. Next she wants to play hide-and-seek, which she has seen others playing in the *dō*, but cannot explain it, so she just gets up, leans against the post and shuts her eyes as she has seen others do. He hides under the Kannon altar, she finds him, and they proceed. Tae-chan, his baby sister, who cannot even say *jan-ken-po*, also tried to join in, and most probably will master it very soon."

Often the toddlers were simply in the way of the older children and nursemaids. In the summer "children are very active in the *dō*. The nursemaids devise all sorts of means to keep their charges out of the way of their games. They tie them to the posts in a sitting or standing position, like horses, persuading them that it will be fun to be tied up. They play blind-man's bluff or will get a sash and try to catch someone and tie her up, provoking much laughter. The smaller babies carried on the back merely run the chance of being knocked down, but the older ones in the *dō* are often left to their own devices. If all else fails they put them on their backs and go on with their own games."

A great deal of children's play centered about the school, once they were old enough to attend, and frequently older children would take their younger siblings or a neighbor's small child. "At seven this morning all the children stopped their games and wandered off to school, in a group like fish, the younger ones being herded ahead. The kids of a hamlet cluster together, but as they go by classmates join up with them. This morning Kawaze came through first, then Oade, and last Kakui."

During the rice transplanting season, the children were all sent off to the school to be looked after by the teachers. "This morning the kids were off to school, pushing their younger charges ahead of them. Today is the first day of nursery school for those between four and six. Some of the children, like the little Fujita girl, stayed home busily rocking her little brother. She was singing a lullaby in her thin little voice to the baby on her back. At the school both children and teachers seemed at a loss. Only a few of the kids were amused by the exercises done to a phonograph record. One teacher complained to me that she had tried to organize some activities but all they did was cry. Some were put in charge of their elder brothers or sisters—or neighbor children—who had brought them to the school. The little Ariyoshi girl was there with her three-year-old sister on her back as usual. The baby cried a lot and refused to be put down, so she just stood apart from the others, clutching her lunch bag and looking on. She had been carrying the child since six in the morning. When her brother went by on his way to class, she called to him, 'Come take her *shi-shi*.' He left the line, lifted the baby off her back and carried her behind a bush. In a moment he brought her back again and rejoined his class." A few days later, "the nursery school seemed much better organized today. The kids were playing in groups, although some were wandering around vaguely, and older sisters were often called out of class to help with them."

"As far as I can see the girls in primary school are treated just like the boys. They participate in sports wearing the same type of shorts, and I think the division of the sexes really begins at the end of the elementary grades." But patterns of play suggest some self-segregation before then. "At the suggestion of the teachers, the children held an athletic meet organized by hamlet, rather than by class. Kakui met on the horse grounds, all in exercise uniforms. All the children were there, as well as some nursemaids with their charges and a few loose preschoolers. Some youngsters were dreadfully lost, wandering about and going into fits of tears. This was especially true of those who could find none of their regular companions, with whom they feel perfectly at ease. The older children ran the show. There were foot-races and relay races, in which the girls usually lagged behind, although there are some good runners among them. They were grouped by age and sex, and no one chose to cross sex lines. The events were over in short order and prizes of candy were handed out.

"The kids hung around and decided to play games. At first only the girls were playing, but the boys finally joined them. The older girls, who had brought their baby sisters, did not seem to be bothered by them in the least, dropping and picking up their charges in the course of play. The babies remained very calm during even the roughest games. The boys left first, all in a group, and the girls started to wander off one by one. Those who stayed behind sat around singing, climbed trees, and so forth, and they decided to play *yado* (inn-keeping). A kitchen was improvised and some girls went off to gather various grasses to represent fish, millet, cakes, rice and bananas. Leaves were collected to serve as plates."

"On Sunday the children were around all day. As you move from hamlet to hamlet you encounter different sets of children. The group around Kawabe's place in Oade consisted of the Ouchi children—a girl of thirteen with her baby sister and her younger brother and sister. The little Tawaji girl was there also. These groups were all girls. No boys were around. It is only after school hours that you see them occasionally playing ball. Occasionally an older boy will show up with a baby on his back, but otherwise after school the boys are said to be playing up in the hills."

Very often such groups were in the general charge of one of the little nursemaids. One such was thirteen-year-old Hayashi Sumiko, "who finished school this spring. She does the cooking at home and is nursemaid to the baby. She is about the neighborhood from seven in the morning to seven at night, with the baby always in tow. The baby, who is about eight months old, is Suzuki's daughter. Its mother, whose other children are eighteen, sixteen, and five, is too busy with them, she says. (Sumiko herself is one of six children.)" Her friend Emiko, also thirteen, described her day thus: "Up at six o'clock, washes face, fixes hair, bows to the god-shelf, eats breakfast, goes to school after a game of one sort or another at the *dō*. After school she plays with other girls—if nothing is wanted at home, she plays until she is called for supper."

"Children who are old enough to go to school all play in groups, usually made up of age-mates in the same class, but sometimes a group will have an age span of three to four years. Preschool children, however, progress gradually toward joining a play group. The young baby is always in its mother's arms or on the nursemaid's back, in which case he participates in all the games by virtue of the fact that nurse and charge are inseparable. As the baby begins to learn to walk, its mother will jokingly let it take part in some child's game that is going on. At about three years, when the child can get around quite well, it is usually attached to its grandmother, for by then as a rule a new baby takes up the mother's attention. Occasionally such a child will be left to the care of its brothers and sisters. He will be told to hold one end of the skip-rope or will be taught by an older sister to play *ishi iri* [hopscotch] lest he barge in and interfere with their games. At this age he has no group of his own, and is always trailing around after the older children, trying to imitate them. Once in a while, if there are several babies of the same age in a neighborhood they will be left on their own while their nursemaids play. The babies will make believe at playing together, but never get very far with it. But a new age-group will appear suddenly on the scene when a few neighborhood children get old enough to play together by themselves. There is one about now, made up of four little boys who just a few weeks ago stopped sticking to their grandmothers and began going about together. They follow the games of the slightly older boys or invent some of their own. With flags, sticks and stones they play all day, running around or building bridges across the stream."

"Children develop very fast after they begin to run around with other kids their own age. Taro-chan now plays with the other little boys all day and his mother complains about the bad habits he is picking up. Today, when he asked her if he could go play, she said, 'Yes, go ahead, but come home before dark.' He is four years old." But the new-found independence was not without its setbacks. "Today Taro-chan had an accident. He forgot to go to the toilet and filled his pants. So great was his embarrassment that he would not go home nor would he allow any of the nursemaids to take him there, but stood and howled every time one of them came near him."

With two of the little boys, both spoiled by their grandparents, this transition was not without an occasional tantrum. "At first neither liked to be left alone, and would sit and yell by the hour because no one would pick them up and carry them around. Gradually they gave up crying and joined the other children, coming to their grandmothers only when in need of help—such as pasting a flag to a stick or joining two pieces of string together. Earlier in the year one of the Eda old ladies used to go around with little Haruo on her back all the time, but now he plays with the other boys while she sits in the sun making straw sandals. With these youngsters, the most frequent cause for tears is a fight among themselves or with an elder brother."

"The two middle Eda boys had a fight. I did not see it, but when I came up the younger one was still scowling and the older one was weeping loudly. Their eldest brother was standing by passively with the baby on his back, but one of the old ladies at the *dō* was much excited for a while. 'What happened?' she inquired, without getting an answer. She complained that the little boy's penis was all red. She made a fuss for a while and then went back to her work. The younger boy and the oldest brother went off and sat in the *dō* pretending to be more or less unconcerned, while the victim walked out to the middle of the road and began to yell. Their parents were away, but occasionally through his sobs one could hear, 'Mommy, mommy!' although he knew quite well that she was not around. Another old lady passing by tried to talk to him, but got nowhere. His sobbing became a bit forced and finally he wandered back to the house alone. He is often teased by his oldest brother, and in fights often loses to the younger one.''

Several months later, "there was another fight down the street, of which I saw only the results. The Ouchi boy was involved, apparently, because he went off yelling. So was the second Eda boy, who sobbed just as he did last winter when he had a fight with his brother. It is a low, monotonous sobbing, and he will pay no attention to anyone. Like the last time his shirttails were out and like the last time his oldest brother was making fun of him. He threw a couple of stones and tried to hit his brother with a piece of straw, but the older boy only laughed and moved away. Their parents, sitting inside the house in plain view, paid no attention.''

IMITATING ADULTS

Many children's games and some of their play behavior involved clear imitation of adult activities. Four months after settling in, "for the first time today I saw some kids playing house, a game called *mamagoto*. The girls, mostly third- and fourth-year students, had spread out some straw mats in front of a house. The little Mori boy and a little girl of two were the 'babies.' They were wrapped up in some blankets and padded garments that the kids had fetched from home, and put to sleep. Cookies were fed to them 'to keep them quiet.' In the back there was a kitchen, they said.''

Another form of playing house was called *kyaku asobi*, to play at entertaining guests. "Some children were playing *kyaku asobi*, making food of grass and serving it on plates of persimmon leaves. There was a father and mother, baby and older sister, but not much was being done beyond fetching more and more grass with which to make more and more food. The Eda girl, the 'mother,' sent everyone else out to gather grass, while she cut it up to serve. She kept saying, 'Go out and get some more. Get plenty more. Then we'll be rich.' This is a direct imitation of her father, who is always talking about rich and poor people.''

There was much imitating of adult behavior. "Today little Mitchan, seeing another baby's running nose, which the nurse never notices because the baby is usually being carried on her back, picked up a tiny piece of paper from the ground and tried to wipe it clean. Even among themselves, little children will stretch out a hand when they want something and say *chōdai* (please). Some of the girls were humming the tunes of songs I have heard women sing at parties. They were also imitating dance steps and mumbling meaningless words that resembled the words of the songs. It turned out that there had been a party in the vicinity recently. The children are always hanging around taking in all that goes on. Tonight at Mori's the children and the nurse who brought over the Eda baby were amusing themselves by taking long drags of cigarette smoke and seeing who could keep it in the longest. The mother paid no attention to them."

"Children are exact replicas of their elders. For example, the other day Yukio-chan was saying, 'Please take my picture,' to me, which was thought very funny by his two little neighbors, the Ariyoshi girl and her friend. So he repeated it over and over, sending them into peals of laughter. They repeated each time the standard expression for such occasions, used when one is amused, and which by its intonation implies, 'What nonsense you are talking.' The phrases were delivered in a sing-song manner, each vowel quite drawn out. They sounded exactly like their mothers on similar occasions in adult conversations."

Sometimes the imitation was graphic and the acts involved considered very private. "Mrs. Kuwagiri is pregnant again, and their youngest child is just two this month. As I sat talking to her, the children played together, the little girl obviously imitating her parents by lying close to her brother and getting him to lie on top of her. Nothing was said when he began playing with his penis."

CHILDHOOD ILLNESSES

Many small children died and many were sick, but there were few cases so dramatic as the following. "In the afternoon I called on Ishikawa in Oade. The oldest daughter, who works out as a maid, was home for the holiday, and her mother said that it is a great help to have her back. It has been very hard without her. They do not keep silkworms because she is so busy with the children—both the oldest daughter and son are out working, two of the children are in school, and of the three still too young to go to school, one is a baby.

"They are tenants, and there is not enough rice to sell. By the time they pay their rent and take care of their *kōgin* they have just enough left to feed the family. They plant a bit of millet and grow some watermelons, and since they have no beans her festival dumplings had no sweetened red-bean stuffing, but a bit of brown sugar instead. To me they tasted fine, but she kept apologizing for having such simple cakes. The house is poor and dirty (here poor and clean is the rare exception). She said that she has not enough milk for the baby. She was also short with the last child, who is now three, but managed all right because she had a bit more than she does for this one. This baby she laughingly calls *Yasē-san* (Mr. Skinny), and indeed he is a rickety child with tiny spider-like limbs, no hair or teeth, and scurvy-like rash. He is pale and very quiet, and his smile in reaction to people talking to him comes as a shock because although he is ten months old, he looks like a baby of two months at most.

"This is the first case of undernourishment I have seen, and it is shocking to compare him to others around him who are older. She says that she has started to give him soft-cooked rice and thought that cow's milk would be good. She asked me about the price. (Some people here do give the bottle when the mother lacks milk. Years ago, when Wauchi's mother ran out of milk, old lady Hayashi had been asked to become the wet-nurse. That was the custom in the days before the vogue for cow's milk, which older people simply cannot abide and even hate the smell of.) Later on, when she served me some watermelon, the baby reached for it. She gave him a little piece, which he sucked on greedily. The other children in this family do not look so emaciated, but all have skin rash. The second youngest is a little devil who is never still, but the next one is quieter and paler.

"Birth control would certainly help here, and although she is a cheerful woman and fond of all her children, I am sure it would be accepted. The more children a family has the more they need and the less they can get done. She cooked some white potatoes in soy sauce and kept telling the children to go outside. She said that she could use some of the things we will be giving away when we leave, for she has never yet owned an aluminum pan. Like many others here, she cooks in a tin can."

"I am always horrified at the deaths of babies because there is no doctor available and the stillbirths that seem to be caused by poor nutrition and too much hard work, but the scene at the Eda's today makes me think that all our talk of the need for proper diet, sanitation, and cleanliness training is just a lot of nonsense. The Eda silkworms began to spin today and had to be taken care of at once, so all the neighbors came over and the kids were recruited to help out. The women brought their babies. Little Mitchan sat by Shoko and was much amused by all the bustle. She would stick her hands into the tray and pull them away from a wriggling worm. Or, picking up some dirt, she would drop it hastily when told that it was dirty. 'That's worm shit,' her mother would say, 'Kaigo-san no be.' Occasionally Shoko would deposit a worm on the little girl's leg and laugh at her jiggling to get it off. Once in a while the baby would say, 'Chichi!' and reach for a breast, whereupon her mother would take her to one breast or another and go right on working."

Suye children were plagued with lice and fleas, which they passed on to the adults. Scenes such as that of Mrs. Fujita and the young Suzuki girls delousing each other were not uncommon. "Today I discovered lice in Clare's hair [and shortly thereafter decided to take her back to Tokyo for the rest of their stay]. Worried as usual I went to buy some kerosene. The Makinos were shocked when I told them its purpose. They laughed and said that all children here have lice. Some people use a special medicine, but as a rule they just let it go. Even grown-ups who have a lot of contact with children get lice, they said, and fleas are common too. Mrs. Tanimoto was also amused when I told her, and suggested combing the baby's hair with a fine comb wrapped in newspaper. She said, which is true, that Clare must have got them from one of the nursemaids."

Early weaning and the mother's lack of milk were both considered to pose grave threats to the child's health. "The Hayashis lost their baby daughter yesterday. They say the baby died because her mother was pregnant again and tried to wean the child too early. It is said to have died of indigestion. This gives significance to Hayashi's stopping at the Kannon *dō* as he went by on his bicycle not long ago. I thought it odd at the time, but now realize that he was praying to Kannon for the child's recovery."

The physical condition of many of the children was the cause of some concern. In Hirayama, the mountain hamlet, "there is a lot of skin disease and noses run all the time. Little children are completely covered with skin eruptions and the mucous runs from their noses into their mouths, but after the third or fourth year in school one seldom sees this. I cannot decide about the health of the kids in this hamlet, but the younger ones do not look very sturdy."

"On my way back from Tontokoro I came across the midwife and walked along with her. She now says that cases of venereal disease are rare. There is the child in Hirayama, of course, who was born healthy, like the other children in the house, so his trouble must be a recent development, which could have been cured if it had been recognized in time. 'I cannot say whether it is the father or mother who is infected.' She remarked that the Hori children have the same trouble, but the baby there is the picture of health. (Of course, I got all my suspicions about the Hori kids from Mrs. Sato, who said, 'It comes from their parents.') It may well be that they have only some kind of skin rash."

Some of the skin diseases of children were the result of poor sanitation, while others developed from dietary habits. "Today, which is a holiday, the women were calling on one another. Tamaki's wife is without doubt the sloppiest thing in Tontokoro. Her untidy hair is always unwashed, her clothes put on any old way, and her baby always has dirt behind its ears and in the creases. Most of the kids have developed dreadful boils and skin inflammations [it is now July], and the babies have horrible looking rashes called sweat-rash (*asebo*). Almost the only ones who don't are the Mori children. Jitsuo-chan started to develop something, which was checked at once by washing and application of medicines and powder. Mori attributes most of the problems to lack of care and dirt. Their baby is constantly bathed and talcumed and is very clean indeed."

In September, "all the children have rashes on their face and body from eating raw chestnuts and persimmon. They get them every fall. Poor little Mitchan, who had almost recovered from her boils, got another from eating chestnuts." Children were always being cautioned about what they ate, but rather ineffectually. "When the younger girl wanted more pickled plums, which had in fact all been consumed, her mother said, 'If you eat too many of those, they will all come out in a lot of *be* [excrement],' and put her hand under the child's buttocks. The older one remarked that if you eat too many persimmons, then no *be* comes out at all, which is quite true, as they are very constipative. To little Mitchan, her mother said playfully, 'Come here, you rash-covered child (*kusaba ko*).' The new boil is on the poor child's head, and it is tremendous. Her mother calls it 'the father of heat-rash' (*usebu no oya*). 'Now,' she says, 'little things will break out all over her.' Others refer to the rash as *kasabo* [syphilitic rash] or *mizubōsō* [chicken pox]. Various ointments and powders are used to treat it."

"When Tamezo's baby had boils, she was taken to the curing priest, who gave her an amulet which she wears around her neck all the time. The Tamaki Giichi baby has been sick for some time now. When she first fell ill, they took her to the doctor, for having made much of their only daughter, they are very worried about her health. She ran a high temperature for a few days, during which period they took very good care of her. Then, when she seemed to be better, they took her out, thinking it would be all right. The mother went to the Hachiman-san festival with the younger boy and the baby on her back. The baby got sick again and this time they decided to try a different cure, so they took her to Taragi to a curing priest for a ceremony to reduce fever. At their first visit to this man, he advised them to switch back to the doctor."

Given the freedom accorded children it is not surprising that many people had suffered injuries in childhood. "The other day I noticed Tsune's hand. She cannot uncurl the middle finger. When she was a baby she grabbed an iron tong stuck in the fire-pit. The doctor grafted some skin from her arm, leaving an ugly scar, and put it on the palm of her hand, but did not straighten out the finger. Later on she had another nasty burn. The mother of a little boy who was there showed me his hand, which was missing two fingers cut off by a thresher."

"While running around the *dō* the other day, the little Fujita girl fell and hurt her wrist. I have not seen it unbandaged, but it sounds as if she may have cracked a bone. Mori tried to fix it and put some medicine on it right away. They continued the application of the medicine for ten days, but there was no improvement. Finally a piece of bone pushed through the skin, so they took her to a doctor in Taragi who treated her and applied more medicine. Most people will try a home remedy first."

DEATH

The death of a child was the occasion for grief, as was that of old women and men, but it was more restrained than that expressed for the young and vigorous who died in their prime. While the Embrees were in Suye, three children died, two in infancy and an older one by drowning.

"Going through Imamura yesterday I discovered a new *rokujizō* [candle stand] by the path and found that it was put there by Irie. Nearby was the new grave, all fresh with a homemade roof instead of a regular *tamaya* [soul house], and homemade paper flowers. There were two paper lanterns, two banner stands (although the banners were gone), the slip of wood with the posthumous name, a tray containing some oil and other offerings, and incense and candles.

"The baby was only eighteen days old, born shortly after I had seen Mrs. Irie lugging those tremendous logs across the footbridge from Nakashima. They do not know what was wrong with the baby. The mother says it was a very healthy baby, but both the older boy and the old man said they thought something was wrong with it from the beginning. At any rate, the baby had cried a great deal and she did not have enough milk even though the old man got something that is sold at the druggist's in Taragi for the mother to drink to increase her flow. At four in the morning the baby was seized by convulsions, rolled up its eyes, stiffened and turned black from the waist down. It was impossible to get a doctor and the old man complained how hard it is to get to Taragi or even Fukada when a doctor is needed in a hurry.

"The baby died and they buried him in a long coffin because he was so small and would feel better lying down. Because this was the funeral of a baby, everything was made at home, and only the lower half of the hamlet attended the services, which is the custom. No outside relatives came because all are far away and it is a busy season. A few here that are related to the family did come. There was no music because it was a child's funeral, they say, and a large funeral takes money. They will have the weekly memorial services anyway. They were flattered that I had called and gave me much *shōchū*. Evidently they feel the loss, because the older boy asked me to take his picture by the grave. I said I would and when I told them that I had already photographed it on my way up, they were pleased. Yet they showed no emotion and discussed the matter calmly. The old man even laughed a bit. Mrs. Irie refused *shōchū* because she does not drink it right after childbirth. This reminded her about *hiaki*, the ceremony of presenting a new baby at the Shinto shrine. What should she do, she wondered, now that the baby is dead? Should she go anyhow? This was her seventh baby, and the first to die. Her husband thought they might just offer *o-miki*. At Shimoda's I told them about the death of the Irie baby. They said it was better that it died young, for when it got to be as old as their baby that died it is hard to forget. [The baby had died just before its second birthday.]"

A few weeks later, Mrs. Eda gave birth to twin boys. "They came at 4:00 A.M. after a short labor and within an hour after the midwife's arrival. The one born second was the smaller of the two, and they did not appear to be identical twins. The one born second is considered the older. Both seemed healthy at first, but this morning the smaller one began to look sickly and refused to drink milk. They called the doctor, who said that the baby was too young to be given medicine. Later the family agreed that it had not been necessary to call a doctor. The baby seemed better for a while, then suddenly began to choke and died. The midwife was there, for she had come to bathe the boys for the naming ceremony. She had washed the sick baby that morning, however, and at the time advised calling the doctor, for she thought it did not look strong. Another bath was considered unnecessary, so before putting the corpse in the box it was sprinkled with water with a branch of *sasa* [bamboo grass] by the relatives.

"I came in about fifteen minutes after the baby died, and everyone was obviously very upset. The mother was lying down in the usual manner with hardly any bedding, and all sorts of rags piled under her head to keep it high. The living baby was next to her, the dead one on the same bed a trifle removed. It looked very much as if it were asleep. She was weeping bitterly and paid little attention to consolations. The midwife, Mrs. Tamaki, and a couple of hamlet women were sitting beside her telling her how sorry they were, but that she should not grieve so because she had been expecting only one baby, and one of the twins was left her. Occasionally they would digress and start discussing some events in the past which were analogous to the present and then return to the current situation again.

"Eda was in the kitchen discussing things with Shimosaka. His eyes were red and he did not conceal his grief. When people arrived they would say, 'You have a child. That is very good,' then add, after being thanked, 'But I hear the little one died. What a pity.' He would thank them again and say how glad he was it had happened suddenly. Then someone, usually old lady Eda, would tell the whole story to the newcomer. With Shimosaka he was discussing how to arrange the funeral and the naming ceremony. The principal problem was that tomorrow is *tomobiki* [an almanac designation punning to 'to pull another along,' and therefore a day in which funerals were never held. In Suye if a person died in the morning on such a day, the funeral was postponed. If he died on an ordinary day early in the morning, he would be buried the next day. If he died late in the day, everything would be put forward a day in order to observe the proper formalities and avoid a rush.] A funeral cannot take place until the death has been registered at the village office, for the corpse cannot be moved until then. Furthermore, a death cannot be registered if the birth has not been recorded, and for that the deceased must have a name. All this caused much complication, but even more troublesome was the fact that the guests had been invited and fish prepared for the twins' naming party.

"It was decided to choose names for both babies and hang them up as is the usual custom, then have a funeral service for the dead baby and a naming party for the living one. While all this was going on, people kept coming in, some to offer rice in condolence, having just heard about the death, others who had not heard with gifts for the naming ceremony. Mrs. Suzuki came with rice flour because she had some extra and it is considered good for the mother. Mrs. Amano stopped by and was surprised to learn of the death. She, like some others, went back home immediately and returned with some rice. The members of the Eda family were caught in a complicated situation of being both guests [at the funeral meal] and hosts [at the naming party]. At any rate, the chief guests were six relatives from Imamura, other kinsmen from closer by, the hamlet people, and the wife of the Eda's go-between. Mrs. Wauchi came late with gifts and was served her festive naming-ceremony meal, but left before the funeral, assisting only briefly when the baby's body was placed in the coffin.

"Eda produced some slips of paper with names for the twins, but Mrs. Tamaki, who has assumed the role of temporary hostess (she is a relative through Mrs. Eda), announced that she had thought up some names the night before. Everyone thought them fine, and indeed she is always suggesting names at these affairs. Others had suggestions, too, all of which would ordinarily have been written out on slips of paper and placed in the cup for a drawing. But hers were simply accepted, and Eda wrote them out on two pieces of paper and hung them up by the god-shelf. He also removed the fish, a *tai*, which had been presented by the fishmonger. It was served later at the naming ceremony, but removed for the funeral. He put a bottle of *o-miki* in the god-shelf and two cups. Then a tray containing incense and a bowl of rice were placed at the Buddhist altar and old man Eda read a sutra while others bowed. (Throughout all this the younger Eda boy slept in the middle of the room, covered with a kimono and another folded under his head for a pillow. Later he was taken up and looked after by the old lady from next door.)

"The midwife was busy. First she bathed the live baby, surrounded by all the women making much noise and praising its looks. Today she dressed the baby, but not in a fancy kimono, and made it up before patting some powder on the dead baby's face too. After the funeral she was given her naming-ceremony meal all alone with the family, passed the baby around as at other such ceremonies, and then went home.

"All this time the mother continued to weep and developed a headache. Her mother, who had come early in the afternoon to take care of her, brought a package of ash from the Buddhist altar and rubbed it on her forehead, saying, 'These are Takatsuka-sama's ashes.' (Takatsuka-sama or Taka-sama is the god at Nishinomura who is good for treatment of illnesses from the waist up. Ashes from there have a marvelous power to clear up headaches. When her first baby was born she was sick for a long time and was treated with these ashes. This time she had wanted to go there, but did not feel up to it, so when Mrs. Shimosaka went there she brought her a handful. Soon her head was better, she said.)

"Men were sent to Menda to make necessary purchases and others were assembling under Shimosaka's guidance. The things that had to be bought or made were a rosary, fan, rope, lanterns, etc. They also bought a piece of new cloth to wrap around the coffin. When discussing the arrangements, the women wanted to know if the village would have to attend, and Shimosaka said that only four or five houses would be needed. It was understood that only close neighbors would come, and only one person from each, but in the event couples came from the whole upper half of the hamlet.

"The Moris called to pay their respects, but brought no rice. They did not participate in the funeral, nor did the Fujitas or the Hayashis. The former were 'too busy with the cocoons' and said they would come the next day to offer condolences. Matsumoto came in to pay his respects and went up to the cemetery to help. Ouchi helped out a little, and his wife was there the whole time. Old man Makino did not come (I think it was understood that only those men would come who had someone to leave at home to look after things), but his son was a pallbearer, as was Nagata. Both their wives were there, left to do their laundry, and returned. The Tanimotos came, she first and he later.

"As soon as it was decided to have the funeral, some men went up to Hirano's to work, the women got busy cooking rice (at first a very small amount for the funeral tray), borrowing cups and trays from neighbors, buying bean curd and seaweed, and serving tea and cakes to all who called. There was a great deal of commotion and old lady Eda fussed a lot, making Eda glare at her occasionally, especially when she forced hospitality on someone and kept worrying aloud lest anyone who called might go away without being served tea.

"When the men started working, Shimosaka came in to see if the baby had been named, then went to register its birth and death at the village office. When he returned the body was moved in front of the Buddhist altar and people sat around a while chatting and smoking. Eda asked someone to remind the men to make a doll. When the coffin was finished they brought it in and Eda made ready to put the body in, assisted by old man Eda, the two grandmothers, and Mrs. Wauchi. The mother, holding the other baby, stood by still weeping bitterly. A basin of water was brought in and each in turn sprinkled the body. Then Eda put it in a sitting position and putting its tiny hands together in the Buddhist attitude of devotion, placed it in the coffin. Everyone gave bits of advice, so the body was removed once and its position shifted. The new white dress with which it had been covered was folded and slipped in under its head. When someone expressed doubt about using the dress, the mother said, 'Put it in. We can spare one dress.' Mrs. Wauchi sent a child out for a flower and when it was brought she placed it in the baby's hand, the fingers being forced open, and Eda put in the rosary and the fan. Before the doll was placed in the coffin, Mrs. Wauchi suggested that a new face be drawn on it, which was done.

"Just as the lid was set in place, Eda remembered that he had forgotten the paper with the baby's name on it, so he took it down from the god-shelf and tried to slip it in under the lid. Mrs. Wauchi objected, saying it might cover the baby's head, so the lid was removed and it was placed beside the body. All through these operations one old woman held some burning incense, which the others said was not considered necessary at this time. Incense is held to purify the air and counteract the odor that may emanate from a corpse.

"After Mrs. Wauchi had her meal and left, more guests arrived from Imamura. It was decided not to serve meals to all, but the parents did have some rice with salt as *wakare gohan* (parting meal). Presently the priest arrived. He is from the local Zen temple although the house belongs to the Shin sect. He had tea, wrote out the posthumous name and started the funeral service. The mother, still holding the other baby, sat out of sight behind the sliding doors.

"The first to offer incense was Eda. Then he took his two little sons up, followed by old man Eda, Uemura, and Tamaki, then old lady Eda, then Mrs. Eda's mother, who took along the Eda little daughter, then old lady Tamaki and two old women, cousins of Eda. Short, disposable straw sandals [*ashinaka*] were prepared, the folded papers to be worn behind the ears distributed, and two men brought the tiny coffin out of the house, followed by the mourners. They waited for Eda to come in front of the line with the tray of offerings. Tamaki and Uemura had brought banners to which pieces of paper bearing their names were attached. (This business of attaching names is very important. One of the Eda women, a relative who was helping today, spent all her time recording from whom the gifts came. The rice brought yesterday was not served, apparently.)

"Mrs. Shimosaka swept the main room thoroughly with a bundle of straw, and a basin filled with salt water was set out. The women began to prepare the food for the meal. They were rather mixed up because none of them knew exactly how many guests there were. They were short of bowls, for two meals were to be served, the funeral feast of *o-nishime* and *yakifu*, and then the regular naming-ceremony meal of fish. Old lady Tamaki cleared things up when she came back from the cemetery. When the priest returned he went in at once to chant another sutra and the relatives, first washing their hands in the salt water, assembled for it. The village men turned up later and went on to the Hirano's, where the priest later joined them. There the relatives were served, but the party was a quiet one, for when I dropped in at Hirano's a little later, they were already eating rice [which means that the drinking had stopped]. Some of the women who had been helping at Eda's were there. They ate in snatches here and there, and I do not know if they got a proper meal.

"At the naming party at Eda's it was decided to give the surviving baby a different name because some feared that keeping the original name, which had been paired with its twin, might serve to 'pull along' this child, too. (Yesterday, when we asked if they wanted a picture of the twins, they said no because later on the surviving child would see it and be reminded of his dead brother—another 'pulling along' belief, I think.)

"Mrs. Eda's mother stayed overnight and was to help out the next day because old lady Eda was wanted at home for the cocoons. This morning the old Eda couple was there, their daughter taking care of the children and helping with the dishes. Some women dropped in to pick up the crockery they had left yesterday. The village headman stopped by for a moment on his way somewhere and offered his sympathies to the father, and asked about the mother and child. Shichihei stopped by to report that a girl related to some people in Kawaze had been hurt when she fell off her bicycle in Menda. There was also some talk about doctors. Eda said that the one they called in was very expensive, charging one yen for the call, during which he only looked at the sick baby. They did not have to call him to come and certify the death, at least [which he did because he had seen the child], which costs another twenty-five to fifty sen. All agreed that he is a good doctor, but had less complimentary things to say about Oka, who is much cheaper.

"Eda told us how he had learned he was the father of twins. Evidently it was taken as a joyful event. He was sitting in the kitchen while the midwife was with his wife. She came out to say that a baby had been born, and he asked if he could go in, but she told him to wait a while. Then he noticed that she had not used the water he had prepared, and realized that another baby must be coming. The midwife had suspected it at once, but said nothing until she was certain. When he asked her point-blank, however, she said yes. When he saw the second child, he was amazed at how small it was. (At once the subject of the Dionne quintuplets was discussed in detail.)

"Then Eda and his father changed into better clothing and went around to thank all those who had helped at the funeral. They stopped for a moment at each house where Eda delivered the usual polite expressions of gratitude, and the two men would bow and move on. Mrs. Eda discussed the experience with the women who dropped in to talk to her. This had been the first pregnancy during which she felt so tired that she could not even fetch water. ('I never can,' put in Mrs. Ouchi, 'I always have to wait for the children to come back from school to do it.') She had wondered why the baby was so active and seemed to have a foot in two different places at once [the twins were in a position with heads opposed, so that one was born feet first, the other head first]. At first they had expected a girl, but later decided that it was so active that it must be a boy. She also said that after the first baby came she somehow did not feel as if it were over and the second one came at once. It all took less than an hour after the midwife arrived and almost immediately after the waters broke. None of the neighbors heard anything during the night.

"All in all the people were very sympathetic and many women wept. At the funeral the young men served as pallbearers repeating exactly the words used by the older men, which is, of course, how they learn the behavior appropriate to all situations. The thing that struck me at the funeral was the lack of interaction between the mother and father. He spoke very little to her and had not much to do with her except when they ate the parting meal. Yet in normal circumstances they are a friendly couple. Was it to avoid becoming emotional in the presence of others?"

Some families observed a Shinto custom intended to insure the survival of younger children if an older sibling dies in childhood. "If one's child dies, one can have the priest conduct a purification ceremony (o-harai) over the next baby born, and pledge it to a god for a specified number of years. Since Tamaki's older boy died at the age of four, the second one was pledged to Kōjin-san for fifteen years. Now, at every Kōjin festival they take rice to the shrine and the priest comes to perform the purification ceremony at their house. He also comes once a year on October 27, the festival of Suwa shrine, and does the same."

Far harder to bear than the death of a newborn infant was that of an older child. "The women were making dumplings for the party to celebrate the end of rice transplanting, when about three in the afternoon Toyama Tawaji came home with the news that a little boy had fallen in the swollen river at Aso. 'Who? Where?' everyone wanted to know. It turned out to be the five-year-old grandson of Hayashi who had accidently been pushed off the bank by his seven-year-old brother. There had been no adults around, and when they were finally summoned it was too late. The search for the body had started.

"Everyone was shocked. *'Odomo shiran! Gurashika na!'* ['I just don't know what to think! How terrible!'] and other exclamations were made, and they recalled that it was just seven years ago that the Kawabe child and Iwaji's own son had drowned while playing at the river. They also recalled how cute the little Hayashi boy was, and how fond of him his grandparents were. (They had little to say about the father, of whom they do not think much. Later someone said to me that he is no good and does nothing. He is an adopted husband. The Toyamas and Kawabes were to say later that they would not go there to offer condolences because the Aso people never come here for that purpose—these two were the sourest of all, but that was much later.)

"After some talk the men were asked to go down to the river while the women thought of offering incense to the house-gods. The search was being organized. People took up positions on the bridges to watch, and along the riverbanks. Boats were being procured and some men were making a raft. Someone went to the curing priest for advice. They went back there in the evening after vainly following his *mamori* (amulet, talisman) in their search.

"The most active hamlets were Aso, Tontokoro, and Imamura. The Toyama servant went out in a boat. (Later Kawaze was accused of a lack of cooperation. They said that only one man came out on the bridge to stand watch, but even he said, 'The child won't float to the surface here,' and soon left. This is not quite true, since others report that there was one man there watching all the time.) The search was concentrated at the bridge called Asago-bashi and carried out by the Suwanoharu people. During the day just anyone watched, but at night a special party was organized consisting of Tontokoro and Aso firemen (in all such cases a young man joins with the hamlet in which he works, if he is an outsider). They watched three at a time, one taking responsibility for each hour of the three-hour shifts. They wore their uniforms. The group assembled in the Tamaki silkworm room, where they slept until their turn at watch came. After it was over, they went to their own homes. Two big gas lamps were projected on each bank, and the men kept a large fire going. All along the bridge, they built a screen of poles, wire, and netting to catch the body.

"According to Take, this was all done the last time, when the Tamaki child drowned, and the body was found on the same day. The Kawabe boy's body had been found at Hitoyoshi, where people searched the estuary as they always do on such occasions. Mrs. Kawabe, however, says that the search went on a whole week that time. At the moment people from Nakashima and Kakui are out on the bridge. Last night's constant rain and today's downpour are no help.

"When I called at the house yesterday the mother, with the younger child on her lap, was alternately crying and sobbing loudly So was the grandmother, who was telling the older boy, 'Now, you cannot take your younger brother to the river. Now, you must not go to the river—you see what happened.' He sat silently and did not weep. [It was he who accidentally pushed his brother into the river.] The only unconscious member of the family was the baby, who was gurgling away as usual. The father was not there. Many had red eyes. They had come to cook for the search party. Things for soup were brought out and the grandmother measured the rice. The old man stopped crying to ask her if there was no more left somewhere else, then corrected her when she measured too short. 'It must be two *shō*, five *gō*.' [One *shō* = 1.92 quarts; one *gō* = .384 pints.] He was going by the proper measurements for a funeral, because Mrs. Kawabe later remarked that the amount for a search-party meal is not set. Much of what went on at this point was as if it were a funeral, although the body had not yet been found. Take says that one does not make a condolence call until the body is found because the family is still worried and upset, but that later the entire village calls. (This seems to be where the Aso people fell short when the Kawabe child drowned seven years ago.) When people come to the house or meet in the street, they at once exchange regrets and make expressions of sympathy, '*Kawaisō natta* [How sad]' and

'*Kinodoku no koto nari mashita* [How pitiable].' It is much sadder than an ordinary death.

"Under the Asago bridge in Tontokoro there was a real camping ground. A large fire was kept going, and the women were serving tea and plates and trays of food. The place had been set up about midnight of the first day. For the first two days the food is supplied by the family, but the work was done by the women of Aso, while men from Aso, Tontokoro, Hamanoue, and the firemen did the searching. When the firemen went to Kinoue, the men stayed on at the bridge. Four of them, naked except for loin-cloths, waded all the way into the river with long poles. They came out shivering, put on dry clothes, and were given tea and *shōchū*. The women had been at it since last night. If the search continues much longer—some say it may last as much as twenty days—the villagers will organize to supply rice and will take rice to the family after the funeral. In the meantime only relatives coming from other villages bring gifts. People have been calling since yesterday to express sympathy. The parents and grandparents have not left the house. Today the grandmother was lying down; the mother has eaten nothing. The villagers say that at such a time 'one becomes mad with grief (*hontō-ni shinke-ni narimasu*).' They were sitting in the main room talking in low voices, bending down once in a while, heads buried in their arms, sobbing. The women helping in the kitchen were much subdued. Candles were lit for the buddhas at the altar. The old man put some *shōchū* in a glass bottle, packed some rice and salt in paper, and sent someone off to offer them to the water god, to ask him to surrender the body. The man took it down to the bridge, scattered some of the rice grains in the water, and left the rest on the bridge near where the child had fallen in. Women were cooking the noon rice for the relatives, while in a different house another group was preparing a meal for the men.

"Those who had not yet finished transplanting went ahead with it, and the events of the last two days did not stop the music at the Oade and Imamura parties to celebrate the end of the work. Various reports are circulated about the curing priest's predictions, and someone said he is predicting another drowning. There is a belief, expressed by all, including the Abe teacher who is so high-hat, that a flood always takes a victim and that the rain will not stop without a drowning." At a party at Kawabe's to celebrate the end of transplanting, "the drowning was much discussed. Every time it came up, Mrs. Toyama would try to conceal her tears by drying her eyes with her kimono sleeves. Their own loss was mentioned and Mrs. Kawabe said that she had so completely lost her mind that she could not remember anything that happened, who went to search, who supplied the rice, anything."

"On the fourth day the child's body was found washed up on the rocks just beyond Hitoyoshi. It was brought to the village office. In the afternoon the firemen gathered there and had a parting meal and drink. Villagers came and hung around for a while. Young Sato thought they should call off their end-of-transplanting party, but it was just changed around a bit. My observation is that these parties are rather a let-down and much quieter than those held in the winter, but perhaps it was because of the child's death."

The funeral itself was held the next day. "The priest came and was served his meal at a neighbor's house, where he later returned to take a nap. The women there sat around talking while the relatives began to gather at Hayashi's. On arriving, each one greeted all present, went into the main room to greet the men seated there, and then found a place to sit. He would then pass his contribution of rice and *shōchū* or a banner with money, to one of the women who was serving the visitors. He was then given tea and cooked beans, and then a black lacquer tray of food, and then a plate of fish and vegetables boiled in soy sauce. By five both the kitchen and the main room were full. The mother and grandmother sat next to the *tamaya*, as did the father at first, but later he moved. They were served last.

"The grandfather, father and the grandfather's brothers sat at the head of the room, then other male relatives. Women sat at the bottom of the room and in the kitchen. None of these callers wore formal kimono except the father's aunt who lives near the bridge where the accident occurred. She came late and had on a special summer one. For the funeral service itself the men changed into *hakama* and *huori* [a divided skirt and short coat worn on formal occasions] as did Mrs. Hayashi of Tontokoro. The mother wore a very pretty pale blue formal kimono, and only she and the grandmother had funeral hairdress. The grandfather began to make the rounds down the line without a cup, pouring *shōchū* for each guest. [On festive occasions one carries one's cup when making the rounds for exchanging drinks.] He was followed by his two brothers and then the child's father. The others just exchanged cups from where they sat. Later the women went up and when all the first round was completed, Mrs. Hayashi of Tontokoro said it was all right to have two drinks. In the midst of this the priest arrived, still in his white kimono, and proceeded to write the posthumous names on the tablets.

"The people relaxed somewhat when the food was cleared, and sat around and chatted. Many relatives, who had not met for some time, exchanged news of the family, discussed the number of children in the various houses and their ages, etc. Then the priest began to change into his formal robes and everybody put on the formal kimono they had brought with them.

"At first the priest prayed at the Buddhist altar, then stood in front of the coffin. For music to accompany his chanting, he had just the bronze bowl. First he dropped some incense onto the coals in the incense brazier, then held up the piece of paper with the child's posthumous name written on it and prayed. He then put the paper on the *tamaya* and resumed his prayers. (Banners had been brought in before this and hung over a pole by the *tamaya*.) After a bit he gave a sign and the grandfather came up, deposited some incense, and knelt to pray for a few moments. He was followed by the child's father.

"Then some confusion arose because the little boy [who had caused his brother's death] refused to go up, and burst into muffled long-suppressed sobs. The priest interrupted his praying and said, 'Somebody lead him up,' but even when dragged up by his grandfather, he made his hand go limp and they could do nothing to make him grasp the incense. He was treated a bit severely the entire time, and made to observe all the rituals. [This may have been due in part to the anger of the adults, of course, but it must be pointed out that it also protects the boy from the possibility of revenge being taken on him by the spirit of the brother he had inadvertently killed.]

"The grandfather's brothers came next, in order of age, then the male relatives on their side, and then after a slight argument, the father's older brother came up, followed by the father's paternal uncle who lives here now near the bridge where the accident occurred. Next were the father's male relatives, the mother, grandfather's brothers' wives by age, and the father's aunt. The child's father went out to fetch the grandmother, who was missing her turn, and the old man from next door came up in the meantime. As each person passed in front of the priest, he bowed to him, and without interrupting his praying the priest returned the bow. When all this was finished, there was a chorus of *namanda*, more praying, and another *namanda*.

"The paper bearing the child's posthumous name was put in the coffin and the lid nailed shut. *Shōchū* was served to the pallbearers, while one of the aunts distributed folded paper to be worn behind the ears of the mourners. Outside, someone passed around disposable sandals which were left on the path on the way back from the cemetery. As soon as the coffin was out of sight straw was fetched with which to sweep the room.

"There were three candles in the stand and five muslin banners and many paper ones. The silk banners were left at the house, hanging over a pole. All were marked by the father who wrote out the relatives' names on them as they arrived. (During the funeral service, food was taken out to the men who were waiting to take the coffin to the cemetery. The women had tea and beans while waiting for the service to end, and had a hurried regular meal while the relatives were at the service in the cemetery.) Upon returning, all washed their hands and feet in a basin of salt water, knelt in front of the Buddhist altar, and went to change. Some went off right away, but others stayed behind to have tea and beans and the same meal over again because the Hayashi were combining the funeral meal with the *detsuki* [ceremony held the day following the funeral] that ordinarily would have been held later. The priest changed out of his robes slowly, and then started to go over to the neighbor's house but was called back to receive his fee. He and the child's father fixed the dates for the memorial services that will be held periodically.

"The relatives were from Suye, Iwano, Taragi, and Itsuki. Although the father is from Itsuki [he is an adopted husband], his parents did not attend, but were represented by his elder brother, a true country hick who made three loud speeches when he arrived, one to the parents (which made the poor mother cry), one to the male relatives, and one to the women during which he had to stop and ask the child's name. With equal loudness he delivered his money to the grandfather. [This is *kōden*, incense money, contributed to a bereaved family by all mourners.] Everyone smiled when referring to him. He was much interested in my presence, and finally decided that I must be a reporter. He asked me to write his name in roman letters, and then said he could not read it. Other Itsuki relatives were the uncle and aunt who moved here not long ago, and whom I had mistaken the day before for the father's parents. They were very active the whole time, especially the wife. Also, a great deal was done by the grandfather's older brother, whom I also mistook for the child's father's father, for it was he who offered the rice, salt and *shōchū* to the water god and fetched the body from the village office."

ELEVEN

The Handicapped, Misfits, Wanderers, and Witches

Among the women of Suye, as among the men, were a number of people who were in one way or another considered to be abnormal. Some were physically or mentally handicapped, while others were the victims of their own inability to adjust to the rather narrow requirements of the society in which they found themselves. Some of them labored mightily to overcome their limitations, but many of them were simply defeated by life. Communities like Suye dealt harshly with such people on occasion, as we shall see.

THE PHYSICALLY HANDICAPPED

Perhaps the outstanding example of a woman who had managed to make a life for herself in the face of extreme adversity was Shimizu Setsuko, forty-six years old, known universally as "deaf and dumb Setsuko." Her story is worth recording in some detail, for it is a noteworthy example of perseverance in the face of very great odds. "Setsuko is a member of a very poor family, although her father's children by his first wife are said to be quite prosperous. She went to a special school in Kagoshima where she learned to understand people and to make herself understood by signs. If she sees a conversation going on, she enquires about it and is told by signs what is being said. She can also read, and is a good dancer even though she cannot hear the music. In one of the more complicated dances at tonight's party, she was showing the other women the steps. Like the rest of them, she smokes. She is somewhat shy and always has to be persuaded to make the rounds with her cup when drinks are being exchanged. The attitude of the other women toward her is very friendly, if a trifle patronizing. When she has trouble making herself understood, she grunts and gets red in the face, but she certainly does not seem at all unhappy."

"Setsuko's first daughter was married about ten days ago. I was interested to find out how the woman had arranged a marriage for her daughter. It turns out that there was a go-between, but since Shimoda's wife can understand her signs better than anyone else in the village, she assisted with the negotiations. The Shimoda couple went to the wedding, where Mrs. Shimoda more or less represented the bride's mother. As a matter of fact, I find it extremely easy to understand the woman. I invited her to our party and she invited me back. I congratulated her on her daughter's marriage, and she thanked me. All this was by signs. For example, she uses her thumb to indicate man, and her little finger to mean woman. For marriage, she holds the two together." These gestures were commonly employed by everyone, but often with strong sexual innuendo.

"One day I met her as she was leading her horse for the third trip that day to the mountains to fetch wood which she had cut. She was walking alone, and I wondered what she thought about as she walked silently the long stretch. She understood me when I told her that I was going to a flower-arranging lesson. I showed her that I could not possibly carry such heavy loads as she does. She shook her head emphatically and by signs explained that she is meant to go to the mountains for wood, while I am meant to do flower-arranging. She is a member of a woman's *kōgin* and yesterday, as the winner, gave the party at her house. She participates in all other events, never missing a meeting at the school and goes to all the lectures the other women attend."

"Setsuko has a different sign for everyone in the village. The Satos are indicated by the gesture of grinding [they own a mill]. For Wauchi the sign is also linked to occupation. For John and me, her gestures are for someone very tall with unruly hair It was explained that 'just the sign for tall is not enough, because in Kakui there are many tall people.' [The disorderly hair is a reference to the only two people in the village who use no oil on it.]"

With this woman and her children lived a blind seventy-year-old woman named Shimoda. "It must be a weird household, yet the unmarried teen-age daughter is cheerful and makes jokes all the time, laughing at both the older women. Setsuko explained that when the old lady had come crying to her, saying that there was no one left to take care of her, she had taken her in. The old lady said many times, 'Setsuko is my host (*tessu*).' Setsuko proudly signed all the man's work she does—getting in all the firewood, ploughing the fields, etc. She and her daughter take care of the silkworms, whereas in all the other families there is some man to help out. She also explained that her husband died, her son was away working, and two of her daughters are married. The really amazing thing is that she differs from the other women in no respect in what she does and how she does it. She even got herself a second husband when the first one died, but he left her."

The other women agreed that she should be proud of her ability to work, but said that she had had three husbands, two of whom died. The third, the father of the youngest girl, had left of his own accord, leaving her solely responsible for making a living for herself and her dependents. Of a very practical turn of mind, she occasionally took measures somewhat out of the ordinary. "Setsuko has created a mild sensation by having special trousers made which she will wear for ploughing, for she does not like to get her bare legs and kimono skirts wet. Lacking any men in the house, she has to plough her own fields. The women say, 'A strong woman that, doing all the man's work.' "

There were also in Suye a number of retarded people, treated not unkindly, but with a pronounced degree of condescension and ridicule. "This morning a strange-looking girl stopped at Kawabe's, selling bamboo shoots. She is fat, dull-looking, and dressed in dirty old clothes. Mrs. Tanimoto was teasing her. 'You are getting so fat! What do you eat, anyway? Haven't come calling on Fumio [a married man of twenty-eight] lately, have you? Has he made a child for you yet? You are eighteen now, and should get married this year. Is it all set?' To all this the girl only giggled slightly or said hmmmm.

"Later I learned that she is from Hirayama and that her mother is Hashiguchi's sister. They used to be a rich family, but when the old people died they lost everything. They send the girl out to sell bamboo shoots and buy rice with the money. She is said to have a mania for men, and that she once was much smitten with Fumio. She used to come around all the time. When he told her once that he could not have intercourse with her because her vagina was too small, the poor girl picked up some corn-silk, blackened it with ink, and stuck it between her legs, apparently having decided that having hair there is a sign of age. (The teasing is one more piece of evidence for my feeling that Mrs. Tanimoto is remarkably tactless and unfeeling.)"

"During the gossip at Makino's, I learned that Osone, the half-wit girl I saw here once, the relative of Hashiguchi who stuck corn-silk on her vagina, has been married. The man was first married to this girl's half-sister, but he disliked her so much that he refused to sleep with her, and now he has got the half-wit instead. One of the women remarked that she is just the kind of girl who will have a child right away." It is not clear whether she was implying that the girl is already pregnant or was too dull to take any countermeasures.

Another peddler from within Suye was a girl who worked for a family that sold fruit. The village women were candid in their low assessment of her abilities. "The Oshiro girl went by and everyone agreed that she is a fool because she cannot add up anything that is not in even weights, such as 50 or 100. Even so, figuring the price for 350 *me* [one *me* = .1325 ounces or .375 grams] of her fruit was an effort. She works for seven *hyō* [one *hyō* = 60 kilograms] of rice a year and three gifts—at *o-bon*, the new year, and transplanting time."

Teasing and condescension were not reserved for females, however. "Toward the end of the naming ceremony for the Shiraki baby, Sasatani Ukichi's younger brother arrived. He is bald and a half-wit. As is the case with most such people, many jokes were made at his expense. He was teased about his baldness, but otherwise was served food and drink like the rest, and made the rounds exchanging drinks with the others. Ukichi remained silent, with an expression of contempt on his face. They say that his brother lives with him and does work in the mountain and other odd jobs."

It should be said that the people of Suye did usually try to find a place for the handicapped. "Araki Toraichi's 'nurse' [for their small children] is a lame boy from Kinoue who apparently finished elementary school before his family sent him out to work. Here he spends a lot of his free time at the school, practicing on the cross-bars and other gymnastic equipment, trying to do hard things such as standing up on a bar, which involves dragging up his bad leg. He is pleased if you admire some difficult stunt, and I have noticed that when sent off on an errand he always runs, evidently hoping that people will forget that he is a cripple."

THE PSYCHOLOGICALLY HANDICAPPED

For some younger children who were considered "not quite right" the future held little promise. "While I was there the old lady who had let her granddaughter fall into the charcoal brazier came calling. The child is always with her. Because of the burns all the back of her head is absolutely hairless. Her legs are not strong, so she cannot walk very well yet. She is also cross-eyed and looks and acts like a half-wit. I do not know if she was made this way by being dropped into the fire when she was two, but she is now five and obviously retarded. She was given some pickle, asked for more, and got more. She asked for tea and got it, then wanted more, and finally drank four cups. She whimpered for still more, was refused by her grandmother, whimpered a while longer, and was finally given two more cups. She whimpered when her grandmother lighted her pipe, was given it, and smoked, taking real puffs on it. Her grandmother kept pulling the child's kimono together in the front to cover her bare legs and middle. Like most of the children here, she did not seem to mind the cold. The pulling of the kimono is done more as a gesture of modesty because none of the preschool children wear pants. It is through the influence of the school that parents sometimes feel it is wrong to leave the genitals exposed."

Later, she was observed in less solicitous company. "The children were playing a variety of hopscotch. The little girl with the burned head was hanging around. She is an utter idiot and even the older kids delight in tormenting her. They call her crazy (*shinke*) and yell at her, which always frightens her so that she runs away to look for help. She, for her part, delights in spoiling their games, stepping on the squares they have marked out and smudging them, and so on. Her mother, who does not look too bright herself, although she is quite husky, just looks on laughing." Toward the end of the Embrees' stay in Suye, there appears the laconic note: "The little girl with the burned head seems much more developed these days." Perhaps, like the bamboo-shoot seller, she was married off in the end.

For a few women marriage had proved to be their undoing. "Sato believes that Shimoda Ichiro's wife is not quite normal. She must have melancholia—she is so quiet. Her father is insane without question. Sato says it is a bad sign that her baby looks so much like her, for she reminds him of the Tsurumi woman who ended her almost complete silence some months after her wedding by drowning herself in a muddy pond." About another woman, there were no doubts at all. "There are rumors that a sister of Kawabe is mad. She was adopted by an aunt in Shirayama who later died. The woman had a baby by an old man, thirty-three years her senior, and then was married to him. She went insane, with a mania for playing with fire and burning things. The other day it was reported that she had died, and Kawabe went there, but returned to say, 'Not yet.' She is said to be confined to a special room in the house."

Less dramatic, but more common, is the condition referred to by the villagers as hysteria (hisuteri). "Mrs. Matsumoto's condition is said to be hysteria, although nothing more specific is said other than that she likes men too much. Mrs. Kawabe did say of herself one day that she herself had trouble with her womb and that it had gone to her head." It is this Mrs. Matsumoto who provides us with one of the rare instances of a truly isolated individual. "At the school athletic meet, Matsumoto was there all morning and his wife came in the afternoon. She sat apart on the low stone wall, used as a seat by many, and did not join the hamlet party on the ground. The women remarked on her presence, saying that she is never seen in public. When I asked why she never comes out, Mrs. Hayashi gave a nasty laugh and said, 'Ha! Indeed, she never comes out. I wonder why?' "

"Yasuo often makes disparaging remarks about these gossipy women. He says that Mrs. Matsumoto apparently does not go out because of hisuteri, but then added, 'On the other hand, maybe she has nothing at all wrong with her, but just dislikes associating with that crowd, so has made up a story about being ill.' He says that her trouble really is jealousy, which is why her husband so seldom goes out alone." It was of this woman that Mrs. Amano said, " 'She likes to talk about sex and brings up the subject at once on any and all occasions. Most probably because she does so much of it,' she ventured. I fear it is the other way around. She said that Mrs. Matsumoto has a 'touch of hysteria' and used to have fits and was always ill, and although she is now much better, she never goes out."

MISFITS

The attitudes and actions of the village women toward the handicapped and misfits gave pause for reflection. There was, for example, Mrs. Tanimoto, the woman who "does not like children. She even had a fence built around her house to keep them out of the yard, but all other living creatures seem to fascinate her. [See pages 229–30.] She croons over her cat and pets it, and delights in telling stories about his violent lovemaking. She positively gloats when telling these stories, and it thrills her when the animal brings in a bird or a rat. She helps him in the business and thoroughly enjoys the scene."

"She says that silkworms are beautiful and she likes the crawling, moving, disgusting mass that the creatures form on the tray. 'Look!' she exclaims, 'just see here,' and she lifts up a wriggling batch of them. She does not treat them with any particular gentleness, however. Just as she enjoys seeing a bird caught, and snips its wings so that it cannot get away from the cat, she is cruel in her remarks to afflicted people like the retarded nursemaid at Origuchi's and treats them like dumb animals."

"If she had children, I imagine that she would by turns drown them with caresses and beat them to death. She always says, 'Just knock him on the head,' to a nursemaid if her charge misbehaves. She is very much a part of society here and not really a misfit, but I think that in a less uniform society she probably never would have married, or if she had, she'd never have been true to her husband. As it is, she goes anywhere she can to find a substitute for a husband. She loves to drink and gets very chummy with men when under the influence."

Later on there is a more general observation. "I suppose it would be hard in this society for a girl who hated housework and who was gifted with a creative mind. The greatest misfit of all would be, of course, a woman who did not like children but had them nonetheless. Bringing women up to be good mothers, society here never disappoints them by leaving them spinsters. Even childless married women are provided for by the system of adoption. There are, of course, exceptions such as Mrs. Tanimoto, who says that she hates children and it so happens has none. But had she given birth, I wonder if she would not have felt quite differently about the matter.

"I once thought that education would unfit girls for staying to work on the farm and make them feel that they are destined for something better, but not all of the girls' school graduates seem to feel that way. There is the Watanabe bride [see pages 159–61] who graduated from a girls' school with an eye to city life, who is unhappy because she was married into a farmer's family. On the other hand, there is the Tawaji girl, a true local product on whom education left no imprint, and who feels silly attending the flower-arranging classes, where the citified girls feel quite at ease. There is a clash between education and farm, no doubt, but its chief result may well be the trouble some young men have finding suitable brides, especially the few who have been away to higher schools."

And still later, returning once again to the theme of the handicapped: "If you can be used around the house, like the crippled boy, or if the family has enough money to send you to a special school and find you a husband, like 'deaf-and-dumb' Setsuko, such a person can stay here and adjust. But if an idiot is useless or otherwise a burden, he gets sent off somewhere, so that in the towns there is an accumulation of homeless half-wits. Often one of them wanders through the village, like the man who was making strange signs at me today. No one knows where he came from, although I have seen him around before. Pilgrims are also sent off by their families and so is the type of man for whom the people of Suye had compassionately built the straw hut [after people of another village had literally dumped him here]. When he died they put a notice in the newspaper, but there was no reply. The deaf woman's son is another type of misfit, the black sheep who ran away from home. I have not encountered one other possible type of misfit, one who is opposed to the established social order. Maybe young Shimosaka could be said to be one of these, for he says that he would marry a girl of his own choosing, were it not for his family. But then he does nothing drastic."

"The blind become music teachers or performers of *naniwabushi* and the crippled go out on the road as pilgrims, along with the old, the diseased, and the mentally deficient. That takes care of all the misfits." This passage concludes with one of the few assessments of the situation that reflects the convictions so thoroughly concealed throughout most of the journal. "Here it is hard to say whether misfits are saved or created, considering the educational system that trains every child to be a militarist and leaves no room for pacificism, a government that suppresses all expression of free thought and expects blind worship of an Emperor whose divine descent is called into question by the most elementary teachings of science and history, and the maintenance of an old-fashioned system of arranged marriages along with increasing levels of education for women and more and more mixing of young men and women, at least in the cities."

BEGGARS, WANDERERS, AND PILGRIMS

Among the most telling indictments of Japanese society at this time are the many short passages in the journal dealing with the appearance in Suye of a miscellany of beggars, wanderers, and pilgrims, many of them turned out by their families. "A musician went through the village yesterday. She played the *shamisen* for rice and a bit of cash. At Torao's she stayed a while and got some *shōchū*. When I went over to ask her where she came from, she said, 'Anywhere. Nowhere.' Teruko referred to her as *kadobiki* [street-corner musician]." But most of them were men. "Early in the afternoon a blind *koto* player from Menda stopped by. His instrument had steel strings and he played it much as one might a mandolin, holding it upright on his knee." And several months later, "the blind *koto* player came again. Our maid was shocked when I sent out five sen, remarking that two would have been quite enough."

"Yesterday we met a queer-looking man with a pair of red horns tied to his head by means of a twisted straw rope like the *shimenawa* at

Shinto shrines. The kids yelled '*Shōki-daijin*'[1] after him, and Tamura says only that he is some kind of beggar. Today another beggar went by. He said that he originally is from Hiroshima, and is not a pilgrim and offers no performance. Dressed in rags, he simply asked, 'Will you give me some food?' There is also an old man, quite out of his wits, with long white hair and a white beard, who is seen here occasionally. His origins are vague and no one can understand what he says. People like to mimic his speech with the words *guzu guzu*."

"Another old man came through yesterday. He said he was born elsewhere, but has been in Kyushu almost the entire time he has been wandering about. He would like to go home, but does not know when he will make it. While telling us all of this he stuttered badly. Then he gave a recitation, and later on I saw him at Komoto's delivering a different one (ours had concerned the Russo-Japanese War) When he finished, he says, '*Yakamashiku shimashita*' (literally, 'I have been noisy,' and offered here as an apology.) In Fukada I saw him at the temple where the priest handed him some money, but I could not see how much it was."

"A beggar, said to be originally from Uemura [a nearby village], went by on his way back from a pilgrimage to Shikoku. He is very old and said something unintelligible about his son. At least one beggar goes by every day, although there are more in summer than winter. Not long ago a strange-looking individual in faded *montsuki* and *hakama* stopped by to deliver a *gundan*, a martial tale, chanted in a loud, forced voice. He held out his fan for the money people gave. He says that he comes from Kanagawa, but stopped farming because of poor health, then set up a shop but failed in business, and started off walking three years ago."

"Many beggars going by these days. There is a strange tall man with white hair and beard who talks to himself of the army and the navy and always looks hungry, although I have never actually seen him beg. Then there is the very decrepit man in rags, also with long hair. The mothers bring their children out to see him and say, 'There! He has a bag and will carry you off in it if you're not good. Finish your rice or he will take it.' Today a man singing comic songs and doing tricks with an old parasol went by. His drum was an old tin can. Some people gave him rice, and he said, 'I am a fool and did not graduate from university.' "

Not all the beggars and wanderers moved on, however. "Mrs. Tanimoto knew nothing about the old man who now works for Hayashi Fumio. 'He was not born anywhere. He just dropped from heaven,' she said. And when Shoko, Fumio's wife, told her that the old man seemed a bit hard of hearing, Mrs. Tanimoto remarked that he was half-baked in general. As a matter of fact, he is a pitiful creature, and likes to tinker with old watches at which he spends his leisure when not running errands for

---

1. "The Demon Queller," a mythical hero of the T'ang dynasty, is usually represented in Chinese military attire, armed with a sword, and carrying a parasol, while hunting imps who seem always to elude him. In Japan, he is a figure of fun and derision.

Fumio or doing some chore, which is always said to have been done wrong. He appears to be a sort of beggar, who lived for a time in the Hashida house in Oade, where they took him in to help with cutting wood."

Some displaced people came to Suye with the intention of staying with relatives. A poignant case of a woman whose plan to do so misfired is presented at some length. "There is a family named Kubo who recently moved into Tontokoro. A few days ago Mrs. Kubo's cousin through her mother came from a village in Yatsushiro County and is staying with them. She is thirty-four and had a four-year-old girl. She is looking for work, and says that she formerly worked in a company and has held various jobs since her youth. Although she comes from a farmer's family, she says she cannot do heavy farm labor, and worked for a long time as a maid. Somehow she got a baby, but this part of her story is unclear. According to her, she left her husband because he drank and now finds it impossible to get a job because she must take care of the child. After leaving her husband, she stayed with her natal family for a time (she has two younger brothers and a sister), but it did not work out and she left there a month ago, finally drifting here. Now she says that she is going on a pilgrimage, but it is clear that she will set out begging. That is why we have so few misfits here; one can always be sent out or go out begging. She asked me for work and expressed her willingness to go with us to Tokyo or even to America."

"I had a visit today from the woman who is going off begging with her child. She wanted me to put them up for the night, and suggested that she might be able to find work in America. She asked if America is more distant than Osaka, and as far away as Manchuria, and it turned out that my explanations meant nothing to her. Tokyo, Osaka, Manchuria, America—any place beyond Kumamoto was all one. She told me again that she had left home to work when she was young. When her mother died she left her job in an Omuta hat factory to attend the funeral and lost the position as a consequence. She had a child by someone in Kumamoto— she does not know who the father is—and lost a job that she had found there. Two years later she was married through a go-between from her village but left her husband because he was a drunkard. She is thinking vaguely of placing her child in an orphanage in Omuta and looking for work somewhere. She really has no idea where she is going, and talked about walking to Hitoyoshi and staying there. Finally, when I gave her the train fare, they left about three in the afternoon. I would guess that she once worked in a house of prostitution because she only giggled when I asked whether the child was conceived while she was serving as a maid somewhere. She had to go home for her delivery she said."

"Today the Kubo woman who lives in Tontokoro wanted to know if I knew what had happened to her cousin and her child. She was surprised to learn that they had gone to Hitoyoshi directly from our house, and said that she had left all their clothing behind." There is no further trace of the pair.

Sometimes women in such desperate straits took more drastic action. "They got into a discussion of Mrs. Matsumoto's sister, who had visited her just a little while ago. As a baby, she was left by some beggar in the *dō* and old lady Matsumoto had picked her up, taken her home, and raised her as her daughter. There is no registration of this unusual 'adoption' but now that the woman is going to have a baby herself, she has to straighten things out so that she can register her marriage and the birth of her child. Both women are much excited, and the village office much bothered, because it is so dreadfully complicated to create a register for people who have no records at all."

OLD TAMA

It is perhaps for the very old, however, that the most desperate fate was reserved. Men and women alike might end their lives completely cut off from their families, barely tolerated strangers in an alien community. One such was "a strange old lady, rather wild-looking and with one leg twice the size of the other. I saw her at Funaba and at first all I could learn about her is that she does not belong to the village and 'goes here and there.' She is called simply old Tama. She is now working as a nursemaid for Hayashi Manzo. She looks like a witch, all ragged and toothless, and covers her tangled white hair with a dirty towel. It seems that the old woman comes from Kume where she has a sister who refuses to feed her, so she works out here and there (at Harumi's during the silk season, for example) or begs. She never married because 'her head is not right.' Her deformed leg is the result of an accident, they say."

"The old woman was at Hayashi's again tonight, her hair still untidy but fixed in the same fancy knot with a bit of red string to hold it in place. Old lady Hayashi Yae treats her like a child. '*Bā-san*, you are getting mud on the *tatami*. Wipe your feet.' '*Bā-san*, it is time to take the baby out.' The latter had to be explained because the old lady did not follow. 'Take her out to urinate. She is too quiet,' said old Yae. When the old woman started asking the baby, 'Do you want to go?' Yae snapped, 'Don't ask her, just take her out.' Finally, she told her that it was time for her to go home to eat, and added in an undertone, 'You can come back after lunch.' The old woman did come back, and when Yae saw her enter the yard, she muttered, 'There she is again. Nothing but a nuisance.'"

"At Origuchi's the old woman from Hayashi's, dressed in a regular kimono, her hair done up in a fancy, tidy knot with red string, was the life of the party. She danced all the time, keeping them amused by her clumsiness. They made remarks about her as though she was not there—'Look, she did think to change step to fit the music,' and the like. Old Yae seemed especially amused and would get up once in a while to do an excellent dance turn, which usually caused the old lady to stop. At the end, Yae would say, 'All right, *bā-san*, now you do it.' After her first long performance, they collected two sen from each person and gave her the donation wrapped in paper."

"Old Tama is still around working for Hayashi Manzo. A pitiful thing, she is talked about in her presence as if she were deaf. When offered tea she drinks it up greedily, cup after cup. People now hire her to do small chores—shell beans, carry something—for a few sen. She cannot tell the coins apart and so believes anything she is told about the amount she is paid. If told that five sen is fifteen, she thinks it is right. Recently she went to Ichibu and gathered a bag of rice and millet on the way there as donations. She sold it to Ochiai Mankichi, who told her that he was giving her fifteen sen, but gave her only five. Today the women were asking her how much she had got. 'Fifteen sen,' she said, and when asked to show it, untied her bag, unwrapped the paper inside, and produced the five sen. She believes that red coins [one-sen coppers] are better than white [which are of higher denominations]."

"Today Tawaji Harumi went by, followed by old Tama. The women wondered if she was walking her to some other place. The poor old woman could hardly walk on her broken *geta*, so took them off and went barefoot. Watching, Mrs. Kato and Mrs. Fujita at once commented on the pitiable way the old hag is treated. 'They could at least buy her a pair of ten-sen *geta*,' they said. 'They'll get what they deserve [*bachi kaburu*] for such mistreatment.' Later Harumi told me that she had been walking the old woman to the Hayashi's again, but that since the baby is sick they did not need her, so she left her with another family for a while. When I dropped in today I asked the Hayashis if the old nurse has returned. They said, 'She went. She has not returned, because she has no place to return to.' Apparently she just went out begging."

WITCHES

There was a darker side to women's nature that went well beyond the negative characteristics normally attributed to them. Despite the contrary claim of the curing priest in Suye, the villagers believed that only women were witches. More specifically, they were believed to be the possessors of a dog-spirit *(inugami mochi)* or less commonly a cat-spirit *(nekogami mochi)*. Unreserved on the subjects of sex, adultery, illegitimate births, and the like, the women of Suye preferred not to talk about witchcraft at all. The very first occurrence of the topic takes the form of the vaguest of references.

"The gist of what the women were saying is that Kakui is on bad terms because there are so many people in the hamlet with quarrels and grudges that go back a long time. 'It's a bad place,' they said, 'quite frightful.' This was a reference to someone having accused someone else of witchery. It all centered around the women of the Sato and Kato families. Mrs. Uchida says that she never repeats anything to those two because it always causes trouble." It is only much later in the journal that any substantial amount of information on the subject begins to appear. Direct acquaintance with witches is initiated in a way that many ethnographers will find familiar.

"Old lady Hashida came over to help Kawabe with their tea-gathering and brought some of her homemade wheat-cake. As we all sat around, I asked if there are any witches in Suye. At once all emphatically replied, 'No!' I discovered only later that old lady Hashida herself is suspected of witchery. Later Fumie told me that she had once been bewitched by her, but would not elaborate. She then mentioned old lady Irie, saying that she is troublesome. Fumie says that all witches' houses have a special Jizō statue or shrine [see glossary] somewhere in the back. At Toyama's it is behind the horse stable; at Irie's it is behind the house itself. According to her there are so many witches in Okaharu [a neighboring village] that people are afraid to take brides from there and the women must marry far away."

While visiting the Ochiai house one day, "I asked him if there are any witches here. Like all the others he laughed and said he did not know. I said that I knew of three, but wondered if there were more I had not heard about. He began to concentrate and it seemed to me that he counted a larger number, so at once I said that I was forgetting one—there are four in all. He agreed, but said nothing more. (I shall be less truthful next time!) When his wife came in, he repeated my question to her. She laughed and told him how embarrassing it had been at Kawabe's the other day, which confirms what I have been hearing about old lady Hashida's being a witch.

"To rid oneself of the effects of witchery, he thought a prayer at any shrine or *dō* would be enough, especially if someone performs a purification ritual. He does not know how witchery is done, but the curing priests are good at dealing with illnesses caused by it. To my question, he answered that he knows nothing of the use in cursing of hair clippings and nail parings, and just throws his own out. I asked if witches have a special deity *(kami)* and he said they do. Usually, when there is a small *dō* in the yard of a house it means that there is a witch there. Then he committed himself by asking, 'Haven't you seen the one behind Toyama's stable?' "

"Mrs. Tanimoto promptly confirmed all the witches I have heard of. She is not sure about Irie, but thinks it is true, since the old lady there is the sister of the recently deceased old lady Toyama. Both Hayashi and Toyama definitely have it, she thinks, because they are related. The Toyama *inugami* (dog-spirit) shrine is right in the house by the domestic Buddhist altar. (Although its exact location is a secret, Mrs. Sato Genzo once told Mrs. Tanimoto about it.) Every day they offer a full bowl of rice—preferably *sekihan*, which is much favored by dog-spirits—since it is thought that the spirit will not go roaming if it is properly cared for at home.

"The Toyama one is a special kind of dog-spirit. It is *fukugami* (deity of good fortune), the kind that brings luck. It works this way. When you sell or give rice, this spirit gets inside it and swells it up so that to the buyer or recipient one measure looks like three. On the other hand, when you receive rice, the spirit jumps on it, making the giver think that he has not yet put in enough, so that the person with the *fukugami* gets more than he should. Those with this spirit become prosperous.

"She thinks that the Hayashi woman is vicious, as is the old lady Hashida, with whom she has no interaction at all for fear of getting into trouble. Then she gave me an account of her own experience. Some years ago, it seems, when people were still living in that house by the shop that is now empty, her husband fell ill and was sick for a long time. One night after the doctor had given him an injection and left, some neighbors came in for tea. Among them was old lady Nagata from Fukada. After some of the callers had left, Mrs. Tanimoto, feeling very tired and sleepy, went down to wash some teacups in boiling water. It was very cold. She accidently splashed some water out of the pan onto the floor and heard some strange sounds—a kind of gurgling and moaning, like a dog in pain. Startled, she looked about, and found that they seemed to be coming from an empty area under the raised floor.

"Terrified, she ran up to tell the remaining visitors about it, and they decided that it must be that there was an *inugami* in the house. Forthwith they summoned the old woman who established the Inari Shrine, who did something over the sick man and determined that he was indeed bewitched. A large bump was forming on his forehead, and it looked just like a great fever blister. Apparently the spirit had escaped from his body through that lump. The next day he felt much better. From this experience she concluded that a witch can leave her dog-spirit behind when she has tea in your house. They had a dreadful shock and have been very careful ever since."

One day, while visiting the Irie's, "I asked Irie if Toyama's Jizō was ever celebrated. He said no. I said, 'I mean the one in back of the house. Isn't that also a Jizō?' He replied, 'No, the one in front is Jizō. The one in back is different.' No further comment was made, but people who live at a greater distance from the Toyama's say that it is indeed a dog-spirit shrine, but then Irie himself is said to have one right in his own house."

Upon occasion, accusations of witchery were made by extreme indirection. "Mrs. Hayashi complained about a photograph John had taken and given her. She had wanted to be photographed with Mrs. Shiraki because they are good friends, but someone else had come along, and as they were talking about making the undesirable three [it was believed that the person in the middle of such a group would be the first to die], instead of getting rid of the third person they had picked a highly undesirable fourth—old lady Hashida. Mrs. Hayashi did not say why they had not wanted her in the picture, but both she and Mrs. Kawabe, who was there, smiled knowingly, as if to say, 'You know why.' "

"Old lady Arasaki said that the old lady at the Soeshima house is a witch, but asked me to tell no one. She is quite sure about it. There is also a witch in Oade, she says, in the house right below Makino, but she does not know the name of the people there. (She must be talking about the Iries, who sit at home all the time.) Only this afternoon I saw the two old ladies Irie and Hayashi coming back from the Fukada temple and stopping at the *dō* for tea. Both are alleged witches, of course."

Gradually more information came out. "Old lady Tamaki gave me some new information about witches. This is how you become *inugami mochi*. You bury a dead dog with only its head sticking out of the earth. Then you offer that head *sekihan* and some other things, which you later eat yourself." It should be pointed out that this does not tally with the more common allegation that the *inugami mochi* inherit their spirits.

One notable case of witchery was that which had made old lady Mori fall ill. She spoke of her troubles on every available occasion. "Old lady Mori was discussing her poor health, as she always does. As she can sleep only on one side because of the pain in her stomach, she says that one side of her face is somewhat larger than the other. She confided that she thinks she is bewitched by a cat-spirit, and I think she has two houses in mind as the culprits. She came to this conclusion because she wants to eat nothing but fish, the only thing that tastes right to her. She reported that on the very day she had first said to her son, 'I must have cat witchery on me,' her daughter in Hitoyoshi had dreamed that their mother was bewitched, which all agreed was a strange coincidence."

"The other morning I found old lady Mori visiting at Tanimoto. As usual she was talking about her illness. It is not a plain one, she said, there is dirty work behind it. Since she began to suspect the possibility of its being cat witchery, she visited Funaba and the priest there said, 'No, it is not *kaze mochi* [an alternative term for *inugami mochi*; *kaze* means wind, and like the wind the spirits are invisible], but there is death witchery here. Two people of two different houses—a man and a woman—have wished death on you by driving nails into a tree *(kugizuki)*.' I asked her how she had determined it was cat witchery *(nekogami* rather than *inugami)*, and she said it is because she has such a craving for fish these days. Anyway, the priest performed a purification ceremony over her. Now she understands why she has been unable to recover from her indisposition. She has no idea who the people are, she says, but it must be said that she spends most of her time telling everyone about it.

"She ran her hand over her bloated stomach, saying, 'Maybe this is where it entered.' All the time she was talking, Mrs. Tanimoto kept sympathizing and saying how awful it was of people to do such things to others. 'So that is why you don't get well,' she said, 'even though you are looking much better these days.' As soon as the old lady had left, Mrs. Tanimoto burst out in a loud whisper, 'She is full of lies and goes around making up those stories to try to persuade people that someone has bewitched her. Of course she means to accuse the Hayashi couple. Anyone can see that!' " Nevertheless, even though Mrs. Tanimoto found no truth in these allegations of cat witchery and made jokes about it, "she does sound frightened when discussing witchery. Her joke on this occasion was made when I questioned her about *nekogami*. She said, 'Why, we have one in the house now,' referring to her beloved pet cat."

Witches might cause a baby to fall ill, and the women thought that such might be the explanation of the Shiraki baby's general lassitude. Occasionally, illnesses with other generally accepted origins were jokingly attributed to dog-spirits. "Both these women have some kind of throat trouble, and it is generally believed that Mrs. Hori's is the result of venereal disease contracted from her husband. Someone made a joke to the effect that both women must be under the influence of *inugami*, since both have throat trouble and the *inugami mochi* is probably jealous of both of them because they are getting too rich. Other cases were brought up. Mrs. Tanimoto had heard that someone wished death on Tomokawa Saya (the daughter in that house), and that her father has been ill so long because the curse was passed on to him. Someone else reported that six nails had been found driven into a tree at the Wakamiya shrine at Fukada. This sort of thing is done not only out of jealousy, but also when people have some grudge against another."

"The women said that witchcraft is practiced only by women and passes from mother to daughter or daughter-in-law. The old lady Tanno, they say, has already passed hers on to her niece, who is known for such activity. They remembered that old lady Nagata was a bad witch. She had seventy-seven dog-spirits, and when she died a goodly number of them survived and passed on to her daughter-in-law."

"Dog-spirits are visualized as little puppies. Sometimes you can see a batch of them rolling about in the back of a house where there is a witch. For example, when Mrs. Tanimoto was only three years old, she used to be nursed by a neighbor woman whose own baby had died. That neighbor had a dog-spirit and Mrs. Tanimoto's mother reported that at night she would sometimes see tiny, fat puppies playing on the baby's chest, licking its breasts in happiness that she had taken milk from their owner."

For all their willingness to gossip among friends about witchery, the women of Suye had ample reason to avoid making any public statements about it, or making accusations that might get back to their target. "On the way back I came across Tawaji Harumi cutting rice. She told me about the fight between her husband Matsuo and his brother Bunzo and when I said that I had heard about it she at once wanted to know who had told me. 'There are no secrets in this village,' she said. Apparently she had said something which the Maeno woman repeated. This had made Bunzo angry, and he had protested to Matsuo, who got mad in turn. 'It was just a fight between brothers, but the Maeno woman was weeping here the next day.' It happened right after the Katakura party, and she said, 'I was so gay the night before, and now all this trouble.' What it was all about she did not say."

It was all about witchcraft accusations, as it turned out. When the Embrees gave their farewell party, to take leave of Suye, "I noticed that Tawaji Harumi did not come. The next day she said that she was detained by guests, but someone reported that her husband had been working as usual yesterday, so she just made up an excuse. Mrs. Tanimoto is sure that she saw Harumi going by, as if coming from our house and she thinks that Harumi had gone to see if the other Tawajis were there, and did not come in when she saw them. The fight is quite a serious one. Harumi has got into trouble before because she likes to talk, said Mrs. Tanimoto. 'And what is bad about it, it is always untrue. She just makes things up.' This time she had said that she is not recovering from her lung disease because Bunzo's wife has bewitched her (Mrs. Tanimoto used the words 'bitten her'). She had told this to the Maeno woman. Now, Mrs. Maeno and Harumi used to be good friends, but after some earlier gossip they had a fight and Mrs. Maeno is no longer loyal. So she went to Bunzo's wife and told her all about it, which caused much trouble. 'You should never say such things about the wife of your husband's elder brother,' said Mrs. Tanimoto. Bunzo's wife said that Harumi herself must be a witch if she goes around spreading such stories. He was very angry and had a fight with his brother. Now Harumi has confided to Mrs. Tomokawa, with whom she is very friendly, that she feels she must ask Matsuo to divorce her because she has caused a fight between brothers and is too upset about it all."

Some accusations of witchery were dismissed as the venomous gossip of old women, and a few people made jokes about real illnesses of embarrassing origin being attributed to witchcraft. But on at least one occasion, the action of a witch was clearly discerned in an event that excited much comment in Suye.

"A very sad thing happened at Tawaji Kichizo's. Three of his horses fell ill today; two of them died within the day and one was still struggling when I arrived at the house. (It died the next morning.) The entire village took it much to heart, and all expressed their shock and sympathy whenever the subject was brought up everywhere one went. People are calling at Tawaji's all day. Toward evening things became more organized when the hamlet women came in to help, and things started to function as they do in all other emergencies. There was much bustling about because no one was prepared for the event, of course, and no one could find the trays or any uncracked tea cups for the more distinguished guests who were sure to call.

"All of Tawaji's brothers, including those from as far away as Menda and Fukada, showed up. They and some men from outside the hamlet, the hamlet head, men from the village office, and the policeman were all entertained in the main room. Women were all in the kitchen and the young men tended to stay out there with them. A full meal was served to the important callers, as well as to the young men who came in from the yard where they were helping look after the still-surviving horse. The women from Oade and Ishizaka contributed rice and prepared food for those who would stay on into the night. Close friends and relatives brought rice or cakes or both, and all expressed deep regret, much as they would on the death of a human. Each was given the full story of the course of the horses' illness and an account of their deaths.

"By nine in the evening the men from the prefectural office had arrived. They examined the still panting horse, but like everyone else were mystified as to the nature of its ailment. The men of the hamlet, led by Tawaji Matsuo, one of Kichizo's brothers, were trying to save the animal by massaging it to restore circulation and pouring water mixed with eggs down its throat. A curing priest was called in from Taragi. He sat in the main room until the men from the prefectural office arrived, and then left, but he was back there this morning.

"The officials and the policeman consulted with Tawaji, asked many questions, and decided to conduct an autopsy on the two dead animals the following morning. They left by eleven in the evening, but the hamlet people stayed at the house all night and were out to help with the autopsy this morning. All three horses—the third having died during the night—were moved into a small grove above the house. While some men set about digging holes, the men from the prefectural office performed the autopsy to the mingled horror and interest of the villagers, who stood about making faces of disgust and revulsion. Said Sato, 'I must wash my hands and feet in salt water when I get home [as one does upon returning from the cemetery].' There had been no use of disinfectants last night until the men from the prefectural office arrived. Then two tubs of the stuff were put out and all washed their hands and feet, and sprinkled their clothing with it. (It was the feet that had to be disinfected, but people here usually wash their feet with their bare hands, so both were treated.)"

The event was clearly a major one, involving many villagers and evoking their deepest sympathies for the loss to the Tawajis. Shortly after it was all over and the horses buried, a group of women were discussing the frightful event. "It must be *kaze*, they said. When I asked Mrs. Goto about the matter the other day, she had been unwilling to talk about it. Nevertheless, she was not at all surprised by my question, because she said, 'I don't know much about such things.' Mrs. Tanimoto said that there is much talk of witchcraft and that the horses' disease is attributed to *kaze*, a word for evil spirit that is always used when referring to illnesses caused by supernatural forces. The doctors remain puzzled, the women said. The trouble seems to start in the legs which causes the horses to fall down. No one can imagine what it is. Mrs. Tanimoto says that on the way back to

Menda the veterinarian from the prefectural office asked the village office agricultural advisor, 'Kuma has witches. How about *kaze* in this case?' "

This report led to the following entry in John Embree's journal: "A rumor has it that Tawaji's horses died of witchcraft and that the veterinarian from the Kumamoto Prefectural Office asked the agricultural advisor of Suye if it might not be *kaze*. The fact is that it was not the vet who asked the question, but the local man from the county office. Furthermore, he asked it in a joking manner." So much for the gossip of old women, or so it would seem, but later on in his journal the following entry occurs: "Sonoda says that he does not know if Tawaji's horses were killed by *kaze*, but he does not seem to doubt the possibility at all." This man is sixty-five years old, and a former village official. And Ella Wiswell's journal provides the final note on this aspect of the issue: "The people at the prefectural office can find no evidence of infection in the materials taken from the Tawaji horses."

Returning now to the conversation with Mrs. Tanimoto about the affair, "I asked her if the Tawajis had enemies or if there are any witches in the hamlet they live in. She said that there might well be witches there, but she does not know if he has any enemies. Enemies are not necessarily part of the picture in such cases in any event. A person might simply be envious of Tawaji's prosperity, make some remark about it, and thereby bring the *kaze* to him. 'They are very rich now,' she said. 'They had four horses and took in a lot of rice last year. They took in so much, in fact, that they had to process and sell it quickly so that it would not go bad. While others here had to buy rice because they had run out, the Tawajis could not use all of theirs, and more is coming in with the current crop.' She also volunteered the information that people do not like to discuss witchcraft because it is frightening and they are reluctant to accuse one another of it because such accusations lead to trouble. Besides, a person is not always aware that she is the cause of the misfortune—that is, she may not even be aware that her envy has caused a death."

At the store a few days later, the subject of the Tawaji horses came up. "The horse dealer who was there suggested witchcraft without my raising the possibility. I had only asked, 'What disease was it?' They said that one of the curing priests from Menda had suggested it might be *kaze*, but they could not understand how such a disease could kill three horses at one time. I asked if witches know they are witches. One man thought not, but others said, 'Of course they do. They have special shrines where they worship, after all.' "

A few days later, "Old lady Tanno said, when I reported rumors of *kaze* in the deaths of the horses, 'Are they talking about it? Maybe it is so,' but she did not raise the possibility herself when I asked what had killed them." So the issue remained unresolved, although it is clear that most people assumed that witchcraft was somehow involved in the tragedy. "Talk about the horses brought out the remark attributed to the veterinarian

that there is much *kaze* in Kuma County, and witches were discussed. All
the women say that there is a kind of *kaze* that makes a strange wheezing
sound, but they could not say exactly when it is made by the spirit. Some
of them have heard it, however.

"They also said that a woman cannot deliver her baby if a witch
is present, and Mrs. Kuwagiri told of an actual case where an old woman
was asked to leave a house because the baby would not come. No names
were mentioned. It is thought that some witches really do not know of
their power, for there are some who have no special shrine in their houses.
But everyone knew of a special shrine in Taragi especially for people who
possess dog-spirits, but none knew when they go there to worship. As for
kaze, it is something vague which they cannot explain clearly. They do not
know how it enters the body, why it runs around loose making noises, or
who puts it into people and when."

John Embree reported one example of exorcism of such a spirit.
"Five years ago the woman at the Inari shrine drove a cat-spirit out of a
possessed man by calling upon the spirit of the fox-god for help, then
beating the man with a stick. The man jumped about, making animal-like
noises. The treatment was repeated every evening for a week until the cat-
spirit finally was driven out. It is said that a curse had been put on him."

Cursing of this type, it was alleged, is done only by women. John
Embree continues: "Sato says that only people who believe in their powers
can be affected by women who put curses on others. He does not believe,
so is not affected. Cursing is done by women only, because they harbor
deep and longer grudges." Yet not all skeptics, as we have seen in the case
of Mrs. Tanimoto, dismiss the matter lightly. "Shimosaka thinks that all
the talk about *inugami* is just talk, although his wife is not so skeptical.
Even he knows the *inugami mochi* by name, and all the details of their
shrines. He told me about the *fukugami* who bring good fortune to the
house, and about *binbōgami* (poor dieties) who bring poverty.

"He insisted that *inugami* are of the house, not of individuals. As
a consequence, all the people in a house make offerings to the spirit to
keep it in the house and prevent it from harming others. There are, he
said, some who have a stone shrine in the house-yard: Hayashi Sao, Soeshima of Oade, and Irie of Kawaze, whose dog-spirit is a very bad one.
There are none at all in Kakui, where there are no very old houses, but
many in Shoya.

"Both he and his wife have heard the rumor that Tawaji's horses
were killed by *kaze*, but he does not take it seriously. When I said that the
curing priest had attributed their deaths to *inugami*, he replied, 'That is
how he makes his living, after all.' "

TWELVE
Conclusions

We have come to the end of our excursion back to the village Japan of earlier generations. The women we have met surely suffered many of the well-advertised disadvantages of their sex in Japanese society. They were accorded no formal authority in village affairs, for the men and perhaps most of the women themselves simply assumed that women could not run their own affairs, much less those of a more public nature. The headship of the Suye Women's Association was assumed by a man from the village office, and although this development was the occasion for some sarcastic comment, the women did not protest his appointment. Men planned the activities of the Association and lectured the women on how to run their households, raise their children, and prepare foods. Even the account books of some of the revolving credit associations formed by and for women were handled by men at the members' request because, the women said, they had no head for figures. The production of silk was almost entirely in the hands of women, but few were allowed to keep the money earned by its sale. Wives enjoyed virtually no degree of financial independence of their husbands, who controlled all but a fraction of the family finances.

Yet it would be a mistake to ignore the extent to which these women—for the most part outsiders to the community into which they had married—formed economic ties, shared labor, and forged bonds of friendship entirely on their own. By dint of careful nurturance of such ties a woman created a network of other women who could be called upon for help in emergencies and assist her when she needed more hands than the members of her family alone provided. We have seen some women marketing produce in town, hiring out as field hands, and engaging in a variety of small income-producing activities as groups, all quite informally organized. While none of these economic activities was as crucial to the financial well-being of the family as were the activities of men, they nonetheless represented an important complement to them.

273

They took their pleasure in tobacco, drink, and sex. Like peasant women everywhere, perhaps, their humor was earthy and their talk of sexual relations straightforward and undisguised. The girls were shy, to be sure, but they did flirt with boys, chased and were chased by them, and occasionally paid the high price of an unwanted pregnancy. Many of the older women drank to excess, finding in alcohol the release of passions too long inhibited by the social constraints on the public behavior of the young. Married women were sometimes adulterous, in sharp contrast to the received wisdom that such behavior was normally limited to husbands in the Japan of the period. What is more remarkable is that they were not always divorced by their husbands who had learned of their affairs. Widows, as we have long known, were considered and often proved to be fair game for philandering husbands and unmarried young men alike.

In discussions of all such matters we encounter one extremely important recurrent theme. Everyone in Suye who expressed an opinion at all observed that in 1935 unmarried young women were less likely to engage in premarital sex and that there were far fewer illegitimate births than had formerly been the case. The schools were universally given credit for making the girls more careful about their liaisons, in part through some very discreet sex education, and by emphasizing the desirability of bridal virginity. Divorce, too, was thought to be far less common than it had been in the youth of Suye's grandmothers and middle-aged women. One explanation was that as marriage formerly had been a rather casual undertaking, divorce was not so serious a matter. However, with the greatly increased scale of dowries and the high cost of weddings, it was widely felt that divorce presented more involved problems of settlement, leading both husband and wife to consider the step much less lightly. Others expressed the view that divorce had declined in no small part because of the rise in the age at marriage. The very young brides of the past—hardly more than girls—had experienced especially severe problems with their mothers-in-law, who had sent them back home or from whom they had fled. For their part, young men were said to have given up their pursuit of village girls in favor of the prostitutes and café girls of the towns. All in all, it seemed to the villagers of Suye that the new generation was altogether more 'serious' than their parents and grandparents had been.

The staggering number of divorces and remarriages that some women went through, often on their own initiative, calls for further examination. Why did men put up with adulterous wives, and how was it that divorced women seem to have been able so readily to find another husband? The answer lies at least in part in the character of the labor-force required by the small shopkeepers' and agriculturalists' households of the time. For the latter, cooperative work-groups and labor-sharing were very important in the peak seasons of transplanting and harvesting, to be sure, but for most of the year and for most purposes a household was responsible for its own affairs. In the small shops self-sufficiency was even more es-

sential. There was a great deal of work to be done, and the absolute min-
imum labor-force was two able-bodied adults. Neither a woman nor a man
could possibly do all of it alone. A man could not make it on his own both
because he simply could not keep up with all the demands on him and
because he literally did not know how to do most of the tasks that women
performed. A woman could not assume the really heavy work of either
kind of enterprise, but if she were physically strong and a good worker,
even the fact that she had young children from a previous marriage was
not an insurmountable obstacle to remarriage.

Behind the frequency of female-initiated divorce there is more than
the ease of finding another husband. Many often-married women had
simply walked out on men they did not like, who drank to excess or
mistreated them, or whose mothers they could not get along with. Some
of them had acquired some assets of their own, which gave them a degree
of freedom denied the propertyless, but the fact cannot be blinked that
there were many strong-willed women of independent mind who drew a
line at what they would bear in terms of domestic conditions. When that
line was crossed they either walked out or threw out their husbands.

Some who stayed despite unpleasant marital circumstances took
control of their households by over-running their husbands. There were,
after all, weak men as well as strong women. Should a man prove to be
incompetent, improvident, lazy, or otherwise unfit to manage the family's
affairs, his wife might very well take over. We have encountered wives
who drank too much, some who were harridans, and others widely known
to be adulteresses, yet who were not divorced by their long-suffering hus
bands. Some of these men loved their wives, to be sure, but others appear
to have realized that all things considered it was unlikely that they could
do better. Others did divorce their wives, of course, and these women
often had to leave their children behind in their husband's house or in that
of their natal families when they remarried. Such secondary unions frequently were contracted with men of lower social or economic position or
with men far older than the women they took as their second, third, or
fourth wives. Among the beggars, wanderers, and pilgrims were women
who for a variety of reasons failed to find even such husbands. They
included the physically and psychologically handicapped, those who had
borne children out of wedlock and lacked either personal sources of support
or helpful relatives, and others whose luck—and their families' patience—
had run out. It must be remembered that this fate was not limited exclusively to women, however. There were, in fact, more men on the road.

It is invariably remarked that Japanese women devote much of
their psychical and psychic energies to the care of their children. In this
regard, Suye women were in no way exceptional. If their lives were not
completely child-centered, they seem to have been very nearly so. Everyone
agreed that a woman would put up with a very difficult marital situation
if there were children, for fear of losing them if she left her husband. The

children were indulged, petted, and made much of by most adults of both sexes. Nonetheless, women frequently said that they wished they had fewer of them, but there is no conclusive evidence that either abortion or contraception was practiced by any significant number of couples. Pregnancy combined with hard work, poor nutrition, inadequate prenatal care, and venereal disease contracted from their husbands,[1] put the health of many young married women at grave risk, yet large families were the rule and however much a pregnancy was regretted, the women seem always to have welcomed the new baby.

As their children finished school and approached maturity, the mothers saw their sons conscripted into military service and many faced the importunities of their daughters who asked to be allowed to seek employment outside the village in the towns and cities. A very few girls had no choice, but were sold by their families into prostitution, out of poverty or the feckless selfishness of their fathers. None of these girls was from a Suye farm household.

Marriage was the goal of all young women and men, and the last major responsibility that the women of Suye discharged for their children was the arranging of their marriages. It was primarily the women who took charge of the negotiations, although the men of the household were always involved at some stage of the process and in almost every case had the veto power. Thus, the mothers' responsibility for their children extended to the moment that they lost them either to other families or to the industries and colonies of Japan of the inter-war years.

They lost all save one, the successor to the headship of the household. At this period the Japanese family passed through a fairly uniform developmental cycle largely shaped by the Civil Code. It was a stem-family and the rules of inheritance and succession were clearly spelled out. By custom, unsupported by the law, there could be any number of generations coresiding in the house, but only one married couple in each of them. It was the duty of the head and his wife to secure the succession in the next generation, preferably if not usually through the first-born son, and to find him a wife. Where there were no sons, an adopted husband would be taken for the eldest daughter, and where there were no children at all (for whatever reason) available to make the link, resort was had to one of the great variety of acceptable forms of adoption. When the senior couple grew too old to manage the affairs of the house and retired, or when the head died, the successor and his wife assumed their duties. The household never ended, then, but was instead conceived to be a kind of corporate entity of indefinite duration.

It is in the nature of household composition and continuity that we find the reasons for the intense concern of women with marriage arrangements. They tended to outlive their husbands by about five years,

1. An anonymous reader has pointed out that if the young women and some of the married ones were as sexually active as seems to have been the case, they may equally well have transmitted venereal disease to the men.

as they still do in Japan today, which meant that at the end of their lives they would be completely dependent upon their successor-son and his wife or another of their married children. We have seen that for some old women of Suye the predictable path was a smooth one, and they died in the care of their child and his or her spouse. We have also seen, in the persons of some other elderly women, the tragic consequences of failure to achieve household continuity. Alone and unwanted, impoverished and ill, some scratched out a living in the village, while others took to the road to beg, or set off on "pilgrimages" from which no one expected or wanted them to return.

It is tempting to suppose that all has changed in the years since John and Ella Embree observed the harsh and lusty lives of these villagers. Certainly there are no places left in rural Japan that even remotely resemble the Suye of forty-five years ago in either the physical conditions of life or the kind of agriculture practiced.[2] Social conditions have changed less dramatically, perhaps, particularly with respect to the position of women and the heavy work-load that rural women still must bear.[3] Nonetheless, the postwar period has seen two developments of undeniable importance with respect to the position of women in Japan. First, the sheer number of women and men engaged in agriculture and resident in rural areas has declined precipitously; second, there have been improvements with regard to the legal, educational, and labor-force status of women.[4]

2. For descriptions of change in village Japan, see Ronald Dore, *Shinohata: A Portrait of a Japanese Village* (London: Allen Lane, 1978); Edward Norbeck, *Country to City: The Urbanization of a Japanese Hamlet* (Salt Lake City: University of Utah Press, 1978); Mitsuru Shimpo, *Three Decades in Shiwa: Economic Development and Social Change in a Japanese Farming Community* (Vancouver: University of British Columbia Press, 1976); Robert J. Smith, *Kurusu: The Price of Progress in a Japanese Village, 1951–1975* (Stanford: Stanford University Press, 1978); and the restudies of Suye by Ushijima referred to in the introduction. It is worth noting that the dust wrappers of the three books by Dore, Norbeck, and Smith all bear pictures of village women rather than men.

3. There is a succinct statement of the classic view of the position of rural women and early postwar changes in their status in Takashi Koyama, *The Changing Social Position of Women in Japan* (Paris: UNESCO, 1961, pp. 76–97. Some years later a short biography of a farm woman accompanied by an insightful analysis of the position of women in a village on the island of Shikoku was published by Gail Bernstein, "Women in Rural Japan," in Joyce Lebra, Joy Paulson, and Elizabeth Powers, editors, *Women in Changing Japan* (Boulder: Westview Press, 1976), pp. 25–50. For the postwar period there are two studies: Linda J. Perry, *Mothers, Wives, and Daughters in Osaka: Autonomy, Alliance, and Professionalism* (unpublished Ph.D. dissertation, University of Pittsburgh, 1976) and Sandra B. Salamon, *In the Intimate Arena: Japanese Women and Their Families* (unpublished Ph.D. dissertation, University of Illinois at Urbana-Champaign, 1974).

4. For useful surveys of these matters, see Masu Okamura, *Changing Japan: Women's Status* (Tokyo: International Society for Educational Information, 1973); Alice H. Cook and Hiroko Hayashi, *Working Women in Japan: Discrimination, Resistance, and Reform* (Ithaca, N.Y.: New York State School of Industrial and Labor Relations, Cornell University, 1980); the articles by various authors in the issue of *Japan Interpreter* 10, no. 2 (Autumn 1975) entitled "Women in a Male Society"; and Merry I. White and Barbara Molony, editors, *Proceedings of the Tokyo Symposium on Women* (Tokyo: International Group for the Study of Women, 1978).

The question that naturally comes to mind is this: Are the lives of the contemporary urban counterparts of these women in all respects more desirable? In some obvious respects they are, of course. Most women of today are spared the crushingly hard labor that broke the health of so many Suye women, and when they are ill they receive far superior medical care. As a consequence their life spans are much longer, now about eighty years as compared to less than fifty in 1935. This means, among other things, that they remain dependent on their adult children for many years after those children marry. But as filial piety is somewhat weakened in contemporary Japan and living quarters are very cramped, not all adult children choose to care for their aged parents, even as was the case forty-five years ago. The problem is rendered all the more acute in that prolonged life expectancy is likely to produce an aged population with a high proportion of the physically and psychologically infirm, for whose care there are inadequate public facilities. The position of Japan's elderly women remains precarious.[5] About sixty percent of those over the age of seventy are women, and the number of households consisting of an elderly couple or a single elderly person living alone has risen sharply (albeit from very low figures) in recent years. Yet as late as 1973, three-quarters of all persons over seventy were living with their married or unmarried children, favoring sons over daughters by a ratio of four to one. Perhaps as many as half of all marriages are still arranged by the families or employers of the young couple. While both women and men are given more say with respect to the final choice of spouse and they no longer marry without some preliminary acquaintance, however brief and superficial, free choice of spouse is still very far from the norm. There has been one major change, however, in that the predominant residential form of the family is now overwhelmingly the conjugal. As a result, most young women—even the wives of first-born sons—are no longer exposed to the tribulations of adjusting to their husbands' households, nor by the same token can they count on the kinds of affective and economic support that the household once afforded their counterparts when emergencies arose.

Today the divorce rate is marginally higher than it was in 1935, but much lower than in the youth of Suye's older women.[6] There are two kinds of divorce petition in Japan, one called mutual consent divorce requested by both husband and wife, the other judicial, which may be filed by either spouse. Mutual consent divorces, which in 1978 accounted for ninety per-

5. These issues are dealt with in a penetrating analysis by Takie Sugiyama Lebra, "The Dilemma and Strategies of Aging among Contemporary Japanese Women," *Ethnology* 18, no. 4 (October 1979): 337–54.

6. In 1883 the rate of divorce per thousand population was 3.39. By 1935 it had fallen to 0.70. The ratio of divorce to marriage in the period 1884–88 was 1:2.71; in 1934–35 it was 1:11.8. See Takeyoshi Kawashima and Kurt Steiner, "Modernization and Divorce Rate Trends in Japan," *Economic Development and Cultural Change* 9, no. 1, pt. 2 (1960): 213–40. The divorce rate in 1978 was 1.15.

cent of the total, are by no means necessarily the result of a mutual decision. The legal position of the wife may be stronger now, but she has little chance of successfully resisting her husband's decision to get rid of her. Lacking financial resources of her own and facing uncertain prospects in the job market, she is unlikely to acquiesce in his demand for a divorce. But men and their families have powerful ways of forcing the issue to which she can offer only slight resistance. The wife who wishes a divorce is also at a disadvantage. The bare majority of judicial divorce petitions, which, it must be remembered, accounted for only ten percent of the total, were filed by women in 1978. Unable to persuade their husbands to grant them the divorce they seek, these women are forced to resort to third-party intervention. Both cases strongly suggest that the wife remains severely disadvantaged in the domestic realm, however improved her legal position. Furthermore, remarriage is still easier for men than for women, in no small part because of the persistence of the view that any woman who has been divorced must have failed to live up to the ideal so long held up to them—to be a good wife and wise mother (ryōsai kenbo). Since it is the woman who is expected to make the adjustments to the marital situation, it is she who is blamed for its failure.

The children of today's women, usually two in number since the legalization of abortion and the widespread adoption of contraceptive practices, survive infancy, are not infested with lice, and are without question far better nourished than the children of Suye. They are not noticeably less indulged by their parents. Indeed, there is every reason to suppose that the mothers of today's society are even more intensely involved with their children than were the women of Suye, for the role of housewife-mother in the contemporary conjugal family is far more narrowly defined than formerly was the case. That role, often supposed to be the classic "traditional" one for married women, is actually of rather recent origin, dating roughly from the early 1920s and the flowering of the white-collar sararīman "salary-man") class.[7] In the postwar decades the housewife-mother role has assumed even greater importance, leading an outspoken feminist to write, "in the past the role of women was much more 'masculine' than it is now."[8]

The housing in which today's women live is superior in every respect, if more cramped, and work-saving appliances are universal. Their husbands tend to hand over their salaries to their wives to manage, as Suye men certainly did not, and there is a very strong sense shared by both husband and wife that the household is her sole responsibility. For

7. See Masashi Fukaya, "Socialization and Sex-Roles of Housewives" in White and Molony, editors (1979): 133–49.

8. Yōko Kirishima, "Liberation Begins in the Kitchen," Japan Interpreter 10, no. 2 (1975): 143.

all that, she remains totally dependent upon her husband's earning power, as he in turn is totally dependent on her domestic managerial skills.[9]

Women of all ages are today far better educated, but for the most part are denied the opportunity to make much use of their learning and training, except in the brief period between graduation and marriage, when the wage differential between women and men is not very great. The increasing numbers of married women in the labor force, however, are generally relegated to dead-end jobs for which they receive compensation that falls far short of that paid men.[10]

Is the young mother of today's urban apartment complex, tied down all day every day with her small children, fan of the daytime television soap operas, and isolated in so many ways from any other kind of intense human contact, in so enviable a position that she can reject out of hand that long-ago way of life of the women of Suye? It is not entirely clear that such is the case, but they do reject what they know of it, for the life of village women in the prewar period is rightly seen to have been too hard and the material conditions of life too mean to persuade anyone that it had any desirable qualities at all. Nevertheless, one need not romanticize that time and place to conclude that it cannot have been altogether a bad thing, after the hard day's work was done, to go with one's women friends to drink and dance in the cool of the evening, waiting to watch the rising of the three-horned moon.

For Japanese women, old pains have been replaced by new, and in terms of relative autonomy and dependency, it is difficult to see that the women of contemporary Japan have progressed as far as they might wish to imagine beyond the hard-working, hard-playing women of Suye. Their pleasures were surely less refined, and the adversities they faced surely were very great, but the women of Ella Wiswell's journal are not the drones,

9. Lebra (1979) argues that the degree of autonomy and dependency of the individual woman fluctuates over the span of her life, the greatest dependency being at both ends of the life cycle. As for the vaunted autonomy of the wife in the domestic realm, she makes the essential point that it is inseparable from her complete economic dependency on her husband. For changing points of view among women with respect to their domestic roles, see Susan J. Pharr, "The Japanese Woman: Evolving Views of Life and Role," in Lewis Austin, editor, *Japan: The Paradox of Progress* (New Haven: Yale University Press, 1976), pp. 301–27. See also chapter 7, "The Family: The Impact of the War on Women," and chapter 8, "The Family: The Changing Roles of Women as Mothers and Wives," in Kazuko Tsurumi, *Social Change and the Individual: Japan Before and After Defeat in World War II* (Princeton: Princeton University Press, 1970), pp. 248–303.

10. While it is true that in 1978, according to the Ministry of Labor, women accounted for one-third of all salaried workers, their earnings were only fifty-six percent of those of men, up from about forty-four percent in 1955. A telling observation concludes the anonymous summary of the Ministry's white paper on the female labor force carried in *Japan Report* 26, 4 (1980): "The white paper states that companies have begun to reassess their female employees as a potential source of talent instead of as a labor force good only for handling routine chores." See also Cook and Hayashi (1980), p. 116, for figures on women's wages and salaries by age, as compared with men's.

depersonalized by the conditions of their lives, whom we are all too often led to believe they must have been. If they were victimized, they were not merely victims.

Ella Wiswell returned to Suye twice after the study was completed, the first time in 1951, the year after John Embree's death, when a memorial service was held for him. She found the parties that followed very much as they had been fifteen years before. The same abandoned gaiety, lively dancing, and heavy drinking were all there, just as she remembered. But when she returned for the second time in 1968, it had all changed. Many of the older women she had known were dead, and the entertainments were as decorous and as formal as any that one might meet with in a citified small town. She felt keenly that a way of life had passed. It is to that way of life, for all its crudities and harshness, and for all its cruelties to some, that this book is intended as a tribute. The women of Suye today would doubtless be mortified to hear of some of the behavior of their great-grandmothers and grandmothers, but we have not resurrected them simply to put them on display, like specimens in an ethnological museum. They were by any lights quite remarkable women, and because no other record exists of their lives, we are setting it out as both a confirmation of and a corrective to assumptions about that way of life made by those who did not know them.

Glossary

Japanese words that appear only once in the text, where they are defined, are for the most part omitted from the glossary. The principal exceptions are certain dialect words and some terms with double meanings.

ame	a molasses-like sweet
asebo	heat rash (standard Japanese: *asemo*)
asobi	play, diversion, recreation, pleasure, fun
ato iwai	an after-party, held after the main affair is over
baba	an old woman; grandma
bachi kaburu	to suffer for one's misdeeds; to get one's come-uppance (standard Japanese: *bachi ga ataru*)
buku	a fool (one of the most insulting words in the language)
bā-san	an old woman; "granny"
bebeka	dirty (baby talk)
benshi	a narrator of silent films
binbōgami	deity who brings poverty (see *fukugami*)
bobo	intercourse; the female genitals (a term used primarily by males)
butsudan	the domestic Buddhist altar where ancestral tablets are kept
-chan	the diminutive form of *-san*, used after the names of children, intimates, and lovers
chinpo	penis
chōdai	"please," the informal form of *kudasai*, used by children and between intimates (see *kudai*)
choppai	intercourse (a term used primarily by males)
dai	the character "large," used to describe the sleeping position appropriate to males, lying on one's back with arms and legs flung wide (see *ku*)
Daikoku	the god of wealth and fortune, often enshrined in farmhouse kitchens
dō	a small building housing an image of a Buddhist deity; a kind of wayside chapel

dodoitsu	a kind of short ballad; a ditty
dōkyūkai	a same-class association, referring to members of the same grade in school; an alumni group
dōnen	age-mates
dōnen kō	a same-age association; a group of age-mates
dōsōkai	a graduates' association; an alumni group
fuda kō	a revolving credit association in which the winner is chosen by lot rather than by bidding
fujin	a married lady, a matron, Madame
fujinkai	Women's Association
fukugami	a deity who brings good fortune (see *binbōgami*)
futon	bedding; comforters
futon kō	a revolving credit association formed to finance the purchase of bedding
geisha	a female entertainer (but here used to mean a relatively high-class prostitute; see *shakufu*)
geta	a thonged wooden clog
gonsai	a second wife, here meaning one taken without divorcing the first (standard Japanese: *gosai*)
gundan	a chanted martial tale
gurashika	hard to bear (standard Japanese probably *kurushī*)
Hachiman	the god of war (Shinto)
haikara	up-to-date; the latest (from English "high collar")
hazukashī	shy, bashful, embarrassed
hiaki	the ceremony of a baby's first visit to a Shinto shrine
higan zakura	a variety of cherry tree (literally: equinox cherry)
hisuteri	a nervous disorder, usually of women (from English "hysteria")
honsai	literally, "real wife" (see *gonsai*)
imonbukuro	a kit-bag for soldiers and sailors
Inari	the god of crops, especially rice (Shinto)
inugami mochi	the possessor of a dog-spirit
Ise kō	the Ise Society, a religious group that worships the deities of the imperial ancestral shrine at Ise (Shinto)
jan-ken-po	a game equivalent to "paper-rock-scissors" or "hunter-fox-gun" (standard Japanese: *jan-ken-pon*)
Jizō	the Buddhist patron and protector of children
kaka	mother; the wife of the head of the household
kami (-sama)	any Shinto deity
kamitate	the naming ceremony for an infant
kanjin	beggar (used in the sense of bogeyman to frighten children)
Kannon	the Buddhist goddess of mercy
Kannon kō	the Kannon Society, a religious group that worships this deity
kao mishiri	a party given for the member households of a hamlet by newcomers to it (literally, "face-showing"; standard Japanese: *kao mise*)
kaze	literally "wind," used to refer to the evil spirits that move invisibly, causing illness and death

kaze mochi	a possessor of *kaze* (an alternative term for *inugami mochi* and *nekogami mochi*, q.v.)
keizai kōsei	economic reconstruction; a program of the central government to promote austerity and village uplift
kintama	the testicles
kō	association, club; a religious group
kōden	"incense money" given to the bereaved family by mourners at a funeral
kogare	the pan-crust produced in making bean curd (possibly related to the standard Japanese term for rice-crust: *o-koge*)
kōgin	a revolving credit association
Kōjin	the earth god; the kitchen god (Shinto); a protective deity
komotsu	childbearing, delivery
komotsu tokoro	the room in the house where childbirth takes place
koshimaki	an underskirt worn with women's kimono
ku	the character for "nine," used to describe the sleeping position appropriate to females, lying curled up on one's side (see *dai*)
kudai	"please"; children's form of *kudasai* (see *chōdai*)
kumiai	an association; a cooperative group
kyaku asobi	playing house (literally: guest play)
mamma	rice (baby talk)
manju	a kind of cake usually stuffed with sweet bean paste; vulva
mattake	mushroom (standard Japanese: *matsutake*)
mekake	a mistress
mikka kasei	a trial marriage (literally: three days' labor)
mochi	a glutinous rice cake
montsuki	a formal kimono
naishōkiki	the "real" go-between who conducts the preliminary negotiations leading to a marriage arrangement (literally: secrets-hearer)
nakaudo	the formal go-between in marriage arrangements
namanda	the short form of the mantra *namu amida butsu* (Hail, Amida Buddha)
naniwabushi	a kind of long ballad
nekogami mochi	the possessor of a cat-spirit
nema	a sleeping-room
nēsan	elder sister, a term often used to address a young woman older than the speaker or of about the same age
ninjin	carrot; ginseng
oba-san	aunt, a term used for any woman older than speaker (*oba-chan* = auntie)
obi	a wide sash worn with kimono
o-bon	Festival of the Dead, observed on the thirteenth to fifteenth days of the seventh lunar month
o-cha iri	a formal call (literally: putting in the tea)
odomo shiran	an exclamation of surprise or shock (dialect); *odomo* or *odoma* = *onore* ("I" or "we"); *shiran* = *shiranai* ("don't know")
o-iwai	felicitations
o-kagura	a sacred shrine dance (Shinto)

okusan	a term for another man's wife, but never used for farm wives
o-miki	sacred wine; sake or *shōchū* (q.v.) offered to any deity
o-mikuji	a fortune-telling slip
saidā	a carbonated sweet drink (from the English "cider")
saiki	the first menstrual flow following childbirth (literally: return)
sakaki	an evergreen plant offered at Shinto places of worship
sakamukai	a party given for someone who has just returned from a pilgrimage or long trip
san san ku do	the ceremonial exchange of cups of sake by the bride and groom at their wedding (literally: three three nine times)
sashimi	raw fish
seinen gakkō	youth schools, a track in the prewar system that included grades seven through fourteen, primarily but not exclusively for boys
seinenkai	Young Men's Association
sekihan	glutinous rice mixed with red beans, served on auspicious occasions
sen	100 sen = 1 yen
senbetsu	a parting gift of money
sewanin	a go-between; the responsible party
shakufu	a serving woman, a term used here to refer to prostitutes of a rank lower than geisha (q.v.)
shamisen	a three-stringed musical instrument, called *shami* locally
shimenawa	a braided straw rope hung at Shinto sacred places
shinke	crazed, mad
shi-shi	to urinate (baby talk)
shōchū	a low-grade distillate of rice
shōji	a sliding paper door on a wooden frame
shojokai	Young Women's Association
sushi	vinegared rice with diced vegetables
tabi	socks worn with *geta* (q.v.) or thonged sandals
tai	sea bream, a fish served on auspicious occasions
taishō	a boss, leader
tatami	a rush-covered floor-mat, approximately three feet by six
tenko	a muster, military inspection
tessu	host, a local term related to standard Japanese *tesū* (trouble, bother, care) or *teishu* (the head of a household)
tokonoma	the alcove in the main room; it contains a hanging scroll, flower arrangement, and other decorative objects
wakare-kai	a farewell party
yakifu	a toasted light cake made of wheat gluten
Yakushi	the healing Buddha
yaya	a baby (baby talk)
yobai	the practice of stealing into a house to visit a woman for illicit sexual purposes
yomego	a bride (standard Japanese: *yome*)
yugawa	a well
zeni	money (an obsolete word for coins)

Bibliography

Anonymous. 1980. "White paper on working women." *Japan Report* 26, 4: 5.

Bernstein, Gail. 1976. "Women in rural Japan" In *Women in changing Japan*, ed. Joyce Lebra, Joy Paulson, and Elizabeth Powers. Boulder, Colo.: Westview Press.

Caudill, William A., and David W. Plath. 1966. "Who sleeps by whom? Parent-child involvement in urban Japanese families." *Psychiatry* 29, 4: 344–66.

Cook, Alice H., and Hiroko Hayashi. 1980. *Working women in Japan: discrimination, resistance, and reform.* Ithaca, N.Y.: New York State School of Industrial and Labor Relations, Cornell University.

Dore, Ronald. 1978. *Shinohata: a portrait of a Japanese village.* London: Allen Lane.

Embree, John F. 1939. *Suye Mura: A Japanese village.* Chicago: University of Chicago Press.

———. 1941. "Some social functions of religion in rural Japan." *American Journal of Sociology* 47, 2: 184–89.

———. 1944a. *Japanese peasant songs.* Philadelphia: Memoirs of the American Folklore Society, no. 38.

———. 1944b. "Sanitation and health in a Japanese village." *Journal of the Washington Academy of Sciences* 34, 4: 97–108.

———. 1944c. "Japanese administration at the local level." *Applied Anthropology* 3, 4: 11–18.

———. 1944d. "Gokkanosho: a remote corner of Japan." *Scientific Monthly* 59, 5: 343–55.

Fukaya, Masashi. 1978. "Socialization and sex-roles of housewives." In *Proceedings of the Tokyo Symposium on Women*, ed. Merry I. White and Barbara Molony, pp. 133–49. Tokyo: International Group for the Study of Women.

Isaku, Patia R. 1981. *Mountain storm, pine breeze: folk song in Japan.* Tucson: University of Arizona Press.

Japan Interpreter. 1975. "Women in a male society." *Japan Interpreter* (Special Issue): 10, 2.

Jones, Thomas Elsa. 1926. *Mountain folk of Japan.* New York: Unpublished Ph.D. dissertation, Columbia University.

Kawashima, Takeyoshi, and Kurt Steiner. 1960. "Modernization and divorce rate trends in Japan." *Economic Development and Cultural Change* 9, 1 (part 2): 213–40.

287

Kirishima, Yōko. 1975. "Liberation begins in the kitchen." *Japan Interpreter* 10, 2: 141–50.

Koyama, Takashi. 1961. *The changing social position of women in Japan*. Paris: UNESCO.

Lebra, Takie Sugiyama. 1979. "The dilemma and strategies of aging among contemporary Japanese women." *Ethnology* 18, 4: 337–54.

Norbeck, Edward. 1978. *Country to city: the urbanization of a Japanese hamlet*. Salt Lake City: University of Utah Press.

Okamura, Masu. 1973. *Changing Japan: women's status*. Tokyo: International Society for Educational Information.

Perry, Linda J. 1976. *Mothers, wives, and daughters in Osaka: autonomy, alliance, and professionalism*. Unpublished Ph.D. dissertation, University of Pittsburgh.

Pharr, Susan J. 1976. "The Japanese woman: evolving views of life and role." In *Japan: the parodox of progress*, ed. Lewis Austin, pp. 301–27. New Haven: Yale University Press.

Raper, Arthur F., et al. 1950. *The Japanese village in transition*. Tokyo: General Headquarters, Supreme Commander for the Allied Powers, Natural Resources Section, Report Number 136.

Salamon, Sandra B. 1974. *In the intimate arena: Japanese women and their families*. Unpublished Ph.D. dissertation, University of Illinois at Urbana-Champaign.

Seki, Keigo, editor. 1963. *Folktales of Japan*. Chicago: University of Chicago Press.

Shimpo, Mitsuru. 1976. *Three decades in Shiwa: economic development and social change in a Japanese farming community*. Vancouver: University of British Columbia Press.

Smith, Robert J. 1978. *Kurusu: the price of progress in a Japanese village, 1951–1975*. Stanford: Stanford University Press.

———. 1981. "Japanese village women: Suye-mura, 1935–1936." *Journal of Japanese Studies* 7, 2: 259–84.

Standless, Mary W. 1959. *The great pulse: Japanese midwifery and obstetrics through the ages*. Rutland, Vt., and Tokyo: Charles E. Tuttle.

Sugimoto, Etsu Inagaki. 1926. *A daughter of the samurai*. New York: Doubleday, Page and Co.

Suzuki, Eitarō. 1940. "*Shakai jinruigaku jō no kenkyū to shite no Embree's Suye Mura to nihon nōson shakaigaku*" [Embree's social anthropological study Suye Mura and Japanese rural sociology]. *Minzokugaku Kenkyū* 6, 3: 353–73.

Tsurumi, Kazuko. 1970. *Social change and the individual: Japan before and after defeat in World War II*. Princeton: Princeton University Press.

Ushijima, Morimitsu. 1958. *Suye Mura in transition*. Unpublished M.A. dissertation. Atlanta University.

———. 1971. *Henbō suru Suye mura* [Suye Mura in transition: a fundamental study of socio-cultural change]. Kyoto: Minerva shobō.

White, Merry I., and Barbara Molony, editors. 1978. *Proceedings of the Tokyo symposium on women*. Tokyo: International Group for the Study of Women.

Yoshino, Roger I. 1955. *Selected social changes in a Japanese village*. Unpublished Ph.D. dissertation, University of Southern California.

———. 1956. "A re-study of Suye Mura: an investigation of social change." *Research Studies, State College of Washington* 24, 2: 182.

Index